Better Homes and Gardens.
YARD & GARDEN
owners manual

contents

1

2

4

5

6

7

contents *(continued)*

8

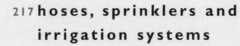

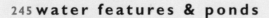
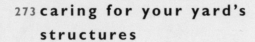

10

11

12

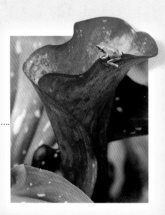

14

13

15

YARD & GARDEN owners manual

Working in the yard and making improvements to it over time is deeply satisfying. Your yard reflects who you are and shows your respect for your neighborhood and community. It may represent a lot of time, effort, and hard work to you, but the results are something you can be proud of and enjoy.

Few publications address how to care for a yard in a straightforward and accessible way, and that's why the Better Homes & Gardens Books editors researched and wrote this book. Each of us has at least three decades of yard work under our belts. We've spent many hours mowing, weeding, pruning, planting, and replanting. Yet we all started out at the same point everyone does: wondering if we were doing the right thing or whether there was a better or easier way to do it. Through the years, we've learned a few tricks and answered many questions. This book is our effort to share those years of experience with you.

paths

annual flowers

fences, gates, and walls

Whether you are a first-time homeowner eager to start gardening or an avid gardener looking for information, you'll find answers to your questions in this book. It could be that your home is brand-new with a landscape that is a blank slate. Or your landscape may be new-to-you but decades old, overgrown, and in need of help. Perhaps you've worked in your yard for years but still have questions. Or maybe you're just taking more interest in it. No matter your situation, this book has been researched and written with you in mind. The beginner to the most experienced pro should find useful ideas in its pages.

About this book

People's lives don't revolve around yard work. For that reason, the *Yard & Garden Owners Manual* breaks down each topic by the tasks that must be done if you want the best results. Then it explains how to ease each job, providing plenty of tips along the way.

Meet the chapters If you're at a stage of life with little time for yard care or have no experience with it, spend time with Chapter 1. It will help you realize that once you know the needs of each element in your yard in general terms, you can start to zero in on a particular element—tree or shrub, fence or patio—so that you provide it with the right care at the right time. Like a photograph coming into focus, you'll develop an understanding of your yard. As you do, caring for it becomes much easier—and much more fun.

Chapter 1 also includes two important suggestions gleaned from years of experience: First, inventory and categorize the basic elements in your yard. Then think about how you can tweak them to save time and effort. For example, reshaping shrub beds or giving them a new edge is one way to ease mowing.

Chapter 2 moves straight to the lawn. There's good reason for this: Lawns are easy to understand. They are often the most obvious landscape element, and during certain seasons they require the most maintenance.

watering

mowing

lawn mower maintenance

fertilizing

insect control

refurbishing your lawn

Introduction

pruning trees and shrubs

Although lawn care can be complex, the most important tasks—mowing, feeding, and watering—are the simplest. The *Yard & Garden Owners Manual* covers the complex as well as the simple.

Also in Chapter 2, you'll begin to see how even though yard and garden maintenance is an ongoing process it can be flexible. Rather than rely on a calendar to prompt a list of chores, you'll learn about routine tasks that help you prevent problems.

You'll learn too that yard and garden care is about understanding the basics and then using them to your advantage. As you'll read in Chapter 2, mowing frequently during the grass's season of fastest growth is vital to a lawn's health. Taking off for a long weekend may mean that you miss a mowing and the grass grows overly long. You could just whack the grass down when you return home, but if you follow the basics and the tips outlined in Chapter 2, you'll be able to mow without setting your lawn back.

Trees, shrubs, vines, and ground covers are long-lived, structural plants, often the most permanent elements in a landscape. Investing money, time, and care in them will reward you and your landscape for many years. We cover how and when to prune these plants in Chapters 3 and 4, along with watering, fertilizing, and watching for pests.

fertilizing

Flowers in pots, beds, and boxes, although less permanent than trees and shrubs, garner the most attention in a yard. In Chapter 5, we present the various categories of flowers—perennials, annuals, bulbs, and container gardens—and give you the basics for growing and caring for each type.

ground covers

Chapter 6 covers food plants, including vegetables, herbs, tree fruits, and berries. Gardeners who find space in their gardens for food plants reap the dividends of fresh wholesome foods. This chapter will help you determine whether food crops are feasible and worthwhile for you to grow in your garden.

Soil is the topic of Chapter 7. Soil supports the roots that support the plants. When the soil is healthy, the plants are healthy, look better, and have fewer pests—making their care much easier.

Tools play an important role in gardening and yard care. Chapters 8 and 9 review some of the newest and some of the most practical tools for gardening, including sprinklers and watering systems. These chapters also emphasize safety and the importance of wearing gloves, ear protection, and sturdy shoes when using power equipment. Good quality tools and observing safety rules make gardening chores manageable and rewarding.

caring for herbs, vegetables, and fruits

growing perennials

repairing a gate

testing soil

composting

Introduction

good advice

Water gardens have a cooling appearance and a soothing sound. For gardeners who have the room and inclination for a water feature, Chapter 10 explains about water features and their routine maintenance.

tips and techniques

" SMART IDEA "

Lawn-care shortcuts

Lawn maintenance is repetitive, which means that saving just a few minutes on mowing, for instance, pays compound dividends. Reducing mowing time by 20 minutes may save at least 4 hours a season. Here are practical ways to cut down on lawn maintenance:

❋ Round corners of borders and beds to make mowing easier.

❋ Convert hard-to-mow or hard-to-water areas to shrub beds.

❋ Replace lawn with ground cover plants on slopes, shady areas, or wherever the lawn is hard to mow.

❋ Fertilize primarily in fall and carefully in spring. Too much fertilizer (or water) in spring and summer causes faster growth, which requires more mowing.

maintaining a water feature

Another aspect of yard care is keeping the nonplant elements in shape, such as fixing a stuck or sagging gate or repairing cracks in a patio. Chapters 11 and 12 explain and show how to maintain yard and garden structures to keep them functional and attractive in your landscape.

Because gardens naturally attract wildlife, Chapter 13 discusses ways to draw the visitors that are beneficial, such as birds and butterflies. It also explains how to discourage pests, such as deer, gophers, and mosquitoes, as well as insect pests of plants.

Throughout this book, you'll find other bits of useful information in photos, charts, and tip boxes. Good-advice tips provide family-friendly tips on safety, saving time, stretching your budget, and keeping the garden healthy. You'll also find tip boxes with more in-depth information on garden gear, doing tasks, plants to try, and more.

lawn furniture maintenance

Finally, there is a collection of our favorite resources, including published and on-line resources.

The information and advice in the *Yard & Garden Owners Manual* will help you create a safe and comfortable outdoor haven while saving time and money. You *can* have the yard and garden you want for yourself and your family, and taking care of it *will* be a pleasure.

critter control

The editors, *Yard & Garden Owners Manual*

meet your garden

To gain the upper hand in your yard, you've got to know its basic parts

Caring for your landscape is a lot like caring for other aspects of your home. To do it well you need to be familiar with the various elements and their basic needs, and you need to organize your efforts in order or priority. When you move into a house, the best advice is to go slowly. Then make changes to suit your tastes and style, indulging your interests in one area and perhaps reducing maintenance in another.

Getting to know your yard

Before you buy a house, give its landscape a complete evaluation. Plants grow (and die), neighborhoods change, and landscapes become outdated. Just as you want to redo rooms in your house as they become out of style, the same goes for your outdoor areas.

Whether you are moving into a house and thinking for the first time about how to maintain the yard, or simply want to be a bit more organized and confident about the maintenance you're already doing, start by categorizing the basic elements of your yard. Then it's a simple matter to plan for—and accomplish—the necessary tasks.

How to evaluate your landscape

The first task in evaluating the health of your outdoor space is to take a walk. This strategy is useful even if you've lived with the yard for years. Walk around, observing with a fresh eye, or maybe enlist the help of a savvy friend or local landscape expert. Look at the house from different perspectives: from across the street or even from a neighbor's yard. With a change of perspective, you may be surprised by what you see or don't see.

Once you have all the aspects of your yard identified and evaluated, it's a short step to determining what kind of maintenance is needed.

■ SMART IDEA ■

View your yard in different seasons

Take more than one season to evaluate your yard. What seems fine in spring or summer might look all wrong in winter. For instance, once deciduous trees have lost their leaves, allowing light through, opening views, you may discover unsightly or damaged areas of walls or house siding. Then again, an uninspiring summer shrub, such as redtwig dogwood, might become the star of the garden in winter, or bulbs that are invisible in summer may appear like magic in spring.

Once you've given some thought to changes you'd like to make, decide which season is most important. Since most people spend time outside in spring and summer, planning for maximum effect in those seasons makes good sense.

Elements of a landscape

Walk around your yard, then draw a rough sketch of your landscape and identify where each feature lies and its approximate size. Then note if they're still functioning as they were intended. For example, a hedge may have been planted to block unsightly views. However, if it wasn't properly pruned and the bottom branches have died, it may need replacing or plantings put in front of it to screen the view.

Finally, assess the condition of each landscape feature. Are the concrete sidewalks heaved and cracked? Does a wooden fence have rotten slats? Is the fruit tree overgrown, with many crowded branches? Determining the condition of each landscape feature will help you to decide whether to leave it as is, repair it, or remove it.

The seven elements

Before you can get a firm grip on the maintenance your yard requires, you have to understand its components.

Lawn Although it could be included in the greenscape group, the lawn is such a ubiquitous part of almost every yard that it warrants its own heading. Your use of the lawn will dictate its size and shape. For example, if you like outdoor activities such as volleyball, a large lawn with a durable grass species, such as turf-type tall fescue, is required. If you like flowers and want a more natural setting, the lawn may be just a green pathway to connect beds of flowers and shrubs. In some yards, lawns may give way to wildflower meadows or disappear altogether in a shady, tree-filled backyard covered with bark mulch and planted in ground cover.

Greenscape Greenscapes—the trees, shrubs, hedges, and foundation plants—are the permanent plants in a landscape.

One important consideration to notice about greenscape features is their size. Have they outgrown their location? For example, a tree may have grown so large that it blocks the light for shrubs, causing them to grow tall and leggy and not flower as well. Foundation shrubs such as yews and junipers may have grown so that they block access to the water faucet or hose bib. An evergreen arborvitae hedge may have grown so tall that pruning it is cumbersome and perhaps even dangerous.

Flower gardens Most yards have some areas devoted to annual or perennial flowers, vegetables, or herbs. Note the sizes of these gardens and think about the time and energy required to plant and maintain them.

time saver • time saver • time saver • time saver • time saver

Save on pruning

Avoid pruning shrubs or trees that outgrow their space by not planting them in the first place. Instead, plant naturally low-growing trees and shrubs. Once trained into shape, they don't grow tall enough to require pruning. Excellent examples include dwarf fothergilla, bush cinquefoil, and globe arborvitae for shrubs and downey serviceberry, redbud and crabapple for trees.

Well-designed landscape

This landscape contains all seven elements: lawn, greenscape (shade tree, hedge, screening shrubs), a flower garden, paths (including the sidewalk), hardscape (patios, pergola, entry, and driveway), a utility area, and a special fountain.

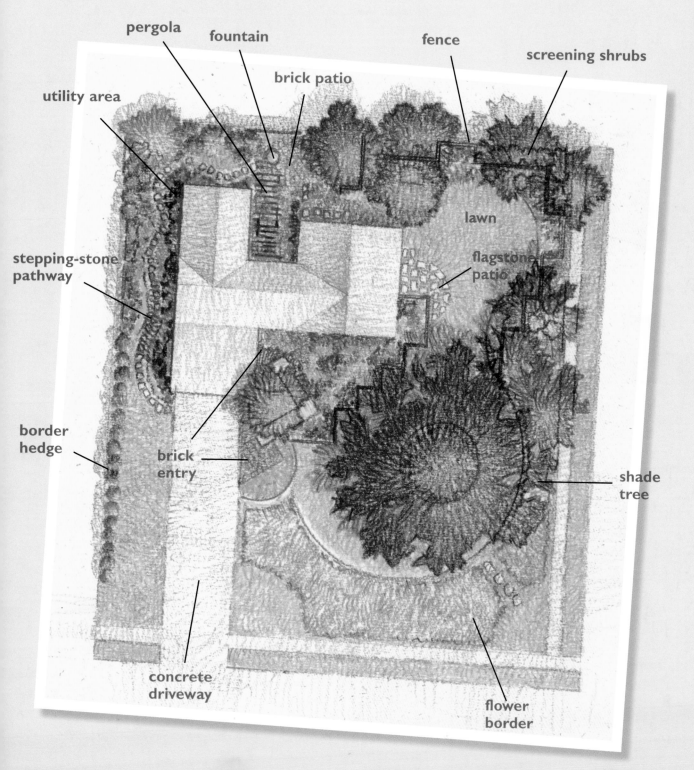

pergola

fountain

fence

screening shrubs

brick patio

utility area

stepping-stone
pathway

lawn

flagstone
patio

border
hedge

brick
entry

shade
tree

concrete
driveway

flower
border

healthy garden · healthy garden · healthy garden · healthy garden ·

Check before you dig

When mapping out your existing landscape, overhead features such as power lines, phone lines, and electrical boxes probably are obvious, but underground ones are not. Where they are located could determine what you build or plant in that area. For example, keep trees with aggressive roots, such as willows, away from septic fields, and locate natural-gas lines before firing up the backhoe. If you're unsure where lines and water pipes are located, call 1-800-DIGSAFE (344-7233).

(Elements of a landscape continued)

Paths As with lawns, paths often hold landscape elements together and create a flow for walking around your yard. When assessing paths, determine if they flow in a way that works best for your uses. Do you want winding paths that meander through the flower beds, or do you need straight, wide paths to move garden equipment and mowers between the different areas of your landscape?

Also, note the materials used for making the path. Bark mulch, stepping-stones, brick, and concrete are common. Each has advantages and disadvantages and specific maintenance needs. Bark mulch paths give the yard a naturalistic feel, but they need refreshing and periodic weeding. Stepping-stone or brick paths offer a more formal look and are safer to travel if you're less sure of footing. However, they'll need regular weeding as grass and weeds grow between the bricks, and perhaps even digging up and resetting if frost heaves displace the bricks.

Hardscape These are the permanent, nonplant features in your yard. Walls, fences, patios, decks, arbors, gates sidewalks, and driveway are all hardscape elements. Pay attention to each feature's condition and whether it fits your needs. For example, stone walls can be an attractive backdrop for a perennial flower border or spring bulb bed. However, they can also harbor critters, such as chipmunks and voles, that may plague a serious fruit or vegetable gardener.

Note the location and size of material used for the driveway. As your family grows or shrinks, you may want to adjust driveway space. In the snow belt, having an open area on which to pile snow near the driveway is a good idea. Shrubs or trees planted too close to the driveway in these areas will be damaged by snowplows and road salt. Asphalt driveways may need resurfacing, and gravel driveways may require a fresh layer of stone every few years.

Utility areas Here's where you put your trash cans, hang the laundry, store tools and supplies, hide the compost pile, or do behind-the-scenes tasks. Consider whether the area's location is convenient so that you will actually use it, allows you to do the tasks you plan on doing, is large enough for your needs, and is sufficiently hidden from view.

Special features Finally, landscapes may have some special features that are technically hardscapes but are more personal and, perhaps, less common. Pools, ponds, decorative statuary, large containers, and fountains are some elements that could be included here. What you do with these pieces comes down to personal taste.

Design ideas for low maintenance

Each landscape has unique features and needs, but there are always adjustments you can make that will reduce maintenance.

A mowing strip Install a 4- to 6-inch-wide concrete, brick, or stone border around planting beds so it is level with the lawn. Run mower wheels along the strip and forget trimming later.

Camouflage unsightly features An appropriately placed grouping of plants can hide less desirable features such as rough walls, air-conditioning units, and trash cans.

Alternative decking Reduce yearly upkeep of a deck by building it of materials such as plastic, composite (recycled plastic mixed with sawdust), or rot-resistant woods. This deck is made of ipe.

Drip irrigation Bring efficiency to landscaping watering: Drip irrigation delivers water to the roots of desirable plants, not weeds. These systems are easily automated.

Evaluate the water system

Are the shrubs and trees in your yard native—or adaptable—kinds that can survive on rainfall alone in your region? If they're thirsty ones, you may find yourself replacing them after the next drought. Check out the irrigation system: Do all the sprinklers work, or do some need to be repaired or replaced? Are faucets easily accessible? Answers to these questions will help you determine your landscape's water needs and your ability to efficiently deliver water to your plants.

Inventory and assess

Once you've drawn and taken notes about your landscape elements, it's time to assess their future. Do you really want apple trees in the backyard? Are the stone paths so weedy they need to be redug and set? Have the foundation plants become so large they're blocking the windows? From your list, determine for each element whether it needs to be repaired, removed, or replaced with something else. For a sample maintenance plan see page 24.

Create lists of the elements you like and will keep and of those that will eventually be removed. Then assess which maintenance jobs you can tackle immediately, which are long-term projects, and which are projects you'll need professional help completing. For the elements that will be removed, consider what, if anything, will replace them. For example, a fence that once blocked an unsightly view may no longer be needed and doesn't need to be replaced. Removing an overgrown evergreen tree in your yard, on the other hand, may open up new planting areas that you previously hadn't considered.

For the elements that remain, you'll need to determine their condition, come up with a yearly maintenance plan, and decide if the plan is something you have the time, energy, and money to tackle. For example, expanding the size of the kitchen garden by digging up some of the lawn is a doable weekend project. Dethatching the lawn to remove dead grass in spring may be a Saturday afternoon project. Expanding the length of a stone wall in the backyard may be a project to chip away at over time. However, removing and replacing a deteriorating stone patio or resurfacing an asphalt driveway may be a job for a professional.

Prioritize and schedule

After you've determined what stays and goes, it's time to itemize your maintenance tasks in order of priority. Your list of things to do around the yard may be long, but don't despair. Tasks such as mowing lawns and trimming hedges are necessary but routine. Other tasks, such as staining the deck or moving some perennial flowers, can be scheduled throughout the season. You don't have to tackle all the projects in a few weekends. It's best to take on projects slowly, as you are inspired. Always leave time during each weekend to enjoy the shrubs, flowers, and vegetables you've worked so hard to maintain. Turning your maintenance list into a second job isn't the point of owning a home. Enjoying your yard is as important as working to improve it.

Laborsaving ways to use plants

Choose plants carefully with an eye to easy maintenance. Look for ones that are naturally neat and well-adapted to the climate and to the location. Then use them in ways that will save time and effort.

Tidy trees Especially in high-use areas such as around patios, plant trees that won't drop fruits, seeds, or litter.

Ground covers Using shade-loving plants under a tree makes more sense than trying to grow turfgrasses, which need lots of sun.

Informal hedges Allowing the shrubs in a hedge to assume their natural size and shape eliminates the need for frequent pruning.

Naturalistic landscaping Using native plants and perennials such as this grouping of fountaingrass and 'Autumn Joy' sedum, reduces labor to little more than a yearly cleanup.

budget stretcher • budget stretcher • budget stretcher • budget stretcher

Water smart

Water conservation is a concern of gardeners everywhere, so it makes sense to look for ways to use less. About a third of the water applied by overhead sprinklers is lost to evaporation. Soaker hoses and drip irrigation systems, which deliver water directly to the soil and to the roots of desirable plants, will reduce the amount of water you use.

Seasonal maintenance schedule

SPRING

Lawns
- Fertilize lightly and repair dead patches.
- Use a preemergent herbicide to reduce crabgrass if needed.
- To revive a weak lawn, dethatch and aerate.
- Edge the lawn around the base of trees, shrubs, and flower beds.

Trees, shrubs, and ground covers
- Replace organic mulch at the base of trees and shrubs. Remove and compost the old mulch.
- Apply an all-purpose fertilizer around the drip line of plants.
- Remove winter trunk protection such as tree guards.
- Prune off any dead, diseased, or broken branches.
- Water new plants thoroughly if the weather has been dry. Check to be sure the water soaks 8 or more inches into the soil.
- Replace dead shrubs and ground covers.
- Prune shrubs that flower in summer.
- Rejuvenate ground covers by grooming, raking, and fertilizing.

Flower and kitchen gardens
- Prepare planting beds by amending the soil with organic matter.
- Plant cool-season flowers (pansies, snapdragons, and primroses).
- Plant cool-season vegetables once the soil is workable. Wait until after the last frost to plant heat-lovers.
- Rake old mulch out of beds and refresh with new.
- Prune (and plant) roses.
- Divide overcrowded perennials and replant or give away clumps.
- Cover yet-to-emerge perennials with a layer of compost.
- Replace old soil in window boxes with fresh potting soil.
- Plant fruit trees and berry bushes. Fertilize existing plants two to three weeks before bloom with a fruit tree plant food.
- Prune vines, such as grapes and clematis, that are overgrowing arbors and trellises.
- Cut back spring bulb foliage as it yellows.

Tools and equipment
- Tune your lawn mower engine by replacing the spark plug and oil; clean the filter.
- Sharpen (or replace) the lawn mower blade.
- Clean and oil pruning tools; sharpen blades if needed.

Water
- Check permanent irrigation equipment for clogging and proper action.
- Reset lawn sprinkler timers.
- Install temporary soaker hoses and drip systems as needed for new plants.
- Check, repair, if necessary, and replace fountain pumps in water features.
- Check water-garden liners for tears, and repair if needed. Fill with water if the level is low.
- Replant overwintered water plants.
- Restock the fishpond.

Hardscape

- Clean wooden decks and protect with sealant or stain.
- Move overwintered furniture and ornaments into the yard.
- Repaint lawn furniture as needed.
- Check paved areas for cracks; repair as needed.
- Add gravel to driveways and mulch to walkways if needed.
- Lubricate swing latches and hinges on gates.
- Check wiring on outdoor lighting fixtures and replace burned-out bulbs. Place saucers under containers on wooden decks to prevent water stains.

SUMMER

Lawns

- Mow lawns, removing only one-third of the grass at one time, and leaving clippings on the lawn.
  Raise the mowing height during the summer months.
- Trim around stone walls and fences. (Avoid using string trimmers near trunks of young trees and shrubs.)
- Alternate lawn-mowing patterns to avoid making strips or ruts.
- If needed, water lawns in the early morning, providing an inch of water a week.

Trees, shrubs, and ground covers

- Weed around the base of plants as needed; add mulch, but keep it away from trunks.
- Periodically check leaves, flowers, and branches for insect or disease damage, and control as needed.
- Water new shrubs and trees once a week, applying water to moisten soil 1 foot deep.
- Trim hedges after their flush of new growth.
- Cut roses for indoors, or snip off (deadhead) faded flowers.
- Prune shrubs, such as lilacs, after flowers die.

Flower and kitchen gardens

- Mulch beds with straw, hay, or grass clippings to conserve moisture.
- Pick flowers for cutting in the morning as they open.
- For best flavor and fragrance, harvest herbs in the morning.
- Harvest vegetables and herbs daily.
- Check all plants regularly for signs of insects and diseases and control pests as needed.
- Water plants in containers regularly when soil is dry a few inches below the surface.
- Fertilize flowers and vegetables monthly to maintain optimum growth.
- Deadhead flowers.
- Harvest fruits when ripe. Prune fruit-bearing shrubs and replant strawberries after fruiting.
- Train vines on a trellis or arbor by tying and occasional light pruning.

Tools and equipment

- Clean soil off cultivators, shovels, and rakes before putting them away.
- Clean out and repair cold frames for fall seeding of vegetables.
- Wipe pruning tools with an oiled rag after each use.

(Seasonal maintenance schedule continued)

Hardscape
- Remove weeds growing between bricks in pathways.
  Repair cracks in asphalt driveways, and resurface as needed.
- Paint or stain the house and outbuildings.
- Adjust outdoor lighting patterns to new plants and new plant growth.

Water
- Control algae and mosquitoes in ponds.
- Adjust the irrigation timer in gardens and lawns for summer weather.
- Keep the birdbath filled.
- Periodically check drip irrigation tubes and pop-up sprinklers
  for clogging.

FALL

Lawns
- Whether you're starting over or renewing, this is the season to seed and
  overseed lawns. In mild-winter areas, overseed by mid-October, about
  the time that warm-season grasses begin to go dormant. In cold-winter
  regions, sow lawn seeds no later than mid-September.
  In cold climates, set the mower to the lowest height the grass can
  tolerate for the final mowing of the season.
- If you do it only once a year, fertilize your lawn now.
  Rake and bag or mulch fallen leaves.

Trees, shrubs, and ground covers
- Plant trees and shrubs such as oak, holly, and beautyberry.
- Mulch newly planted conifers and keep them well-watered.
- In cold areas, protect tender roses by cutting back canes to within a foot
  of the ground, and then covering them with soil. Protect tender climbing
  roses by wrapping their canes in burlap, laying them on the ground, and
  covering them with soil or mulch.
- Clean up rotten fruits and fallen leaves around fruit trees; they may
  harbor diseases.
- Rake fallen leaves and compost them.
- Root-prune trees and shrubs you intend to move in the spring.

Flower and kitchen gardens
- Cut back perennials to approximately 6 inches above the soil.
- In cold areas, dig and store nonhardy bulbs such as dahlia and gladiolus.
- Divide and replant overcrowded perennials.
  Protect tender crops, such as basil and impatiens, from frost. Or remove
  them altogether, replacing them with cool-season annuals such as
  pansies and snapdragons. In mild-winter areas, cool-seasons annuals
  provide fall-through-spring color.
- Harvest vegetables before the first frost.
- Once the vegetables are gone, work compost into vegetable gardens.
- Plant spring-flowering bulbs such as tulips and daffodils.

Tools and equipment
- Dip blades of shovels, hoes, and trowels into a bucket of oily sand, and oil
  wooden handles.
- Clean debris off power tools.
- Winterize gasoline engines by running them until empty, or by filling the
  tank with gas and adding fuel stabilizer. Remove spark plugs, pour a
  teaspoon of oil into the cylinder, turn the engine over several times, then
  replace the spark plugs.

Hiring a landscaper

Although you may be able to tackle most landscape and outdoor projects, there are times when it's smarter to call a professional. When hiring landscapers, ask if they are bonded, insured, and have been accredited by a trade association. Ask friends, neighbors, garden centers, or nurseries for referrals. Put in writing the exact nature of the work, the cost estimate, and how to resolve any differences that may occur.

Water

- **Drain permanent water systems. Pull up and store temporary soaker hoses and drip systems.**
- **In cold areas, drain pools and ponds.**
- **Prepare water gardens and fish ponds for winter.**
- **Lift and store water pumps.**
- **Winterize and cover swimming pools.**
- **Store hoses and portable sprinklers.**

Hardscape

- **Store (or cover) outdoor furniture.**
- **Clean paths of slippery leaves.**
- **Inspect outdoor lighting fixtures and outlets for weather damage, and replace burned-out bulbs.**
- **Clean and store temporary arbors, stakes, and trellises.**

WINTER

Lawns

- **Avoid walking on dormant or frozen lawns.**
- **Try alternatives to salt, such as sand or kitty litter, to minimize damage to lawns.**
- **If the lawn is green all winter, apply a light dose of nitrogen fertilizer in late winter.**
- **Mark the edge of the lawn with stakes in cold areas so snowplows can avoid turning over turf when removing snow.**

Trees, shrubs, and ground covers

- **Water newly planted evergreens if rain and snow are lacking.**
- **Select bare-root roses; plant as soon as possible.**
- **In late winter, prune fruit trees; spray with dormant oil.**
- **Protect trees from rodent damage by wrapping trunks with tree guards.**
- **Protect tender foundation shrubs from snow and ice by wrapping them in burlap or erecting wooden covers.**

Flower and kitchen gardens

- **Check wintering bulbs in storage, and discard any that are soft or rotten.**
- **Order annual, perennial, herb, and vegetable seeds.**
- **In mild-winter areas, fertilize flowers with a fast-acting fertilizer.**
- **Pot prechilled amaryllis and daffodil bulbs for indoor forcing.**

Tools and equipment

- **Repair broken trellises and arbors.**
- **Organize tool storage and workshop areas.**

Water

- **Order pond plants and fish for spring.**
- **Check irrigation lines for cracks and bad emitters.**
- **In warm areas, adjust automatic watering timers to reflect reduced need.**

Hardscape

- **Keep decks and patios free of snow.**
- **Repair stone walls and patch concrete walls, weather permitting.**
- **Repair cracked birdbaths and fountains.**

Sample maintenance plan

Feature	Function and size	Condition	Action plan
Large asphalt driveway	enough space for three cars	needs resurfacing	hire professionals in spring
Arbor leading to side-yard flower beds	entryway to garden and backyard; an adequate 3 feet wide	one support post beginning to rot; others likely to follow shortly; covered by overgrown grapevine	hire contractor to replace posts; restain to protect all wood; remove grape and plant new ornamental vine, maybe clematis
Backyard lawn	play space for kids, pets; 3,000 square feet	thin in spots near the deck; lots of crabgrass in summer	fertilize, aerate, and reseed bare spots this fall; use preemergence herbicide in spring
Flower beds	100-square-foot bed along the house	flowers don't grow well; soil seems infertile; bed is small	add compost to soil; plant flowers instead of vegetables in nearby beds
Foundation shrubs	good color in spring; some shrubs are overgrown; the rest are OK	rhododendron, lilac, pieris, and boxwood; all are healthy	prune rhododendron and pieris after they bloom; cut out $1/3$ of the largest lilac stems in winter
Maple in front yard	large shade tree on south side of house keeps house cool in summer	healthy	leave it be; mulch around base
Wooden deck in backyard	plenty of room for entertaining (600 square feet).	good condition but shows wear; needs new preservative stain	do it early so it can be enjoyed for the summer
Toolshed	good size for mowers and tools; 10×10 feet	good shape	plant evergreens in front of shed to block view from house
Deciduous hedge on western and southern property boundary	blocks view in the summer only	overgrown	keep trimmed, but eventually replace with evergreen hedge for year-round privacy
Old stepping-stone path on east side of house	pathway to backyard; individual stones are set into lawn	uneven, overgrown with grass	remove and reseed bare areas this spring
Raised vegetable and herb garden	at 800 square feet, too large for two people	good soil; stone walls in good shape	use half for flowers and the rest for edibles
Pine trees on eastern property boundary line	large trees partially block views of neighbors	trees have grown too large, and lower branches are dead, exposing views into neighbor's yard	hire arborist to prune trees, then plant rhododendrons to fill in and restore privacy

caring
for your
lawn

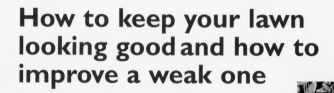

How to keep your lawn looking good and how to improve a weak one

No lawn is perfect. But basic attention to mowing, fertilizing, and watering pays dividends greater than you might expect.

Keeping a healthy lawn

There's nothing in the garden like a lawn. Large or small, it frames your property and welcomes friends and visitors. Lawns also cushion footsteps, cool the air, and prevent erosion. For the practical-minded, lawns are the most perfect outdoor play surface known, great for romping children and pets, and the backdrop for a variety of games. Landscape designers appreciate how lawns tie outdoor elements together, connecting the house to the shrubs and trees, then to the surrounding community. In short, everything looks better with a well-kept lawn.

When it comes to maintenance, there's no doubt we expect a lot of our lawns. For instance, we expect them to look good from spring to fall (or year-round in mild-winter climates), despite vast differences in seasonal growing conditions. Years ago, maintaining an attractive lawn required an obsessive obedience to schedules and details. But that's no longer the case. New grass varieties need less water and less fertilizer to look just as good as the best of the old-time grasses. Even where water shortages are a fact of life, you can have a lawn, as long as you choose the right kind of grass and keep the size manageable.

You can keep lawn care from being burdensome. Once you get into the habit of providing the required basics—and there are only a few—you'll be amply rewarded with a beautiful lawn. That's when you'll discover that caring for it is more joy than chore.

■ SMART IDEA ■

Lawn-care shortcuts

Lawn maintenance is repetitive, which means that saving just a few minutes on mowing, for instance, pays compound dividends. Reducing mowing time by 20 minutes may save at least 4 hours a season. Here are practical ways to cut down on lawn maintenance:

■ Round corners of borders and beds to make mowing easier.

■ Convert hard-to-mow or hard-to-water areas to shrub beds.

■ Replace lawn with ground cover plants on slopes, shady areas, or wherever the lawn is hard to mow.

■ Fertilize primarily in fall and carefully in spring. Too much fertilizer (or water) in spring and summer causes faster growth, which requires more mowing.

Which season is your lawn?

Cool-season grasses:
- Optimum temperatures for growth between 65° and 75° F
- Peak growth in spring and fall
- Limited winter dormancy
- Good cold tolerance
- Some shade tolerance

Warm-season grasses:
- Optimum temperatures for growth between 80° and 95° F
- Peak growth late spring through summer
- Usually dormant in winter
- Limited cold tolerance
- Minimal shade tolerance

Kinds of grasses

Turfgrasses are classified in various ways, but the most useful for gardeners is to consider them in terms of the climate they prefer. In this sense there are two types: those that grow best during the heat of midsummer, and those that grow best during the cooler temperatures of spring and fall.

Warm-season grasses The most common warm-season grasses are bermudagrass, St. Augustinegrass, zoysiagrass, bahiagrass, carpetgrass, and centipedegrass. Native grasses, including buffalograss and blue gramagrass, are also in the warm-season camp, as is the salt-tolerant specialty grass seashore paspalum.

Warm-season grasses are best adapted to the southern regions of North America. These are areas with hot summers and mild winters, and occur roughly south of a line drawn through northern sections of North Carolina, Tennessee, Arkansas, Oklahoma, and Texas, then through New Mexico and Arizona to the West Coast.

All of these grasses grow best during hot weather, and become dormant and brown during cold weather. Actual cold hardiness— the grass plants' ability to withstand low temperatures—varies. St. Augustinegrass will die at temperatures near 18° F, whereas blue gramagrass is hardy to -20° F. Warm-season grasses are also generally more drought-tolerant than their cool-season cousins.

Cool-season grasses Bentgrass, Kentucky bluegrass, fine fescues, tall fescues, and perennial ryegrasses grow well in regions north of the line described above, as well as at high elevations farther south. They grow best in the cool temperatures of spring and fall. Their growth stalls during spells of high heat in midsummer, and they are dormant, often covered by snow, through winter.

The region where you live may be neither the hottest nor coldest but somewhere in between. In terms of turfgrasses, this is called the transition zone. Here you have the option of growing either warm- or cool-season grasses, or a combination of the two.

Season of peak maintenance Schedule planting or any maintenance activities that tear up the lawn (dethatching, aerating, renovating) just prior to the grass's season of optimum growth. If your lawn is warm-season, plant or renovate in late spring; if cool-season, do those tasks in early spring or early fall.

Grass types

Knowing the type of grass you have tells you a great deal about how to care for it, including when and how much to fertilize, and when to adjust mowing heights. Here are six of the most common turfgrasses.

Hybrid bermudagrass
(Cynodon hybrids), a warm-season grass, grows equally well in the Southwest, Southeast, Mid-Atlantic region, and Lower Plains states. It is heat- and drought-tolerant and forms a luxurious, fine-textured lawn that stands up to the wear-and-tear of a growing family.

Zoysiagrass *(Zoysia* spp.) is a tough, aggressive, creeping warm-season perennial with good heat-, wear-, and some shade-tolerance. Leaf texture ranges from coarse to fine. Zoysiagrass will survive cold climates but is brown more than it is green when grown there.

St. Augustinegrass *(Stenotaphrum secundatum)* is a warm-season grass best adapted to the warm humid regions of the Southeast. This shade-tolerant grass is fast-growing, deep-rooted, and coarse-textured, with broad blunt-tipped blades.

Tall fescue *(Festuca elatior)* is the best cool-season grass for transition regions. It is more heat- and drought-tolerant than other cool-season grasses, but it is not as cold tolerant as Kentucky bluegrass. Newer turf-type tall fescue varieties form a dense, beautiful lawn that, like bermudagrass, stands up to the wear-and-tear of family life. Tall fescue does reasonably well in shade.

Kentucky bluegrass *(Poa pratensis)* is by far the most popular cool-season turfgrass. It is cold-hardy, often remaining green through winter. During periods of high temperatures and low rainfall in summer, Kentucky bluegrass will go dormant and turn brown. Once temperatures moderate, the grass will recover.

Perennial ryegrass *(Lolium perenne)* is a fine-textured, dark green cool-season grass. It is grows well in shady spots. Because it germinates in three days, it is often combined in seed mixes to act as a nurse grass. Or it may be used in a mix with Kentucky bluegrass to create a beautiful wear-tolerant grass. It's main limitation is that dull mower blades shred its leaf tips.

29

Mowing

For most homeowners it's something like paying taxes: You can either do it yourself or hire it out, but either way you've got to do it. It may seem odd to coddle lawns with water and fertilizer, only to relentlessly cut them back, but the fact is we mow lawns for some good reasons.

The habit was likely set decades ago when keeping down the growth around the homestead was plain good sense. Mowing eliminated hiding places for snakes and insects. Later, a well-kept greensward became a status symbol because relatively few had either the space for a lawn or the time to care for one.

The main reason we mow today is to keep the grass looking good. Because grasses evolved on plains that were grazed by animals, grasses have adapted over time to being cut back. In response to cutting, they grow out sideways, producing more blades. The result is a neat, dense turf that most people think is attractive.

Mowing correctly is one of the most effective ways to improve the quality of your lawn. Taken for granted because of its apparent simplicity, mowing has as much impact on lawn quality as fertilizer and water. Consistently cutting at the right height, at the right frequency, and with a sharp mower will help produce a thicker lawn with fewer weeds.

How to mow

Start by comparing the recommended height for your type of lawn in the chart with the actual height of your lawn. Then consider the cardinal rule of mowing: Avoid removing more than one-third of the

Cutting corners

If your lawn has lots of corners that force you to stop and back up while mowing, round them off on the first pass, leaving them unmown. Mow in a circular pattern, working toward the center. Once you're done, go back and finish off the corners and odd angles. This way the corners slow you down only once, not on every pass.

Cool-season grasses

Grass	Inches high
Annual ryegrass	$1\frac{1}{2}$–$2\frac{1}{2}$
Bentgrass	$\frac{1}{2}$
Canada bluegrass	$3\frac{1}{2}$
Fine fescue	2
Kentucky bluegrass	$1\frac{1}{2}$–$2\frac{1}{2}$
Perennial ryegrass	2
Rough bluegrass	$2\frac{1}{2}$
Sheep fescue	3
Tall fescue	$2\frac{1}{2}$-$3\frac{1}{2}$

Warm-season grasses

Grass	Inches high
Bahiagrass	3-4
Bermudagrass	1-$1\frac{1}{2}$
Blue gramagrass	2-3
Buffalograss	$1\frac{1}{2}$
Carpetgrass	1-2
Centipedegrass	1-2
St. Augustinegrass	$2\frac{1}{2}$-4
Dwarf St. Augustine	$1\frac{1}{2}$-$2\frac{1}{2}$
Zoysiagrass	$\frac{3}{4}$-$1\frac{1}{2}$

leaf blade height at one time. If your lawn is 3 inches tall, your cutting height should be no lower than 2 inches. Or put another way, if the optimum cutting height for your lawn is 2 inches, mow before it's 3 inches tall.

Adjust the cutting height of your mower on a flat surface, such as a driveway. Measure from the ground to the blade with a measuring tape to ensure the cut will be at the right height. You can check up on the mower by inserting a ruler into the lawn in several places around the yard. (Or use your index finger and estimate.)

Cutting too low forces the grass plants to use stored energy reserves to produce new leaves. But these energy reserves are limited and become depleted if plants are forced repeatedly to recuperate from low mowing. The result is a weak, weed-prone lawn.

An occasional mowing that's too low is a setback but one from which the lawn can recover. But if you routinely cut off more than a third of the grass—either by setting the mowing height too low or by not varying your mowing schedule to suit your lawn's rate of growth—you can expect your lawn to thin out, become weedy, and perhaps invite pests and other problems.

If you leave town for vacation, consider having the lawn mowed in your absence. But if that's not practical and you're faced with a 4-inch-tall lawn that should be 2 inches, raise your cutting height to at least 3 inches. Three or four days later, mow again, but lower. Repeat until the lawn is back to where it's supposed to be.

▪ SMART IDEA ▪

Cut that noise!

Lawn mowers are loud. Even the latest models of gasoline mowers produce about 85 to 95 decibels. Mildly annoying at a distance, this level of noise can create permanent hearing loss close up. If you've got to shout to be heard, the noise is damaging your ears.

Hearing protection will preserve your hearing and make mowing more comfortable and less stressful.

Manufacturers of hearing protectors must indicate how many decibels their product will handle. Their figures come from laboratory ratings. Assume that if the device has a noise reduction rating of 30, it will eliminate about 15 decibels. Hearing protectors are available in two basic styles: plugs and earmuffs.

What about clippings? To reduce the demand on landfills, many communities now prohibit disposing of clippings in the trash. Clippings must be either composted (and used as a mulch) or, most conveniently, left in place on the lawn.

Leaving clippings on the lawn has some advantages. It saves time and energy. When you leave the clippings, the nutrients in them are recycled. These nutrients are eventually returned to the soil, where they become available to the roots of the plants.

(Mowing continued)

Choosing the right mower

Rotary mowers These are the most popular because of their low cost, easy maneuverability, and simple maintenance. The spinning mower blade cuts the grass blade on impact. Most rotary mowers cannot produce a high-quality cut when set to cut lower than 1 inch. They are, however, versatile and work well on taller grasses and weeds, for mulching grass clippings, and for general trimming.

Mulching mowers are rotary mowers that are designed to chop the clippings into small pieces and leave them on the lawn. The differences between a standard rotary mower and a mulching mower are that mulching mowers have a doughnut-shaped deck and a multipitch blade. The modified blade and deck chop the cut grass into smaller pieces than conventional rotary mowers.

Reel mowers These cut with scissors-style, spiral-shaped rotating blades (usually five) and a stationary bed knife. Those with a motor are more expensive, and are heavier than rotary mowers, but they are preferred for low-cut, high-quality lawns such as golf greens and stadium turf, where appearance is especially important. Reel mowers work well at cutting heights of 2 inches or less and for stiff, wiry grasses such as bermuda- and zoysiagrass. They do not cut well when grass is especially tall or the ground is uneven. Sharpening reel mowers is best left to a professional mower repair service.

All mowers have to conform to safety standards. The most significant is the so-called "deadman" control, which stops the engine and blade almost the instant the handle is released. All mowers have a safety flap at the rear of their deck.

Mower size

Most homeowners are well-served by a mower in the 19- to 22-inch range. Larger mowers will save time on larger lawns, but they're also heavier, more expensive, and slightly more awkward to store. If your property is large or hilly, consider a model that's self-propelled.

Riding mowers and garden tractors are best suited for large, relatively flat properties. What you gain in mowing speed is often offset by a loss of maneuverability. Most of the ones marketed to homeowners are rotary mowers. Garden tractors are slightly larger than riding mowers; they can accept powered attachments, such as snow throwers or tillers. Given their greater power, they also offer larger-diameter decks, so they may be suitable for the largest properties. Automatic—called *hydrostatic*—transmissions, a seat with back support, and air-filled tires are desirable features of riding mowers.

Mow smart

- **Check the area before mowing, making sure there are no sprinkler heads poking up, and no toys or tools lying in the grass.**
- **Fill the gas tank only when the mower is cool and sitting on pavement. Spilled gas will kill grass and damage the soil.**
- **Mow during daylight, and watch for debris in front of the mower.**

Two basic mowers

Mowers are common yard maintenance tools. If you maintain your own lawn you need one. There are two basic types: rotary and reel.

Reel push mowers
Constructed of lightweight metals, these mowers are ideal for very small properties. Like reel mowers, they cut grass cleanly with a scissoring action and are not practical for rough or uneven ground.

Rotary mowers The most common type of lawn mower is the rotary. A single spinning horizontal blade cuts by impact. Height is easy to adjust in high-end models.

Sharp is better

Your mower blade can never be too sharp. A dull blade will rip the leaves, producing jagged edges and giving the lawn an overall light-brown to whitish color. If your blade is sharp and the mower still doesn't cut well, check the blade orientation. In its normal position, the blade should spin clockwise (viewed from the top).

(Mowing continued)

Mower maintenance

The best way to ensure that your mower will last many years is to set up—and follow—a comprehensive maintenance schedule. Your owner's manual is a good place to start.

Read the manual. Most tell you what you need to know. Pay close attention to the viscosity and equality of oil recommended for the engine. The wrong oil can cause overheating and excessive wear on the internal parts, which may, in turn, shorten the engine's life.

Keep the air filter clean. A dirty filter causes the engine to work harder, which wastes energy. It also may permit particles to enter the internal workings of the mower, wearing them down and causing pitting of the blade. The mower may burn oil like a poorly maintained car engine.

Inspect or change the spark plug either at the beginning or end of each mowing season. Use a spark-plug gauge to check the gap; most manuals list the gap thickness. Take care not to damage the porcelain insulator. If the porcelain is cracked, replace the plug.

At the end of the mowing season, ready the machine for the winter. After the last mowing, allow the engine to cool completely. Drain most of the gasoline from the fuel tank, then run the mower until the fuel system is completely dry. Or add a fuel stabilizer to the tank. (Consult the owner's manual first; using an additive may void the warranty.)

Drain and properly dispose of the old crankcase oil and replace it with fresh oil according to the manufacturer's recommendations. Remove the spark plug using a spark-plug wrench. Lubricate the cylinder by pouring a teaspoon of oil through the spark-plug hole (again, check the instructions in your owner's manual). Slowly rotate the engine several times by turning the crankshaft or pulling the starter rope, to distribute the oil. Replace the spark plug with a new one, but don't reconnect the spark-plug wire until the next spring.

Thoroughly clean all dirt and debris from the machine. If you have a self-propelled mower, grease the rear height-adjuster brackets. Check and tighten the blade and engine-mounting bolts. This is also a good time to inspect and sharpen the blade.

Store the mower in a clean, dry place, well away from appliances with pilot lights or other potential ignition sources.

Step-by-step maintenance

Tune up your lawn mower at least once a year in spring by cleaning, checking the engine, and sharpening the blade.

1 **Keep deck clean** If grass is the least bit wet when mowed, it will stick to the underside of the deck. Mowers with clogged decks won't cut or mulch properly. Brush away clippings after each use.

2 **Change engine oil** Drain old oil through the drain plug on the engine, or by tipping so oil drains out of the fill plug. Check the manual for recommended oil; 30-weight detergent oil is typical.

3 **Check air filter** If dirt and grime are visible, the filter needs cleaning or replacement. Clean foam filters with warm soapy water; squeeze dry and add 2 teaspoons of oil.

4 **Sharpen blade** Disconnect the spark plug so the engine can't start. With the mower on its side, loosen the nut with a wrench. Wedge a block of wood between the mower housing and the blade. Use a grinder or hand file to sharpen the blade, following the original bevel.

5 **Balance blade** An unbalanced blade wobbles as it spins, which could damage the motor. Center the blade on a cone so that it swings free. Let it settle. Mark the light end, then hand file the heavier end. Recheck the balance.

6 **Check spark plug** At the beginning or end of the mowing year, inspect the spark plug. Remove it with the tool supplied with the mower or with a long-neck socket and wrench. Use a spark plug gauge to check the gap (your owner's manual will list the correct gap size).

35

Fertilizing

Like all plants, lawns need nutrients to survive. Left on their own, grasses would survive, but the lawn wouldn't look well-kept. Have your soil tested to determine exactly what nutrients your lawn needs.

Nitrogen, phosphorus, and potassium are considered the primary mineral nutrients, because plants use them in the greatest quantities. (Essential general nutrients—carbon, hydrogen, and oxygen—come from the air and water. The 10 other nutrients that plants require are generally more abundant in most soils than the tiny amount plants actually need.)

Fertilizers contain nitrogen, phosphorus, and potassium in proportion to the amounts grass plants use. Nitrogen (N) is the most important element for a lawn that gardeners can do anything about and it is the nutrient upon which most lawn fertilizer recommendations are based. It encourages rapid growth and promotes dark green color. Turfgrasses require more nitrogen than other nutrients. Nitrogen is also prone to washing out of soils *(leaching)*. So it is the key nutrient in lawn fertilizers. Typical lawn fertilizers contain three to four times the amount of nitrogen as other nutrients.

The relationship between the percentages of nitrogen, phosphorus, and potassium in a fertilizer is called its *ratio*. For instance, a fertilizer with an analysis of 21-7-14 has a ratio of 3-1-2. Lawns are best served by fertilizers with ratios in the range of 3-1-2 or 4-1-2, although it's not critical that your fertilizer be exactly these ratios.

Slow-release nitrogen Most commercial lawn fertilizers combine forms of nitrogen that are fast- and slow-release. The portion of slow-release nitrogen is listed on the fertilizer bag as water-insoluble nitrogen, sometimes abbreviated WIN or CRN for controlled-release nitrogen. If no WIN is listed on the fertilizer label, assume that all of the nitrogen is water-soluble or quickly available, unless the nitrogen includes sulfur-coated urea.

The nitrogen contained in slow-release fertilizers becomes available over time, so the fertilizer can be applied less frequently and at higher rates than quickly available kinds. Properly applied, slow-release fertilizers are less likely to burn a lawn than quickly available kinds. In most areas, the benefits of a soluble fertilizer last about four weeks, compared to six to eight weeks for a slow-release fertilizer.

Another benefit of slow-release fertilizers is that they are less likely to run off into streams and sewers and leaching is reduced.

budget stretcher • budget stretcher • budget stretcher •

One lawn, two programs

If you have a large lawn and don't want to invest the time or resources to fertilize all of it, manage a small portion optimally and the rest minimally. Note which area is most used or most noticed, and focus on it, fertilizing three or more times a year. Fertilize the remaining lawn once or twice, in late summer and fall.

Reading the fertilizer label

Choose a product with an **N-P-K** ratio of 3-1-2 or 4-1-2, with at least half the nitrogen slow-release, then apply the amount recommended in the label directions.

The three prominent numbers on any fertilizer are the analysis of the fertilizer. The numbers are the percentages of nitrogen, phosphorus, and potassium—always in that order—in the bag. The numbers may not add up to 100 percent because of other materials in the mix.

Manufacturers are required to show the various forms of nitrogen in the bag. An important part of this listing is the percentage that is water-soluble and the percentage that is water-insoluble. The greater the percentage of water-insoluble nitrogen, the slower-acting the fertilizer. A fertilizer with one-third of its nitrogen in a water-insoluble form is considered slow release. Ammoniacal nitrogen and urea are water-soluble forms of nitrogen.

The sources of primary and secondary nutrients in the fertilizer are listed after the guaranteed analysis.

Guaranteed Analysis

Winterizer™   22-3-14   F643

Total nitrogen (N) 22%
    5.7% ammoniacal nitrogen
    8.9% urea nitrogen
    6.8% other water-soluble nitrogen*
    0.6% water-insoluble nitrogen

Available phosphate (P_2O_5) 3%

Soluble potash (K_2O) 14%

Sulfur (S) 10%
    10% combined sulfur (S)

Derived from: urea, methyleneurea, potassium sulfate, ammonium phosphate, and ammonium sulfate.

*Contains 4.9% slowly available methylenediurea and dimethylenetriurea nitrogen.

All secondary nutrients and micronutrients contained in the fertilizer are listed.

Don't burn your lawn

Contact with a water-soluble fertilizer may "burn" the grass, leaving it looking scorched. Avoid fertilizer burn by fertilizing only when grass blades are dry. Water the fertilizer into the soil right after application. And don't apply too much fertilizer. This concentrates fertilizer salts in the lawn's root zone.

(Fertilizing continued)

Ways to apply fertilizers

There are three basic types of spreaders for dry fertilizers on home lawns: drop spreaders, broadcast spreaders, and hand spreaders.

Drop spreader Drop spreaders dispense the fertilizer straight down to the lawn through openings at the base of a hopper. If you're in a hurry, they are best suited for fertilizing small areas. Use them where you need to precisely apply fertilizer, such as around flower and shrub beds, near water gardens, or along pavement.

These spreaders apply materials in a well-defined, straight path 18 to 24 inches wide. The amount of fertilizer they apply depends on the size of the opening, the type of fertilizer, and the speed at which the spreader is pushed. Drop spreaders are not as easy to maneuver around trees and shrubs as broadcast spreaders.

To avoid leaving stripes when using a drop spreader, overlap each pass slightly. Newer drop spreader models have an arrow that you align with the wheel tracks of the previous pass. Without an arrow, pivot the spreader at the end of the pass so that the wheel is just inside the previous track. Take care to overlap just the wheels and not the hopper.

Broadcast spreader Broadcast spreaders, also called rotary or cyclone spreaders, have a rotating disk that throws fertilizer in a semicircular pattern as the spreader is pushed. This type is best suited for covering large areas quickly. The distribution pattern is not as uniform as provided by a drop spreader—more fertilizer falls near the hopper than at the edges—but it is better than a hand spreader. Newer broadcast spreaders let you adjust the spread to one side or the other so you can avoid getting fertilizer where you don't want it.

Hand spreader These are a type of rotary spreader. They are inexpensive and useful in small areas. They hold only a few pounds of fertilizer and are imprecise because most people don't have the arm strength to hold the hopper and crank the handle steadily without wobbling.

Application tips Apply header strips at the end of the lawn or around the edges of an irregularly shaped lawn. Then fill in between the headers. Push the spreader rather than pull it. Walk in a straight line as you push. Set a steady, moderate pace and maintain it. Start walking, then open the hopper. Close it as just you come to a halt, or when turning, backing up, or when you reach a section that you've already applied.

Lawn spreaders

Grasping a handful of fertilizer from the bag and trying to spread it evenly with flicks of your wrist will result in patchy fertilization. Any one of these spreaders will do a better job.

Drop spreaders let fertilizer fall straight down (exaggerated in the photo). This ensures accurate application. Note where material falls and overlap wheel tracks only to avoid streaks. Drop spreaders cover less space with each pass than broadcast spreaders, so take longer to cover large lawns.

Hand broadcast spreaders are convenient for quick applications of small amounts of fertilizer.

Broadcast spreaders are preferred for large areas. They hold more material than drop spreaders and broadcast a swath up to 6 feet wide, covering big lawns quickly. However, the fertilizer may fall in gardens and other areas where you don't want it.

(Fertilizing continued)

How much fertilizer to apply

Several factors affect which nutrients and how much of them you will need to supply. The type of turfgrass, soil, and length of the growing season are most important. The longer the season, the more fertilizer the lawn will need. The amount of rain and watering are contributing factors because water tends to wash the key nutrient, nitrogen, from the soil. Finally, your own standards matter. Do you want the lawn to look its very best all season, or is a less than perfect lawn acceptable? Your lawn will look better with the more fertilizer it receives, but it will also require more maintenance.

One pound per thousand An almost universal standard recommendation for lawns is to apply 1 pound of actual nitrogen per 1,000 square feet of lawn area. The term "actual nitrogen" simply refers to the pounds of nitrogen in a quantity of fertilizer. If the analysis of a fertilizer shows it contains 20 percent nitrogen, then a 50-pound bag of fertilizer has 10 pounds of actual nitrogen in it.

To calculate the amount to apply of any fertilizer, divide the amount of actual nitrogen needed by the percentage of nitrogen specified on the fertilizer bag. For example, to apply 1 pound of actual nitrogen to a lawn using a 16-4-8 fertilizer, divide 1 pound by 16 percent (.16). In this case, you would use 6.25 pounds of fertilizer.

Most turfgrasses provide a high-quality turf with 2 to 3 pounds of nitrogen per year. For a low level of maintenance, they will get by on 1 to 2 pounds of nitrogen. Bermudagrass and zoysiagrass vary from these requirements. Supply bermudagrass with 3 to 6 pounds of nitrogen and zoysia with 2 to 5 pounds of nitrogen on a high-maintenance level. For low-maintenance levels, supply both with 1 to 3 pounds of nitrogen.

When to fertilize

The best time to fertilize depends on many factors, including where you live, the kind of lawn you have, and the quality of lawn you want.

Timing is important Fertilizer is applied to warm-season and cool-season grasses according to their growth cycles. The most important time to fertilize cool-season grasses, such as Kentucky bluegrass and tall fescue, is late summer and fall; the most important time for fertilizing warm-season grasses is mid-spring to midsummer.

Too much nitrogen fertilizer in spring on a cool-season lawn is detrimental, because it leads to excessive leaf growth at the expense of stored food reserves and root growth and may increase injury from

healthy garden • healthy garden • healthy garden

Going organic

You can make your own fertilizer for your lawn using natural materials. Here's how much you'll need of four commercially available organic materials to deliver 1 pound of actual nitrogen to 1,000 square feet:
Pounds of natural fertilizer needed:

cow manure: 50
cottonseed meal: 15
alfalfa meal: 20
blood meal: 7

summer diseases and drought. Similarly, excessive late-summer and early-fall applications of nitrogen to warm-season turfgrass without applying adequate amounts of phosphorus and potassium can lead to winter injury.

Fall fertilization keeps cool-season grasses growing longer into cold weather, stimulating the lawn to thicken. As the grass slows its growth in fall, it stores carbohydrates to help it survive winter and to get off to a fast start the next spring. Fall fertilizing provides the nutrients that cool-season grasses need to form carbohydrates.

Growth for warm-season grasses peaks in midsummer, then tapers off until the fall frost. Make the first application two to three weeks after the grass turns completely green in spring, using a quick-release form of nitrogen. Fertilize warm-season grasses for the last time six to eight weeks before the expected date of the first frost.

Be wary of fertilizing any lawn in summer. The practice is likely to force a flush of succulent growth, which will leave the lawn either growing faster than you can mow it, and more vulnerable to diseases.

Grasses growing in heavily shaded areas require only one-half to two-thirds as much nitrogen as grasses growing in full sun. Because cool-season grasses in shade can best use nitrogen when sunlight reaches the grass leaves, time your fertilizer application to when the most light reaches the lawn, such as after most leaves have fallen from deciduous trees in fall.

The easy-going option If you expect to have a picture-perfect lawn, naturally you'll use more water, fertilizer, and time to make it so. But if all you want is to keep the lawn alive and halfway decent, here's what to do:

For cool-season lawns, fertilize once in fall. For somewhat better results, fertilize once in late summer and again in fall. Avoid fertilizing in summer and fertilize little, if any, in spring.

Fertilize warm-season lawns once in late spring, and once in early summer.

For either type of lawn, choose slow-release fertilizers, and leave the clippings on the lawn after mowing. Lawns receive significant amounts of nitrogen, potassium, and other nutrients from clippings and they do not cause thatch.

budget stretcher • budget stretcher • budget stretcher •

Watering smart

■ **Water early in the morning. Less water is lost to wind and evaporation then so more reaches the lawn.**

■ **Reduce the need for water by going easy on fertilizer.**

■ **Raise the cutting height on the mower by a half-inch or so. Taller plants grow deeper roots and use water more efficiently so you won't have to water as often.**

Watering lawns

With few exceptions, lawns need watering. Exactly when and how often depend on several factors: local climate and weather, the type of grass, the soil type, and how the lawn has responded to the way you've watered in the past.

In general, lawns need 1½ inches or more of water per week in summer. More specifically, you want to apply enough water to wet clay soil to a depth of 4 to 6 inches, loamy soil to 8 inches deep, and sandy soil to 12 inches deep. Bermudagrass and native grasses such as buffalograss require much less water while some bluegrasses need at least that much if not more to avoid summer dormancy. If the water comes from rain, fine; if not, you must provide it.

Lawns in dry climates predictably need the most regular and consistent irrigation, while lawns where growing-season rainfall is generous need the least. This is the main reason that lawns in the arid West and Southwest are generally smaller and more precious, but even in the Midwest, East and Southeast, extended periods of drought are common, and you'll have to make up for the missing rainfall.

Water your lawn when the soil begins to dry out but before the grass wilts, or loses resilience. At the wilting stage, areas of the lawn begin to change color, displaying a blue-green or smoky tinge. Footprints on the lawn remain visible rather than bouncing right back. Ideally, water the lawn before these signs of wilting are so obvious.

The best time of day to water a lawn is early morning (4 a.m. to 8 a.m.). Evaporation is minimal, so water use is optimal, and that time of day is usually the least windy. Mid-morning to late afternoon temperatures are higher and wind more likely, so more water is lost to evaporation. Early evening or night watering is not recommended, because during warm nights, wet grass blades are highly susceptible to disease.

Water deeply and infrequently. A light sprinkling every couple of days will do your lawn little real good. Watering that wets only the top layer of soil encourages the roots to stay shallow. Then, when a drought hits, the roots can't access deeper water.

Recovery from severe drought During periods of severe drought when water use restrictions are in effect, you may be obliged to let the lawn go dormant. Many healthy cool-season lawns

When to water

After you've observed your lawn for a season or two, it will be easy to see when and where water is needed. Until you can spot the symptoms of drought easily, use these tools and techniques.

Screwdriver test If you can easily push a long screwdriver 6 to 8 inches into the soil, most likely the soil is adequately moist.

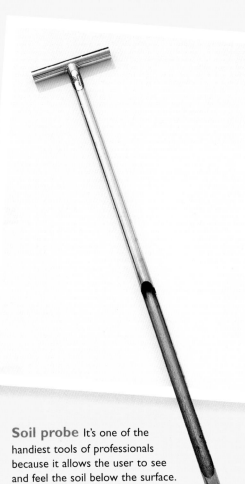

Soil probe It's one of the handiest tools of professionals because it allows the user to see and feel the soil below the surface. Simply press the probe into the ground and pull out a core of soil.

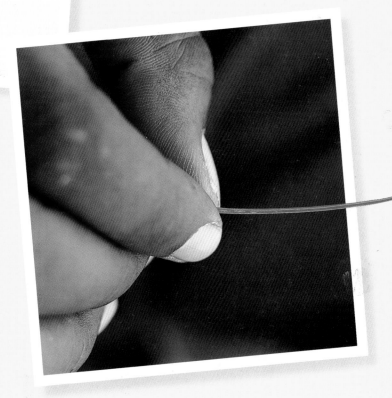

Rolled gray-colored blades You may have to look closely, but when leaf blades roll up and the lawn takes on a gray cast, you are seeing signs of drought stress.

(Watering continued)

can still recover in fall given a soaking rain and cooler soil, though the drought may take a toll. To aid recovery, fertilize in fall with slowly available or organic nitrogen and let the grass grow somewhat taller than you might otherwise before mowing. If the lawn does not fully recover, reseed before the lawn goes dormant for the winter.

How long to water

How long the sprinklers should run depends on two things: the type of sprinkler and the type of soil.

Measure your own sprinkler setup: Place straight-sided containers (soup cans work well) or rain gauges around the lawn. Turn the sprinklers on for 20 minutes, then measure the amount of water captured in each container. Divide 1 inch by the amount measured in the least-filled can. Then multiply the result by the amount of time you ran the water. For example, say you measured $\frac{1}{4}$ inch: $1 \div \frac{1}{4} = 4$, and $4 \times 20 = 80$. Run your sprinklers for 80 minutes to give your lawn an inch of water.

This equation works best for a loamy soil. Depending on soil composition, water may drain so rapidly that the soil remains dry, or so slowly that water puddles and runs off. A sandy soil may absorb 2 inches of water in an hour, while a clay soil absorbs only a quarter inch. The solution for both is to split the total into several waterings. Water sandy soil twice a week, a half-inch at a time.

For clay soil, cycle the water. As soon as you see water running off the lawn, turn the sprinklers off for an hour or so, giving the water time to soak in. Then restart the sprinkler and repeat until you've reached the target amount. Aim to apply $\frac{1}{2}$ inch of water in one day twice a week. This style of on-again, off-again watering is essential when dealing with a clay soil and sprinklers that put out water faster than it can be absorbed.

A day after watering, double-check a few locations in the yard to see how well your irrigation program is distributing water to the root zone. Use a probe to extract a sample of soil, or cut a slender 6- to 8-inch deep wedge with a shovel. You can replace the wedge without damage to the lawn.

Check your water meter Use the water meter attached to your house to check how effectively water is applied. It measures water in cubic feet. When no other water is being used in the home, water a known area for a set amount of time. One inch of water over 1,000 square feet is 624 gallons, or 83.2 cubic feet.

budget stretcher • budget stretcher • budget stretcher • budget stretcher

Sprinklers with a brain

Automated sprinklers are great labor savers, and generally do an efficient job of watering, until they come on after a week of wet weather. You can prevent that by connecting the timer to a soil moisture sensor. It will override the timer and allow the sprinklers to operate only if the soil is dry.

How much to water

The weather, your soil, the type of grass, and even how you fertilize influence your lawn's water needs. The goal is to ensure the entire root zone is moist. Usually that means about an inch of water each week.

Poor system design

Underground sprinkler systems should be designed with sprinkler heads that direct water to the lawn only. Watering on windy days will defeat a good design.

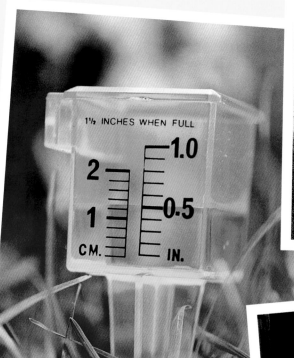

Rain gauge Measure rain to ensure the lawn receives enough water and you're not assuming the rain was enough.

Can test Set cans around the lawn to see how evenly sprinklers apply water. (Use the same-size can throughout.) By testing just once you may learn how to adjust your sprinklers to compensate for unequal distribution.

Rejuvenating weak lawns

Thin, weedy, or weak lawns can often be salvaged without having to start over. You may be surprised how easy it is. Often it's simply a matter of fertilizing, watering, and mowing properly. Sometimes eliminating weeds will speed the process.

The most common cause of a so-so lawn is lack of nutrients. To know for certain, fertilize the lawn at the preferred time of year, and watch for the results. If the lawn looks better within a month, you've fixed the problem.

The information in this chapter can keep you from getting to a point where your yard needs resuscitation. And if you begin taking care of a neglected lawn properly, it will gradually improve.

Patching

Your lawn may be in good condition with only a few troublesome spots, such as a weedy patch or a bare spot. In this case, you need to replace or repair only the damaged area.

The damage may result from a one-time accident, such as spilled gasoline or dog urine. If not, try to figure out what has led to the damage. Unless you correct the underlying cause, the same damage will reoccur.

Once the source of the problem is addressed, prepare the soil for the new seed, sod, or plugs. Completely remove grass and weeds in the problem area, plus a little extra. Next, prepare the soil as thoroughly as you would if you were planting a new lawn—that is, cultivate it to a depth of 4 to 6 inches, and remove any weeds or debris. Add several inches of compost or other organic matter and mix it in. Finally, rake the surface smooth, at the level of the surrounding turf if sowing seed or planting plugs, or about ½ inch lower if planting sod.

Sow seed and cover the area with a thin layer of weed-free mulch. Keep the area moist until after the seeds germinate. If you want the area to look better right away, patch it with a section of sod. Cut a piece of sod to fit the space that needs to be repaired and tuck it into place. Water it thoroughly after planting, and follow up with daily watering during hot weather.

healthy garden · healthy garden · healthy garden · healthy garden ·

Bumpy lawn?

If your entire lawn is mildly bumpy, like walking on cobblestones, spread a ⅛ inch layer of native soil over it in spring, then go over the lawn with a roller. For a dip that creates havoc for your mower, cut around the sod that covers the area and gently lift it. Set it aside. Add enough soil to fill the depression to the correct level. Put back the sod. Water daily until roots develop.

Rejuvenation steps

If your lawn is thin and weak, or if perennial weeds have taken over, you can plant a new lawn in as little as one or two weekends. The best time? Late summer to early fall (cool-season), or spring (warm-season).

1 Remove old lawn Cut the dead lawn and weeds as low as you can to remove as much old plant material as you can. If the old lawn includes many perennial weeds, kill them first by spraying with an herbicide such as glyphosate.

2 Dethatch and aerate Cut through old, matted, dead grass and thatch with a dethatching machine, then rake up and dispose of debris. Follow by aerating (shown).

3 Sow seed and fertilizer Choose a high-quality seed of a type that's adapted to your region and sow at label recommended rates. Follow with a starter fertilizer that is high in phosphorus.

4 Rake, roll, and water Rake the new seed and fertilizer gently with a steel rake to ensure seeds are in close contact with soil, not trapped above it. Then roll with a water-filled roller to press seeds firmly against the soil. Until seeds germinate, water frequently enough to keep the seedbed moist.

Getting to the core

Aerating is most effective when the soil is soft and the coring tools can penetrate 2 to 3 inches to remove a solid core of soil. Aim for 20 to 40 holes per square foot. Some power machines may require you to make multiple passes.

(Rejuvenating weak lawns continued)

Aerating

The soil in many lawns, particularly those that are heavily used and growing on clay, can become compacted. (Sandy soil rarely becomes compacted.) Compaction affects how well your lawn grows. It restricts the movement of air and water to roots. It restricts root growth. And it is one of the conditions that may lead to thatch.

The soil under lawns tends to compact readily because, unlike garden soil, it is virtually never worked or turned after it is installed. Aerating is one way to prevent compaction or to break it up once it begins. Aeration promotes better moisture and air penetration into compacted soils. It helps establish a deeper and healthier root system and also stimulates the microbial activity involved in decomposing the thatch layer.

Aerating consists of pushing a narrow, hollow tube into the soil. A core of soil is extracted, leaving an open hole. This can be done with hand or power tools. Either way, it causes little damage to the lawn. Most lawns need aerating only once a year or once every two years. The rate depends on your lawn, how it is used and the soil type. If you maintain your lawn to a high standard, or if your soil is heavy and tends to compact, it may need aerating twice a year.

To be effective, the aerator must have hollow tines or spoons that bring cores of soil to the surface. If your lawn is small, you can use a foot-pressure aerator that you push into the soil like a shovel. Rent a power machine if your lawn is more than a few hundred square feet. It can aerate large lawns in little time.

Water the lawn deeply prior to aerating so that at the time you're ready to work the soil is moist. Soil that is either too wet or too dry will prevent the tool from working properly.

It's best to run a core aerator over the lawn several times in different directions to break up compacted soil as much as possible. Leave the cigar-shaped cores on the surface of the lawn for a couple of days to dry, then rake them up. It takes about six weeks for grass to fill in the holes left by aerating.

The best time to aerate cool-season lawns is between late August and early October. The next best time is in the spring. Follow with regular, frequent watering. (In spring, wait until you've mowed the lawn twice before aerating.) The best time to aerate warm-season lawns is in late spring or early summer, though anytime that is followed by four weeks of good growing weather is fine.

Dethatching

Thatch is the layer of dead grass stems, roots, and debris that builds up just below the green surface of the lawn, on top of the soil at the base of the blades.

A thin layer of thatch is no problem. A layer that is ½ inch thick or less is normal and no cause for action. If thatch is thicker than that, water may be blocked from reaching the soil and will run off.

Causes of excessive thatch are numerous: Poorly aerated soil, excess nitrogen, and too much water are common. It may also result from activities that kill earthworms and microflora which break down organic matter, such as overzealous use of pesticides. Some varieties of lawn grass are more prone to developing thatch than others.

There are several ways to deal with thatch. For lawns with moderate levels, aerating may do the trick. Or for extra insurance, use a *cavex rake,* noted for its unusual semicircular tines. Its knifelike blades cut through the sod and pull out thatch. For large lawns with serious thatch problems, the most effective solution is a vertical mower. Resembling a heavy-duty power mower, it has a series of spinning vertical knives that cut through thatch.

Dethatching often results in a large volume of debris that must be removed from the lawn. If the debris is weed-free and you have not used herbicides or pesticides on your lawn, compost it.

The best time to dethatch cool-season lawns is late August to early October, depending on your location. At that time, the grass is growing vigorously and should recover quickly. In addition, few weed seeds are likely to germinate at this time. A light application of fertilizer (½ to ¾ pound actual nitrogen per 1,000 square feet) and regular watering will speed the lawn's recovery.

Dethatch warm-season lawns in late spring or early summer after they've completely greened up and are growing rapidly. At this time, the lawn should recover quickly.

• SMART IDEA •

Getting air to lawn roots

The roots of all plants need air as much as water, which is why aerating is so important. Aerating a lawn is a way to cultivate your lawn's soil without damaging the lawn.

The best time to aerate is a day or two after a soaking rain or heavy watering, when the soil is moist but not soggy.

Aerating with manual equipment is often best, because you can go slowly enough to ensure that cores are removed. If you use a heavy machine, watch to be sure the coring tools are actually extracting cores of soil and not just punching holes. Avoid tools that are designed to punch holes without removing cores.

What about moss?

Moss and algae thrive in shade— exactly where grasses grow poorly. Remedies such as copper sulfate or ferrous sulfate stain paving and may not be effective. Another option is to prune overhanging limbs to allow more light to reach the grass. Or replace the mossy lawn with shade-loving plants.

Lawn problems

Weeds or the dead spots caused by insects or disease, can make your lawn unsightly. Here are some typical causes of lawn problems and how to fix them:

Environmental problems

Poor drainage In sections of lawn that are always wet, grass will struggle and weeds such as ground ivy will thrive. *Solutions:* Alter the watering pattern, or improve drainage, perhaps by regrading.

Poor watering Too much or too little water can harm a lawn. *Solution:* Check how much water you're applying (see pages 42–45). After watering, check to see how far the water has soaked in.

Slopes There's too little water near the top and too much at the bottom. *Solutions:* Replace the sprinkler with one that applies water very slowly, like a gentle rain, so that the water can soak in before it runs off. Consider replacing the grass with a ground cover.

Shade Most lawn grasses grow poorly in shade, although some specialty grasses are shade-tolerant. *Solutions:* If trees cause the shade, pruning them will allow more light to pass through. Plant shade-tolerant grasses: fine fescues in cool-season areas, St. Augustinegrass or zoysiagrass in warm-season areas.

Low mowing Cutting your lawn too low or too often, removing more than one-third of its height at once, creates openings for pests of several kinds. *Solutions:* Raise the cutting height of your mower. (See page 30 for optimum heights for different grasses.) During the seasons of most rapid growth, you may need to mow more frequently than every seven days.

Weeds

Keeping lawns completely free of weeds is not practical for most people. There will always be a few weeds showing up. The issue is, what kinds or how many you can tolerate.

Weeds are generally classed into three broad categories based on their life cycles.

Annuals These are are weeds that produce seeds in one season. The classic example is crabgrass. It likes heat and is able to outcompete cool-season grasses in summer if given the slightest advantage. Other annual weeds prefer cool weather, so they predominate in spring and fall, or through winter where winters

Lawn insects

Healthy lawns can support a few pests, but if there are too many, some degree of intervention may be necessary.

Grubs Larvae of beetles, they have white bodies, brown or tan heads, tiny legs, and are usually folded into a C-shape. Control with pesticides specifically labeled for this pest and for use on lawns.

Sod webworms Adults (shown) are gray-white moths that fly low over lawns at dusk. Their caterpillars live in thatch. Control with pesticides specifically labeled for sod webworm control.

Mole crickets These gray-brown insects have short, shovel-like front feet which they use to dig irregular tunnels. Digger wasps are a parasitic control; encourage them by planting the wildflower southern larraflower. Chemical control is difficult but possible, if directions are followed exactly.

Hairy chinch bugs These are small, black bugs (about 1/3-inch-long) with white wings folded over their back. Control by removing thatch, and by keeping the lawn moist to encourage beneficial fungi. Chemical controls are also available.

(Lawn problems continued)

are mild. Examples of these include henbit, common chickweed, and annual bluegrass.

Biennial These weeds require two years to produce seeds. These weeds emerge and grow the first year, overwinter as a dormant rosette of leaves, and resume growth and produce seeds the second year. Wild carrot (Queen Anne's lace) and common mullein are examples.

Perennial These weeds emerge, grow, and produce some structure that enables the plant to overwinter and resume growth year after year. These plants typically reproduce by vegetative mechanisms as well as seeds. Common examples include quackgrass, nimblewill, ground ivy, plantain, and dandelion.

Other classifications Finally, weeds are classified as either broad-leaved or grassy. Broad-leaved weeds (botanically *dicots)* have branching leaf veins. Grassy weeds *(monocots)* have parallel leaf veins. The difference is important, because some herbicides work on one kind and not the other.

Preemergence herbicides interrupt seedling emergence, so they must be in place before weed seeds germinate. These are used most successfully to prevent crabgrass, which mostly germinates all at once, about the same time as forsythia blooms. Postemergence herbicides kill growing weeds. Selective herbicides kill targeted weeds and leave other plants unharmed; nonselective herbicides kill all plants.

Insect and disease problems

Although many types of insects are normally present in a lawn, most of them are not harmful to turfgrasses. Close examination on your hands and knees is the best way to identify insect pests in a damaged lawn. You may be able to see the insect in action. To determine whether insects are a problem, both shoots and roots should be examined. Some turf insects, such as white grubs, are active only underground. Common insect pests in turfgrasses are lawn moths (sod webworms), cutworms, armyworms, skippers, chinch bugs, leafhoppers, white grubs, and billbugs. Nematodes and rodents cause occasional problems.

For most homeowners, lawn diseases are not a major problem. Most can be traced to overwatering or to selecting the wrong grass for a given climate. Another cause is applying too much water or too much fertilizer. Focus on the basics of watering, modest fertilizing, and regular mowing, and you'll encounter few, if any, problems.

healthy garden • healthy garden • healthy garden • healthy garden

Insect indicators

Most lawns have a variety of insects living in them that cause no problem. But if your lawn has dead spots *and* if it's popular with skunks or browsing birds such as starlings, crows, or grackles, chances are that sod webworms or grubs are plentiful enough to cause damage.

3

tree&
shrub
care

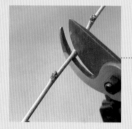

Long-lived trees and shrubs add character to your yard. Here's how to care for them.

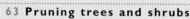

Trees and shrubs are the most valuable and long-lived plants you own. Maintaining them properly keeps them healthy and looking their best. When problems do occur, knowing what to look for and what to do may prevent the loss of a valued landscape plant.

Caring for trees and shrubs

Deciduous trees and shrubs lose their leaves in autumn; evergreens retain their foliage year-round. These characteristics, and others, determine the best way to prune, water, protect, and fertilize your trees and shrubs.

Deciduous trees and shrubs Many deciduous plants offer attractive flowers or fruit, colorful or unusual foliage, and beautiful forms. They often serve as landscape accents or focal points. Care should make the most of the plant's ornamental features and maintain its attractive natural form. Some require specific pruning, watering, and fertilizing techniques.

Evergreen trees and shrubs Evergreens block sun and wind, and screen unwanted and intrusive views year-round. As hedges, they define boundaries. Some evergreens have ornamental flowers, fruit, or foliage. The two types of evergreens—those with needles and those with broad leaves—have different pruning and fertilizing requirements.

Shade trees Most grow tall and wide with spreading limbs, and lose their leaves in autumn. Some shade trees are evergreen. Providing adequate fertilizer and water, protecting them from injury, and pruning damaged and poorly placed limbs are the keys to maintaining them.

Hedges Closely planted rows of evergreen or deciduous shrubs provide a living wall or boundary. Gaps in a hedge signal entry points and transitions between spaces, and may frame attractive views. Windbreaks of densely planted shrubs and trees, especially evergreens, can help moderate the microclimate in your yard.

· SMART IDEA ·

Observe your new landscape

When you move into a home with established landscape trees and shrubs, observe them for six months to a year before doing more than maintenance pruning, such as hedge-trimming or removing dead, damaged, or diseased wood. Use the time to note the plants' season of bloom, growth habits, health, and vigor.

If the previous owners hired a landscape service, ask to see the maintenance records, which may include pesticide and fertilizer applications, pruning schedules, and plant species. These details and landscape history can help you establish your own maintenance schedule.

Uses for trees and shrubs

So essential and useful that they're often taken for granted, trees and shrubs are the most permanent element in a landscape. Four key functions they provide include:

Backyard shade Shade trees moderate the climate, noticeably lowering temperatures and reducing cooling costs.

Fence and wall Planted closely together, trees and small shrubs form a hedge to mark boundary lines. Low hedges like this simply divide space; taller hedges create privacy.

Beauty Many trees and shrubs compete with the showiest perennials for breathtaking flower displays. A specimen tree makes a lovely focal point for a landscape.

Direction Trees and shrubs combined with other plants can be used to direct foot traffic, make entryways inviting, and divert the eye from unsightly views.

Tree and shrub maintenance calendar

Most trees and shrubs need only seasonal or annual maintenance.
The timing and frequency of care depends on the climate and
particular plants. Use the following checklist as a general guide.

Task	Reason	Why now?
SPRING		
Prune pines	appearance; control growth	pinching soft spring shoots is the best way to control shape and size
Prune storm- or frost-damaged plants	safety; plant health and appearance	dead branches look shabby and provide entry points for pests
Shear hedges	shape up just prior to spring growth	spring growth quickly covers pruning wounds
Mulch	weed control	spring is peak weed season
Fertilize	improve growth	most landscape plants benefit from spring and early fall fertilization
Replace dead or dying trees and shrubs	as needed	improve appearance of landscape and control possible spread of diseases
SUMMER		
Shear hedges	maintain shape	summer's warmth and heat promote growth that mars the shape of the hedge
Prune spring-flowering shrubs	maintain shape and promote next year's flower crop	promotes growth of new branches that will flower next spring
Prune shade trees	tree health and shape	regrowth will be less than after dormant season pruning
Watch for pests and diseases	most are easy to manage if caught early	common pests are most active in summer
Water as needed	maintain plant health	periods of drought are common in all regions during summer
FALL		
If rains have been light, soak soil to 18-inch depth	plants are more winter hardy if they're well-watered	ensure that plants enter winter in good condition
Apply low-nitrogen fertilizers	give slow-acting materials plenty of time to work into soil	ensure that plants enter winter in good condition
Wrap or shelter tender plants	wind protection	exposure to icy winds causes most damage
WINTER		
Water evergreens on sunny days, or provide shade	winter survival	evergreens often suffer drought on sunny days when soil is frozen
Prune shrubs that bloom in summer	to reshape the plant and to promote more blooms	pruning spurs growth of new wood, which carries the buds for summer blooms (Spring pruning removes those buds.)

57

Nitrogen fertilizer

Fertilizers release their nitrogen quickly or slowly, depending on the form of nitrogen in the product. Ammonium nitrate, ammonium sulfate, calcium nitrate, potassium nitrate, and urea are quick-release nitrogen forms. Controlled-release forms may include the initials **WIN**, which stand for water-insoluble nitrogen.

Fertilizing

In home landscapes, trees and shrubs often benefit from additional nutrients. Some plants, especially hybrid roses and fruit trees, require more fertilizer than other trees and shrubs. Trees and shrubs absorb nutrients through their roots in a zone around their trunk or stem that is about twice the diameter of their branch spread. Leaves can also absorb liquid nutrients.

How much to fertilize

Natural soil usually contains all of the nutrients that locally adapted plants need, but the soil in your yard could be deficient for your shrubs and trees. Consider testing your soil and adding supplements in any of the following circumstances:

- **Your house is newly constructed. Builders often truck in poor-quality soil that lacks organic matter and adequate nutrients to fill the finished site.**

- **Your trees and shrubs grow in spaces where soil is limited, such as between a street and a sidewalk, in a small pocket surrounded by pavement or other hard surfaces, or in a container. Small spaces limit access to nutrients.**

- **Trees and shrubs are young. Fertilizing helps them become established more quickly.**

- **You grow plants with special needs, such as fruit trees or acid-loving plants. Trees and shrubs growing outside their naturally adapted climate may have special requirements.**

When plants need more nutrition than the soil can provide, they may or may not show obvious symptoms. Nutrient-deficiency symptoms often mimic signs of other problems, such as pests, disease, physical damage, air pollution, or water stress. Deficiency signs can include stunted twig or shoot growth compared to growth in previous years; twigs dying near the ends of the branches; fewer flowers and fruits; and smaller, off-color, or paler green foliage compared to that of nearby plants of the same species.

A soil test can help determine if your tree or shrub needs additional fertilizer. Test for soil nutrients and pH with a do-it-yourself kit, or send a soil sample to a professional soil-testing lab, such as those operated by state and county extension services. Obtain soil lab sampling kits at garden centers or farm supply stores, or by calling your local extension service.

Depending on the results of the soil test, the testing lab may recommend adding nutrients or other soil amendments, such as sulfur or lime, to increase the effectiveness of the fertilizer. Sulfur lowers the soil pH and lime raises it. Nutrients are most available to roots when the soil pH is in the middle range. Although modifying the soil pH is often worthwhile for lawns, shrubs, and vegetable and flower gardens, it is less practical for long-lived trees. In some soils (such as one naturally high in lime, as in the Southwest), adjusting pH is a slow process that may take years, and the change is often short-lived. When planting new trees and shrubs, consider those that thrive naturally in your current situation instead of trying to change it.

Fertilizer types and how to use them

Solid and liquid fertilizers come in many formulas to suit particular plants and situations. Some are designed for the growing needs of specific kinds of trees or shrubs, such as fruit trees, evergreens, rhododendrons, or roses. General or all-purpose fertilizers are suitable for most kinds of trees and shrubs as well as other landscape plants.

Granular fertilizers These come as small, dry pellets and are usually the least expensive and easiest to apply. Some dissolve quickly in the soil and give plants a fast boost. Controlled-release fertilizers dissolve more gradually, providing a steady source of nutrients for several months. Many brands combine both controlled- and quick-release forms.

The easiest way to apply granular fertilizer around trees and shrubs is to scatter it on the soil's surface with a spreader, then water to help it dissolve into the soil. Use this method in places where the fertilizer is unlikely to wash into a waterway in a heavy rain. Avoid this problem by burying the granular fertilizer in holes drilled 1 to 3 feet apart and 4 to 8 inches deep, spaced uniformly around the tree. Start the holes 2 to 3 feet from the trunk and extend them to 3 feet beyond the drip line. Divide the fertilizer evenly among the holes, then fill the holes with compost.

• GOOD PLANTS •

Caring for the acid-lovers

Most plants in your yard prefer a slightly acidic soil pH, just below neutral 7. But a handful of landscape stars need soil that is more acidic and is high in organic matter. Depending on your soil and water pH, these plants may need fertilizers formulated for acid-loving plants.

To help lower the pH and keep it there, maintain a 2- to 4-inch mulch layer of shredded bark, pine needles, or chopped leaves—especially those from oak—out to the drip line to hold the soil moisture and provide organic matter. Some plants and their preferred pH include azaleas, camellias, mountain laurel, and rhododendrons, 4.5–5.5; star magnolia, 5–6; daphnes, 6.5–7.5; witch hazel, 6–7; glossy abelia and Oregon grapeholly, 6–8.

(Fertilizing continued)

Fertilizer spikes made of compressed granular fertilizer; these are inserted into the soil with a hammer. Space them evenly throughout the plant's root zone. Manufacturers offer formulations for specific plant types, such as fruit trees, roses, and evergreens. Spikes cost more than an equal amount of loose granular fertilizer, but they are tidier to use. Their disadvantage is that they do not distribute the nutrients evenly throughout the root zone. Use spikes for mature trees growing in lawns, and where you don't want to scatter fertilizer on the soil's surface, such as on slopes and near streams and ponds.

Liquid and water-soluble fertilizers These types release their nutrients quickly for immediate plant absorption. They are especially useful for correcting specific nutrient deficiencies, such as iron deficiency in oaks, but their effect is temporary. They may be applied to the soil's surface, injected into the soil with a special tool, or sprayed on the foliage.

The advantage to injecting liquid fertilizer into the soil is that it gets the nutrients right into the root zone and adds water to the soil. You can purchase an application tool that attaches to your garden hose. Inject the fertilizer solution 6 to 9 inches deep in holes spaced about 2 to 3 feet apart. To spray liquid fertilizer on foliage or the soil's surface, use a hose-end sprayer attachment.

The best fertilizer formulas for woody plants generally have ratios of three or four parts nitrogen to one part phosphorus, and one or two parts potassium. Commercial examples include formulas such as 15-5-10 (3-1-2) and 12-4-8 (3-1-2). The amount of fertilizer needed and the best time to apply it depend on several factors, including the age and desired growth rate of the tree or shrub. Fertilizer products differ, so read package labels for additional details.

Newly planted trees and shrubs do not need fertilizing immediately. If they were planted in fall, wait until early spring to fertilize. Spring-planted trees and shrubs can be fertilized six to eight weeks after planting. Spread 1 tablespoon of controlled-release granular fertilizer containing 10 to 12 percent nitrogen around the perimeter of the planting hole for a tree or shrub that was in a 1-gallon or an 8-inch-diameter container. Use 2 to 3 tablespoons for larger trees.

Young or small trees and shrubs, especially hedges, benefit from fertilizer to speed their growth. Twice a year, in early spring and autumn, apply 1 to 1½ pounds of actual nitrogen per 1,000 square feet, or use the recommendation for newly planted trees. See the instructions on page 62 on how to calculate the amount of fertilizer to apply.

safety alert · safety alert · safety alert · safety alert · safety alert

Fertilizer safety

Quick-release fertilizers can harm trees and shrubs growing in drought conditions. A day or two before applying fertilizer to dry soil, water the root zone of the plant thoroughly to a soil depth of at least 8 inches. After applying the fertilizer, water again to dissolve the nutrients into the soil.

Fertilizing trees

Regular fertilization keeps trees and shrubs vigorous and pest-free. The dripline area marked in the picture shows the area to fertilize.

Auger Use a soil auger to bore 2- to 3-inch holes about a foot deep, and 3 feet apart under the tree's dripline. Pour 5 ounces of 12-4-8 fertilizer mixed with enough compost to fill the hole into each hole.

Hand-held spreader Spread about 3 pounds of an all-purpose fertilizer containing 10 percent nitrogen over 100 square feet.

Fertilizer spikes These are a convenient way to ensure mature trees have access to basic nutrients. Follow product directions regarding the number to use.

(Fertilizing continued)

Mature trees and shrubs need less fertilizer than younger plants. If they are growing in a lawn that receives annual fertilization, you do not need to give them any additional nutrients unless a soil test indicates otherwise. If they do not get nutrients from other sources, apply 1 to 2 pounds of actual nitrogen per 1,000 square feet of soil surface once a year.

To calculate the right amount of a specific fertilizer to use around your tree, divide the desired amount of nitrogen by the percent of nitrogen listed on the container. For example, if you want to apply 1½ pounds of actual nitrogen and you have a bag of 12-4-8 fertilizer, divide 1½ by 0.12 to get 12½ pounds of fertilizer per 1,000 square feet.

If you want to spread fertilizer in a smaller area, divide the desired area by 1,000, then multiply the nitrogen per 1,000 square feet by the result. For example, if you want to apply fertilizer at the rate of 12½ pounds per 1,000 square feet, but your area is 100 square feet, divide 100 by 1,000 to get 0.10. Multiply 12½ by 0.10 to get 1.25 pounds of fertilizer per 100 feet.

The best time to apply fertilizer is in the early spring after the ground thaws but before leaf growth begins. Be wary in cold-winter climates of fertilizing too early.

Watering

Trees and shrubs often seem such a natural part of the landscape it's easy to forget that although they usually get all the water they need from rainfall, in some situations they may need additional moisture. Symptoms of water stress include wilting leaves, dropping flower buds, and stunted growth. In any of the following situations, pay particular attention to the water needs of your trees and shrubs:

■ **Trees or shrubs are less than five years old. Young plants need moist, but not saturated, soil for the first few growing seasons, until their roots become well-established. After their first growing season following planting, allow the soil to dry between waterings to help the plants adjust to natural conditions.**

■ **Trees or shrubs are planted in containers or in soil pockets surrounded by paving. Plants with limited root zones need watering more frequently than those with larger root systems.**

budget stretcher • budget stretcher • budget stretcher • budget stretcher

Making leaf mulch

Make mulch from the leaves that fall in autumn. Rake the leaves into long piles about 6 inches deep and the width of your lawn-mower deck. Mow over the pile to shred them; collect shredded leaves in the mower bag or rake them up. Spread shredded leaves 2 to 4 inches deep around landscape plants.

- **The shrub or tree species has shallow roots or large leaves.** Azalea and dogwoods, for example, have most of their roots close to the surface, where the soil dries out quickly. Large-leaved plants, such as magnolia and hydrangea, lose more water through their foliage than smaller-leaved plants and must absorb more through their roots.

- **The shrub grows under a tree or roof overhang.** Plants in these places usually can't get enough natural precipitation.

- **The weather has been hot, dry, or windy.** Although many trees and shrubs are naturally adapted to these conditions, those growing outside their natural environment may not be. Unusual weather may affect all plants, regardless of their adaptability.

As a rule, if the soil is dry at a depth of about 6 to 8 inches within the root zone, it's time to water. Trees and shrubs grow most of their absorbing roots in the top 12 inches of soil, and roots can extend out two to three times wider than the leaf canopy. Water deeply, moistening the soil down to at least 8 inches, every one to two weeks to encourage deeper, more drought-resistant roots. Shallow watering promotes roots that grow close to the surface, where they need more frequent irrigation.

Pruning trees and shrubs

Pruning trees and shrubs is more successful when you have a goal in mind. Most often your goal is to improve or maintain plant health and vigor while retaining the plant's natural shape. When pruning formal hedges, however, uniformity and wall-like growth are the goals. The pruning method that you use depends on the type of plant, its growth habits, and what you hope to accomplish.

Tree and shrub anatomy

Before you prune, it's important to understand the different parts of shrubs and trees and how each grows and interacts with other parts. The following definitions list the components of a tree, from the largest and most central parts to the smallest, outermost ones:

- **Trunks are the main, woody stem between the roots and leafy canopy. Many trees naturally have multiple trunks; others, such as spruce trees, have a single trunk.**

· HOW-TO ·

Easy soil moisture test

A wide variety of gauges and meters that are designed to measure soil moisture are available. But the direct—and simple—approach remains one of the best. Insert a new wooden paint stir stick 6 to 10 inches into the soil near the plants you need to keep watered. Leave the stick in place for 30 to 60 minutes. The soft wood absorbs soil moisture and darkens slightly. Pull it out and note the depth of the moisture on the stick. If the stick is dry, apply water until the top 8 inches of soil within the root zone are moist. Irrigate slowly, allowing the water to penetrate into the soil without running off. Check the soil moisture depth again a day later to be certain that the root zone is moist.

(Pruning trees and shrubs continued)

■ Scaffold limbs are main branches that grow outward from the trunk. The ring of bark at the base of the scaffold limb, where it joins the trunk, is called the collar.

■ Secondary branches and twigs grow from the scaffold limbs. Although smaller, they also have collars where they join the limb.

■ Shoot buds grow on twigs and branches and develop into new twigs and leaves. When shoot buds expand, they leave telltale scars on the twigs.

■ Flower buds are often larger or fatter than shoot buds. They may grow on new twigs that were formed in the current year or develop on older stems from previous years. Some trees and shrubs grow flower buds that bloom in the same year that they form. Other tree and shrub species form flower buds that don't bloom until the following year. To promote flowering, it's important to know how and when your trees and shrubs form flower buds and bloom before you prune them.

■ Terminal buds grow at the tip of each twig and branch. As they expand, they leave a ring around the twig. Measuring the distance between the end of the twig and the nearest ring shows how much the twig has grown that year. Often, you can see how much the branch has grown in previous seasons by measuring the number of rings and the distance between them. Terminal buds produce hormones that suppress the growth of shoot buds farther down the stem.

Shrubs grow multiple stems from a crown, the place where the stems emerge from the roots just below the soil's surface. In most shrub species, each stem grows for a number of years before it declines and is replaced by new, younger stems that grow from the crown. Shrubs also have shoot buds, flower buds, and terminal buds that function the same as those on trees. They do not have scaffold limbs, but most do have twigs and branches that grow from the main stems.

Pruning techniques and tools

Pruning trees and shrubs involves two basic kinds of cuts.

Thinning Use thinning cuts to help retain the natural shape of a plant. With this technique, you cut a branch or twig back to the trunk, limb, or branch from which it grows. To promote healing, make the cut just outside the collar on the stem you are cutting back. Thinning cuts generally do not cause vigorous new growth, because you remove the entire stem and all its buds. Use thinning cuts to remove dead, diseased, damaged, and crowded branches and twigs, and those that cross one another.

Heading A heading cut removes the terminal bud, leaving a stub that contains dormant shoot buds. Make the cut just above a shoot bud, so that removing the terminal bud ends its dominance over other buds, allowing the others to expand and grow. These cuts change the natural branching pattern. When several shoot buds on a

Pruning safety

Wear appropriate clothing and safety gear while pruning. Leather gloves can prevent nicks and cuts from pruning shears, saws, and sharp thorns. Safety goggles keep sawdust and twigs out of your eyes. Ear protection avoids hearing damage. When operating a chain saw, also wear long pants and closed-toe leather shoes.

Pruning basics

Where you cut is just as important as when you cut. That's why you need to understand these basic cuts. Once you do, you'll be able to anticipate the effect of cutting at different places and realize your pruning goals.

Heading cut Cutting at any point on a stem results in a cluster of new growth below the cut. For best results, avoid leaving stubs. Using a hand pruner, cut just above a bud. Select the bud carefully to direct growth.

Thinning cut To thin a plant, remove a branch all the way back to a main branch, the trunk, or the ground using a hand pruner. Thinning encourages the branches that remain to grow while maintaining the plant's natural shape.

Shearing Shearing is a type of heading cut done with pruning shears. It is used to shape plants, usually into hedges but may include fanciful forms. After shearing, growth resumes just below the cut, resulting in a dense outer shell of leaves covering a leafless interior.

(Pruning trees and shrubs continued)

twig expand at once, the resulting growth will be denser, which is desirable in hedges, for example, but not a shade tree. Use a heading cut to change the direction in which a branch grows. If a branch or twig is growing toward the house, prune it back to a branch or bud that points away from the house.

Call a professional to prune limbs that grow among or near overhead wires, that are large enough to damage property, or that you cannot prune without a ladder.

It's important to use sharp, clean tools to prune, because they make cuts that heal quickly. Always use the right-size tool for the branch you are pruning to avoid damage to the tool and to the plant. Tools that you need to prune trees and shrubs include the following:

- **Hand pruners cut twigs and branches up to ¾ inch in diameter.**

- **Loppers make cuts between ¾ inch and 1½ inches in diameter. Their long handles allow you to tackle higher branches, and reach into the center of crowded shrubs.**

- **Shears, whether manual, electric, or gasoline-powered, prune many stems at once, making an even surface on hedges. They can cut stems up to ½ inch in diameter.**

- **Pruning saws cut limbs more than an inch in diameter. Some pruning saws are mounted on poles for reaching high branches.**

Pruning priorities

Prune to improve the health, safety, and appearance of landscape plants. Keep these priorities in mind:

Prune off all dead, damaged, and diseased branches, stems, and twigs before you tackle any other pruning task. If the plant is dormant and you aren't sure what's alive and what's dead, wait to prune until the buds begin to swell in spring or until the plant is in full leaf in early to midsummer. Cut back to a living, undamaged branch or bud.

Remove crowded stems and branches and those that cross other branches. Crowding promotes disease and insect infestation, and branches and stems that rub against one another can open wounds in the bark. They also limit the amount of sun that reaches into the plant, weakening the shaded branches and twigs. On shrubs that send up many shoots from their crowns, you can prune dead, broken, crowded, or unhealthy shoots right back to the ground.

healthy garden • healthy garden • healthy garden • healthy garden

Post-flowering cleanup

Some ornamental shrubs benefit from having their spent flowers removed. This procedure, called *deadheading*, promotes repeat flowering in some species, especially roses. Plants with unattractive flower stalks, such as lilac and rhododendron, look tidier too. Use pruners to cut the stems back to a healthy bud.

What to prune

Trees and shrubs need pruning for many reasons. Young plants benefit from training and shaping; mature plants need problems fixed. Here are some common reasons to prune.

Overhanging branches Limbs leaning precariously over your house invite problems. Hire a qualified arborist to do this job to avoid damaging your home.

Storm damage Remove broken limbs as soon as possible. A qualified arborist will be able minimize further damage to either the house or tree.

Watersprouts These fast-growing, flexible shoots drain energy from the tree and mar the shape of the plant. Remove them by cutting them off at their base.

Overhead wires Utility wires and tree branches are a bad mix. Never prune them yourself. Hire an arborist who is certified to work in such situations and around electricity.

Dead limbs They are an entry point for pests and diseases. Removing them with a pruning saw improves both the tree's appearance and health.

Crossing branches Branches that cross rub against each other, creating wounds which are entry points for pests. Remove one of the branches.

Narrow crotch angle Tight crotches like this can break in strong wind or heavy snow. Remove the weakest branch or keep the one growing in the desired direction.

Suckers These are similar to water sprouts, but arise from the tree's roots. Remove them whenever they appear. Cut as close to the ground as possible.

Poorly spaced limbs The small branch in the center is weakly attached and grows the same direction as the one at right. Cut it off at the collar.

(Pruning trees and shrubs continued)

Prune out dangerously or inconveniently placed limbs and shoots. Remove branches that rub against the house or crowd the sidewalk, for example.

Prune off suckers that grow from the base of the trunk of a tree and water sprouts that grow straight up from horizontal limbs. Suckers and water sprouts drain energy and detract from the natural form of the tree. Those on ornamental flowering trees may not produce flowers, or may have flowers and growth habits that differ from the rest of the tree.

Promote blooms

Correct pruning can increase the quality and quantity of flowers that shrubs produce and help shrubs remain vigorous and attractive in all seasons. Before you prune a flowering shrub you need to know when it forms flower buds and when it blooms. If you aren't sure, observe the shrub during the growing season before pruning it, or talk to the staff at a garden center or nursery, a Master Gardener, or your local country extension agent. You can prune dead, damaged, crowded and poorly spaced stems and suckers at any time.

In general, shrubs fall into two categories: those that bloom in spring and early summer and those that bloom in mid- to late summer. Here's when to prune each kind:

■ **Shrubs that bloom in spring to early summer usually form flower buds the previous year. Prune these shrubs right after they finish blooming. If you prune them after they have formed flower buds for the following year, you may cut off their flower buds and lose the next season's bloom. Spring-blooming shrubs include lilac, barberry, forsythia, smoke tree, spring-blooming spirea, mockorange, cotoneaster, euonymus, viburnum, weigela, bigleaf hydrangea, and oakleaf hydrangea.**

■ **Shrubs that bloom in mid- to late summer usually do so on the new twigs and shoots that grew in the spring. To increase flowering, you want to promote vigorous spring growth and lots of new shoots. Prune in late fall to early spring, when the shrubs are dormant. In climates where freeze damage to plants is common, you can wait to prune until the buds just begin to swell. Summer-blooming shrubs include roses, butterfly bush, beautyberry, hibiscus, summer-blooming spireas, and glossy abelia.**

In many roses and some other shrubs, shoots of a flowering variety have been grafted onto the vigorous roots of another variety to ensure hardiness. The graft union, where the roots and top parts were grafted together, is usually knobby and swollen in appearance and located near the soil level. Remove any shoots that grow from below the graft union as soon as they appear, because they will not produce desirable flowers and may weaken the plant.

safety alert • safety alert • safety alert • safety alert •

Bee safety

Bees perform important functions in nature and can be welcome visitors to your garden. Although most don't intentionally sting people, play it safe by planting bee-attracting flowering trees and shrubs, such as linden, fruit trees, and butterfly bush, away from swimming pools, patios, play areas, and walkways.

Pruning shrubs

Shrubs need pruning to control size, maintain healthy vigorous growth, and maximize flowering. Shrubs used as hedges need regular shearing to maintain size and shape.

Formal hedges Shear mature evergreen hedges in spring before growth begins. New leaves will hide pruning cuts. Or prune during or just after the spring growth spurt. Don't shear after late summer—the growth that results will be more vulnerable to winter injury.

Pinch conifers Pinching new growth is the easy way to maintain size and promote density. These are new shoots of spruce.

Rejuvenate Mature shrubs, such as lilac or butterfly bush, benefit by pruning for continual renewal. Each year at pruning time, remove one-third or fewer of the oldest stems, cutting as close to soil level as possible with loppers.

(Pruning trees and shrubs continued)

Maintaining clipped hedges

Formal hedges consist of individual plants that are pruned as one large mass to achieve uniform appearance. If you have an established hedge, shear it throughout the growing season to promote dense growth. Certain species need only a few trimmings early in the growing season; others need regular shearing over a longer period.

As a rule, trim a hedge whenever it begins to look unkempt. If it has large leaves that show the effects of pruning for a long time, prune in early spring so that pruning wounds will be covered quickly. If leaves are small and pruning wounds insignificant, prune just after growth spurts in later spring. At that time, growth is slowing and the effects of pruning will last longer.

Properly pruned hedges are wider at the bottom and narrower at the top. Hedges trimmed this way allow sunlight to reach top to bottom, and shed snow more readily. Hedges that are wider at the top cast shade on lower leaves, causing the lower portions to lose leaves.

If your hedge has bare spots, is overgrown, or is less dense than you want it, you may be able to renovate it, depending on the type of shrub. Vigorous shrubs tolerate heavier pruning. These may grow back even when cut nearly to the ground. Slow-growing shrubs may take years to recover if pruned too heavily in one season. And some evergreens, such as hemlock, pine, and fir, may never recover if you remove all the current season's wood, because they have no buds on their old wood.

Once you know the type of shrub making up the hedge, you can renovate it following these guidelines.

Shrubs that tolerate severe pruning Cut the shrubs to within 6 to 20 inches of the ground, depending on the size of the stems and vigor of the species. Smaller stems usually recover and sprout more quickly than larger-diameter stems. As new growth develops, prune often to encourage a dense, bushy hedge that is broader at the base than at the top. Vigorous shrubs include privet, firethorn, barberry, bayberry, spirea, forsythia, boxwood, yew, and holly.

Slower-growing shrubs Remove about a third of the oldest—the longest and thickest—shoots each year for three years. Prune them just above the ground. As an alternative, prune each shoot a bit lower or narrower than you want the hedge to be when it's mature.

Plants that do not grow new shoots from old wood You may have to replace the overgrown specimens and start over.

time saver • time saver • time saver • time saver • time saver • time saver

Easy-care hedges

Instead of pruning a high-maintenance clipped hedge, let your shrubs keep their natural form. Space shrubs so that they touch at maturity without crowding. Prune with thinning cuts so shrubs retain their natural shape and vigor, but avoid shearing.

Pruning conifers

Growth habits and pruning considerations differ for conifers and broad-leaved trees. Most conifers need pruning only to remove dead, damaged, or diseased limbs and to correct errant growth.

Whorled branching Spruces, firs, pines, and other conifers that have three or more branches at each node grow new branches from only the tips of each branch. Cutting into existing growth leaves a hole that won't close up. To control size and density in these conifers, prune the new growth, called a *candle,* as it expands.

Random branching Arborvitae, juniper, yew, and and other conifers that have latent buds along their stems can be pruned anywhere. These you can head, shear, or thin as much as is required or desired.

Prune conical-shaped conifers only to remove competing leaders. Those with less symmetrical forms can have branches pruned to create more openness, and lower branches can be removed to have room underneath for other plants.

All conifers will grow more densely if you lightly shear off new growth each spring. To help control the size of needled evergreens, clip them back during their main growing season in spring.

Conifers have two types of branching patterns, which require different pruning methods. Most conifers grow from a single, central trunk. Sometimes, however, competing leaders will form. Remove these by cutting them off at their base as soon as you see them. If the central leader is injured, you can train a new one by gently bending an upper limb into a vertical position and tying it to the trunk or a stake. Remove the tie when the new leader can stand on its own, usually within a year.

• SMART IDEA •

Hire an arborist

Pruning even a modest-sized tree is a big job ... and it can be hazardous. The margin of safety shrinks if the tree grows close to the road, power lines, or a structure. To play it safe, tackle only limbs that you can reach easily from the ground. If you use a ladder, prune only relatively lightweight limbs. For more challenging jobs that require climbing or cutting near power lines, call an arborist. Certified arborists and foresters can help diagnose and correct insect, disease, and nutritional problems as well. Look in the Yellow Pages under Arborists, Foresters, or Tree Services, or seek recommendations at a tree nursery. Ask for references, proof of insurance, professional certifications, and a written estimate.

Rejuvenating ornamental shrubs

When shrubs outgrow their space, begin to look unkempt and shabby, or produce fewer flowers, you can often bring them back to their former glory by corrective pruning. For most shrubs, it's best to accomplish the renovation over a period of several years. Do not remove more than a third of the plant's stems in one year.

(Pruning trees and shrubs continued)

The first step is to go through the list of pruning priorities, removing the undesirable wood. Next, depending on the amount of wood you removed in the first step, prune up to a third of the remaining healthy shoots. Either cut the oldest stems at the ground, or prune the stems to a point a bit lower than you want the plant to ultimately grow. Use thinning cuts at the recommended time of year for your shrub's season of bloom. In subsequent years, repeat this process until the shrubs reach the size and appearance you desire.

You can turn some large shrubs into small trees by pruning and training them over a period of two to three years. Use this technique to create an interesting focal point in your landscape, to preserve an overgrown but otherwise attractive shrub, or even to produce a shade tree for a small yard or patio.

1. In the first year, choose the stem that you want to become the trunk of the new tree. Prune all other stems to the ground. For a multitrunk tree, leave two or three stems to grow.

2. In the second year, use thinning cuts to remove the lower twigs and branches from the trunk, and remove any new stems that have sprouted up from the ground. Decide which of the remaining stems will make the best scaffold branches, and remove the rest. (See "Shaping young trees" below.)

3. As the tree grows taller in subsequent years, continue to shape the plant and remove competing shoots.

Good shrub candidates for turning into small trees include Russian olive, pussy willow, pagoda dogwood, and cornelian cherry.

Shaping young trees

Young trees need shaping to establish a healthy branching structure that will keep them thriving and trouble-free as they mature. When viewed from the top, healthy limbs radiate out from the trunk-like spokes from a wheel hub. The limbs should be spaced up and down the trunk so that each has room to mature without crowding or crossing another. At the point where each limb attaches to the trunk, the limb should be smaller in diameter than the trunk, and the angle at which the limb is attached should be somewhat U-shaped. Limbs that attach in a sharp V angle or that are bigger than the trunk are more likely to break under stress, especially as they grow larger.

Shaping should begin at planting. When you plant a tree, remove broken and crossing limbs and any that have a larger diameter than the main trunk. If the tree has multiple leaders, choose one and

Colorful stems

Shrubs with colorful stems, including red-osier and yellow twig dogwood, green-stemmed kerria, and willow, show their best colors on young shoots. Prune out older, less colorful stems each spring, or cut the whole shrub back to 6 to 10 inches from the ground to promote new growth.

Ensuring good shape

Saplings need encouragement to develop into handsome, vigorous, mature trees. All it takes is some attention to training in the first three or four seasons of the tree's life.

Select scaffold branches. These are the large branches that will form the tree's main framework. Choose limbs that are distributed around the trunk, not too close together, and not directly above one another.

Before This tree has developed two main trunks, excess twiggy growth on lower trunk, and suckers from roots.

After One main trunk was chosen and the other cut off at ground level, along with suckers. Low branches on the trunk were cut off at their collars, and main scaffold branches were selected and shaped.

Well-shaped tree The difference between well-trained trees and poorly trained trees can be dramatic.

73

Promote natural shape

Instead of removing the lower branches from conifer trees such as firs and spruces, leave them intact. They balance and enhance the trees' natural appearance. If the branches interfere with weeding or mowing, spread an organic mulch around the tree.

(Pruning trees and shrubs continued)

remove the others. In second and subsequent years, select the best-placed limbs and remove the others, never taking more than a fourth of the tree canopy in a single season. Prune off undesirable branches while they are young, if possible, to keep the wound small.

Use thinning cuts, pages 64 to 65, taking care not to leave a stub or injure the ridge of bark at the point of attachment. Locate this collar and make the cut flush with the branch-side edge of the ridge. Not all trees have easily identifiable collars. In this situation, make the cut parallel to the trunk without cutting into the trunk bark or leaving a stub.

The best time of year to prune trees depends on the kind of tree and your climate. In general, prune in winter before dormant trees resume growth, or wait until midsummer to prune trees that bleed sap excessively, including maples, birches, and walnuts. Use hand pruners, loppers, or a pruning saw to make clean, smooth cuts. See page 196, for more information on pruning tool selection and care.

Repairing storm damage

Prevention is the best strategy when it comes to dealing with storm damage. Train trees properly when they are young so that they develop good, strong branching. Water properly to ensure a good root system. Minimize winter injury by avoiding late summer fertilization. Protect newly planted trees in winter by wrapping their trunks with commercially available tree wrap. Vandalism and accidents that cause similar injuries can be treated the same ways. If damage occurs anyway, take time to assess the situation before plunging in with the chain saw. First check for unsafe conditions. Look for large limbs that could fall, damaging property and harming people. Make sure no overhead wires are involved. If you see a downed or damaged wire, stay away from it and call 9-1-1 or the utility company. Do not attempt to work with any part of the tree until the utility company deems it safe. Call in a professional arborist to remove the largest, most dangerous limbs.

Damage may occur in the following ways:

Heavy snow or ice loads break or split limbs, especially on trees with brittle wood, such as silver maple and poplar, and on evergreens. If possible, knock off snow with a long pole or roof rake before breakage occurs. If you are able to do so safely, remove broken limbs yourself, using a thinning cut, otherwise call a professional.

Removing large limbs

Remove a heavy branch with three cuts to avoid bark tearing as the limb falls, a common cause of long-term damage to trees.

1 Cut under the branch. Make the first cut from underneath the branch, 6 to 12 inches from the trunk. Saw about one-third of the way through the limb.

2 Cut from the top. Next, set the saw 2 to 4 inches beyond the undercut. Saw completely through the branch from the top. If the bark on the underside tears, it will peel back only to the point of the undercut.

3 Remove the stub. Find the collar, the ridge of bark or the swollen area where the limb meets the trunk. Remove the stub by cutting just outside the collar. To get the right angle of cut, you may have to saw from the bottom.

4 Smooth the edges. Clean wounds heal quickly. Use a sharp knife, wood rasp, or coarse sandpaper to clean and smooth rough bark at the edge of the cut. This encourages the formation of callus tissue, which encloses the wound. Paint, tar, or other wound dressings should be avoided.

Pruning dwarf conifers

Some needle-bearing evergreens remain small by growing very slowly—sometimes less than an inch per year. Prune these special plants only to remove dead branches or limbs that grow much faster than the rest of the branches. Prune carefully to retain the shrub's natural shape.

(Pruning trees and shrubs continued)

Wind may split two trunks, or a limb and a trunk, at their point of attachment. Narrow crotch angles are especially vulnerable and should be removed before breakage occurs. Prune limbs using the three-cut method in "Removing large limbs," page 75. Call a professional to remove or repair split trunks and hard-to-reach limbs.

After a lightning strike, the bark on a tree may split, tear, or pop off completely. If the bark is damaged all or most of the way around the trunk, immediately call a professional, who may be able to save a valuable tree by grafting. Usually, however, a tree that has lost bark around the entire circumference of the trunk will die.

If the bark is torn only part of the way around the trunk, repair it using a sharp knife to trim the loose bark back to where it firmly attaches to the wood. If possible, trim the wound into an elliptical or pointed oval shape, which will let water drain freely.

Strong wind or flooding may uproot trees or cause them to lean. You or a professional can rescue small trees (25 feet or less in height), if at least half of the roots are still in the soil, by straightening and staking the tree in an upright position. This procedure may require a winch or other equipment. Larger trees require professional assistance and probably should be removed.

Removing trees and stumps

In most situations, it's a good idea to call a professional arborist to remove trees. Trees with rotted, cracked, or weak wood, a heavy canopy, or a distinctive lean may not fall where you expect. Unless the tree is 8 inches or less in diameter and growing well away from buildings, overhead wires, roads, and other valued trees and shrubs, you may cause unintended property damage or personal harm by trying to remove it yourself. An experienced arborist can take the tree down in sections, remove the stump, and clean up the debris.

To remove a tree yourself, following these steps:

1. Decide which way you want the tree to fall. Check for obstacles. Remember that the tree may not land exactly where you intend. Keep observers, especially children and pets, at least three tree lengths away from the area.

2. Notch the tree on the side of the fall by making two wedge cuts that meet at a 90-degree angle with a saw. The depth of the wedge should be about one-quarter of the diameter of the trunk.

3. On the side of the tree opposite the wedge, make a saw cut that's horizontal to the ground and about an inch above the center of the notch. Do not cut all the way through the tree. Leave a hinge of 1 to 1½ inches to help control the fall.

4. If the tree doesn't fall on its own or if the saw binds, drive wedges into the cut with a mallet. Quickly move at least three tree lengths away as the tree starts to fall. Do not try to control the fall once the tree begins to move.

You can remove small stumps yourself by digging around the tree and cutting through the main roots with an ax or chain saw. For fast and efficient stump removal, hire a tree service with a stump grinder. Stump-dissolving products, for sale at garden centers, may take years to completely remove a stump.

Pests and problems

Familiarize yourself with the appearance and growth habits of your healthy plants so that you will recognize unusual symptoms. Early intervention can prevent small problems from becoming serious. Keep in mind that not all problems have a practical solution, and others aren't serious enough to warrant treatment.

Symptoms to watch for:

- **Sticky residue on leaves and on surfaces under the plant. Cause: Probably sooty mold growing on aphid honeydew.**

- **Black, gray, brown, or white powder or spots on foliage and twigs. Cause: Suspect disease.**

- **Wet streaks or oozing sap on the bark. Cause: Disease or injury.**

- **Sunken or swollen areas on limbs, discolored twigs, or mushrooms growing on limbs or tree trunk. Cause: Heartwood is rotting. If the tree is large, it may need to be removed.**

- **Leaves turning yellow in the wrong season. Cause: Suspect disease, injury, nutrient imbalance, water stress, or possibly air pollution.**

- **Leaves brown around the edges or between the veins. Cause: Most likely water stress or heat damage; possibly wind or nutrient imbalance.**

▪ SMART IDEA ▪

Chain-saw safety

Chain saws may be the noisiest and are definitely the most dangerous power tool gardeners routinely use. So first of all, approach chain saws with a healthy dose of respect. When you do use one, wear proper safety gear, which includes safety glasses or goggles, heavy-duty gloves, hearing protection, sturdy shoes, chaps to protect legs, close-fitting, long-sleeved clothing, and a hard hat. Always use both hands to operate the saw, and keep the blade below shoulder height. Never climb a tree with a chain saw (raise and lower it by rope), or use one from a ladder. Use a pole-mounted pruning saw to cut overhead limbs. Keep children, other people, and pets out of the area where the tree or limb could fall.

(Pests and problems continued)

■ **Dead or dying branches. Cause: Disease, insects, or water stress.**

■ **Wilting foliage. Cause: Suspect water stress, disease, damage, or insects.**

■ **Holes in leaves, or leaves, twigs, or bark eaten. Cause: Suspect insects if leaf damage; animals if bark damage.**

To confirm the causes, and to get information about prevention or control, contact an arborist, an expert at a local nursery, or cooperative extension office agent. Be prepared to identify the affected plant, describe the growing conditions (soil, moisture, drainage, pH, and sun and wind exposure), and explain where the plant is growing, how long it's been there, when the problem first occurred, and whether other plants nearby are also affected. It's also important to report anything unusual that's happened in or near your yard, such as construction, excavation, or chemical applications.

Insects, disease, environmental damage, and animals, especially humans, pose the main threats to trees, shrubs, and other plants. The following sections describe the most common problems and their solutions. Turn to Chapter 13 for information about controlling pests.

Insects, snails, and slugs

Insects damage trees and shrubs mainly by sucking, piercing, chewing, or boring into the leaves, fruit, flowers, roots, and stems.

Sucking and piercing insects These insects leave a sticky sap residue under the tree or on the leaves, raised bumps, sunken or puckered areas on leaves or fruit, and silvery or speckled patches on leaves. These insects include aphids, scales, thrips, and lace bugs.

Chewing insects The larvae of beetles, moths, butterflies, and other chewing insects, leave holes in the foliage, fruit, flowers, and small stems. They often eat entire leaves and soft twigs or graze on plant roots. Examples include Japanese beetles, spruce budworms, and tent caterpillars.

Boring insects Very damaging to woody plants, boring insects burrow into wood or under the bark, usually to lay their eggs. After hatching, the larvae often eat the inner bark. Borers sometimes leave a telltale pile of sawdust at the entrance hole. Examples include Asian and eucalyptus longhorn beetles, bronze birch borers, peach tree borers, and some weevils.

Snails and slugs These members of the mollusk family, eat tender leaves, leaving a shiny slime trail behind them. They frequently hide amid mulch, wood, or other garden debris during the day and come out to feed at night.

healthy garden • healthy garden • healthy garden • healthy garden

Sticky tree sap

Trees that drop sap on your car or patio are probably infested by insects. As they feed, aphids and scale insects secrete a sticky substance called honeydew, which drops from the leaves. If possible, wash off the tree with a strong spray of water. If the tree is too large for that, call an arborist.

Deer and rodents

Voles, mice, and rabbits eat the bark of shrubs and young trees, especially in winter, often girdling and killing them. Protect plants by encircling them with wire mesh hardware cloth. Keep mulch and weeds away from tree trunks and shrub stems to discourage mice. Deer and other large browsers have voracious appetites for some trees and shrubs, especially in areas where other food sources are scarce.

The best strategies include planting only deer-resistant shrubs and trees or installing barriers to prevent deer access. Deer-resistant shrubs include barberry, boxwood, butterfly bush, Carolina cherry laurel, Oregon grapeholly, cotoneaster, euonymus, heavenly bamboo, mountain laurel, juniper, lilac, rock rose, spirea, California lilac, tree peony, and viburnum.

Diseases

Trees and shrubs that suffer mechanical damage or environmental stress, or grow in soil or climates where they are not suited, are more susceptible to disease. You can prevent many plant diseases by following these tips:

- **Buy disease-resistant trees and shrubs. Ask an expert at a nursery for advice when choosing new plants.**

- **Choose locally adapted plants that thrive in your climate, soil, and sun conditions.**

- **Avoid working with disease-prone shrubs and trees, such as roses and dogwoods, when their leaves are wet.**

- **Remove diseased plant trimmings and leaves promptly from your yard. Do not compost diseased leaves or shred them for mulch.**

SMART IDEA

Controlling pests naturally

Most gardeners encounter only a few of the many pests that can damage favored plants. Using a few simple techniques, you can reduce insect pest problems on trees and shrubs without using pesticides. For example, a blast of water from your garden hose knocks off aphids and spider mites. If crawling caterpillars or ants are a problem, spread a sticky pest barrier on a 4- to 6-inch-wide strip of plastic and tie it around tree trunks (where you won't bump into it accidentally). Surround plants with a 1- to 2-inch-wide copper metal strip to foil slugs and snails. Stop gophers by planting shrubs and bulbs inside a buried hardware-cloth cage. For more ideas, see Chapter 13.

Fungi, bacteria, and viruses are the major cause of plant diseases, and they can attack all parts of trees and shrubs. For help fighting most diseases, especially those affecting valuable trees, call an arborist or a forester for diagnosis and treatment.

Fungal diseases are spread by air- or water-borne spores, on insects, or on contaminated plant parts. Some diseases, such as verticillium wilt, and fireblight, can be spread by pruning tools. If your tree has either of these diseases, disinfect cutting tools by dipping them for 15 seconds after each cut into a disinfectant of Lysol or Listerine, or a household bleach solution (1 part bleach diluted with 9 parts water).

Disease resistance dividends

When replacing trees and shrubs, look for disease-resistant varieties. Plants that resist disease live longer in your yard, may require less maintenance, and need fewer pesticide applications. Check plant labels or ask an experienced nursery worker for recommended varieties of plants, especially roses and flowering crabapples.

(Pests and problems continued)

Environmental problems

Pollutants in air, water, and soil affect trees and shrubs greatly. The symptoms of environmental damage often look like those caused by a disease or nutrient deficiency and can be difficult to diagnose.

Air pollution damage usually shows up on foliage. Common causes of injury include drifting herbicides, seaside and road salt spray, ozone from car exhaust, and sulfur dioxide from coal and oil-burning industries. Symptoms include distorted and discolored leaves, brown needles and leaf edges, and bleached or dead areas on foliage. Natural-gas leaks and landfill gases, such as methane and carbon dioxide, are toxic and may kill plant roots. Consult an expert for positive identification and solutions.

To prevent herbicide damage, follow the label instructions carefully when using herbicides containing dicamba and 2,4-D, such as those found in some "weed and feed" lawn-care products. The product labels recommend avoiding their use within the drip line of trees and shrubs. Some trees, including linden, dogwood, redbud, box elder, and Siberian elm, are especially sensitive to these products.

Physical damage

Trees need protection from threats to their roots, trunks, branches, and foliage, and also to anything that compromises their ability to absorb nutrients and water. The most common threats include:

Mechanical injury Scraping a tree trunk or shrub stems creates an entrance for diseases and insects. Bark injury also disrupts the flow of water and nutrients within the tree.

Bark constriction Ropes and wires wound around trunks and limbs tighten trees grow in diameter. They constrict the flow of water and nutrients, killing the restricted part of the plant. Remove tree support wires within a year. Avoid tying anything around limbs and trunks.

Soil changes Heavy foot traffic and parking or driving vehicles around trees and shrubs compact soil, squeezing out air and water. Compacted soil reduces roots' ability to grow. Avoid parking or driving around trees and shrubs. Mulch to cushion the soil surface.

Piling soil over a tree or shrub's root zone, or removing soil, damages roots and can kill the plant. Most roots grow in the top 12 inches of soil, where air and water are plentiful. Adding soil suffocates roots; removing it exposes them. Digging that cuts roots may cause plant decline or death if it cannot absorb enough water or nutrients. Oaks are especially sensitive to soil changes around their roots.

Protecting existing trees

Trees are essential to the landscape and represent years of investment in time and energy. Here are simple steps that help keep them in good health.

Keep lawn away Grasses compete with trees for nutrients, and mowing or trimming too closely often damages trunks. To prevent: Plant ground cover or mulch to the drip line.

Protect tree roots Create a barrier to keep heavy equipment out of the area above tree roots. If passage is essential, put down a layer of bark mulch covered by plywood extending beyond the drip zone.

Maintain mulch Refresh a 2-inch layer of mulch in spring to minimize weeds, moderate soil temperatures, and reduce moisture loss.

Use straps or rope Hanging a hammock by nailing it to the tree or latching it to eye screws installed in the trunk is damaging. Instead hang it from a broad strap wrapped around the trunk.

Damage repair Trees heal themselves by covering wounds with new growth that begins just under the bark. Speed healing by using a sharp knife to clean the edge of the wound, leaving bark smooth and tight against the wood.

Replacing trees and shrubs

When you replace a tree or shrub, or choose new ones to add to your landscape, first decide what you want the plant to do. Consider whether you want shade, privacy, a colorful focal point, attractive flowers, foliage or fruit, a hedge, or year-round greenery.

Although trees and shrubs initially cost more than other landscape plants, they can live for many years, making them a sensible long-term investment. It pays to invest in the best-quality plants available.

Transport all trees and shrubs under cover, either inside your vehicle or protected with a tarp. Exposing leafy plants to wind in the back of an open truck damages them. Do not leave plants in a closed vehicle when interior temperatures will rise above 90° F.

If you cannot plant them right away, store potted and balled-and-burlapped plants in a cool, shady place away from direct sunlight and wind. Water as needed to keep the root ball moist, and get the plants into the ground as soon as possible. To store bare-root plants, follow the directions provided by the supplier.

How to plant

Dig the planting hole twice as wide and slightly shallower than the root ball. Avoid digging too deeply then filling in the hole. Roots need to sit on stable soil. This is because plants often sink as they settle into loose earth. Then the trunk may rot, roots suffocate, and the tree could die. Gauge depth by measuring the height of the root ball from top to bottom. Dig the hole slightly shallower than your measurements, leaving the soil in the bottom of the hole undisturbed.

Lift plants by the root ball—not the stem or trunk. Leave natural burlap in the hole, but pull it away from the root ball and bury it completely when backfilling. Loosen circling roots. Adjust the plant height as necessary.

Fill the planting hole three-quarters full with the soil you removed. Water thoroughly to settle the soil. Add soil, if needed, up to the top of the root ball. Form a saucer by building up a 4- to 6-inch ring of soil around the planting hole to retain water.

Mulch after planting to hold moisture and reduce weeds, but keep the mulch away from the plant trunk or stems.

safety alert · safety alert · safety alert · safety alert · safety alert · safety alert

Planting safety

Prevent trees from interfering with overhead wires by planting the right tree in the right place. Inside the zone that spans 15 feet on each side of an overhead wire, choose trees that remain less than 20 feet tall. Within 50 feet of the zone, plant trees that will not grow more than 40 feet tall.

4

vines &
ground
covers

Vines cloak the vertical plane while ground covers hug the horizontal. Here are the basics of caring for them.

Vines scramble up walls, fences, trellises, and trees, adding vertical splashes of color and texture to your landscape. Vigorous, well-established vines often need regular pruning and maintenance to keep them healthy and attractive. Ground covers carpet the soil, protect slopes, and cover difficult terrain with greenery that grows where turf is neither wanted nor practical. Most need only occasional fertilizer, water, and pruning.

Vines

Vines grow rapidly, some expanding their shoots as much as 10 to 15 feet each year. Many have spectacular flowers and ornamental foliage. Their vigorous and decorative characteristics make them ideal for adding a quick cover-up or vertical drama in the garden.

Types of vines

Vines are broadly categorized as annuals, which live for only one growing season, or perennials, which grow for many years. Each type has its own maintenance needs.

Annuals Annual vines such as morning glory, grow from spring-planted seeds or cuttings, and bloom in summer. The entire plant dies with the first freeze or cold weather. Most grow no taller than about 10 feet, making them suitable for training on temporary trellises or supports. They need little pruning. Keep the soil watered, and fertilize them in spring and early summer to promote rapid growth.

Perennials Perennial vines are either herbaceous or woody. Herbaceous perennials, such as perennial sweet pea, grow back from hardy roots each spring. These are a good choice where you want seasonal flowers and greenery without winter stems. Similar to annual vines, herbaceous perennials require little pruning and can grow on temporary trellises. Woody vines, such as grapes and wisteria, have hardy stems and branches, like shrubs and trees that grow larger and heavier over time. Most require sturdy, permanent supports, such as wood arbors, and most need annual pruning.

• HOW-TO •

Rescue wooden posts

Wooden trellises decay over time and eventually need mending to keep them safe and sturdy. If the support posts are rotting where they meet the ground, you can repair the supports without replacing the trellis. Place new, preservative-treated support posts into the ground next to the old supports, taking care not to damage the vine's stems and roots. Use a post hole digger to get each hole deep enough (24 to 36 inches), and place gravel or stones in the bottom. Then begin backfilling around the post, tamping as you work. The new supports should extend about 18 to 24 inches above ground. Bolt the old posts to the new posts, using two stainless-steel bolts for each leg of the trellis.

Vines for small spaces

In small yards, sometimes the only way to grow is up. Vines take up little room on the ground, making them ideal plants for tight spaces and postage-stamp-size gardens. Take advantage of a fence to add vertical dimension to your garden. No soil? No problem! Plant a vine in a patio-size pot.

(Vines continued)

How vines climb

Vines grow long, flexible stems that either sprawl on the ground or climb up vertical supports toward the sunlight. Vines support themselves with several different mechanisms. It's useful to know these climbing methods so that you can choose the most suitable and attractive supports for each vine.

Twining stems The stems of twining vines wrap around supports as they grow. Often, vigorous and long-lived, herbaceous and woody twining species, such as wisteria, climb anything they can get their stems around. They may strangle trees and shrubs if allowed to climb them. Annual twining vines, such as morning glory and moonflower vine, remain more easily within bounds. Support twining vines with trellises, arbors, and fences.

Some tough, fast-spreading, twining vines can easily escape from gardens and wreak havoc, strangling trees in the countryside. Among the worst are porcelain berry *(Ampelopsis brevipedunculata)*, oriental bittersweet *(Celastrus orbiculatus)*, Japanese honeysuckle *(Lonicera japonica)*, and moonseed *(Menispermum canadense)*.

Tendrils Many vines have tendrils that coil around slender supports. A few, including clematis, have leaf stalks that act like tendrils. Vines with tendrils and tendril-like structures grow best on wire fences, trellis nets, and shrubs. If they grow into trees and shrubs, they generally do no serious harm to trees and shrubs, although large vines may shade the foliage of their host plant.

Clinging rootlets Vines with these support mechanisms can climb nearly any vertical object, because they attach themselves with special pads or roots, called *holdfasts*, that adhere tightly to any surface. Long-lived adhering vines, such as Virginia creeper and Boston ivy, are difficult to remove once established. Support these vines on brick or stone walls. Do not let them grow on wooden buildings, because they hold moisture against the wood and prevent building maintenance, such as painting. Old vine sections that come loose from their support cannot reattach themselves. Only young stems grow new holdfasts.

Sprawlers and ramblers Although not true vines, many members of this group of plants, such as roses and bougainvillaea, use thorns on their long, stiff canes to scramble or climb a suitable support. Some, such as winter jasmine, merely have long, trailing stems that weave through neighboring shrubs or cascade to the ground. Tie these climbing plants to garden supports to keep them off the ground.

Using vines

Loose-stemmed opportunists, vines grow where other plants can't: hugging a masonry wall, arching over a pergola, or spilling over a retaining wall. Among this extremely varied family of plants you can find selections to fit a variety of landscape uses.

Bold beauty Hardy vines such as clematis can climb up a trellis or post, then spread out into neighboring shrubs.

Fragrance Several tender vines, such as star jasmine, and hardy ones including roses and wisteria, add fragrance to patios and gardens.

Cloak a wall An expanse of stuccoed wall is an ideal candidate for either a clinging vine growing from below, or a draping one growing from above—such as bougainvillea.

Soften structures A classic role vines play in gardens is covering pergolas and arbors, blurring the structures' hard edges and making them look more natural.

Cover-up Functioning like makeup for the yard, vines make quick and practical covers for anything worn-looking.

Trellis smarts

Trellises become heavier and heavier as vines grow and mature. Anchor trellises securely in the ground or brace them against a wall or fence for support. Orient them in the same direction as the prevailing wind to prevent toppling.

(Vines continued)

Supporting vines

Knowing how vines climb helps you choose the most appropriate support to keep vine and support maintenance to a minimum. Some—such as kiwi and wisteria—will quickly overwhelm a small trellis. Left unchecked, Boston ivy will grow over and cover the windows of your house; they can almost lift the shingles on your roof. Smaller, more refined vines, such as most clematis, on the other hand, can grow unrestrained through shrubs and over temporary supports without harm. The following survey will help you match vine to support structure.

Trellises Trellises vary in construction from sturdy, permanent structures to temporary, seasonal panels covered in netting. At their simplest, trellises consist of two posts spanned by slats, which may be wood, metal rods, ropes, or wire. Trellises can be any width or height to accommodate the mature size of a vine or to fit any space. They make attractive garden walls or screens and can even substitute for hedges where space is tight.

Lightweight wire or string trellises work well for annual vines, such as morning glories, nasturtiums, and sweet peas. Use permanent wooden or metal trellises, typically attached to posts sunk securely into the ground or attached to a building, for large, heavy vines. A good rule of thumb is that the larger and heavier the vine, the sturdier the trellis must be.

In windy sites, anchor the trellis securely and orient it in the same direction as the prevailing wind. Once the vine covers a trellis, it will catch the breeze like a sail if it faces the wind.

Pergolas or arbors Pergolas and arbors consist of a roof, usually slats or lattice, supported by posts. They differ mainly in size; pergolas are large and architectural while arbors are small and cozy. Both are ideal for supporting long-lived, twining and rambling woody vines. The sides of pergolas and arbors can be covered with trellis for privacy or left open to admit light and air. Plant vines at the support posts and train them to sprawl on the roof.

Trees Small as well as mature shade trees make good hosts for twining or rambling vines. Lightweight perennial and annual vines with twining tendrils may safely scramble through shrubs and small trees as long as the vine doesn't overburden the limbs or shade the foliage. Plants that hold on with their thorns, such as roses and bougainvillea, can produce an attractive effect. On the other hand, ivy or winter creeper on the trunk may promote crown rot, and wisteria is likely to grow too large for most trees to support.

Buildings and walls Vines that have clinging rootlets can grow on buildings and walls. Leafy vines help moderate summer temperatures and can reduce the need for air-conditioning. However, they can also increase the amount of maintenance on the structure. Walls made of stone or masonry blend softly into the landscape when covered in vines. Whether on walls or structures, clinging vines may need regular pruning to stay in bounds.

Take care to prune clinging vines growing on a brick or masonry home away from wooden trim. Keep them off gutters and roofs, where they collect debris and loosen shingles. If you choose to pull down clinging vines, be aware that holdfasts will remain.

Don't train clingers onto buildings with wood or vinyl siding. Try twining and tendril climbers or ramblers instead. Grow them on a trellis you can take down so you can maintain your home. The trellis must be firmly anchored so it stays in place in all weather, no matter the weight of the vine. Leave several inches between the trellis and the siding to allow for air circulation and room to prune. You can also train rambling roses and twining vines on wires or heavy string until they reach the top of the wall, where they can scramble freely.

Pole tripods and garden pillars These look elegant when covered in flowering annual or perennial vines or rose canes. Sweet peas, pole beans, morning glory, clematis, and gourds add a vertical accent to your flower garden when trained to one of these temporary structures.

Fences All styles of fencing make ideal supports for twining vines, ones with tendrils, and those with long, scrambling stems. Vines with tendrils are easier to remove from chain link and wire fences than those with twining stems. Use wire or other netting systems to hold vines in place on solid board fences and to train vines to the top of a rail fence.

Woven textile netting This material is often sold for growing vegetables such as cucumbers. It also works well for annual flowering vines. Support the net on a wood or metal tube frame and place it in a sunny place where you want a spot of seasonal color.

· HOW-TO ·

A simple wire trellis

A simple wire trellis can, in the space of a couple of seasons, become a dense green screen. The basic scheme of wire stretched between posts is economical, unobtrusive, and perfect for twining vines. Here's how to make a 6-foot-tall screen: Install 8-foot, pressure-treated 4×4 posts 8 feet apart, sinking them 2 feet into concrete in the ground. After the concrete sets, install screw eyes at 24 and 48 inches high on the insides of both posts. Attach turnbuckles to screw eyes on one of the posts. Twist 12-gauge wire onto the turnbuckles and to the screw eyes on the opposite posts. Tighten the turnbuckles until the wire is taut. Nail a board across the top of the posts for extra bracing.

healthy garden • healthy garden • healthy garden • healthy garden

Covering bare stems

As vines grow taller, their lower stems often become bare and unsightly. With multistemmed vines, such as clematis, prune one or two stems to buds close to the ground to encourage lower stems. As an alternative, bend a tall, leafy stem back toward the ground and tie it to the support.

Maintaining vines

Perennial vines need more pruning than annual vines, but annuals must be replanted each year and fertilized more frequently. Both kinds benefit from mulching to control weeds and stabilize soil moisture and temperature, as well as watering in dry weather.

Fertilizing

Most vines require annual fertilizing to maintain their vigor. Fertilize vines according to their growth stage and type. After applying, scratch the fertilizer lightly into the top half-inch of soil with a garden rake. Water it into the soil, taking care to prevent the water from running off.

Established vines Vines that have been in place for two to three years are best fertilized in autumn or early spring by sprinkling the fertilizer in a 10×10-foot square around the vine, starting 6 to 12 inches from the vine's stems. To cover this 100-square-foot area, use 2 to 3 pounds (4 to 6 level cups) of low-nitrogen granular fertilizer, such as 5-10-10 or 5-10-5.

Vigorous vines Large, fast-growing vines, such as trumpet vine *(Campsis radicans)* and wisteria, do not need annual fertilizing. Additional nutrients only encourage excessive stem growth and inhibit the vines from flowering.

Watering and mulching

When natural rainfall is less than an inch per week, check the depth of the moisture in the soil. Use any method that's convenient for you. A soil probe that extracts a core of soil allows you to see and feel the soil several inches deep. Or simply open the soil with a trowel or small shovel. Once you can see that the soil is dry to a depth of 6 to 8 inches, water deeply.

Pruning and training

Annual vines need less pruning than perennial vines because they live for only a short time. Vigorous woody vines may require two or more prunings a year. Follow these guidelines for the different stages of vine growth:

Newly planted vines These usually need little pruning. Remove any badly damaged or dead stems, cutting them back to a healthy bud. For a bushier plant, wait until the vine has grown at least three to five sets of leaves, then prune the tip bud to promote branching. Guide newly planted twining vines toward the support by tying strings to the support and to small stakes near the base of the plant.

Young vines You can encourage vines to cover their support more quickly by pruning off the tips of their shoots so that buds farther down the plant expand and branch out. For most vines, make the cut just above a fat, healthy bud or group of buds. As the vine grows, arrange the stems on the support to cover it evenly and to give each stem space to expand. Loosely tie the shoots in place with twine, if necessary, and remove unwanted stems at the vine's base.

Mature vines Vines can become tangled and congested if they are not pruned annually. Prune them to remove dead and unproductive stems and to reinvigorate the plant. Start with one stem at a time, tracing it to its ends. If it is dead or no longer healthy, remove it in sections by cutting out manageable pieces. Cut it back to the base of the plant or to a branch or bud. Repeat with additional stems as needed. Take care not to damage healthy stems as you work.

Twining vines may be too difficult to prune by removing individual stems. In this case, it may be better to cut the whole plant back to branches or buds within a foot or two of the ground and unwind the dead vine from the support. Not all vines will tolerate this treatment, especially those with thick, woody stems. It works best with vines that send up many shoots from their roots, including some clematis and passionflowers. If you are not sure how your vine will react, cut only a stem or two and watch for a season to see if it sprouts new growth.

You can also renovate old vines by cutting out one-third of their stems each year for three years. As the new growth sprouts, train it to replace the older shoots.

To improve flowering, prune vines that bloom in spring to midsummer right after they finish blossoming to ensure bloom the following year. Prune vines that bloom in mid- to late summer on the current season's new growth during the previous winter's dormant season, before spring growth begins to encourage new shoots.

Wisteria, climbing roses, and clematis vines have special pruning and training requirements that ensure the best flower display. Follow these step-by-step instructions for each:

· HOW-TO ·

Painting around a vine

To paint a vine-covered trellis without harming the vine, plan to do the work either before or after the growing season, in early spring or autumn. Remove the vine by carefully unwinding the tendrils and stems, or untying the canes of roses. Prune tangled and clinging vines by cutting individual stems back to strong buds and branches. Old, woody stems cannot reattach themselves to the trellis, so the pruning will encourage new, self-supporting growth. Lay the longest, flexible stems on the ground, taking care not to break them, and of course avoid stepping on them as you work. Paint, let dry, re-tie canes and stems to the trellis, and wait. Your vine will quickly cover the like-new trellis.

safety alert · safety alert · safety alert · safety alert · safety alert

Thorn protection

Protect yourself from thorns while pruning rose and bougainvillea by wearing tough gauntlet gloves that cover your hands and lower arms. For extra protection, wear long sleeves, pants, and safety glasses to prevent scratches and eye injuries.

(Maintaining vines continued)

Pruning wisteria Wisteria vines are vigorous growers in favorable conditions and develop heavy, picturesque trunks over time. They may take seven years or more to begin flowering after planting. Because wisteria grows so large and vigorously, train it to sturdy support, such as, a trellis made of heavy lumber. To train wisteria, prune recently planted vines to one central trunk or leader, with scaffold limbs spaced about 18 inches apart. Each scaffold limb may also have branches. Tie them to the support in a horizontal position.

For the first three years, remove any competing leaders and unwanted limbs and branches as they appear. In midsummer, shorten the branches by half their length. In winter, prune the central leader back to about 30 inches above the topmost limb. Also remove about one-third of the growth from each branch, leaving the spurs and two or three fat flower buds on each limb and branch.

Once established, wisteria vines need regular pruning several times a year to produce the dramatic hanging clusters of fragrant purple-pink to white flowers for which they are famous. In summer, the vines form flower buds on spurs that grow on old wood. The flowers bloom the following spring. Prune wisteria after it finishes flowering by cutting back the limbs and branches by half and removing leafless stems. If you are training the vine on a trellis, tie the branches in a horizontal position to encourage flower buds to form on the spurs. Remove any crowded or unwanted shoots.

Pruning climbing roses Climbing roses fall into two groups: those that bloom in mid- to late summer on this year's growth—called climbers—and those that bloom in spring to early summer from buds formed in the previous year—called ramblers. You must prune each group differently, so if you aren't sure which kind you have, wait to prune until you have observed when they bloom.

For the first two to three years after planting, train both kinds by selecting a number of main structural canes and tying them to the support in an angled fan or a horizontal pattern. Choose three to five canes for the first year and add more canes as the plant matures, if you wish. Let them grow for the first two to three years, removing only dead, unwanted, and spindly canes.

Here is where the groups diverge: Prune rambling roses, which flower on one-year-old canes, after flowering, by cutting the main canes back to buds about 16 inches from the ground. Then, throughout the summer, tie the newly developing shoots to the support at a horizontal angle. This encourages flower buds to form. Over the years, some structural canes will become less vigorous.

Pruning an established vine

Vines need regular pruning to keep them in bounds and to promote or enhance flowering. The best time to prune is later winter or early spring. These are three techniques to use with vines.

To encourage branching on leggy stems, head back the stems to within 2 feet of the ground.

Heavy, woody vines should be cut back to a basic framework, leaving two to three buds. Do this in winter for summer bloomers, and after flowering for spring bloomers.

Cut overgrown vines showing signs of reduced flowering or less vigor back to within 2 to 3 inches of the ground. Clematis, honeysuckle, and roses respond favorably to renovation.

Climbing roses in cold climates

In climates where winter wind and cold kill rambling and climbing roses, protect the vining canes by untying them from their support and laying them on the ground. Peg them down with U-shaped wires. After the ground freezes, cover the entire plant with 8 inches of soil or mulch.

(Maintaining vines continued)

Remove up to a third of the structural canes each year, pruning out the least vigorous ones. Train replacements from the shoots that grow from the plant's base.

Prune climbing roses during the dormant season, usually in winter, to encourage lots of new shoots. Climbers bloom on the side branches that grow from the main structural stems. Cut each side branch back to two or three buds. Also remove spindly or dead wood. After flowering, remove spent blooms, cutting them back to a healthy leaf.

Pruning clematis Clematis vines also fall into different pruning categories based on when they bloom. Some bloom only in spring from buds formed the previous year. Others bloom in mid- to late summer on the current year's new stems. A third group does both, repeatedly flowering from spring to late summer on old and new wood. Plant catalogs and pot labels usually tell you when to expect flowers and when to prune, or you can observe the plant for a season before pruning. After planting a clematis, prune it back to a pair of fat buds about 12 inches from the ground to encourage multiple shoots to develop.

Prune spring bloomers right after they flower, removing just the ends of overgrown vines and taking out dead wood. This group usually needs minimal pruning. Among the spring bloomers are alpine clematis, sweet autumn clematis, and anemone clematis.

Mid- to late-summer-blooming clematis, such as 'Jackmanii' and 'Hagley Hybrid', can be cut down in the early spring to pairs of fat, healthy buds about 12 inches from the ground. Wait to prune until the buds just begin to swell to be sure that they are viable.

Reblooming clematis include most of the popular large-flowered varieties, such as 'Nelly Moser', 'The President', 'General Sikorski', and 'Duchess of Edinburgh'. This group blooms on old wood in spring and early summer, then repeats the bloom later in summer on new shoots. Prune reblooming clematis in late winter. Cut back the vines only to the top pair of fat green buds, and remove dead stems. If the stems become bare near the base after a few seasons, remove one-third of the stems, pruning them to a pair of buds near the ground each year. Untangle and remove the severed vines carefully, cutting them out in sections.

No matter the type, clematis that becomes completely tangled and overgrown can be cut down to within a foot of the ground. Select the most vigorous shoots that emerge after pruning and train them to the support. Remove all other shoots and begin annual pruning according to the correct schedule for your vine.

Replacing and planting vines

Before planting, assess the soil where you intend to grow vines. Most vines prefer or require moist, fertile soil that's rich in organic matter. Soil next to buildings, especially under the eaves, tends to be infertile and dry, and the soil under trees may also be dry due to competition from the tree roots. In most cases, you will need to add organic matter to the soil and loosen it to encourage hearty root growth. Amend the entire planting bed, not just the backfill soil for the vine.

Choose a spot that will be easy to irrigate as needed, especially if you are planting a large, long-lived vine, such as wisteria or trumpet vine. Take advantage of warm south- and west-facing walls to grow heat-loving vines and those that need extra winter protection in your climate. Vines that thrive in shade grow well on north- and east-facing walls.

Unless you are planting the vine near an existing support, such as a wall or tree, it is important to install the support before you plant. After you have the trellis or other support in place, follow these step-by-step instructions to get your vine off to a good start.

1. Dig a hole 12 or more inches from the support. Vines that form heavy trunks can be planted farther away, while annual vines can be planted closer. If planting near a tree, look for a space between the large roots near the base of the tree.

2. Make the planting hole about three times the diameter of the root ball (potted plants) or root spread (bare-root vines). For most vines, the depth of the hole should be about the same as the root ball or length of bare roots, so that the crown—the point where roots and shoots meet—will be just at the soil's surface. As you dig, pile the soil on a tarp for easy cleanup.

3. Add and thoroughly mix composted manure, compost, moist peat moss, or rotted leaves into the soil of the planting bed, depending on the quantity and quality of your soil. Poor-quality soil next to buildings particularly needs amending, whereas fertile garden soil may need little. The amount of organic matter should equal about 20 to 30 percent of the backfill. You may also mix in a high-

• SMART IDEA •

Trellis of opportunity

Lightweight vines, such as clematis, sweet pea, and morning glory, can easily use a large shrub, such as lilac, smoke tree, or camellia, for support. And heavier vines, such as a rambling rose or bougainvillaea, will scramble up a tree in no time. In fact, a vine might be the best way to deal with the stump of a dead tree (as long as it's not in danger of falling). Train the vine on twine or chicken wire wrapped loosely around a tree trunk until the vine reaches the branches. To ensure that the vine gets enough water, either plant the vine outside the root zone of the host plant or install drip irrigation to keep it watered. If planting under a mature tree, tuck the vine into the soil between large roots close to the trunk.

(Maintaining vines continued)

phosphorus fertilizer to aid root growth, and a slow-release fertilizer according to package instructions.

4. Consult the care tag on the vine for individual planting instructions. In general, for bare-root plants, make a cone of soil in the center of the hole. Firm it well to prevent the plant from settling. Set the plant on the top of the cone and spread the roots over it to check planting height. At the same time, check that the width of the planting hole is sufficient to accommodate the vine's roots.

When draped over the mound, the crown of most plants should be at ground level or up to an inch below it, depending on the plant species and its requirements. In cold climates, some plants, such as roses, should be planted more deeply to protect the crown from winter weather. In all climates, set the crown of clematis 3 to 4 inches below the soil surface to encourage stronger rooting.

Check the planting height; if it is too low or high, add or remove soil to the cone of soil and check again. If the planting hole is so narrow that existing roots are forced to bend or crimp to fit, enlarge the hole. Trim overly long or damaged roots.

5. For vines in containers, gently slip the root ball out of the pot. Don't pull on the stem; if the plant seems stuck in the pot, cut the pot away with heavy shears. Take special care with bougainvillaea, which has fragile, brittle roots. Set the root ball into the hole, and adjust the hole depth as needed to bring the crown to soil level or slightly below it. Add the backfill to the hole, firming gently, until the hole is three-quarters full.

6. Fill the hole with water to settle the soil. Let it drain. Hold the vine in place as you water, adjusting it gently if needed. Fill the hole to the top with soil and firm gently. Build a saucer around the vine with a 4-inch-high ring of soil. Fill it with water and let it drain.

7. Mulch the vine by filling the saucer area with a 2- to 3-inch layer of bark or other organic mulch, keeping it 2 to 3 inches away from the vine stems.

After you plant the vine, begin training and pruning. In most cases, prune off only dead and damaged parts at planting time. To encourage more stems to grow, pinch off the tips of expanding vines after they have grown at least several sets of leaves. Guide the vine gently to the support by forming a figure-eight loop with garden tape or a strip of soft cloth around the stem and tying it to the support. As the shoots grow, continue tying them to the support as needed.

Vine or ground cover?

Some vining and long-stemmed plants can grow as either vines or ground covers, depending on where you plant them and how they are trained. Woody perennials such as English ivy, bougainvillea, and rambling roses can either climb a trellis or sprawl over the ground.

Training a new vine

Right after planting you can begin training a vine. Make sure that supports are secure, and cut or pinch plants back to compensate for roots lost through transplanting.

Pinch tips Remove growing tips and reduce the number of flower buds on new vines by pinching them off. This will focus the plant's energy on new, branching growth.

Cut off broken or dead stems It is typical for new plants to include some old stems from previous seasons, or stems that were broken in the process of moving from nursery to home.

Tie to support Use soft material and tie in a loose figure eight which will provide support but not constrict the growth of the expanding stem.

(Maintaining vines continued)

Guide to caring for favorite vines

Common name	Climbing method	When to prune	Blooms on	What it provides
DECIDUOUS (Hardy most everywhere)				
Dutchman's pipe *(Aristolochia macrophylla)*	twining	late winter	old wood	large foliage
Trumpet vine *(Campsis radicans)*	twining	late winter	new wood	flowers
Clematis *(Clematis spp.)*	tendrils	varies by type	old and new, varies by type	flowers, seeds
Climbing hydrangea *(Hydrangea anomala)*	clinging	late winter	new wood	foliage, bark, flowers
Virginia creeper *(Parthenocissus quinquefolia)*	clinging	early spring		foliage, fall color
Boston ivy *(Parthenocissus tricuspidata)*	clinging	early spring		foliage, fall color
Climbing roses *(Rosa spp.)*	rambling	summer	old wood	flowers
Grapes *(Vitis spp.)*	tendrils	winter	old wood	foliage, fruit
Chinese wisteria *(Wisteria sinensis)*	twining	spring, summer, winter	old wood spurs	flowers
EVERGREEN (Tender unless noted)				
Cross vine *(Bignonia capreolata)*	tendrils	early spring	new wood	flowers
Bougainvillea *(Bougainvillea spp.)*	rambling	early spring	new wood	flowers, foliage
Carolina jessamine *(Gelsemium sempervirens)*	twining	after bloom	old wood	flowers, fragrance
English ivy *(Hedera helix; hardy)*	clinging	early spring	no blooms	foliage
Chinese jasmine *(Jasminum polyanthum)*	twining	early spring	old wood	flowers, fragrance
Trumpet honeysuckle *(Lonicera; hardy)*	twining	after flowering	new wood	flowers
Passionflower *(Passiflora spp.)*	tendrils	spring	new wood	flowers
Star jasmine *(Trachelospermum jasminoides)*	clinging	early spring	old wood spurs	flowers, fragrance
ANNUAL (Grow anywhere)				
Purple hyacinth bean *(Lablab purpureus)*	twining	as needed		flowers, fruit
Cup-and-saucer vine *(Cobaea scandens)*	twining	as needed		flowers
Morning glory *(Ipomoea tricolor)*	twining	as needed		flowers
Cardinal climber *(Ipomoea × multifida)*	twining	as needed		flowers
Scarlet runner bean *(Phaseolus coccineus)*	twining	as needed		flowers, fruit

Caring for ground covers

Ground covers are shrubs, vines, and perennials that spread horizontally over the soil. Some spread quickly and need annual pruning and physical barriers to keep them in bounds, whereas others spread more slowly and need much less maintenance.

Ground cover types

Ground cover plants grow and spread in several ways. How they grow determines the maintenance and care they need.

Creeping underground Ground covers that spread by creeping underground stems and roots that send up new shoots can cover a lot of area. Examples of ground covers that spread by underground roots and stems include pachysandra, lily-of-the-valley, sweet woodruff, St. Johnswort, and creeping lilyturf. Some are herbaceous perennials, which die to the ground each autumn; some are evergreen perennials; and some are shrubs.

Spreading aboveground Branches, stems, or aboveground runners that root where they touch the ground allow plants to spread over large areas, forming new plants as they go. Eventually these ground covers form dense, uniform mats that hold soil against erosion and inhibit weed growth. Vines that spread this way, such as English ivy, must be pruned regularly to prevent them from climbing trees, walls, and buildings and to form a uniform surface. Other ground covers that spread by rooting stems and branches include cutleaf stephanandra, rock rose, and common periwinkle. These do not climb but need occasional pruning to stay tidy and contained.

Clump-forming These ground covers do not send out creeping stems or roots but instead increase in diameter each year, gradually spreading wider and slowly covering more ground. This easy-to-maintain group includes many hardy perennial plants, such as daylily, hostas, heaths and heathers, and English lavender. Most need little pruning other than the removal in spring of old stems and leaves from the previous year. Regular watering and annual fertilizer help them fill in more quickly and resist insect pests and diseases.

Sprawlers These wide-spreading plants have sprawling branches that make them effective and easily managed ground covers. Other than watering, fertilizing, and pruning to remove dead, diseased, and damaged limbs, this group needs little maintenance. Examples include ground-covering and rambling roses, junipers, Russian cypress, and broom.

budget stretcher • budget stretcher • budget stretcher • budget stretcher •

Gentle restraint

Keep aggressively spreading ground covers in their place by installing lawn edging between ground covers and adjacent lawns and gardens. The deeper the barrier, the better to prevent creeping roots from spreading. Trim the edges regularly to stop them from growing over the top of the barrier.

Using ground covers

Many kinds of low growing plants—perennials, shrubs, and vines—have the capacity to blanket the soil with a dense cover of foliage. They do it different ways, according to how they grow.

Clumping perennial Hostas bridge the gap here between lawn and woodland.

Creeping underground shrub
Ground covers that spread with underground stems, such as aaronsbeard St. Johnswort, quickly carpet large areas.

Sprawling evergreen shrub These are often low-growing and irregularly shaped. This is Russian cypress, a hardy evergreen.

Spreading aboveground vine
English ivy can be an alternative to lawn in a shady landscape.

Sprawling flowering shrub Climbing roses and low-growing shrub roses serve admirably as ground covers, and their colorful flowers are a bonus.

Fertilizing and watering

In the first year or two after planting ground covers, it's crucial to keep the soil moist and fertile to maximize their growth so that plants fill in quickly. After ground covers become established, especially if they are well-matched to the growing conditions of your yard, they should need watering only during times of unusual drought. When rainfall is less than an inch per week, check soil moisture by inserting a clean paint stirring stick 10 inches into the soil. Leave it for an hour. Pull it out and check the depth of moisture on the stick. If any of the top 6 inches of soil is dry, irrigate until the soil is moist to a depth of 8 inches. Use a sprinkler or drip irrigation for even coverage on new and established plantings. Apply the water slowly, especially on hillsides, to allow the water to soak in without running off.

To achieve rapid growth in young ground cover plantings, spread a fertilizer that contains more nitrogen than phosphorus and potassium, such as 10-6-4. After the plants become well-established, usually after three years, the vines may not need annual fertilization. Evaluate the vines' appearance and growth rate before fertilizing. Have the soil tested so that you apply the right fertilizer in the correct amount.

Autumn is the best time to fertilize, but wait until the following spring to fertilize fall-planted ground covers. Early spring, before the plants begin to grow, is the second-best time to fertilize. Always apply fertilizer to dry plants, because particles that stick to wet foliage can burn the leaves. Spread the fertilizer evenly over the entire planting, using a handheld rotary spreader, then water thoroughly to wash the nutrients into the soil.

Weeding and mulching

Prevent weeds in new ground cover plantings by spreading a 2- to 3-inch layer of shredded bark or other organic mulch between the plants, taking care to keep it away from the stems. Preemergence herbicides, such as trifluralin or corn gluten meal, are an option, but are less effective than a thick mulch. If weeds release seeds or become established in the ground cover area, they could be time-consuming to eradicate.

Apply herbicide in spring as the soil begins to warm up but before weeds have germinated. The timing for corn gluten meal is important. It must be applied before weed seeds germinate. But if you apply it too early, soil microbes will limit its effectiveness. Corn gluten meal is also most effective during periods of drought.

Whichever herbicide you use, rake it into the top half-inch of soil, and reapply in summer if needed.

time saver • time saver • time saver • time saver • time saver • time saver

Weed blocks

Landscape fabric is one of the best physical weed controls in ground cover beds. It allows water to pass into the soil, but stops weeds. Roll the fabric over the bed and hold it in place with large metal staples. Use a knife to cut slits for plants. After planting, cover the fabric with a layer of mulch.

Pruning ground covers

Compared with most plants, ground covers need little regular care. Occasionally, cutting back to rejuvenate, groom, or restrain is needed.

Mowing If the ground is level, mow pachysandra (above), lilyturf, St. Johnswort, and wintercreeper euonymus in early spring. Set your mower to its maximum cutting height.

Grooming Use hand shears to reach into plants in order to remove dead branches.

Cutting back Where ground isn't level enough for mowing, or if plants are too tall, use a line trimmer.

Edging Spreading plants will naturally overtake a pathway. Hedge shears are the simplest method for small areas. Electric shears and line trimmers are other options.

(Caring for ground covers continued)

Established ground covers with dense foliage shade the soil, which prevents most weeds from sprouting and growing. Those with less dense foliage, such as recently renovated ground covers and herbaceous perennials before they fill out in spring, may need weeding until they become dense. Pull the weeds by hand or use a hoe, if possible, taking care not to disturb the ground cover roots. After the ground covers fill in their area, they no longer need mulching and require only occasional weeding.

Renovating ground covers

Ideal ground covers look uniformly dense and full. To keep them looking their best, most need annual pruning or trimming to encourage bushy, compact growth, to remove dead, winter-killed growth from the previous year, and to restrain vigorous expansion. The methods to use for pruning and renovating a ground cover depend on the type of plant it is and how it grows.

Deciduous perennial ground covers These die to the ground in autumn and look best if you prune away all the dead material and rake it up before the plants resume growth in spring. Some spread by creeping underground stems and others form clumps. Remove the old foliage with hand pruners, a string trimmer, or a lawn mower, depending on the ground cover and size of the area. It's important to remove only the dead foliage and stems without cutting into the living crowns. If your mower cuts too low, rent a high-wheeled mower. Edge the ground-cover area to prevent creeping plants from escaping into the lawn or other areas where they are not welcome.

· HOW-TO ·

When tough weeds invade

Established and vigorously growing ground cover beds are rarely weedy. The plants shade the soil and effectively crowd out weeds. Occasionally perennial weeds get a foothold. Broadleaf ones, such as field bindweed, are persistent and have no convenient chemical control. Herbicides containing glyphosate (Roundup) kill weeds and ground cover alike. Spray the weeds if you can cover the ground cover leaves with plastic or otherwise keep the spray off them. Grassy weeds such as bermudagrass can be selectively killed when growing in broadleaf ground covers. Look for herbicides containing sethoxydim (Vantage) or fluazifop (Fusilade), and be sure that your ground cover is listed on the label as safe to spray.

Evergreen perennial ground covers Wintercreeper euonymus, English ivy, pachysandra, and other evergreen ground covers spread and grow from underground shoots or rooting branches. They can be sheared in early spring, at the beginning of the growing season. Prune to remove the overgrown or worn-looking top growth while encouraging the remaining stems to sprout into vigorous new growth. Cut about 6 to 12 inches above the ground, depending on the plant and its growth habits. Use a string trimmer or a mower on its highest deck setting, if it cuts high enough, or rent a high-wheeled mower to prune large areas. (Continued on page 106)

Dividing and replanting ground covers

Any ground cover that spreads from expanding clumps or spreading stems can be divided. The result is new plants you can use either to expand the planting area or to replant thin areas.

1 Dig up Lift the parent clump and shake off most of the soil.

2 Separate Depending on the plant, either gently pull plants apart or use pruning shears to cut them apart. Throw away the old and weak plants, keeping the most vigorous for replanting.

3 Amend soil Refresh the soil and give the plants a good start by adding weed-free compost.

4 Plant Set the new plants in place, spacing them so they have room to spread. Cover the bare soil between plants with mulch, then water.

Guide to caring for favorite ground covers

Common name	What to do when	Spacing	What it needs
SPREADERS UNDERGROUND			
Wild ginger (*Asarum europaeum*)	divide clumps in spring to propagate	12 inches	shade, moist soil, wind protection
Lily-of-the-valley (*Convallaria majalis*)	rake in early spring	8–12 inches	shade
Barrenwort (*Epimedium* spp.)	trim in late winter	12 inches	shade
Sweet woodruff (*Galium odoratum*)	rake in early spring	8–12 inches	shade
Oregon grapeholly (*Mahonia aquifolium*)	trim dead branches anytime	2 feet	moist, acid soil; shade
Japanese spurge (*Pachysandra terminalis*)	mow if needed in spring	8–12 inches	shade, moist soil
Dwarf sweet box (*Sarcococca hookeriana humilis*)	trim dead branches in spring	2–4 feet	shade
SPREADERS ABOVEGROUND			
Manzanita, bearberry (*Arctostaphylos*)	prune in spring if needed	12–48 inches	moist, acid soil
Cotoneaster (*Cotoneaster horizontalis, C. apiculatus,* or *C. adpressus*)	dead branches anytime	3–5 feet	sun; moist, well-drained soil
Trailing African daisy (*Osteospermum fruticosum*)	cut back sprawling plants in early fall	2 feet	sun, average soil
Sedum (*Sedum* spp.)	none needed	12–15 inches	drought-tolerant
Creeping thyme (*Thymus* spp.)	shear after flowering	12 inches	sun; dry soil
Dwarf periwinkle (*Vinca minor*)	shear in winter if needed	12–18 inches	shade, moisture
CLUMPERS			
Heath, heather (*Erica* spp., *Calluna* spp.)	shear after flowering	18–24 inches	sun, moist soil
Cranesbill (*Geranium* spp.)	rake in early spring	12–24 inches	sun to part shade, moist soil
Daylily (*Hemerocallis* spp.)	rake in early spring	12–18 inches	sun
Creeping lilyturf (*Liriope spicata*)	mow or shear in early spring	12 inches	partial shade
Bush cinquefoil (*Potentilla fruticosa*)	prune in spring if needed	1–2 feet	sun, drought-tolerant
SPRAWLERS			
Dwarf coyote brush (*Baccharis pilularis*)	old stems in autumn	2–3 feet	heat- and drought-tolerant
Rock rose (*Helianthemum nummularium*)	shear in spring and after bloom	24–30 inches	drought-tolerant
Creeping juniper (*Juniperus horizontalis*)	dead branches anytime	4–5 feet	sun; well-drained soil
Russian cypress (*Microbiota decussata*)	shear in spring	5–8 feet	shade; well-drained soil
Ground cover roses (*Rosa* spp.)	dead branches in spring	4–5 feet	sun; moist, fertile soil
Trailing rosemary (*Rosmarinus officinalis* 'Prostratus')	shear after flowering	3–4 feet	sun; well-drained soil

(Caring for ground covers continued)

For small plantings, use hedge shears. Remove the clippings from the bed, if possible, for best appearance. It's not necessary to prune each year if the ground cover is thriving and under control. Many ground covers need mowing only every few years, and some require no mowing at all.

Sprawling shrubs Juniper, Russian cypress, and other sprawling shrubs, which don't root at the stems, need pruning only to remove dead and damaged wood and to redirect their growth. Use hand pruners to make thinning cuts, as described on page 64.

Replacing and planting ground covers

Occasionally, one plant or even a section of plants in a ground cover will die out, requiring you to replant. But before you do, try to determine the cause: too much or too little water or shade, or the presence of a pest are common. Before replanting, correct the situation and avoid losing more plants.

Remove the dead ground cover roots and stems in the bare spot. Prepare the soil by hand pulling or hoeing weeds. When planting a ground cover that spreads by rooting branches or by underground shoots, spread 1 to 2 inches of compost over the soil and work it into the top 6 to 8 inches of soil with a garden fork, taking care not to disturb the roots of nearby ground cover plants. When planting clumping perennials or shrubs with spreading limbs, add compost to the individual planting holes instead of amending the entire area.

Where you obtain the replacement plants depends on how your ground cover grows and spreads. Purchase replacements for sprawling shrubs at a garden center or nursery. Match the existing ground cover species and variety to maintain the uniformity of the planting. Take a piece of the ground cover with you if you don't know the name of the plant.

For ground covers that form clumps or spread by creeping, rooting stems, you can divide rooted pieces from a mother plant. Use a trowel or spade to dig up rooted stems from a healthy part of the ground cover and cut the pieces from the mother plant.

If you must replant a large area, calculate how many plants you need to cover your site. The goal is to space plants so that they will fill in the bed by the end of the third growing season or by the time they reach their mature width, which could take longer. For the recommended spacing, refer to the plant-care tag, check the ground cover chart on page 105, or ask a knowledgeable nursery or landscape worker.

time saver • time saver • time saver • time saver • time saver • time saver

Harness the sun

It's critical to eliminate weeds before planting ground covers, but hand pulling, hoeing, and using herbicides have drawbacks. Instead, solarize the weeds out of the soil during the warm, sunny time of year. Mow the weeds close to the soil, then cover with a clear plastic sheet, sealing the edges with boards or soil. Leave the plastic in place until the weeds die.

Putting the plants at a closer spacing yields faster cover, but as the plants mature they become crowded and will need more frequent watering and pruning. You may have to remove some plants.

To determine the number of plants you need, follow these steps:

1. Calculate the area of the planting bed in inches by multiplying length times width. If the bed is 60 inches wide and 120 inches long, for example, its area is 7,200 square inches or 50 square feet.

2. Calculate the area needed per ground-cover plant, in square inches, by multiplying the recommended spacing times itself. A plant that is spaced 12 inches from its neighbor, for example, needs 144 square inches.

3. Divide the area of the planting bed by the area needed per plant. In this example, 7,200 square inches divided by 144 square inches equals 50. So you need 50 plants to fill in the bed.

Use the following chart to determine how large an area you can cover with 100 plants, based on planting distance.

How much ground 100 plants cover

Planting distance apart (inches)	Area covered (square feet)
6	25
8	44
12	100
18	225
24	400
30	625
36	900
48	1,600
60	2,500

After preparing the soil and obtaining the ground cover plants, follow these instructions for spacing and planting them.

1. Mark the spots where each plant will go. Use a tape measure or yardstick to set the distance between plants. For large areas, stretch a string between two stakes to establish straight rows. Mark the first spot with chalk, lime, or flour, starting at one corner of the area, and

Bare-root budget

Covering a large area with ground cover plants can be expensive, but buying bare-root plants in bulk saves money. Some local garden centers and many mail-order plant nurseries offer dormant bare-root shrubs and perennials for a much lower cost than potted specimens. Plants resume growing and spread quickly after they're set out.

Ground cover roses

There are many rough-and-ready roses that serve well as ground covers, providing utility as well as scent and flowers. New—and some heirloom —varieties bloom almost continuously all summer and need little pruning. Disease-resistant ground-covering roses include Baby Blanket, 'Charles Albanel', Electric Blanket, Fuchsia Meidiland, Flower Carpet, Gourmet Popcorn, Jeepers Creepers, Napa Valley, Ralph's Creepers, Red Meidiland, Royal Bonica, and White Meidiland.

(Caring for ground covers continued)

continue to mark spots in the first row. For the second row, place the first mark halfway between the first and second marks in the first row so that the three form an equilateral triangle. Continue marking in this manner so that each plant will be equidistant from its neighbors. Staggered row planting encourages the plants to fill in more quickly and evenly.

2. At each marked planting spot, use a sharp knife to cut an **X** just large enough to install the plant in the landscape fabric.

3. With a trowel or shovel, dig a hole for each plant. Make the hole just large enough to accommodate the root ball and leave the crown of the plant at the soil's surface.

4. Plant the ground cover according to the needs of its type. If planting on a slope, make a small half-saucer for each plant with a mounded ring of soil under the fabric on the downhill side to hold water.

5. Replace the landscape fabric around the plant, then spread 2 to 3 inches of organic mulch, such as shredded bark or pine needles, over the fabric. Keep the mulch away from the plant stems.

6. After planting, keep the soil moist until the plants become well-established, usually within one or two growing seasons. Check the soil moisture frequently by digging down to the root depth if natural rainfall is infrequent and you do not regularly irrigate. On steep hillsides, water carefully to avoid runoff and erosion. Either water slowly using drip irrigation or cycle the sprinklers on for a few minutes, then off to let the water soak in, then on again. Repeat until the soil is moist to a depth of at least 6 inches.

7. Refresh the mulch as needed to keep it thick and heavy enough to cover and block weeds. Remove the weeds that do appear weekly until the ground cover becomes dense enough to crowd and shade them out. Pull by hand or use a hoe. If you use an herbicide, read the label carefully to be sure that it is safe to use around your ground cover plants, and follow the application directions exactly.

Pests and problems

Pests that commonly attack vines and ground covers are the same as those that bother other landscape plants. Insect infestations and diseases in ground covers, however, can be more severe and harder to control than problems with individual plants, because ground covers grow together densely and usually cover a large area. Monitor vines and ground covers throughout the growing season for signs of insect and animal pests, diseases, and environmental stress. Treat the problem promptly to prevent its spread.

Symptoms and causes

Symptom	Likely cause
Sudden wilting of a vine, part of a vine, or a section of ground cover	suspect a gnawing animal, mechanical damage, or disease; also check soil moisture
Sticky or shiny residue on ground cover, vine leaves, and surfaces under a vine	suspect insects such as scales and aphids; also check overhanging trees and shrubs for pests
Mottled, stippled, or silvery foliage	suspect spider mites
White, gray, or black powder on leaves	suspect mildew fungus
Brown or black leaf spots	suspect fungal or bacterial disease
Holes in leaves and on leaf edges	suspect snails, slugs, or chewing insects
Brown foliage, especially at the ends of evergreen branches	suspect weather damage from drying wind, cold, and winter sun, and also disease or insects

Here are the most common pests and some of the most susceptible vines and ground covers:

Aphids These ⅟₁₆ to ⅛-inch long, pear-shaped insects congregate on the newest, softest leaves and stems, where they pierce the tissue and suck the sap. Aphids excrete sticky honeydew, which attracts ants and encourages a sooty-looking black fungus to grow on the foliage. Aphids also spread viral diseases among plants. Commonly infested plants include ajuga, lantana, and rose.

Scales Look for hard, oval shells on stems and leaves. These insects exude honeydew and are often difficult to control, because their shell protects them from pesticide sprays. Plants that are susceptible to infestation include wintercreeper euonymus, juniper, pachysandra, and English ivy.

Spider mites Nearly microscopic spider relatives spin fine webs on leaves and stems and pierce the foliage. Leaves have a silvery, yellowish-brown, or stippled appearance. Spider mites commonly attack cotoneaster, wintercreeper euonymus, juniper, lantana, rosemary, and Virginia creeper.

Ground cover invaders

It is a fine line between an invasive plant and a perfect ground cover. Both usually outcompete nearby plants to dominate an area. A few former star ground covers are now considered problem invasives. Examples are ajuga, goutweed, moneywort, and wintercreeper. Check with a local botanical garden or conservation organization before planting them.

(Caring for ground covers continued)

Slugs and snails These mollusks live under mulch and garden debris by day and come out to eat tender leaves and shoots at night. Look for holes in leaves and shiny slime trails. They attack English ivy, daylily, hostas, and many other ground cover plants.

Thrips Tiny, ⅟₁₆-inch-long, narrow insects pierce and suck the sap out of leaves and flowers of many plant species, giving them a streaked or stippled appearance. Thrips-prone ground covers include wintercreeper euonymus and rose.

Weevils, beetles, and grubs Adult and immature beetles chew holes in leaves and roots. Adult weevils pierce stems, leaves, and roots, often laying their eggs inside the tissue. Vulnerable plants include English ivy, speedwell, grape, and Virginia creeper.

Voles and mice Small rodents often burrow, nest, and live under the protection of ground cover plants. They also eat the stems and roots of some vines, including clematis. Look for tunnels, pieces of chewed stems, and sudden wilting.

Mildew A fungus that thrives in hot, humid, still air causes powdery white or black patches on foliage. Ground covers are especially vulnerable. Mildew-prone species include pachysandra, rose, and speedwell.

Root rot This fungus lives in damp soil and infects the roots of vulnerable plants, including ajuga, bearberry, and juniper. Look for wilting and plant collapse.

Leaf spot Fungal infections appear as tan or brown spots on foliage and dying stems. Bacterial infections start at water-soaked spots on leaves that turn brown to black. Affected vines and ground covers include bearberry, English ivy, pachysandra, rose, speedwell, Virginia creeper, and dwarf periwinkle.

Winter wind and sun Evergreen ground covers and vines, including lilyturf, English ivy, rose, and rosemary, may suffer injury from winter wind and sun, which dry out their foliage. Look for papery brown leaves, especially at the tips of stems.

Repairing winter-damaged evergreens

Evergreen vines and ground covers with winter-damaged brown leaves and stems can be pruned or sheared to remove the unsightly dead parts. In early spring, use hand pruners or hedge shears to trim stems back to healthy tissue. Trim grassy perennials, such as lilyturf and mondo grass, to just above the ground.

flower
gardens

Can you have more flowers and do less gardening? Sure. Here's how.

Well-tended flower gardens add the flair, color, and personality that define your yard and make it yours. The life cycles of different kinds of flowering plants determine their care needs. Annual plants live for just one year or growing season, while perennial plants and bulbs live for several years. The charts and guides in this chapter will help you plan ahead and give each type of plant the care it needs to thrive.

Perennial plants

Most perennials bloom at a particular time of year, usually for two to four weeks, although some have longer bloom periods or flower more than once per year. The time of year in which perennials flower and their individual growth habits influence when you must do certain maintenance tasks, such as pruning, staking, and dividing. Giving perennial plants what they need at the right time increases the quantity and quality of their flowers and foliage.

Seasonal care

Spring chores get the yard and garden season off to a fresh start. It's the time of year when perennial flower gardens usually need the most attention as you clean up from winter and prepare for the growing season ahead. Summer tasks, including pruning, watering, and fertilizing, help the flower garden look its best and keep potential problems under control. Autumn cleanup prepares the garden for winter and the following spring. Winter is the dormant time for cold-climate perennials, but it remains an active growing season in warm-winter climates.

Throughout the growing season, check plants at least twice a week. Look to see if they need water, remove any spent flowers, and keep an eye out for symptoms of insects and other pests and diseases. Remove weeds as you see them. Use the calendar on page 114 to plan your maintenance tasks. Look in the following pages for details on how to do each activity.

■ SMART IDEA ■

Simplest bed edging

The oldest, simplest, and easiest way to edge a garden is by making a trench around the bed.

Mark the outside edge of a straight garden border with a taut string between stakes. For a curving line, use a garden hose to mark the border. Then dig the trench with a spade or an edging tool. Starting at one end of the garden, push the spade straight down into the soil about 3 to 4 inches. Pull back on the top of the handle to pop out a wedge of soil. Continue working this way down the line. At the end, you should have a nearly vertical edge with an edge that slopes into the planting bed. Regular edging prevents lawn grasses and creeping weeds from growing into the garden.

(Perennial plants continued)

Perennials maintenance calendar

What to do	Why
SPRING	
Cut back the dead stems from last year	garden appearance, pest prevention
Pull emerging weeds and add fresh mulch	prevent future weeds; improve growth, appearance
Neaten the edge of the garden	appearance; stop creeping weeds
Divide summer- and fall-blooming perennials	improve plant health, flowering, appearance
Fertilize with granular flower-garden formula	improve growth
Prune off spent spring-blooming flowers	plant appearance; prevent pests
Shorten stems of tall, fall-blooming plants	reduce need for staking; make plants better-looking
Install plant supports	prevent top-heavy plants from collapsing
Install irrigation around thirstiest plants	more consistent watering improves plant growth; reduce maintenance
Scout for pests, diseases, and other problems	catch problems early when easy to treat
Test the soil for pH and nutrients	improve plant health
SUMMER	
Pull weeds before they set seed	remove the source of future weeds
Water whenever rainfall is inadequate	plant health
Deadhead spent flowers; trim sprawling stems	maintain plant health and growth
Continue watching for pests and problems	catch problems early
Divide spring-blooming perennials	improve plant growth and bloom next season
Fertilize, and replenish mulch	maintain vigorous growth; prevent weeds
Add plant supports as needed	prevent drooping or broken stems
AUTUMN	
Transplant six weeks before the ground freezes	allow roots to establish before winter
Pull or dig up remaining weeds	remove seeds, places for pests to hide over winter
Water before the ground freezes if the soil is dry	ensure plants are healthy prior to winter
Protect late-flowering perennials from frost	extend bloom
Cut dead stems to the ground	garden appearance
Remove and store plant supports	appearance; preserve equipment
Apply winter mulch after the ground freezes	prevent freeze-thaw cycles that damage plants
WINTER	
Mulch tender perennials	protect them from freezing; assist winter survival
Scout for rodent damage	prevent serious damage
Reset frost-heaved plants	aids their survival if done before spring arrives
Maintain growing routine in warm-winter climates	garden appearance

Using perennials

The uses for perennials are as broad and free-ranging as they can be for any plant. Grow them alone as specimens or en masse as ground covers. Or mix them up in any combination that delights you. There are no rules. However, there are some common styles that people have used for years. These are four.

Cottage style An informal mix of closely planted perennials such as delphiniums, foxgloves, hollyhocks, irises, phlox, and roses has an old-fashioned flavor.

Prairie style These plantings emulate the native tall-grass prairie of North America. Ornamental grasses such as maidengrass are prominent in this garden style, along with perennials such as black-eyed Susan.

Shade garden style Foliage predominates, but many flowering plants thrive. The style works with the colors of leaves and textures of plants to create the framework of the design. Occasional flowers add sparkle and excitement.

Exuberant style This no-holds-barred style mixes bright colors and bold textures, and it has something in bloom at all times. By combining perennials with differing bloom seasons, your garden will be covered in blossoms from spring to fall.

115

(Perennial plants continued)

Maintaining perennials

Some garden tasks must be done every few days or at least weekly throughout the growing season; other jobs need attention less often. Use the following guidelines to maintain your perennial garden.

Water Most perennials need about an inch of water per week during the growing season. Drought-tolerant plants need less; moisture-loving species may require 1½ to 2 inches of water. Use a rain gauge to measure rainfall each week, and supplement with irrigation to bring the total amount of water to at least 1 inch. Monitor weekly weather conditions and the plants' growth stage. Increase the amount of water when plants are growing rapidly and when hot, windy weather increases evaporation and plants' water needs. During the driest weeks, check plants daily for wilting, and water them until the soil is moist to a depth of about 6 to 8 inches. Turn to Chapter 9 for information on how to water gardens effectively.

Fertilize In early spring, just as perennials begin to emerge from the soil, apply a granular all-purpose 5-10-5 or 5-5-5 fertilizer at the rate of 1 pound per 25 square feet. If you use a 10-20-10 or 10-10-10 formulation, apply one-half pound per 25 square feet. Sprinkle the fertilizer around the plant clumps, and avoid getting it directly on the plants. Wash the fertilizer off the leaves to avoid burning the foliage. Water the garden to help dissolve the fertilizer into the soil, but avoid puddling and runoff, which could cause the nutrients to spread unevenly. Repeat the fertilizer application once more about a month later.

Weed, mulch, and edge Begin weeding as soon as the ground thaws or weeds begin growing in spring. Use a sharp hoe to slice weed seedlings off just below the soil's surface, disturbing the soil as little as possible to avoid injuring perennial plant roots or encouraging new weed seeds to sprout. Pull larger weeds by hand, using a taproot weeder to uproot the long taproots of dandelion, burdock, chicory, and others. Pull weeds before they flower and set seed. Remove as many weed roots as possible when pulling up weeds that grow as perennials, such as quackgrass, Canada thistle, and bindweed. Rake up and discard the dislodged weeds to keep their seeds and roots from spreading in your garden. To prevent weed seeds from growing, apply a preemergent herbicide, such as trifluralin (Treflan, Preen) or corn gluten meal (Safe 'N Simple, WOW!), to the soil in spring as soon as the ground thaws or begins to warm up and before weeds have germinated. Rake it gently into the top half-inch of soil. Reapply in summer and fall, at the interval recommended in the package instructions.

time saver • time saver • time saver • time saver • time saver • time saver

Finding time

Perennials don't require any more time than other plants, and big jobs are rare. But if the prospect of growing perennials is daunting, practice this simple technique: Walk your garden every other day or so, and observe. See what the plants need. Snip off a faded flower here, and pull and weed there, and you're done.

Basic perennial care

Step 1 is choosing plants that are well-adapted to your region and garden. Provide the water plants need. Then follow up with the tasks shown here, and your perennials will thrive.

Mulch A 1- to 2-inch-thick layer of shredded leaves, compost, or shredded bark between plants works miracles. It will block weeds and help plants survive heat and drought.

Fertilize Most perennials grow best in nutrient-rich soil. Use your favorite type of fertilizer—organic or synthetic. Work it into the soil in early spring.

Groom Regularly snipping off spent flowers before seeds form stimulates most perennials to bloom again. However, there are perennials, such as stonecrop, with good-looking seedheads and these you might elect to leave in place.

Winter protection In cold climates, drape pruned evergreen branches over tender plants. They'll trap snow, which insulates and protects plants from wind.

Filling in with annuals

Perennial plants take up to three years to grow to their mature size, which leaves bare spots in the garden until they fill in. Plant annuals among the young perennial plants to add color for the first summer or two. The annuals also shade the soil and help keep weeds at bay.

(Perennial plants continued)

Mulch prevents weeds from growing, moderates the soil temperature, and helps hold moisture in the soil. In spring, remove and discard old mulch that may contain weeds and weed seeds as well as disease organisms. If the old mulch is free of weeds and diseases, rake it lightly to break up any crust and smooth it out. Add new mulch to the garden in a layer 2 to 3 inches thick. Keep the mulch away from plant crowns and stems to allow them to grow freely. Use locally available natural mulches, such as bark, seed hulls, and shredded leaves or pine needles. In fire-prone areas, use nonflammable mulch, such as gravel, near buildings.

Keep the edge between the garden and lawn or paved areas neat and well-defined by trimming the grass with a string trimmer or grass shears along the edge whenever you mow. For yards without installed plastic or metal edging, make a tidy boundary with a special edging tool or sharp square-pointed spade. Push the blade straight down about 3 to 4 inches into the soil at the edge of the lawn and tip the handle so that the wedge of soil pops out toward the garden. Rake up and compost the dislodged soil and turf. Edge the garden early in spring and repeat monthly as needed.

Prune and deadhead Removing spent flowers is called deadheading, and it should be done at least once a week, and more often if possible. The practice encourages plants to continue blooming and keeps the garden looking tidy. Use sharp scissors or hand pruners to snip off individual flowers and stalks. For perennials that send up naked flower stalks from the ground, such as daylilies, cut off individual flowers as they fade, then cut the flower stalk to the soil when the last flower bud has finished. After flowering, plants with leafy stalks, such as delphiniums and hollyhocks, should be cut off just below the lowest flower to a set of healthy-looking leaves or new flower buds, leaving as much foliage intact as possible. Add the clippings to the compost pile, or put them in the trash if they contain insect pests or diseases. Leave old flowers on plants that produce ornamental or bird-attracting seedpods, such as globe thistle and purple coneflower.

To encourage shorter, bushier summer- and fall-blooming plants, such as New England aster, garden phlox, and chrysanthemum, pinch off an inch or two of the growing tips when the plants reach about a foot high in early summer. Pinching encourages the shoots to branch and grow more flowers. Repeat the pinching two or three times until midsummer. To keep the garden healthy and tidy, prune off broken stalks and diseased or dead stems whenever you see them. Some perennials, including oriental poppies and catmint can be cut to within a few inches of the ground when they finish flowering; they may produce a fresh mound of leaves.

Supporting tall flowers

Many perennials need help to keep their tall or heavy flowers up high. If heavy rains or strong winds are likely in your area, supporting structures are essential.

Recycled prunings Twiggy prunings cut from a shrub form a skeleton over which perennials will grow. By bloom time, the support branches will be completely hidden.

Hoop cages Many types of stakes are on the market. Most are made from heavy, coated wire. They range in style from this set of interlocking stakes, which you use to ring a plant, to single stakes for single stems to cross-hatched "plates" with legs. Emerging stems grow through these and are held securely upright.

Stakes and string Bamboo stakes and string or twine are versatile and inexpensive. Use them for single stems (right) or full clumps. Ring a clump with three to five stakes. Tie string to one stake, then encircle the clump, wrapping around each stake one or two times. Finish up by crisscrossing the clump with the string to form a star pattern.

Single stem stakes Push the bamboo into the soil a few inches from the stem you wish to support. Tie one end of the string to the stake then loosely loop it around the stem, making a figure 8 between stem and stake. Tie the loose end to the stake.

119

Garden clothes

Gardening is an easygoing activity, but if you'll be doing a lot, give some thought to your clothes. First, wear a cap or hat to protect your face, neck, and head from the sun. (In addition, be sure to wear sunscreen.) Wear heavy shoes or boots, especially if using a shovel or any kind of equipment. Finally, wear gloves, particularly if you'll be digging in rough soil or applying fertilizers or mulch.

(Perennial plants continued)

Stake and support Tall perennials and those with top-heavy stems need support to keep them upright and looking good in the garden. In spring, before plants get too tall, place wire grow-through supports and plant cages over clumps of floppy perennials, such as peony, garden phlox, and tall shasta daisy varieties. As the plants grow, their foliage will hide the supports. Each week, guide any wayward stems back into the cage.

Stake the individual stalks of tall delphiniums, hollyhocks, and other tall perennials, especially in windy sites, by loosely tying the individual stalks in several places with cloth strips or purchased plant ties. Stakes should be nearly as tall as the plant stalks when inserted into the ground. As an alternative, surround the plant with a cage made of interlocking wire bars or wood stakes and twine. The cage should be at least half the height of the plant. Remove the supports in the fall and store them for the following year. Turn to page 119 for illustrations and more information on plant supports.

Divide and replant As perennial plants grow, they may begin to crowd their neighbors, become less vigorous, die in the center of the clump, or produce fewer flowers. When any of these situations occur, the plants need to be divided into smaller pieces and replanted. Perennials that spread rapidly, such as obedient plant and bee balm, must be divided every two to three years to control their growth. Plants that increase in size slowly or are hard to transplant, including peony, bleeding heart, and butterfly weed, rarely need division. For best results, divide spring-blooming plants in fall and midsummer- to fall-blooming plants in spring.

Divide a perennial by either digging up the whole plant or taking pieces from the outside of the clump, being careful not to disturb surrounding plants. Loosen the soil around the whole plant or part of the plant with a garden fork and lift it from the ground. If necessary, wash the soil off to expose the roots and crown. Whether digging the whole clump or taking outside pieces, use either a sharp spade to slice or a garden fork to pry the clump apart. Make sure all pieces contain roots and shoots. For plants that form dense clumps, such as daylilies and hostas, insert two garden spades, placed back-to-back, into the clump and pry apart.

Discard the oldest and least vigorous portions of the plant. Keep the remaining pieces cool and moist until replanting. Prepare planting holes by loosening the soil and mixing in a shovelful of compost. Make a hole with a spade or trowel and set the plant crowns at the same soil depth as they previously grew. Spread the roots in the hole and firm the soil gently around the roots. Water thoroughly to

Dividing a daylily

Daylilies are tough plants and can take lots of abuse. But after five years or so, clumps become so dense and crowded that flowering slows down. That's the time to divide.

1 Dig around clump
In early spring or in fall after blooming ends, dig around the clump a few inches beyond the leaves. A sharp spade and boots or shoes with heavy soles will make the job easier.

2 Pry clump apart
Intertwined roots make a dense clump that is hard to pull apart. Prying it apart with back-to-back forks is a traditional method; or use a spade to cut through the clump.

3 Separate crowns
Use your hands to pull apart and separate 6- to 8-inch-wide clumps or, for the maximum number of plants, individual fans. Each clump needs at least one fan of leaves with roots attached.

4 Replant Space larger clumps about 2 feet apart, smaller ones 6 inches apart. Keep new divisions moist, fertilized, and mulched through their next summer. Bloom will be sparse, but the following season and several to come will compensate.

(Perennial plants continued)

eliminate air pockets. Protect from direct sun for a few days to prevent wilting, if the plant has foliage.

Newly planted and divided perennials sometimes pop out of the ground in winter as the soil freezes and thaws. If frost heaving occurs in your garden, press the plant back into the ground, if possible, and mulch it heavily with soil or bark mulch to protect the roots from drying out. After the ground thaws, replant the perennial.

Scout for problems Insects, animal pests, diseases, and environmental distress can affect your garden plants in any season. At least once a week, walk through the garden and look for anything unusual. An insect pest here or there should not cause you any particular alarm, and often waiting and watching is a better course than immediately spraying. Picking or brushing or washing insects off plants will suffice to remedy most problems. Before you take any significant actions to stop an insect, look at the pictures of common pests on page 331, and also the pictures of beneficial insects on page 335.

Inadequate or excess water causes wilting and pale foliage. High temperatures, herbicides, strong sunlight, and air pollution may discolor leaves of sensitive plants or cause spots and dead patches. Symptoms of insect, slug, and snail pests include holes in the leaves; sticky or shiny residue; and distorted, speckled, or streaked flower buds, flowers, leaves, or new shoots. Look for symptoms of disease, too, such as leaf spots; sudden wilting; rusty, powdery white, or black residue on leaves; brown flower buds; dying leaves; stunted or distorted growth; and slimy black or brown plant parts.

Larger pests, such as rabbits and deer, eat the leaves and shoots of many perennials. Entire plants or parts of plants may be eaten. Rodents and other burrowing animals eat plant roots and stems close to the ground. Look for burrow entrances and raised tunnels if you find perennial shoots chewed off at ground level or plants suddenly wilting and dying or able to be pulled easily from the ground with few roots remaining. See Chapter 13 for more information on identifying and controlling animal pests.

Replacing perennial plants

When a plant dies or needs to be replaced, look for a new plant that shares the cultural needs of surrounding garden plants to make caring for your garden easier. Keep moisture-loving plants in one section of the garden, for example, and those that tolerate dry soil in another to keep irrigation needs to a minimum.

Planting weather

Planting (or transplanting) leafy perennials and annuals in the heat of summer can stress the plants and cause wilting. Choose cloudy or rainy days to keep the plants from drying out. Water plants well before the move, and keep the soil moist for the rest of the growing season.

When selecting replacements, look for vigorous new growth. Avoid potted plants with wilted, discolored foliage or roots growing out the bottom holes. Smaller, more compact plants usually recover from transplanting more quickly than larger plants in full bloom. Nurseries sell plants in containers ranging from 2-inch cells in a six-pack to gallon-size pots. Smaller plants are more economical but take longer to reach mature size.

In cold climates, the best time to plant container-grown perennials is in the spring. In warmer regions (Zone 5 to Zone 11), spring or fall planting is equally good. In mild winter regions, fall is the best time for planting.

Container-grown perennials may have roots growing in circles. To facilitate their transition to the garden, tease any bound or circling roots away from the root mass with your fingers.

To replace a plant, remove all remnants of the dead plant from the garden. Dig a new planting hole and mix a shovelful of compost into the backfill soil.

Plant bare-root perennials when they are available in your area, usually early spring. Mail-order nurseries will usually send perennials after washing soil off their roots, in part to reduce postage expense. First make sure that bare-root plants don't dry out. If they're in a plastic bag, add a few tablespoons of water to the bag. Set them out of the sun in a cool, shaded location. Just prior to planting, soak roots in a bowl or bucket to make sure they are fully rehydrated. Set the plants on a small mound of soil in the center of the planting hole and spread the roots out. Gently pat soil over roots as you backfill.

Gently remove a container plant from its pot and set it into the hole so that the crown is at the same soil level as it was in the pot. Firm the soil gently around the plant roots and water thoroughly. Keep the soil moist for several weeks. Protect the plant from direct sun and wind for the first week or two if it has tender foliage.

· HOW-TO ·

Dividing bearded iris

While one of the longest-lived and easiest-to-grow perennials, bearded iris need dividing every three to five years. Otherwise, they become overcrowded and flowering is diminished. The best time to divide them is in midsummer after they've flowered. Gently lift the thick underground stems, called rhizomes. Tease or cut apart the clumps and discard the oldest sections. Cut back the leaves of the youngest, healthiest sections to one-third their original height. Each transplant should have a fan of leaves, a healthy rhizome, and several roots; discard all the rest. Replant by setting the rhizome on top of a mound of soil in a planting hole. Adjust height and add soil so the rhizome is only barely covered, and water.

flower gardens

(*Perennial plants continued*)

Caring for 17 favorite perennials

Perennial	Water; light	Fertilizer	Support	Pruning	Division	Pests and problems
Yarrow (*Achillea* hybrids)	low; sun	low	grow-through	deadhead flower stalks to ground	spring or fall, every 4–5 years	few (insect- and deer-resistant)
New England aster (*Aster novae-angliae*)	average; sun	average	grow-through	pinch tips 2–3 times until midsummer	spring, every 2–3 years	Japanese beetles, deer, rabbits, powdery mildew
Astilbe (*Astilbe* × *arendsii*)	high; shade	high	none	deadhead flower stalks to ground	rarely needed	spider mites, rust, powdery mildew
Bellflower (*Campanula* species)	average; sun	average	usually none	deadhead to strong leaf bud	fall or spring, every 3–5 years	rabbits, woodchucks
Coreopsis (*Coreopsis* species)	average; sun	low	grow-through	deadhead flower stalks to ground	fall or spring, every 2–3 years	few
Purple coneflower (*Echinacea purpurea*)	average; sun	average	none	deadhead flower stalks to ground	fall or spring, every 4–5 years	few
Blanket flower (*Gaillardia* × *grandiflora*)	average; sun	average	stake tall varieties	deadhead flowers if desired	spring, every 2–3 years	few pests; crown rot in wet soil
Cranesbill (*Geranium* species)	average; sun	average	none	shear to ground after flowering	spring, every 5–6 years	few pests; leaf spot may occur
Ornamental grasses (many species)	average; sun	average	none	cut back in spring	spring, every 4–5 years	voles
Daylily (*Hemerocallis* hybrids)	average; sun	average	none	deadhead flower stalks to ground	spring, every 4–5 years	slugs, snails, rabbits, deer, leaf diseases
Hosta (*Hosta* hybrids)	high; shade	average	none	deadhead flower stalks to ground	spring, every 7–8 years	slugs, snails, rabbits, deer
Bearded iris (*Iris* hybrids)	average; sun	average	stake tall varieties	deadhead flower stalks to ground	midsummer, every 4 years	iris borers, wind damage
Shasta daisy (*Leucanthemum* × *superbum*)	average; sun	high	grow-through	deadhead flower stalks to ground	fall or spring, every 2–3 years	aphids, plant bugs, stem rot
Bee balm (*Monarda didyma*)	average; sun	average	grow-through	deadhead flower stalks to ground	divide to control plant spread	powdery mildew, plant bugs
Peony (*Paeonia lactiflora* hybrids)	average; sun	average	grow-through	deadhead flower stalks to leaf	fall, every 8–10 years	botrytis infection on leaf, flower
Garden phlox (*Phlox paniculata*)	average; sun	high	grow-through	deadhead to strong leaf bud	spring, every 3–4 years	powdery mildew, spider mites, nematodes
Black-eyed Susan (*Rudbeckia* species)	average; sun	average	none	deadhead flower stalks to leaf	spring, every 4–5 years	few pests, self-sows readily

Annual plants

Annual garden plants require regular care. At least once a week, deadhead flowers, water, pull weeds, and check for pests and diseases. Fertilize monthly and stake and support as needed.

Water Most annuals prefer moist soil, although some thrive in more arid conditions. Whenever weekly rainfall falls short of the usually required 1 to 1½ inches of water, or the soil feels dry around the plant roots, irrigate the garden until the soil is moist to a depth of 6 to 8 inches. Plants need more frequent watering during hot, windy weather.

Fertilize Annuals benefit from more frequent fertilization than perennial plants because they grow quickly and expend much energy in their flowering. Use a slow-release fertilizer at planting and again at midseason, following the package instructions. Some annuals, including geraniums and petunias, need feeding every two to three weeks. Stop fertilizing in late summer.

Weed, mulch, and edge Annual garden plants need the same weed and mulch maintenance as perennials. Turn to page 116 for more information. If you plant annual seeds directly in your garden, avoid using preemergence herbicides, which prevent seeds from growing.

Prune and deadhead To keep most annuals blooming, remove the spent flowers before the plants develop seeds. Once they set seeds, many plants stop blooming. Check plants often, and cut or pinch off the old flowers. Some "self-cleaning" annuals, including ground-cover petunias, have been bred to flower continuously without deadheading.

Stake and support Usually only the tallest and most top-heavy annuals need staking or supporting, although plants in gardens that experience heavy rains and wind may benefit from supports for lower-growing annuals, too. Stake tall, slender-stemmed annuals such as larkspur and painted tongue. Install stakes at planting time and guide plants into them as they grow. See page 119 for information on how to use stakes and supports.

· GOOD PLANTS ·

Cheap and easy color

It's tempting at the garden center to grab the prettiest, newest, or otherwise most exciting plants. But it's smarter to look for the plants that give the most color for the least effort. For lots of color without deadheading or weekly watering, look for these "self-cleaning" annuals: Wave petunias, Million Bells (Calibrachoa), celosia, wax begonia, moss rose (Portulaca grandiflora), ornamental grasses, and impatiens. If you live where summers are hot and dry, grow drought-tolerant annuals. Some of the best include: blanket flower (Gaillardia × grandiflora), California poppy (Eschscholzia californica), moss rose (Portulaca grandiflora), verbena (Verbena × hybrida), and African daisy (Arctotis and Dimorphotheca species).

(Annual plants continued)

Care calendar for annuals

Annual plants complete their entire life cycle in one year. They begin as seeds in spring, grow rapidly to maturity, bloom for many weeks in summer, then die in the fall. Many annuals continue flowering nonstop until frost if they receive adequate water, fertilizer, and pruning. Because they live for only one growing season, annuals must usually be replanted each year. Exceptions occur in mild-winter climates where some annuals live through winter.

What	Why
SPRING	
Pull up and discard last year's annuals	garden appearance
Eliminate weeds from the flower bed	prevent future weeds, appearance
Prepare the soil with fertilizer and compost	improve growth
Transplant annuals or sow seeds outdoors	give plant full season to grow
Prune off flowers from new transplants	improve root growth and flowering
Set up irrigation system if needed	save labor and improve growth
Deadhead spent flowers	promote rebloom; improve appearance
Protect from unexpected frost and freezing	as needed to ensure survival
Mulch, water, and fertilize after planting	improve growth
Install supports for tall or floppy annuals	prevent broken stems
Scout for pests and problems often	catch problems while small
SUMMER	
Deadhead spent flowers	promote rebloom; improve appearance
Prune untidy and overgrown stems	improve plant appearance
Fertilize with low-nitrogen fertilizer	sustain vigorous growth and bloom
Pull or hoe weeds weekly	reduce competition and future problems
Plant fall-blooming annuals in late summer	extend bloom season
Water when rainfall is less than an inch per week	ensure plant survival
Scout for insect and animal pests and diseases	catch problems early
AUTUMN	
Protect plants from frost	extend bloom season
Continue to eliminate weeds	reduce weeds next year
Water as needed when rainfall is inadequate	plant health
Pull up and discard plants after the killing frost	garden appearance

Using annuals

The best thing about annuals? They let you change your color scheme or planting plan every year—or more often if you want. Build an entire garden with annuals, or use them to fill in and provide accents throughout your yard, or grow them in containers. Here are a few ideas.

Colorful coverup In the space of a few months, trailing annuals such as nasturtium will cover an old tree stump or more. Plant them in baskets, or where they can sprawl over walls.

Cut flowers Many annuals, such as zinnias, often make the best cut flowers. They bloom prolifically so there are plenty of blossoms for indoors and out. And the cut flowers are usually long lasting.

Knock-out color Annual seed is so inexpensive you can fill nearly every inch of your yard with color. Planting the shortest annuals in front and the tallest in back shows off all the plants to best effect.

Showy leaves Annuals are usually about colorful flowers, but not always. Red-leaved amaranthus are backed by purple castor beans. Orange marigolds complete the picture.

(Annual plants continued)

Scout for problems Many of the animals, insects, slugs, snails, and diseases that bother perennials also attack annuals. See page 122 and consult Chapter 13 for information on identifying and controlling problems.

Choosing and planting annuals

The chief drawback to annuals—that they only live for a year—is also their biggest virtue. Every planting season is an opportunity for a new look and new colors in your garden.

When shopping for annuals, choose sturdy, vigorous plants with no wilting, brown leaves, or broken stems. Slip a plant out of its container and check the roots, which should not circle tightly around the outside of the ball of soil. Plants without flowers will recover from transplanting more quickly, because more of their energy will go into growing strong roots. Prune off any flowers at planting time by pinching them back to flower or leaf buds.

Container sizes range from small cell packs to gallon-size pots. Smaller plants usually recover from transplanting more quickly than larger plants. Choose the smaller sizes, especially early in the season, when you need lots of plants for mass planting or want to stretch your budget. Buy the large container sizes for specimen plants, when you need an immediate impact, or late in the season when small plants wouldn't have time to mature.

Transplant annuals into fertile, weed-free soil after frost danger has passed and the soil has warmed. Protect plants from the earliest frosts in autumn to keep your garden blooming into fall. When unseasoned frost threatens, cover the plants with bedsheets, cardboard boxes, or garden fabric until the danger passes. Remove the protection during the day if the temperature rises above freezing.

Space the plants in the garden so that they will slightly overlap their neighbors at maturity. If plants will grow 12 inches wide, for example, allow 12 inches between the centers of neighboring plants. Look for plant labels that provide plant width, or check the list on the opposite page for information on some popular annual plants. Slip plants out of their pots, gently loosen circling roots, and plant at the same soil level as they grew in the pots. Press the soil gently around the roots, and water thoroughly to settle the soil. Apply mulch around the plants, but keep it away from the plant stems.

time saver • time saver • time saver • time saver • time saver • time saver •

Planting sticks

When establishing a mass planting of evenly spaced annuals or ground covers, a planting stick is a useful tool. Cut a stout twig, bamboo stick, or piece of scrap wood to the needed length and use it to space your plants accurately. The sticks come in handy for planting seeds, too.

Caring for 18 favorite annuals

Most annuals need about an inch of water per week and monthly fertilizing. Plants with low water or fertilizer requirements should receive about half an inch of water per week and feeding every other month.

Annual	Water; light	Fertilizer	Support	Pruning	Problems	Spacing
Ageratum (*Ageratum houstonianum*)	average; sun	average	stake tall varieties	shear spent flowers	few	8–12 inches
Snapdragon (*Antirrhinum majus*)	average; sun	average	stake tall varieties	pinch early stem tips, deadhead	rust, mildew	6–12 inches
Bidens (*Bidens ferulifolia*)	average; sun	average	none	none needed	few	12 inches
Million bells (*Calibrachoa*)	average; sun	high	none	none needed	few	12 inches
Celosia (*Celosia* hybrids)	average; sun	low to average	stake tall varieties	none needed	few	6–12 inches
Spider flower (*Cleome hassleriana*)	average; sun	average	none	deadhead	few	1–3 feet
Coleus (*Solenostemon scutellarioides*)	average; shade	low	none	pinch off flower stalks	aphids	6–18 inches
Cosmos (*Cosmos* species)	average; shade	low	stake tall varieties	deadhead for more flowers	wind, rain breakage	1–3 feet
Gazania (*Gazania rigens*)	low; sun	low	none	deadhead	few	8–12 inches
Impatiens (*Impatiens* varieties)	high; shade	low	none	shear to promote branching	few	12–18 inches
Sweet alyssum (*Lobularia maritima*)	average; sun	average	none	shear spent flowers	few	6 inches
Geranium (*Pelargonium*)	average; sun	high	none	deadhead	few	12–18 inches
Petunia (*Petunia x hybrida*)	average; sun	high	none	deadhead	few	1–3 feet
Salvia (*Salvia* species)	average; sun	low	stake tall varieties	deadhead	few	1–2 feet
Fan flower (*Scaevola aemula*)	low; sun	average	none	deadhead	few	15 inches
Marigold (*Tagetes* hybrids)	average; sun	average	stake tall varieties	deadhead	few	6–24 inches
Pansy (*Viola × wittrockiana*)	average; sun	average	none	deadhead	few	4–6 inches
Zinnia (*Zinnia elegans*)	average; sun	average	stake tall varieties	pinch branches, deadhead	mildew	6–12 inches

Flowering bulbs

Bulb plants store food in swollen underground parts, making them easy to grow and adaptable to a wide range of growing conditions. Some are winter-hardy in even the coldest climates, whereas others must be lifted from the soil, stored for the winter, and replanted in spring. Different kinds of flowering bulbs bloom from early spring throughout the summer and into autumn. Some bulbs, including elephant's ear and caladium, display colorful and dramatic foliage. Spring-flowering bulbs make ideal companions for annual flowers, which can be planted right on top of the bulbs after the bulbs' foliage ripens in early summer.

Bulb maintenance calendar

Bulbs that remain in the ground year-round require little maintenance. The following chart summarizes bulbs' annual maintenance schedule.

What	Why
SPRING	
Deadhead spent flowers; leave the foliage intact	ensure the bulbs store energy
Fertilize naturalized bulbs	promote next year's growth
Water deeply if needed	good growth
Plant summer-flowering bulbs	summer color
Install supports for tall summer annual bulbs	prevent blooms from falling
Scout for pests or problems	make fixes early
SUMMER	
Fertilize spring-flowering bulbs after flowering	aid bulb development
Check for disease and insect pests	catch problems early
Remove yellowed leaves from spring bulbs	grooming
Deadhead summer flowers; leave the foliage intact	divert energy into bulbs
Water deeply if needed	sustain good growth
Stake or support tall, heavy plants	best display
Divide spring bloomers	ensure bloom next season
AUTUMN	
Plant spring-flowering bulbs	spring color
Fertilize naturalized bulbs	promote next year's growth
Mulch after the ground freezes	prevent freeze-thaw cycles
Lift tender bulbs and store for the winter	they won't survive otherwise

Kinds of bulbs

Many of the plants people refer to as bulbs actually are not bulbs at all, botanically speaking. Though their shapes, sizes and origins vary, each is packed with all the energy needed to grow and bloom. The following are four of the most common types of "bulbs."

Bulb A compressed and dormant flower bud waits inside, stretching out from the top as soon as soil warms in spring. Many bulbs are adapted to surviving periods of cold.

Tulip It's likely the most well-known flower that grows from a bulb. Other flower bulbs include lilies, amaryllis, ornamental onions, milk-and-wine lilies, and daffodils.

Corm A corm is a stem that has changed into a mass of storage tissue. Unlike bulbs, corms are solid, and multiple buds may grow from the top. Many corms are adapted to surviving periods of seasonal drought.

Gladiolus Flowers growing from corms include gladiolus, crocus, bugle lily, monbretia, and blazing star.

Tuberous root Like stocking the cold cellar, some plants pack their food reserves in sections of roots that retain a growing tip at one end.

Anemone Because Greek anemone (or windflowers) produce tuberous roots, they are sold as bulbs. In gardens, they behave like perennials. Other tuberous-rooted bulbs include dahlia, ranunculus, sweet potato, and daylily.

Rhizome Rhizomes are underground stems that store nutrients and help the plant spread in a garden.

Bearded iris Rhizomes grow new shoots and roots from their tips while leaving the older portion behind to rot. Bearded iris are among the showiest of plants that grow from rhizomes. Others include African lily, lily of the valley, and canna.

(Flowering bulbs continued)

Maintaining bulbs

Hardy bulbs probably require less care than nearly any other landscape plant, but occasional maintenance keeps them looking tidy and flowering profusely from year to year. The plants commonly referred to as bulbs are actually many different kinds of plants. But they are grouped together and called bulbs for convenience because they all spend a season underground and dormant.

Water All bulbs need adequate water throughout their growing season. If your bulbs grow in a mixed flower garden that includes perennials or annuals, the water you provide for them will be enough for bulbs, too. Whenever rainfall has been less than an inch per week, water bulbs to make up the difference. Most bulbs have deep roots, so be sure that the irrigation or rainwater penetrates at least 8 to 12 inches deep. You may stop additional watering after the bulb foliage ripens and turns yellow.

Fertilize All perennial bulb need good nutrition during their periods of active root and leaf growth. Mix a slow-release bulb fertilizer, such as 9-9-6, into the planting soil when planting bulbs, using 1 tablespoon per square foot. In established bulb gardens, sprinkle 1 level tablespoon of fertilizer per square foot or ½ cup per 10 square feet around bulbs growing in the garden as soon as the shoots emerge from the soil in spring. If you added fertilizer to the planting hole, you may skip additional feeding for the first year.

Dahlias, lilies, and other summer-flowering bulbs have nutritional needs similar to perennial plants. Add 1 tablespoon of fertilizer per square foot to the planting soil when planting annual bulbs, such as dahlias. Then fertilize them once a month during the summer with a lower-nitrogen formula, such as 5-10-10, spread at the rate of 1 pound per 25 square feet. Stop feeding in mid- to late summer, or about six weeks before the first expected frost. Naturalized bulbs growing in lawns do not need additional feeding, especially if you use lawn fertilizer.

Prune and deadhead Removing spent flowers prevents the bulb plants from developing seeds, so more energy goes to root and bulb development. Snip or pinch off individual flowers when they finish blooming and begin to collapse, leaving the flower stem intact. When cutting flowers for a bouquet, leave as much of the stalk and foliage intact as possible. Some bulbs, such as grape hyacinth, Spanish bluebells, and flowering onions, self-sow readily from seed. Let the seed heads mature if you want to increase your bulbs by seeds instead of dividing the clumps of bulbs. Leaving the seed heads on the plant may prevent the bulbs from increasing in size.

healthy garden • healthy garden • healthy garden

Start begonias early

Pot your stored or purchased begonia tubers in March or early spring. Plant the eyes or sprouts about 2 inches below the soil's surface. Place in a sunny window and keep the soil just barely moist. Transplant into window boxes and hanging baskets in May.

After spring-flowering bulbs finish blooming, the foliage continues to make food for the bulbs until it begins to decline and turn yellow or brown in midsummer. Although the ripening foliage may look unattractive, leave this foliage intact for about six to eight weeks, until it is no longer green, then snip it off if you wish. Do not braid the foliage or mulch over it; both practices reduce the leaves, ability to trap sunlight. If you have naturalized bulbs in your lawn, avoid mowing over the foliage for about four to six weeks, until it begins to turn yellow, to give plants time to prepare for dormancy.

Stake and support Only the tallest and most top-heavy bulb plants, such as dahlias, gladiola, crown imperial, and some bearded iris, regularly need staking or supporting. In windy yards and places that receive heavy rains, use supports with lilies and other topple-prone species. Support dahlias with a cone-shaped tomato cage. Use wire snips to cut the legs off the bottom of the cage, then place the cage upside down over the newly planted tuber. Bend the removed wire legs into U shapes and use them to peg down the cage. Tie the cage to a sturdy post for additional support if needed. For gladiola, lilies, and tall bearded iris, use individual flower stakes and soft plant ties to secure the stems.

Lift and store tender bulbs To keep frost-tender bulbs, such as begonia hybrids, caladium, and dahlia, from one year to the next, you must store them for the winter in a nonfreezing place. When the tops begin to turn yellow, or within a week or two after frost kills the foliage, dig the bulbs with a garden fork. Throw away damaged and decayed bulbs, and prepare the rest for winter storage.

• HOW-TO •

Dividing daffodils

Large-flowered daffodils produce new bulbs every year, gradually becoming more crowded and producing fewer, smaller blooms. The remedy is to dig and divide the clumps; the benefit is having many new daffodil bulbs to plant elsewhere. The best time to lift the bulbs is right after leaves have died down. Gently dig up the clump with a garden fork, taking care not to pierce or bruise bulbs. Keep the bulbs and roots from drying out as you work. Brush off soil with your fingers and separate loosely connected bulbs. Discard bulbs that are damaged or soft. Replant immediately in fertilizer-enriched soil, 5 to 8 inches deep, then water deeply. Or dry the bulbs for a few days, then store and replant them in fall.

The best way to store bulbs depends on the individual plant. Hard, dry bulbs with papery husks, such as those of gladiolus, freesia, and crocosmia, are relatively easy to overwinter. After digging, let them sit for a week or so until the stems and wiry roots are dry.

Remove any loose stems and soil, put the corms into a mesh onion bag, and hang it in a dry cellar or other place at about 45° F. Avoid plastic bags, which trap moisture.

(Flowering bulbs continued)

Soft rhizomes and tuberous roots, such as those of tuberous begonia, dahlia, canna, and calla lily, are more likely than corms to dry out or decay in storage because they have soft skin and contain lots of moisture. After digging, let them dry for a day or two in an airy, nonfreezing, shady place. Cut off the stalks 4 to 6 inches above the bulb and brush off as much soil as possible. Then place them in a single layer in a cardboard box and cover them with slightly damp wood chips, shredded peat moss, or vermiculite. Store in a dry place at about 45° F.

Check stored bulbs once a month throughout the winter and throw away any that show signs of decay. Never store bulbs near ripening fruit, which gives off bulb-damaging ethylene gas.

Scout for problems Deer, chipmunks, gophers, voles, and other animals enjoy eating the emerging shoots, leaves, flowers, and bulbs of bulbs. If your bulbs have been chewed or are missing after they sprouted, the likely suspects include deer, rabbits, and woodchucks. If gophers are endemic in your area, consider planting bulbs in protective wire cages. Netting suspended over bulb beds will protect shoots and flowers for larger animals.

If animal pests are unremitting, plant only the kinds that they won't eat. Daffodils, crown imperial, crocus, and flowering onion are left behind as critters favor tulips and lilies.

Insects that attack summer-blooming bulbs include general pests such as aphids, cutworms, earwigs, and snails and slugs. There's more about them in Chapter 13, beginning on page 323.

Pests specific to bulbs include gladiolus thrips, iris borer, lily beetle, and narcissus fly. Both leaves and flowers of gladiolus infested with thrips look withered, and plants are often stunted. Several sprays are available to control it, including acephate (Orthene), and the microbial insecticides that contain *Beauveria bassiana*.

Prevent iris borer by keeping iris beds clean, primarily by removing dead leaves in spring before the insect lays eggs. The bright red lily beetle is a new pest in much of North America. It feeds on the leaves of lilies and fritillary and can defoliate them quickly. There is no currently recommended control spray, but watching for the beetles and destroying them by hand is sufficient in most gardens. Narcissus fly is a bumble-bee size fly that lays eggs near leaves. Planting bulbs deeply provides protection.

healthy garden • healthy garden • healthy garden • healthy garden •

Bulb markers

After spring-flowering bulbs bloom, their foliage often withers and disappears, leaving no trace above ground. While bulbs are still in bloom, insert labeled plant stakes to mark the positions of daffodils, tulips, and other bulbs so that you won't accidentally disturb them when planting annuals and perennials.

Basic bulb care

Bulbs need little more than water to get them growing and blooming their first year. But to sustain bulbs over the seasons and keep them looking their best, fertilize and groom them each year.

Water Giving bulbs plenty of water at the right time is key. Water after planting bulbs in fall to get their roots growing. During the bulbs' growing and blooming season, water when soil is dry. When bulbs are dormant, let soil dry out.

Remove dead stems As long as leaves are green and healthy they're adding to the bulb's underground food reserves. Wait until foliage dies back before removing it.

Remove spent flowers To prevent bulbs from investing energy into developing seeds instead of bulbs, snip off spent flowers at their base as they fade.

Fertilize In fall, after planting, scatter a bulb fertilizer or compost over the bed to ensure optimum spring growth. Repeat each spring, just as shoots emerge from soil.

135

(Flowering bulbs continued)

Caring for 15 favorite bulbs

Of the dozens of kinds of bulbs available, the ones listed in the following chart are the most popular. Nearly all bulbs require well-drained soil that receives about an inch of water per week during the growing season. The section on fertilizing bulbs on page 132 describes the feeding requirements for an average spring- and summer-flowering bulb. As a rule, all bulb blooms should be deadheaded to ensure that all the bulb's energy fuels growth of the bulb and not developing seeds.

Bulbs	Water; light	Fertilizer	Support	Pests and problems	Planting depth
Flowering onion (*Allium* species)	average; sun	low	none	few (deer-resistant)	4–5 inches deep
Tuberous begonia (*Begonia* hybrids)	high; shade	average	none	mildew, slugs, thrips, botrytis	tops at soil level
Caladium (*Caladium bicolor*)	high; shade	average	none	snails, slugs	2 inches deep
Canna (*Canna* × *generalis*)	high; sun	high	none	slugs, Japanese beetles	3–4 inches deep
Autumn crocus (*Colchicum autumnale*)	average; sun	low	none	few	3–4 inches deep
Crocus (*Crocus* species)	average; sun	low	none	few	4–5 inches deep
Hardy cyclamen (*Cyclamen hederifolium*)	average; sun	low	none	few	½-inch deep
Dahlia (*Dahlia* hybrids)	high; sun	high	stake tall varieties	mildew, slugs, aphids, Japanese beetles, wireworms	3–4 inches deep
Gladiolus (*Gladiolus* species)	average; sun	average	stake tall varieties	thrips, botrytis, wireworms	4–6 inches deep
Amaryllis (*Hippeastrum* species)	average; sun	average to high	none	bulb rot, mealybugs, thrips, mites	8 inches deep
Hyacinth (*Hyacinthus orientalis*)	average; sun	average	none	botrytis	4–6 inches deep
Iris (*Iris* species) rhizome and bulb types	average; sun	average	stake tall varieties	iris borers, wireworms	set just below surface, bulbs 3–5 inches deep
Lily (*Lilium* species)	variable; variable	average	stake tall varieties	thrips, lily beetle, viruses, botrytis	3 times the bulb height
Daffodil (*Narcissus* species)	average; sun	low to average	none	snails, slugs, narcissus fly	5–8 inches deep
Tulip (*Tulipa* species)	average; sun	average	none	rodents, aphids	6–8 inches deep

Container gardening

Growing plants in decorative pots, hanging baskets, and window boxes allows you to garden in even the smallest space. The smaller volume of soil holds less water and plant food, however, which means that container gardens need more attention and regular maintenance than in-ground gardens. The container itself also benefits from seasonal care to ensure that it will survive winter's cold weather.

Maintaining plants in containers

Keeping your container garden looking its best requires regular maintenance. Growing potted plants close to your living space also requires more detailed attention to their appearance and grooming.

Water When plants have matured and the weather turns hot and dry in midsummer, it's not unusual to find that plants need watering every day and sometimes twice a day. Moving plants to a shadier spot will decrease their water requirement. Always apply the water slowly, checking to be sure that it's reaching all parts of the soil and not just running down the inside of the container and out the drainage holes. Dig into the center of the pot to check the soil moisture if plants seem to dry out quickly. If the soil becomes too dry to easily absorb water, soak smaller containers and hanging baskets in a bucket or tub of water for 15 to 20 minutes.

Fertilize Plants growing in cramped quarters also need more fertilizer than plants in the garden. For lowest maintenance, choose a nutrient-fortified potting soil. If your potting soil does not contain fertilizer, add a controlled-release type, and use it at the recommended rate. Mix it thoroughly into the soil before planting. As the effectiveness of the controlled-release fertilizer becomes apparent, supplement it with a water-soluble type.

Prune and deadhead Pinch off spent flowers at least twice a week as they finish blooming to encourage more flowers to develop. Trim or prune back straggly or unhealthy-looking stems. If a plant dies, pull it out and replace it. If plants become too crowded as they grow, you may need to remove some to make room for others to

• SMART IDEA •

Easy-reach watering

If you grow a lot of container plants, watering them can become a time-consuming chore. Various elaborate drip watering systems are available to make the task convenient, and even automatic. Using a sprinkler designed for the job will help, too. One of the best sprinklers for containers is a watering wand, which has a shower-type spray head on a 3-foot-long pole. For window boxes and baskets that are out of reach, look for a hose extension wand. Telescoping hose extensions can reach 12 feet or higher, depending on the model. If you can't find one of those, check the paint department or window cleaning section of a home improvement store for an extension pole that attaches to a garden hose.

(Container gardening continued)

flourish. Refer to the other sections in this chapter for more specific information on pruning annuals, perennials, and bulb plants.

Stake and support Floppy plants and vines need support to remain attractive in containers. Stake individual stems or plants with a length of bamboo and soft plant ties. For vines, install a trellis inside the pot or on a wall adjacent to it. Clumps of weak-stemmed plants can be supported by inserting lengths of bamboo around the inside perimeter of the pot and winding twine around them to form a cage. Regardless of the type used, take care to anchor the support securely, and position the container out of strong wind. Winds can easily topple pots that contain trellises or tall supports.

Container upkeep

Place containers on pot feet or pedestals to improve drainage, discourage slugs, and prevent staining or rotting of wood decking. At the end of the season, discard annual plants and tip the soil onto the compost bin or garden. You may want to transplant hardy perennials to the flower border and prepare bulbs for winter storage. Wash the pots thoroughly with a mild disinfectant, such as well-diluted bleach and allow them to dry before storing. Store ceramic and terra-cotta pots in a dry, nonfreezing place for the winter to prevent them from cracking. Move potted plants that you plan to overwinter to a place in the house where they will receive at least eight hours a day of bright light.

Planting in containers

Most people plant new container gardens each spring, choosing annuals, perennials, and bulbs to grow in baskets, boxes, and patio planters. The combination of plants, container, and soil mix determines the amount of maintenance the container garden will need throughout the summer.

Plants When matching plants to your container, consider how large the plants will become in relation to the amount of soil the pot will hold. Too many plants in a too small container will increase your upkeep by requiring more frequent watering and pruning.

Containers When purchasing a container, consider its ease of maintenance, including its size, material, color, and ability to drain water. All containers should have a way for excess water to drain away from the soil to keep the plant roots from rotting. If the pot does not have drainage holes, drill some in the bottom. Larger containers hold more soil and water than smaller ones and, therefore, need less frequent watering, but they weigh more. Choose containers that will not easily tip over when exposed to wind.

time saver • time saver • time saver • time saver • time saver

Automatic watering

Keep your plants watered without a fuss by setting up an automatic drip irrigation system. It will help to water your hanging baskets, window boxes, and patio planters every day or when you go away on vacation. Schedule watering times to meet the demands of thirsty container gardens.

A garden in a pot

Start with a container large enough
to accommodate a variety of plants,
then choose plants with colors that
work with the house or garden.

Contrasting textures
Combining textures, such
as the fine-textured
marguerite and bold
flowering cabbage
and medium-
textured
fern, creates
interest.

Work with color A single
color planting like this is more
attention grabbing than a mix
of colors. Choose colors that
complement or blend with
each other.

Trailing plants Vines and other
plants spilling over the rim of the
pot visually softens the container.
The trailing plants here include
glacier ivy and sedum.

139

Clay pot sealer

Decrease the watering demands of porous terra-cotta planters by sealing the inside of the pots with polyurethane spray. Clean and dry the pot thoroughly, then spray the inside surface with polyurethane. Let dry overnight before adding potting soil and plants.

(Container gardening continued)

Pots made from porous materials, such as unglazed terra-cotta, and moss- or coconut-fiber-lined baskets, lose moisture rapidly and need much more frequent watering than containers made from glazed or impervious materials. To prolong their life, paint the inside of terra-cotta pots with a sealer before planting. Use tar-like roofing compound, terra-cotta sealer, or epoxy sealer.

Soil mixes Commercial potting soil mixes provide the best ingredients for growing plants in containers. They are made of peat moss or composted bark and smaller amounts of other ingredients, such as perlite, that improve fertility, drainage, moisture retention, and aeration. Avoid using regular garden soil in your containers, because it packs together too tightly, cannon drain quickly enough, and contains disease organisms that become problems in pots.

Follow these steps to planning and planting your container:

1. Start with a clean container. Put large, heavy pots in their permanent positions, and raised slightly to improve air circulation and drainage. Cover drainage holes with window screen to prevent soil from washing out.

2. Use a moistened soil mix with added controlled-release fertilizer. Partially fill the container, firming it gently as you work.

3. Set the largest plant in place first, rotating it in place until it shows its best side forward. Add more potting mix.

4. Arrange smaller plants or bulbs on the soil's surface in a pleasing composition, with draping plants at the edge. Leave about half as much space between plants as you would if you were planting them in the garden.

5. Slip plants out of their nursery pots and loosen any tightly wound roots. Take care not to pull on the plant stems. Set the plants into the container at the same level that they previously grew. Add or subtract potting mix as needed so that the final soil level in the container is 1 to 2 inches below the pot rim.

6. Irrigate thoroughly so that the potting soil is thoroughly moistened. Use a hose-end bubbler or gentle spray to avoid disturbing the soil.

harvest
gardening

The freshness and flavor of homegrown vegetables, herbs, and fruits are unbeatable!

Harvest gardening is like marriage. It takes effort to start a fruit or vegetable garden and effort to keep it going. But that work produces lots of benefits and a sense of satisfaction along the way. The key to reaping the benefits of your hard work is to keep your garden in top condition throughout the growing season.

Keeping a vegetable garden

Caring for a vegetable garden doesn't have to be time-consuming, but it should be routine. The payoff is tremendous: great-looking vegetables that bring the taste of summer to your table.

Vegetable garden care

The more fertile, and friable the soil, the better that vegetables will grow. Organic matter, such as compost, is what makes the difference. It builds soil fertility as well as improves friability. Till it into the soil before planting.

Another, more gradual method of building soil is to grow cover crops. The tradeoff is they take up space and they take time. Plant them during the off-season, or do one section of the garden at a time, using a fast-growing, warm-season crop, such as buckwheat. About a month after sowing, and before plants go to seed, till the crop into the soil.

Bed style Planting in raised beds allows you to plant more crops in a smaller space. The beds drain quickly after a rain, and warm up faster than surrounding soil in spring. Also, raised beds allow you to concentrate fertilizer and water exactly where the plants' roots are. Raised beds are essential where soil water drainage is poor. To make a raised bed, scrape soil into a 3- to 4-foot wide mound 8 to 10 inches high. Slope the edges, or use landscape timbers, bricks, or other materials to restrain the soil. (Do not use pressure-treated wood.)

Another option where soil is poor or non-existent, is to grow vegetables in tubs. Many varieties of tomato, pepper, eggplant, bush

■ SMART IDEA ■

When tomatoes see red

Preliminary research shows that colored plastic mulch can produce surprising results. It used to be a matter of clear and black; the former warmed soil more, the latter stopped weeds. Now consider: Red plastic mulch may bump up tomato yields by 20 percent, and melon yields have spiked with dark green mulch by 35 percent. Dark blue mulch may punch up cucumber yields by 30 percent, and silver mulch may increase pepper yields by 20 percent. All plastic mulches, no matter the color of plastic, warm the soil, so don't use them around cool-loving plants, such as lettuce and broccoli. Mulch on top of the plastic with organic materials (after the soil initially warms in spring) to help keep the soil cool.

healthy garden • healthy garden • healthy garden • healthy garden

Dressing on the side

When giving plants a midseason boost of fertilizer, apply 1 to 2 tablespoons of 10-10-10 granular fertilizer per plant or 1 to 2 pounds per 25-foot row. Place it 6 to 8 inches from plant stems. Instead of fertilizer, you could sidedress rows with 2 to 3 inches of compost. Apply liquid fertilizer such as fish emulsion on the foliage and soil by adding it to the watering can when watering.

(Keeping a vegetable garden continued)

summer squash, carrot, cucumber, and most greens will grow well. Use as large a container as possible, such as a half whiskey barrel. Fill it with potting soil, not garden soil and place it in the sunniest spot in the yard. Keep containers well-watered; fertilize regularly.

Water Much of vegetable gardening is about watering, especially in warm, dry regions. During the first few weeks after seeds germinate or seedlings are transplanted, watering is critical to keep plants growing strong and to avoid transplant shock. Deep watering encourages roots to grow deeper in the soil, where they're better protected and have access to water.

When to water depends on weather conditions and your soil. Sandy soil dries faster than clay, and sunny, windy conditions dry soil quicker than cloudy, cool weather. Don't depend on plant wilting to signal water need. Intense heat or soggy soil may cause temporary wilting. Check soil moisture by actually feeling at the soil 3 or 4 inches down. If it's dry, water.

Watering is critical at different growth stages for different vegetables. For example, broccoli, cauliflower, and cabbage are most dependent on soil moisture when the heads are forming. Carrots, onion, and radish plants need water most when roots are enlarging. Squashes need it when flowering and setting fruit. Peppers, tomatoes, and eggplant must be well-watered from flowering until harvest.

Soaker hoses and drip irrigation systems provide a slow, constant supply of water. They conserve water, applying it exactly where needed. Overhead sprinklers can provide a garden with a rainlike soaking but lose water to evaporation and to the broad spray, which waters everything in its path, including walkways.

Weed No one relishes weeding. But if done well early in the season, it can help you avoid work later. There are two types of weeds with which vegetable gardeners have to contend: annual and perennial. Annual weeds germinate quickly in spring and summer after the soil is turned. Soil contains thousands of dormant annual weed seeds, such as lamb's-quarter and pigweed, waiting for the right sun and moisture conditions to grow. It's easy to kill the young seedlings after germination by cultivating with a lightweight hoe, such as an oscillating hoe. Lightly work the top few inches of soil to dislodge the weeds. Repeat this light weeding every week or so until the vegetables are large enough to shade out new weeds.

Vegetable gardening techniques

Maintaining a vegetable garden is mostly like any other kind of gardening, but more concentrated. The plants grow fast and have immediate needs for water and fertilizer. Here's how to help:

Amend soil Including both organic matter and nutrients, compost makes the best all-around amendment.

Water consistently Succulent vegetables, such as lettuce, need soil that is consistently moist.

Manage weeds Weeds compete with vegetables for water, nutrients, and light. Keep them in check, especially early in the season.

Fertilize Because they're growing fast, vegetables need a steady and abundant supply of nutrients.

(Keeping a vegetable garden continued)

Perennial weeds, such as quackgrass and dandelion, should be dug out more vigorously, to remove as much of the root system as possible. For this purpose use a taproot weeder or Cape Cod weeder (see page 201). Avoid letting weeds go to seed; you will battle them for years if you do.

Fertilize Applying fertilizer while plants are growing is called side-dressing. Side-dressing crops can lead to a fuller harvest. Unless you're growing a leafy vegetable such as spinach or lettuce that requires lots of nitrogen, use a fertilizer that has a balance of nitrogen, phosphorus, and potassium. Avoid overfertilizing fruiting crops such as tomatoes, eggplants, and peppers. Too much fertilizer results in leafy growth at the expense of the fruit. For these, use a tomato fertilizer and follow label directions. (For more, see page 165).

Tomato supports

Tall tomatoes such as 'Better Boy' and 'Sweet 100' produce best if supported. Drive a single stake next to a young tomato transplant, and loosely tie the plant to it with cloth or twine. Or make your own tomato cage. Use a section of 12-gauge, 6-inch-mesh wire fencing that's 5 feet high and 7 feet long. Roll it into a cylinder, then bend the ends of the wire on one side of the cylinder with pliers and hook them over the mesh of the other side. Cut off excess wire with wire cutters.

Vegetable	When to fertilize
Broccoli	3 weeks after transplanting
Cucumber	When vines first form and flowers appear
Eggplant	3 weeks after transplanting
Lettuce, Swiss chard, spinach	3 weeks after germinating
Melon	When vines first form and again 3 weeks later
Onion	3 weeks after setting out, when tops are 6 to 8 inches tall, and again when bulbs swell
Pepper	3 weeks after transplanting
Potato	When plants bloom
Squash, pumpkins	When vines first form and again 3 weeks later
Sweet corn	3 weeks after germinating and again when tassels appear
Tomato	3 weeks after transplanting, at flowering, and when fruit sets.

Mulch Among a gardener's best labor- and timesaving devices are mulches. They prevent weeds from growing, and help conserve soil moisture, reducing the amount of watering. Mulches are organic or inorganic. Organic mulches, such as hay, straw, bark chips, chopped leaves, pine straw, and grass clippings, eventually break down in the soil. They are best applied after vegetables are established and you've done a few initial weedings. Inorganic mulches, such as black plastic, won't break down in the soil, and have to be removed annually, but they conserve moisture and stop weed growth. Lay plastic mulches down before planting heat-loving crops such as melons, tomatoes, and peppers. The plastic helps warm soil which will increase the growth rate of your vegetables.

Annually refresh the soil with compost. On fertile soil, a 1- to 2-inch-thick layer of compost worked into the bed yearly before planting is plenty. On gardens that are performing poorly, work in a 3- to 4-inch-thick layer for best results.

Propping and pruning

Tomatoes, peas, and pole beans produce more and better-quality fruits when the plants are off the ground. Tie tomatoes to stakes or grow them in tomato cages. Trellis pea varieties that are taller than 3 feet, such as 'Sugar Snap', on a chicken-wire or nylon-mesh fence. Support pole beans, such as 'Romano', on 6- to 8-foot-tall poles formed into a tepee. Evenly space the poles 1 foot apart in a 3-foot-diameter circle, drive them 1 foot into the ground, and tie the tops of the poles together with twine.

Sweet corn and Irish potatoes thrive with extra soil mounded around their base. Hilling keeps cornstalks from falling over in the wind. For potatoes, hilling creates more space for spuds to form tubers. Hoe the soil around rows of plants up to the top leaves once they emerge from the soil and again three weeks later.

Succession planting

To harvest your favorite vegetables throughout the season, periodically sow a small crop through the growing season. For example, sow a small crop of bush beans, carrots, and lettuce every two weeks until midsummer. After harvesting the first crop, pull the plants and put in another crop that will mature before the first frost. Start planting cool-season crops such as spinach and broccoli in mid- to late summer for late fall to winter harvest.

When planting in the middle of summer, it's best to start with transplants (six- to eight-week-old seedlings). Summer weather and insects are too much for germinating seeds. Transplants of vegetables such as lettuce, cabbage, and broccoli are often found in garden centers in summer or can be started indoors at home. Some vegetables, such as carrots, beets, and beans, are best planted from seed. When sowing seed for a succession crop, make sure the soil

▪ SMART IDEA ▪

Beds hot, frames cold

Hot beds and cold frames are structures for starting, growing, and holding plants. They look similar, but hot beds have a heat source and are warm enough to start seeds and protect seedlings on the coldest of nights. Cold frames are cool with no heat source. They're an intermediate step in which to hold and harden off plants before moving them to the garden. To build a simple cold frame, place three bales of hay in a C-shape against a building in a sunny location, forming a 3×3 foot box. Place plants in the box and cover the opening with a window sash or a sheet of clear plastic in a wooden frame. Prop the top open on sunny days to vent heat, and close it at night and on cloudy days to hold heat.

(Keeping a vegetable garden continued)

remains moist during germination, and watch for pests. If you have only a few open spaces in your midsummer vegetable garden, tuck in an extra broccoli or lettuce seedling. You'll be surprised at how much more you can produce from a small garden by planting in open spaces as they become available.

Season extending

Temperatures below 70° F in spring or fall will slow production of many crops. Continue the harvest season by protecting plants with row covers, tunnels, and cold frames. Floating row covers are made of lightweight material that can be laid right over plants. They let in air, water, and sunlight but block animals and insects, and they keep plants 2 to 2½° F warmer, a small but critical gain. Drape row covers over frost-sensitive and low-growing crops before cold weather threatens. For taller crops, such as broccoli, install wire hoops along the row and drape the row cover over the hoops to cover the plants.

Vegetable pests

The first line of defense against insects, animals or diseases is prevention. Keeping them away is a lot easier than dealing with them once they've arrived. Lay floating row covers over plants to prevent insect pests from reaching them, and when you can, plant insect- and disease-resistant varieties.

If pests reach the plants, try low-impact controls. Start with cultural techniques. Pull up and destroy infected plants or cover to prevent spread of a disease. Hand-pick insects or use repellents. Crushing Colorado potato beetle eggs before they hatch can prevent a full outbreak. If these preventive efforts fail, use the least toxic pesticide sprays available to control specific pests. Read the label on the pesticide to ensure both the pest and plant are listed, and follow the application rates and timing as directed. Some of the safest sprays to use are *Bacillus thuringiensis* (Bt) for cabbageworms and insecticidal soap for aphids and whiteflies. See Chapter 13 (beginning on page 323) for more about pest control.

Following are some of the most common pests you'll find on vegetables, and their controls.

Mexican bean beetles These ladybug look-alikes have a tan-yellow shell with 16 black spots. The larvae feed on bean leaves and pods. Control by handpicking eggs and spraying larvae with an insecticide containing pyrethrin.

Cabbageworms and loopers These green caterpillars are hard to see on their favorite plants (broccoli, cauliflower, kale, and cabbage)

---

healthy garden • healthy garden • healthy garden

Cover crop basics

A cover crop is any plant grown to prevent erosion and improve soil. There are four kinds:
1. Hardy legumes, such as hairy vetch, are sown in fall and turned under in spring.
2. Tropical legumes, such as perennial peanut, are sown in late summer in the north, or fall in mild-winter areas.
3. Grasses, such as ryegrass, are sown in fall and turned under in spring.
4. Annuals, such as buckwheat, are sown in spring or summer and turned under before flowering.

Gallery of vegetable pests

Most garden insects are innocent bystanders, and a few are helpful. These, however, are all known troublemakers.

Mexican bean
beetle larva

Mexican bean
beetle adult

Mexican bean
beetle damage

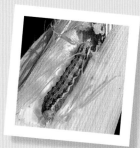

corn
earworm

cutworm

striped cucumber
beetle

spotted cucumber
beetle

bacterial wilt

Colorado potato
beetle adult and eggs

Colorado potato
beetle larvae

tomato
hornworm

tomato
hornworm eggs

cabbage root
maggot adult

cabbage root
maggot larvae

flea beetle

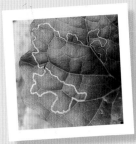

leaf miner

(Keeping a vegetable garden continued)

but can cause massive damage as they feed on the leaves. Spray Bt at the first signs of the caterpillars.

Corn earworms Small fat worms feed on the tips of mature corn ears. The damage looks disgusting but doesn't affect edibility; simply it cut off. To control, smother young larvae by placing a dropperful of mineral oil on the tip of the ear after silks wilt and turn brown.

Cutworms Cutworms are active at night, feeding on stems of transplants such as broccoli and peppers. In the morning, the plant is toppled and the insect is gone. Prevent damage with a barrier. Wrap transplant stems with a 2-inch-wide collar made from a paper cup, centering it 1 inch below and 1 inch above the soil surface.

Cucumber beetles These small, yellow-and-black beetles have either striped or dotted shells. They attack seedlings and mature plants of squash, cucumber and melon. Their feeding leads to a killing disease called bacterial wilt. Protect young plants by covering them with floating row cover. Spray older plants with pyrethrin.

Colorado potato beetles Large brown-and-yellow-striped adult beetles feed on eggplant and potato leaves; however, the soft-bodied, young do the most damage. Control this pest by crushing the orange eggs, found on the underside of leaves, and by spraying a Bt strain specifically formulated for potato beetle larvae (*tenebrionis* or *san diego* strains).

Tomato hornworms These large green caterpillars with a hornlike protrusion feed on tomato, pepper, and eggplant leaves and fruit. The occasional hornworm can be handpicked and discarded. For large numbers of small, young caterpillars, spray plants with Bt.

Root maggots Root maggots are the larvae of small flies that lay eggs on plant stems near the soil surface. Various types eat cabbage, onions, radishes, broccoli, cabbage, and cauliflower. Prevent damage by placing tar paper squares around the transplants or cover young plants with floating row cover to prevent the adults from laying eggs.

Flea beetles Small, shiny black beetles hop around, feeding on young leaves. Their damage looks like holes from a shotgun blast. To control these pests spray with insecticidal soap or use row cover.

Leaf miners These tiny wasp larvae tunnel and feed within the layers of a leaf. Swiss chard, spinach, and beets are among their favored hosts. Pick off and discard tunneled leaves, or cover plants with floating row cover to prevent the adults from laying eggs.

healthy garden • healthy garden • healthy garden • healthy garden

Attracting good bugs

To lure beneficial insects into your garden to control pests, provide a water source such as a birdbath, and the plants they need for food. Some of the herbs and flowers these helpful insects prefer include alyssum, cilantro, fennel, and marigold. See Chapter 13 for more information.

Diseases

Diseases are best prevented by growing resistant varieties (check descriptions on seed packages and in catalogs), removing crop debris in fall, leaving space between plants so air circulates around them, and removing weeds that may harbor disease.

Some problems that appear to be diseases may be something else. For example, blossom-end rot on tomatoes is caused by a calcium deficiency due to fluctuating soil moisture. Mulching around plants and keeping soil moisture constant are the best ways to prevent the condition.

Harvesting

Harvest when plants are dry; working around wet plants can spread disease. Use a sharp knife to cut tomatoes, melons, and other fruits from their stems. Harvest in the morning when plants are less likely to be stressed from heat.

For many vegetables, such as beans, summer squash, cucumber, and melon, the more you pick, the more they produce. If allowed to grow too large, the seeds inside mature, signaling the plant to stop producing. Pick the vegetable while it's still small; if you aren't able to eat it when it's ready, give it away or preserve it. The flavor of many vegetables is best when picked young.

Fall cleanup

Remove all plant debris from the garden in fall. Compost it unless it was diseased or insect-ridden. Put that material in the trash. Pests may survive composting and end up in your garden again next year.

· HOW-TO ·

Zapping leaf blight

Leaf blights on tomatoes, such as early blight and late blight, cause leaves to yellow and drop before their time. You'll still get tomatoes, but fewer of them, and blighted plants don't look very good. Minimize the effects of blight by mulching around the base of plants to prevent disease spores from splashing onto the leaves during rains or overhead watering, by removing infected leaves at first sign of the diseases, and by spacing plants farther apart to increase air circulation around the leaves. If tomato blight is a major problem where you live, plant resistant varieties. Preventive sprays of copper fungicide applied in early summer can reduce the spread of these diseases.

Spread 1 or 2 inches of organic material over the soil, and cultivate it in. Soil microbes will break it down into usable compost by spring. By turning the soil and incorporating organic materials in fall, you'll speed decomposition, expose overwintering insects to the elements, and improve the soil so that water penetrates it more deeply. Soil tends to be dry in fall, making it easier to turn, and it will be one less task you'll have to tackle in spring.

Contain aggressive herbs

Herbs such as mint are aggressive spreaders that will take over an area if allowed. Plant these herbs in a corner where they can spread into an otherwise barren area, or restrain them in a container.

Success with herbs

Traditionally, herbs have been grown in a separate garden to be used for culinary or medicinal purposes. However, with home gardens shrinking, many gardeners now grow herbs in flower, vegetable, and container gardens, and even use them as ground covers. Considering the variety of annual, biennial, and perennial herbs available, it's easy to see how herbs can fit into many settings. Keeping them growing their best is the key to harvesting full-flavored herbs for your kitchen.

Herb garden care

Knowing an herbs' background helps in growing them. For example, many common herbs, such as thyme, rosemary, oregano, and sage, hail from the Mediterranean, where temperatures are mild and soils rocky and well-drained. Mimicking these conditions in your garden will help these herbs develop their best flavor. Other herbs, such as mint and lovage, prefer wetter soils.

To keep all herbs growing strongly, soak the soil when it's dry to 4 inches deep and add compost to the soil each year in fall or before sowing seeds in spring. Overfertilizing herbs used for food and fragrance can cause them to be less pungent and could encourage pests such as aphids. Apply a sidedressing of fertilizer only if leaves turn yellow. Some herbs, such as basil, tarragon, chives, and lovage, need more fertility. Fertilize once a month starting in spring with a soluble low-nitrogen fertilizer such as fish emulsion.

Weed and thin Weeding the herb bed is similar to weeding vegetables. Carefully cultivate annual weeds as they germinate, hand-pull tenacious perennial weeds when found, and avoid letting any weeds go to seed. Perennial herbs, such as oregano and lavender, have more extensive and widespread root systems than annual herbs, such as basil and fennel, so care should be taken when working around these plants not to disturb the roots.

Annual herbs such as cilantro and dill spread their seed around a garden. Plant them once and you'll likely have them for years. If you decide to keep the seedlings that appear, thin so they have room to grow to maturity. Perennial herbs, including chives, lovage, mint, oregano, thyme, rosemary, tarragon, and lavender, need periodic pruning and winter protection in cold climates.

In spring, trim some of the woody growth off lavender, sage, thyme, and rosemary to shape and rejuvenate the plants. Chives, lovage, mint, sage, and tarragon are hardy perennials able to withstand harsh winters to USDA Zone 5 with little protection. However, rosemary (hardy to USDA Zone 8) should be grown in containers and brought indoors in colder regions.

Control pests Aphids, whiteflies and mealybugs are sap-sucking pests. Spray insecticidal soap to control them. Soft, succulent herbs, such as basil, rot easily in cool, wet soil. If summers in your region are cool and wet, grow herbs in raised beds or containers with well-drained soil. Caterpillars, such as the parsley worm, eat parsley and dill. Handpick individual caterpillars or leave them to form into beautiful swallowtail butterflies. Beetles, including Japanese beetles, are attracted to basil. Trap or handpick beetles in the morning to control this persistent pest. See Chapter 13 for more about dealing with pests.

Harvesting and drying herbs

When and how you harvest herbs makes a difference in their potency. Most herbs taste or smell best when harvested in midmorning, when the weather has been clear and dry for a few days. Wait until the dew has dried off the leaves. Many herbs reach their highest oil content just before flowering. Here are tips for when to harvest the most popular herbs:

Basil Harvest just as the plant starts to bud. Snip off branches instead of individual leaves to stimulate more growth and new leaves later in the season. Remove flowers to encourage leafy growth.

Chives Harvest six weeks after planting or as established plants sprout in spring. Snip leaves as needed. Ball-shaped lavender flowers are edible; remove them before they set seed. Chives self-sow rampantly.

Cilantro Harvest when leaves are 4 to 6 inches tall. The whole plant is edible, and seeds—coriander—are harvested when they're dry and pinched open. Hang seed heads in a bag to catch the seeds.

Dill Harvest eight weeks after planting. For dill seeds, cut seed heads when they're light brown. Dry them in paper bags for a few days, shaking the seeds loose from the heads.

Fennel Harvest anytime. Keep the flower stalk trimmed to stimulate leaf production. Cut Florence, or bulb, fennel, as soon as bulbs enlarge but before the plant sends up a flower stalk. The leaves of Florence fennel can also be used to season dishes. Harvest them anytime.

safety alert • safety alert • safety alert • safety alert •

Body-friendly pruners

Pruning woody herbs and stems can be tough on your hands, wrists, and arm muscles. Select pruners that feel comfortable in your hand and have sturdy grips. Newer-styled hand pruners, with ratchets and gears, reduce the amount of effort needed to make a pruning cut.

Gallery of herbs

Fresh herbs are essential to fine cooking, and they are easy to grow. All that's needed is a few square feet of soil near the kitchen door, or a pot for the porch.

basil and
chives

Florence fennel

rosemary
and dill

tarragon and
peppermint

sage and flat-leaf
parsley

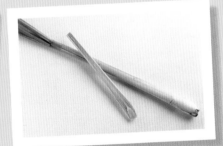

lemongrass

winter savory
and oregano

marjoram and
curly parsley

thyme and
cilantro

Lemongrass Harvest after four to six bulbous stems have formed. Cut the whole stem, strip off the outer leaves, cut off the top of the stalk, and use the tender inner leaves.

Mint Harvest as needed, cutting back plants occasionally to rejuvenate them. The highest oil content in the leaves occurs at full flower in midsummer.

Oregano Harvest leaves as needed. Trim plants back before flowering to promote bushier growth.

Parsley Harvest as needed. Cut entire stalks from the outer portion of the plant. Dig and pot plants in fall to be brought indoors for winter use.

Sage Harvest as needed. Wait until the second year after planting to harvest leaves heavily.

Thyme Harvest all summer as needed. Use leaves and sprigs (young stems with leaves attached). Trim plants in spring to stimulate new growth.

Rosemary Harvest sprigs before flowering. Shape plants in early spring.

Tarragon Harvest in early summer for best flavor. Prune back vigorous plants in early spring to reduce height by a third.

Marjoram Harvest when flowers appear in early summer. Cut plants back to the soil line. Cut a second time in midsummer.

• HOW-TO •

Drying herbs

Most herb leaves and stalks dry readily, so it is a preferred way to preserve their color and flavor. Here's all there is to it:

1. Harvest complete stems; gently wash leaves.
2. Hang stems upside down in a warm, well-ventilated room with low humidity, out of the bright sun.
3. Strip leaves from stalks when they crackle or crush when touched.
4. Store whole leaves in an airtight container such as a jar or sealable plastic bag.
5. Cut off and place ripening seed heads of dill and cilantro (coriander) in a bag.

A few herbs, including cilantro, dill, and chives, are best preserved in some other way, such as by freezing.

Planting herbs

Herbs fit well in any open space in your vegetable or flower garden, in containers, or even in window boxes. Look for places in your garden or containers where annual flowers or vegetables have finished producing. Tuck in a few basil plants among the beans or some fennel to succeed pansies. The herbs will thrive as long as they receive at least six hours of direct sun; grow in compost-amended, well-drained soil; and are protected from pest attacks. Perennial herbs such as chives and thyme can be started in summer or fall. For a second crop of annual herbs such as basil and dill, start them in midsummer so that they mature before the first frost.

(Success with herbs continued)

Seeds or plants? When growing a second crop of herbs, start them from seed or buy transplants. Transplants are more likely to survive the vagaries of the weather. Some herbs, such as French tarragon, can only be started from plants. Most other herbs can be started from seed, either sown directly in the garden or started indoors. A seed-grown plant will take longer to reach maturity, however, seeds are much less expensive than transplants. When sowing seed, cultivate the bed well, removing old plant debris. Sprinkle the seed on the bed and lightly cover with soil. Keep moist with daily waterings if necessary, or cover the bed with a row cover to protect the germinating seedlings and retain moisture.

Herbs indoors

You can enjoy the flavors and scents of herbs year-round indoors, even in the coldest climate. Either bring established plants indoors to overwinter in the warmth of your home, or start a windowsill kitchen garden of culinary herbs in fall to use throughout the cold season.

Perennial and biennial herbs such as rosemary, mint, thyme, chives, and parsley can be dug from your garden, potted in fall before the first frost, and grown outdoors for two to three weeks before moving them inside for winter. To acclimate outdoor plants, keep them well watered, fertilized, and growing in a partly shaded area so they adjust to the lower light levels indoors. Inspect plants carefully for insects, and spray them with the appropriate pesticide, such as warm and soapy water, while they're outdoors. Once indoors, grow them in a sunny window or under grow-lights that are on for 14 hours a day. Because they grow less indoors, reduce watering and fertilizing. Use tepid water, and allow most herbs, except rosemary and mint, to dry out between waterings. Mist plants and circulate the air with a small fan. Check every few days for insects that may have hatched since the plant was brought indoors, and spray to control them. If you have sprayed the plants with a pesticide, rinse leaves diligently before using them.

To start an indoor windowsill herb garden, choose dwarf varieties of herbs that you enjoy cooking with and are able to grow well indoors, such as 'Spicy Globe' basil, 'Fernleaf' dill, and dwarf garden sage. Fill 4-inch-diameter pots with moistened potting soil, place a few herb seeds in each pot, and lightly cover with soil. Once the seeds germinate, thin to one seedling per pot and grow on a sunny windowsill or under grow-lights. Keep well-watered and fertilize regularly with a balanced plant food. Harvest leaves as needed.

healthy garden • healthy garden • healthy garden • healthy garden

Keeping rosemary indoors

If you live where rosemary doesn't grow outdoors year-round, bring it inside for the winter. Lightly prune plants before bringing them in. Indoors, provide plenty of light for at least 12 hours a day. Usually this means ensuring plants receive all the natural light available plus supplemental fluorescent light. Water so the soil stays damp but not soggy.

Fruit garden basics

If started right and given annual attention, fruit trees can produce for years. And if you don't have room for trees, berries provide luscious fruit in small spaces.

The essentials of fruit-tree care include watering, fertilizing, pruning, training, weeding, and controlling pests. Although each type of fruit tree may have special needs, these general guidelines are good for all.

Fruit garden maintenance

Fruit trees need regular care, such as feeding, pruning, mulching, and watering. The critical period for watering is between fruit set and ripening. During this period, ensure the tree receives at least an inch of water per week. If it doesn't rain, irrigate.

Prevent competition from grass and weeds, which reduces yield. Remove sod and weeds from the tree trunk to the dripline, and beyond if possible. Prevent grass and weeds from growing back under the tree canopy with organic mulches. Spread the mulch 4 to 6 inches deep under the tree, keeping it away from the trunk.

Established fruit trees often require little fertilizer beyond a yearly addition of compost to aid growth. For young, non-bearing trees, a spring application of a complete fruit tree fertilizer based on a soil test helps the tree grow strong to the bearing age. You can tell whether a young tree is receiving enough nutrients by its growth. If leaves are pale green and new growth is less than a foot long per year, provide supplemental fruit tree fertilizer in spring. If the leaves are lush and dark green, fruit production is low, and the fruit is soft and bland-tasting, reduce or eliminate fertilization.

Apply either ground dolomitic limestone or sulfur to adjust soil pH, according to soil test recommendations. Some fruit, such as citrus, also need micronutrients such as manganese and iron to grow properly. Check out the fruit tree websites listed in the Resources section, page 355, for specific fertilizer recommendations.

• HOW-TO •

Pruning a neglected tree

If you inherit an abandoned tree, it probably needs rejuvenation pruning. Fruit trees are usually resilient to heavy pruning. You can prune out up to one-half of the branches of peach and Japanese plum trees in a single year, and one-third of apple, cherry, and European plum trees. If you have one of those trees, follow these steps:

1. Remove all water sprouts and suckers.
2. Remove dead, damaged, diseased, and split limbs.
3. Remove large, crowded limbs from the center of the tree.
4. Head back branches around the tree to force growth outward versus upward.
5. Thin smaller branches that are shading other branches or crossing them.

Lawn fertilizer alert

Growing a fruit tree in a lawn is possible, but it's hard to fertilize both the fruit and the lawn just right. Fertilizing the lawn enough means giving the fruit tree too much. Fruit trees that get too much fertilizer are more pest-prone, and they set fewer fruits of lower quality. Spread less fertilizer on lawns under fruit trees, or better, keep the area under the tree mulched and free of lawn.

(Fruit garden basics continued)

Fall and winter care

Fall is a time to ready fruit trees for the winter. The trees need to use their energy to store starches to get them through the winter. Anything that stimulates growth, such as fertilizing or pruning, short-circuits this process and can lead to winter injury. In fall, cut back on watering, and put away your pruning tools. If you have a very dry fall, continue watering trees after the leaves drop.

Protect trunks of young trees by wrapping them with tree tape or painting the trunks with white latex paint. Otherwise, in winter, dark-toned bark can expand during the day while exposed to bright sunlight. Once the sun sets, the bark temperature drops dramatically, causing it to split.

Pruning

All fruit trees need annual pruning to create properly shaped and productive trees. This is especially critical for nonbearing young trees when the main structure is forming. Pruning priorities listed in Chapter 3 are important for fruit trees. But the goal in pruning them is to get light into the tree canopy. This encourages first fruit set and development. Home gardeners are often concerned they'll prune too much, but that is rarely a problem. Timing, however, is critical. Prune fruit trees in late winter and again in summer if needed.

Remove dead, diseased, and broken branches anytime. Make clean cuts with sharp pruning tools. When cutting back to the main trunk, leave a 1- to 2-inch-thick branch collar to promote proper wound healing.

Thinning and heading back are the two types of pruning cuts. Thinning cuts remove entire branches such as suckers or water sprouts (one-year-old branches that grow vertically up from the tree base or a main branch). Heading back cuts stimulate and direct new growth and keep the tree compact. Make heading back cuts just above a bud that's facing in the direction you want the new branch to grow.

Two pruning systems—central leader and open center—produce strong branches capable of supporting the fruit load, yet they leave the tree open enough so light can reach the interior branches.

Central leader training produces a tree with a Christmas-treelike shape. The central trunk continues straight up, and lesser scaffold branches are arranged underneath and around it. Ideally, the scaffold branches aren't directly above one another. Fruits often trained to a central leader include dwarf apples, pears, cherries, and

Training fruit trees

All trees need pruning to maintain size and appearance. Fruit trees also need pruning to sustain good health and provide optimum harvests.

Open center Train peaches, nectarines, and Japanese plums to an open center. This training also takes three years. It involves removing the leader, thinning the scaffolds, and opening the center so that sunlight reaches all parts of the tree.

Central leader Train apples, pears, and European plums to a central leader (trunk). This involves three tiers of broad-spreading scaffold branches and one central leader. It takes three years of heading the best, strongest branches to train the trees.

159

(Fruit garden basics continued)

European plums. A variation of the central leader is the modified central leader. In this technique, the central leader is maintained until four or five scaffold branches are developed, then it's removed.

Open center pruning results in a tree with a vaselike shape. The central leader is removed when the tree is only two or three years old, and scaffold branches are allowed to grow around the tree. Remove branches inside the vase to open the center of the tree to light for fruits developing there. Apricot, Japanese plum, peach, and nectarine are fruits that are often trained to an open center.

Thinning and harvesting

Fruit trees routinely set more fruit than they can possibly mature, then naturally abort most of these excess fruits in early summer (called *June drop*). However, some varieties still benefit by hand-thinning. Thin to remove overcrowded, small, diseased, and damaged fruit when fruits are ½ to 1 inch in diameter. At the end of the season, you will have fewer but larger fruits. Below is a listing of the most common fruits, and when and how to thin young fruit and harvest mature fruit.

Apple Thin four to six weeks after bloom, leaving the "king" fruit in the center of the cluster. To harvest, cup the fruit, lift it upward, and twist it off the tree without removing the stem.

Apricot Leave three or four healthy fruits per cluster. Harvest when fruits are fully colored and slightly soft when pressed.

Cherry Doesn't require thinning. Harvest fruits when fully colored.

Citrus Most citrus mature over a period of months. Taste full-size fruits for ripeness. Many fruits can remain on the tree once ripe and not rot. Clip off the fruits with a hand pruner when harvesting.

Peach Four to six weeks after bloom, leave fruits spaced 6 to 8 inches apart. Harvest when fully colored. Fruits slip off tree with a slight twist when ripe.

Pear Leave fruit 6 inches apart. Harvest when full-size but still hard. If left to ripen fully on the tree, they will rot. Mature fruit should break away easily from the branch when lifted.

Plums Japanese plums should be left 3 to 4 inches apart, European plums 2 inches apart. When fruits are slightly soft when squeezed and slip off the tree easily, begin harvesting.

time saver • time saver • time saver • time saver • time saver • time saver

Fruits in containers

Many fruit trees come in dwarf versions that grow well in containers. Here's how:
1. Plant the tree in a container of well-drained soil mix made of peat moss, sand, perlite, and compost.
2. Keep the tree well-watered, letting the soil dry out between waterings; fertilize monthly.
3. In cold-winter climates, move the container into an unheated garage for the winter. Maintain citrus in a greenhouse or sunroom.

Keeping berries

Berries provide great benefits in a small space. They cost little to plant and maintain, produce fruit within a few seasons at most, and give you a ready supply of fruit that's fresher than what you will find at the grocery store even when in season.

Berries are perennial plants that require varying degrees of care. Once established, raspberries, blackberries, blueberries, and grapes can grow for years with minimal additions of water and fertilizer. Strawberries require more care for good production. They multiply easily, often producing more berries than you can eat fresh. This will allow you to dry, freeze, or make jam from the excess for winter use.

For best production, size, and flavor, water berry plants well, especially as the fruits are developing. Yearly applications of compost and mulch help keep weeds at bay and soil moist. Beside compost, annual additions of a complete fertilizer in spring based on a soil test will ensure a continued yield of high-quality fruit.

Berry maintenance

Each type of berry has special growing considerations. Here are some special techniques for the top five types of berries. Check the Resources section, page 355, for websites with more detailed information on berry care.

Blackberry and raspberry Trellis plants on a coated-wire fence strung 3 feet off the ground. Or train one plant up a single post. Prune to remove bearing canes after production is finished. Grow fall-producing everbearing varieties to extend the season.

Blueberry Prune mature blueberry bushes annually in late winter, removing one or two old, poorly bearing branches. Keep the soil pH around 5, by amending it with soil sulfur, and maintain a mulch.

Grape Prune most varieties in late winter. Remove all but two or four main canes, each 12 buds long and with four side shoots each. Tie all four canes to a trellis or fence.

Strawberry Strawberries require more attention than other berries. Place mother plants 12 inches apart in rows that are also 12 inches apart, on raised beds amended with compost. During the first year, pinch off all berries and daughter plants, which will divert energy from establishing the mothers. In the second year, after harvest, till under the patch and replant. Protect plants through winter with a 5- to 6-inch-thick layer of hay or straw.

healthy garden • healthy garden • healthy garden • healthy garden

Rodent-proofing

Mice and other voles gnaw on the bark of trees in winter, when other foods are scarce. Protect the trunks of young trees with hardware cloth. Sink the lower end 1 to 2 inches into the soil, and extend it to just above the expected snow line. Be sure to check the wrap the following spring, making certain it's loose enough to allow for growth.

Training berries and grapes

Small fruits are easier to grow than tree fruits.
Yearly pruning is the main chore.

Blackberries Cut the old canes of most types of blackberries to the ground after harvest. Tie new canes that develop in spring onto a support, such as a wire fence.

Blueberries Prune in late winter, removing tangles or broken branches. Saw the oldest, least productive branches off at their base.

Grape vines Train the main trunk up a post, then tie two to four horizontal canes along supports. In late winter, prune side shoots on these canes to two or three buds. Inset is a spring shot showing the results.

Strawberries For best production, plant two beds in alternate years. Prune off all fruits and runners the first season after planting, and harvest the following spring. Replant after harvest.

Gallery of fruit pests

In most areas fruit trees and their developing fruit are as attractive to pests as to gardeners.

cherry fruit fly

cherry fruit fly damage

plum curculio adult

plum curculio damage

peach tree
borer adult

peach tree
borer larva

peach tree borer
damage to trunk

peach tree borer
damage to fruit

raspberry cane
borer adult

raspberry cane
borer eggs

wilt caused by
raspberry cane borer

raspberry canes
killed by borer

codling moth adult

codling moth damage

apple maggot adult

apple maggot damage

apple maggot trap

healthy garden • healthy garden • healthy garden • healthy garden

Controlling fruit diseases

Many diseases, such as fire blight, apple scab, and black rot, affect fruits. But before reaching for the sprayer, use these simply measures: Eliminate weeds from around your plantings, cut back on fertilizer, and avoid injury to trunks with mowers or string trimmers. In the case of fireblight, sterilizing pruners between each cut by dipping them in a 10- to 20 percent bleach solution pays big dividends.

(Fruit garden basics continued)

Fruit and berry pests

Some insects, such as aphids and scale, are general pests discussed in other sections of this book. The following are a few of the most common fruit problems. This information is enough to get you started. For detailed controls and proper timing of sprays see websites listed in the Resources, or check your county extension service.

Apple maggot A pest of apples, plums, cherries, and pears, look for misshapen fruit with brown insides and small white worms (maggots). Remove dropped fruit early in the season, place maggot traps, and spray by late June or early July.

Codling moth A pest of apples, pears, and apricots, this larvae leaves tunnels and rotten flesh in the fruit it attacks.

Cherry fruit fly Small misshapen fruits with rotten insides and white maggots are signs of this pest. Cultivate under trees in fall to kill over wintering insects, set up yellow sticky traps to monitor adult population levels, and use approved sprays before adults lay eggs.

Peach tree borer A pest of peaches, cherries, plums, and apricots, it bores into tree trunks, opening the tree to diseases that can kill a tree. Physically remove worms with a wire poker; spray pesticides.

Plum curculio Attacking apples, peaches, cherries, pears, plums, and apricots, this weevil leaves a C-shaped scar where it lays eggs on fruit. Larvae feed inside the fruit. Catch and kill curculio adults after fruit sets. Place a white sheet under the tree, then in the morning, shake the tree. The insects will fall on the sheet.

Raspberry cane borer Larvae bore into the raspberry cane, killing the plant. Adults girdle the cane, forming two rings around wilted canes. Prune out and destroy infected canes below the lower ring.

Choosing and planting fruit

To reduce maintenance, select disease-resistant, hardy varieties adapted to your region. Fruit trees often come as dwarfs or grafted onto semidwarf rootstocks. The resulting smaller trees are easier to care for yet produce plenty of full-size fruit. Even though some fruit trees, such as 'Northstar' sour cherry, are self-fertile, most fruits and berries will produce better if at least two varieties grow nearby.

Once you've decided on the type and variety of fruit, select a full-sun location with well-drained, fertile soil away from cold pockets. Plant as described in Chapters 3 and 4 (beginning on page 53).

7

managing
soils &
composts

The basics of soil maintenance

Stone that has crumbled over eons is the main ingredient in soil. Different kinds, ranging from granite, limestone, and sandstone to volcanic rock, account for the regional differences in the mineral content and alkalinity of soil. In addition to minerals, soil contains organic material and living organisms, which affect its fertility, how easy it is to dig, and how it drains. Use this chapter to discover how these ingredients combine to create the strengths and weaknesses of the soil in your yard.

What is soil?

Soil is the layer of the earth that sustains plant and animal life, helps regulate where water goes, cycles nutrients, helps filter pollutants, and supports structures. The mineral particles in soil are different sizes, and the predominating size accounts for the type of soil in your yard. Most soils are a mix of different-size particles and not pure sand, silt, or clay. The largest particles are sand, followed in decreasing order by silt and clay. The other solid ingredient in soil is a combination of decayed organic plant and animal matter, called *humus*.

Soil types

Sandy soil This type has the largest, most loosely packed mineral particles. Air and water travel easily through it. It is easy to dig. Problems arise because sandy soil tends to be infertile and dry.

Clay soil This soil is comprised of the smallest, most tightly packed mineral particles. It is fertile soil that holds water well. Problems can arise because when clay soil is wet, it is sticky. Clay drains poorly, so soluble nutrients may not reach plant roots. Dry clay soil can be hard and bricklike, making it difficult to work and for roots to grow.

Silty soil Particle size in silty soil falls between those of sandy and clay soils. Problems can arise when the soil is primarily silt because compaction from rain, irrigation, or traffic, causes a condition called *capping,* which prevents water and air from moving through the soil.

· HOW TO ·

Knowing your soil

Soil structure is the shape the soil takes based on its physical and chemical properties. Soil texture depends on the distribution of various sized particles. These tests will give you an idea of what you're working with.

■ Squeeze a handful of soil. If it sticks together in a ball it indicates clay is present. If it immediately falls apart or become dusty when squeezed, it is sandy. These may indicate poor texture.

■ Dig a 1-foot-deep hole. Check the size of the soil crumbs at different depths. Ideal soil structure should look crumbly; the crumbs should be about $1/32$ inch in diameter.

■ Halfway fill a jar with soil. Then slowly add water to the jar's brim. Clay, silt, and sand will separate (coarse materials at the bottom, finer materials at the top). This gives an indication of soil texture.

healthy garden • healthy garden • healthy garden • healthy garden

Correcting soil pH

To correct soil pH by increasing soil acidity or alkalinity, use these amendments according to soil-test or manufacturer's recommendations.

To increase acidity:
Garden sulfur, iron sulfate, aluminum sulfate, peat moss, or pine needles

To increase alkalinity:
Dolomitic limestone, crushed oyster shells

To neutralize acidity:
Compost, leaf mold, and manure

(What is soil? continued)

Improving soil texture

The amounts of sand, silt, or clay in soil interact and together make up the soil's texture. It's difficult and usually impractical to change texture. Altering texture of a clay soil, for instance, is possible by adding sand. But huge amounts of sand are required, at least a 3-inch layer of sand worked into 6 inches of soil. And the attempt may backfire: Adding too little can result in a concretelike soil.

A better strategy is to aim to improve soil structure, which is the way soil particles hold together. Incorporate humus (decomposed organic matter) and other organic materials such as compost, peat moss, and shredded leaves. Organic matter improves structure by "gluing" soil particles into larger granules. This in turn improves tilth, aeration, water retention, drainage, fertility, pH, and workability.

How organic matter improves soil The benefits of organic matter go beyond improving soil structure. Beneficial soil organisms, including earthworms and bacteria, eat organic matter, breaking it down into humus and plant nutrients. Like a glue, humus causes soil minerals to arrange themselves better, and it also serves as a pH buffer, working to neutralize acidic and alkaline soils.

How soil pH affects fertility The pH of soil (technically, a measurement of its hydrogen potential) indicates its acidity or alkalinity. Ideally the soil should be neutral to slightly acid for best plant growth. (The pH scale runs from 0 to 14, with 7 being neutral.) Plant roots absorb nutrients dissolved in water, and the pH of soil affects solubility of the nutrients. If the pH is too low or too high, nutrients become less available.

The most key nutrients are available to plants in slightly acid soil, with a pH between 6.3 and 6.8. That range is also a healthy environment for soil organisms such as earthworms. Few yards have ideal soil pH. The solution then is to grow plants adapted to the pH of the soil in your yard.

Soil Tests

A typical soil test tells you the pH and the presence of nutrients nitrogen, phosphorus, and potassium. Soil tests can be done with over-the-counter products, such as soil-probe meters or solution-based test kits (see Resources, page 355). A laboratory soil test is more thorough and accurate than a home-test kit, and will include recommendations on how much of various nutrients or amendments to add. These are available through private companies or county extension services.

Testing soil

The ways to test soil range from simple to scientific. Simply feeling soil reveals its texture. Laboratory testing is the most accurate way to measure pH and nutrients.

Clay soil

Squeeze a handful of moist soil into a ball If it holds its shape and feels smooth, the soil contains a high amount of clay.

Sandy soil

When a moist handful of soil is squeezed and falls apart, the soil is sandy.

Soil tests

Scrape away the top inch of soil from six to nine spots in your yard and dig a scoop of soil from each one. Mix all the samples in a bucket. Measure I cup of this mix and send it to your county extension office.

A soil probe

provides a quick way to test soil a foot or more below the surface without creating a large hole. Use a probing tool to check moisture, to reveal the presence of layers such as hardpan, and to take samples of soil tests.

Soil amendments

If your soil is tested by a laboratory, the report will include specific recommendations that usually include some type of soil amendment. Soil amendments can be either organic or inorganic.

Organic amendments

Organic amendments improve soil structure, provide nutrients, and slightly acidify soil pH. They include materials such as compost, manure, and peat moss.

- **Compost: partially decomposed organic matter. It may be homemade or come from a commercial or municipal source. Use it to improve soil structure, aeration, and drainage and to promote soil microbes. It's also useful as a mulch and as a slow-acting fertilizer.**

- **Composted fir bark: ground, composted tree bark. Use it to lighten the soil, as mulch, and as a slow-acting fertilizer. In areas of the southeast United States, composted pine bark is preferred.**

- **Leaf mold: shredded, partially decomposed leaves and tree litter lightens soil and promotes soil microorganisms in soil.**

- **Manure: aged and dried waste from cows, sheep, and chickens. It serves as both a fertilizer and organic amendment. Fresh manure can burn plants and should not be used.**

- **Peat moss: partially decomposed plant material harvested from bogs. Use it to lighten the soil, improve water retention, and acidify the soil for acid-loving plants such as azaleas.**

Inorganic amendments

These are minerals mined from the earth and used to improve structure and correct soil-mineral deficiencies. Buy inorganic soil amendments at home and garden centers, from specialty gardening catalogs, and through websites (see Resources, page 355).

- **Aluminum sulfate: powdered bauxite that has been treated with sulfuric acid. Use it to acidify the soil and to intensify the blue flower color of hydrangeas.**

- **Gypsum: calcium sulfate. It is used to open and loosen soils with naturally occurring sodium (as in table salt) or soil that has been damaged by sodium.**

- **Limestone: calcium carbonate, dolomitic limestone, or calcium magnesium carbonate. Use it to raise pH of acidic soils.**

- **Sulfur: the pure element. Use the powdered form to lower pH.**

Using soil amendments

Most people put plants where they enhance the house, where it is convenient, or where they fit in—near a water spigot, in a sunny

Potting soil tips

Improve potting soil with these sterile ingredients:
Hydrogel crystals: Granules made from pH-neutral polymers absorb water and turn into a gel that releases water slowly to roots, reducing watering frequency.
Perlite: Expanded volcanic rock lightens weight and increases drainage.
Vermiculite: Expanded mica chips increase water and fertilizer retention.

Organic and inorganic soil amendments

Feed the soil and let the soil feed the plants. It's an old axiom that makes sense. Use soil amendments to maintain a healthy soil that is slightly acidic, moist but not soggy, and well-aerated.

Sulfur Use 18 pounds over 1,000 square feet to lower the pH of an alkaline loam soil from 7.5 to a more desirable 6.5.

Gypsum Use it as a calcium fertilizer to prevent blossom-end rot in tomatoes; it's also a good sulfur fertilizer. It cannot adjust pH like limestone, but it improves soil structure in soils that are high in sodium.

Limestone Use this to raise the pH of acidic soil from 5.5 to a more favorable 6.5. The application rate depends on several factors. Have your soil tested at a lab.

Compost Homemade or commercial, it is the soil cure-all. Work it into new planting areas at the rate of one-third by volume (a 2-inch layer into 6 inches of soil). Also use it as a mulch or slow-acting fertilizer.

171

healthy garden • healthy garden • healthy garden

Time to test

Soil samples can be taken any time during the year for checking pH, phosphorus, and potassium. Nitrogen typically is not tested because it is so active. Collect soil samples 3-6 months before planting. Results will arrive in plenty of time to allow you to apply amendments or recommended fertilizers before planting.

(Soil amendments continued)

area, or in an empty spot in the yard. Soil condition is an afterthought. In fact, there may not even be any good soil in the yard, because topsoil is often removed or compacted during the construction of new homes. It is unlikely that your yard has ideal soil, but you can correct many of its shortcomings by incorporating organic or mineral soil amendments.

If you choose only one amendment, make it compost. Composted organic soil amendments are nature's all-purpose remedy for poor soils. They can be applied any time of the year, and as often as needed, because they are decomposed and release nutrients so slowly that they won't chemically burn plants. Organics applied in the spring will condition soil and release nutrients over the growing season. Lay them on the soil's surface as a topdressing or mulch from which, over time, soil organisms will carry nutrients into the soil. Or you can speed things along by working organic material into the soil.

Dried organic material, such as shredded leaves, peat moss, and bark, decomposes slowly. During composting, microbes use up some nitrogen from the soil. Supplement dried amendments with a nitrogen-rich fertilizer, or apply them in fall, when plants need less nitrogen. Use oak leaves and pine needles, which have an acidifying effect, around acid-loving plants.

Mineral amendments are not very water-soluble, so they travel slowly through the soil, where microbes gradually convert them into soluble nutrients that roots can absorb. Some amendments, such as lime, can burn plants upon contact, so they should be applied only in forms that are safe, such as ground limestone, and at rates recommended by soil-test results or package labels. The best time to apply mineral amendments is in fall, so that they will have all winter to work into the soil and become available to plant roots. Sprinkle them on the soil's surface or work them shallowly into the soil.

The most common mineral amendments are ground limestone to raise soil pH, and ground sulfur to lower soil pH. Both are mined and offered in powdered as well as pellet form. Look for products in pellet form; they will be easier to apply and less messy.

Reading weeds

Weeds, like other plants, grow better in some soils than others. By noting which weeds are growing in your yard, you can learn about your soil. Here are some common lawn weeds and what they can tell you about your soil.

Dandelion is a widespread lawn weed that thrives in acidic soils as well as in hard, compacted soils.

Chickweed prefers low soil nitrogen, moist soil and is often a spring arrival in flower and vegetable beds.

Plantain thrives in compacted or heavy clay soil. Its long, tough taproot can penetrate nearly impervious soils.

Nutsedge prefers poorly drained or overly irrigated areas and is a major lawn weed in southern and coastal areas.

Chicory prefers fertile soils that have been recently cultivated.

Mustard grows best in alkaline soils.

Fertilizers

A fertilizer is any material that contributes plant nutrients to soil. Some fertilizers are also soil amendments, because they improve soil structure, and others can be used as mulch.

The three most important, or primary, nutrients in fertilizers are nitrogen, which is responsible for green leaves and stems; phosphorus, which is responsible for healthy root, flower, and fruit development; and potassium, which makes plants disease-resistant and helps flowers and fruit develop. Commercial fertilizer packages list the percentages of their primary nutrients with the initials N (nitrogen), P (phosphorus), and K (potassium). A fertilizer that lists all three primary nutrients, for example 10-10-10, is called a complete fertilizer. The 10-10-10 fertilizer is a balanced formula; the nutrients are in equal amounts. A 10-6-4 formula is higher in nitrogen.

Organic fertilizers

These are made from decomposed plant or animal materials. Their nutrients are slowly released as the materials break down in the soil. Depending on what they are made from, they can provide one or more nutrients. Organic fertilizers can be purchased separately or in packaged blends from garden centers, specialty catalogs, and on the Web (see Resources, page 355). They include:

■ **Blood meal: dried, powdered animal blood, with an analysis of 12-0-0.**

■ **Bonemeal: steamed and ground animal bones, having an analysis of 4-12-0; slightly alkaline.**

■ **Cottonseed/soybean meal: ground cotton seeds, with an analysis of 6-2-1; contains some micronutrients.**

■ **Fish emulsion: a commercial concentrated liquid made from fish, having an analysis of about 5-1-1.**

■ **Manure: ranges in analysis from 4-4-2 (chicken manure) to 2-1-2 (cow manure), and contains micronutrients. Compost fresh manure before applying, or buy aged, packaged manure.**

■ **Seaweed extract: a commercially packaged liquefied seaweed concentrate, with an analysis of 1-0-1. Use it to provide many micronutrients.**

Mineral fertilizers

Nutrients are very slowly released from mineral fertilizers by weathering and erosion. Examples of mineral fertilizers include:

■ **Borax: a source of the micronutrient boron, which promotes disease resistance and improves food crops.**

healthy garden • healthy garden • healthy garden •

Time to fertilize

Choose a mild, calm day to apply fertilizer. Wind scatters fertilizer, especially if you use a broadcast spreader, causing some plants or parts of a lawn to get too much, and other areas to get too little. Heat stresses plants and fertilizer adds more stress. To prevent damage, avoid fertilizing during the heat of the day, during a drought, or anytime plants are stressed.

- Epsom salts: contains 10 percent magnesium and 13 percent sulfur. Use it to correct deficiency diseases.

- Granite meal: ground granite contains from 1 to 4 percent potash (potassium).

- Greensand: about 6 percent potash and many micronutrients; mined from coastal minerals.

- Gypsum: about 22 percent calcium and 17 percent sulfur. Use ground gypsum to condition clay soil.

- Iron sulfate: about 20 percent iron and 11½ percent sulfur. It promotes green leaf color and flowering. Apply around acid-loving plants.

- Rock phosphate: a source of phosphorus and micronutrients. Works best in acidic soil, because acid helps release the phosphate. Use it to condition soil.

Synthetic fertilizers

These manufactured products are more nutrient-rich than organic or mineral fertilizers. The nutrients in some are soluble, which means the nutrients are immediately available to plants. Some are controlled-release, meaning they dole out their nutrients over a period of time. Read packages for formulations and directions before purchasing.

The biggest difference between synthetic and organic fertilizers is that, although slower-acting, organics improve the soil structure, microbial activity, and nutrient content of soil. Over time, soil is improved, and less fertilizer is needed. Synthetic fertilizers improve plant growth quickly, but continued use won't improve the soil; if overused, they may discourage beneficial microbes. Synthetic fertilizers fall into five broad categories.

· HOW TO ·

Four ways to fertilize

Check out the following methods to find the one most likely to benefit the plants you want to grow.

Broadcasting: distributing granular fertilizer by hand or by using a hand-crank or push-model mechanical fertilizer spreader. Fertilize sizable lawns by broadcasting fertilizer with a mechanical drop spreader.

Foliar feeding: spraying diluted fertilizer onto plants.

Side-dressing: putting fertilizer on the ground beside plants. This is a good method of fertilizing established plants and food crops that are planted in rows.

Top-dressing: scattering fertilizer evenly over an entire growing bed. This method is usually used on new planting beds.

- Dry granules: use to spread over soil or lawns. The best kinds are homogeneous granules, meaning each particle contains all nutrients.

- Controlled-release: granular or pellet. Nutrients are released over weeks or months. Ideal for containers and flower beds.

- Tablets or spikes: meant to be driven into the soil; long-lasting. Good for containers and shrubs.

- Soluble: powder or liquid concentrates. Dissolve them in water and pour on soil.

- Foliar: soluble, dilute fertilizers with nutrients that leaves can absorb.

(Fertilizers continued)

How to use fertilizers

To make the best use of fertilizers, you need to know the nutrient requirements and growth cycles of your plants, have your soil tested to reveal soil-nutrient deficiencies, then use a fertilizer that provides the proper nutrients at the proper times of the year.

When to fertilize Use fertilizers for correcting soil-nutrient deficiencies and replacing nutrients that plants use. To decide if you need to fertilize, look for signs of nutrient deficiency, including slow growth, yellowing or discolored foliage, or lack of flowers or fruit. Have your soil tested; it's the only way to know for sure.

Applying fertilizers

Annuals and container plants These plants continually grow and bloom, and therefore have ongoing nutritional needs. Apply soluble, balanced fertilizer, such as 10-10-10, or a formula high in phosphorus, such as 5-10-5, at half strength biweekly to supply an ongoing source of nutrition. For extra insurance, incorporate slow-release fertilizer into the soil at planting time.

Lawns Apply a high-nitrogen lawn fertilizer according the the type of turfgrass and your maintenance level. Apply lime (to correct soil pH) in fall. Avoid fertilizing during hot summers or droughts to avoid damaging grass.

New beds Before planting, incorporate soil conditioners and slow-acting fertilizers. After the plants are in the ground, you can give most a head start by applying a fast-acting, soluble fertilizer. Each spring, spread compost, or granular or controlled-release fertilizer, over the soil to replace nutrients as plants use them.

Perennials Stop fertilizing in midsummer in cold-winter regions, and late summer in warm-winter areas, to allow perennials to prepare for winter dormancy.

Trees and shrubs To avoid transplant shock, do not fertilize newly planted trees. Keep the soil around them moist the first year, and fertilize once the following spring with a balanced fertilizer. By the third season, trees should need no additional fertilizer.

time saver • time saver • time saver • time saver • time saver • time saver

Timing tilling

Timing tilling properly can save a lot of soil maintenance in the long run. Squeeze a handful of soil into a ball. If the ball crumbles easily, the soil is ready to be tilled. If it sticks together, it's too wet. If it crumbles and won't form a ball, it's too dry.

Cultivating

Working the soil is essential to preparing new beds and removing weeds. Digging aerates the soil and makes it easier to sow or plant. When it comes to tilling, however, it is better to do too little than too much. Overcultivating, working soil at the wrong time, or compacting it when tilling damages soil structure and plant roots, and threatens beneficial soil organisms.

Working the soil

The best time to work the soil is a few days after a light rain, when the ground is moist but not so wet that it clumps, which destroys pores. Walking on prepared beds compacts the soil; lay down boards temporarily to distribute your weight.

The first step is to lay out the perimeter of the area to be filled using stakes, string, a tape measure, or a garden hose. For a geometric area, measure the dimensions and stake the corners. Tie strings to the stakes to outline the bed and till inside the borders. To lay out a circular bed, drive a stake into the center of the bed and tie a string to it that is half the diameter of the bed. Tie a stake to the unattached end of the string and, pulling the string taut, walk in a circle, marking the outline with flour or lime. To outline a free-form bed, lay a garden hose on the ground to create the shape and sprinkle flour along the hose. Remove the hose and till inside the lines.

Next, remove weeds, and remove and compost sod, because if you grind weeds or grass into the soil, you'll be inviting them to grow back.

· HOW TO ·

Tea time for plants

Manure tea is a fast-acting organic "soup" that is rich in micronutrients. When all the right microbes are living in the soil, plant roots are better able to gather the nutrients that the plant needs. A plant's need for nutrients varies through the season and over its life. A vigorous population of soil microbes searches out the nutrients, providing them to the plant as needed. Research has shown that plants given a manure tea need much less regular N-P-K fertilizer. Here's how to make your own: Put a heaping amount of manure in a "tea bag" (burlap works well) and steep in water for several days. Remove the bag and dilute liquid to the color of weak tea. Water with it, or spray it on foliage to discourage leaf diseases.

How to till Rototilling is the most efficient means of preparing a large bed or renovating a lawn. Use a heavy-duty tiller for starting a large bed; reserve less powerful mini tillers for small beds and for weeding and cultivating established beds. Tilling is a fast way to

(Cultivating continued)

incorporate organic matter and loosen clay soil to a depth of 6 to 8 inches. After tilling, check the soil deeper than 8 inches. If it is hard, loosen it with a garden fork. Wear protective clothing when tilling: sturdy, lace-up shoes; earplugs; and goggles.

Till garden soil for a specific purpose, such as incorporating organic matter or loosening soil prior to planting.

Digging Working soil by hand is practical for preparing small beds. If necessary, remove weeds and rocks with a heavy-duty, short-handled combination pick and hoe called a mattock. Loosen the soil with a garden fork. Strip sod by sliding a spade or shovel just under the surface of the soil and prying it up. When the soil is clear, distribute amendments over it. Using a shovel with a pointed blade, dig up and turn amendments into the soil. Digging to the depth of a shovel blade is called single digging. Digging two blades deep is called double digging and is usually reserved for poor soils or beds that will not be renovated for a long time, such as those for perennials.

Solarization If you are not in a hurry, "cook" grass and weeds in an easy process called solarization. This method does not disturb soil structure. First, mow the grass short and cover it with plastic tarps. Any kind will kill vegetation by blocking out light, but clear plastic speeds up the process by using the sunlight to steam the weeds and grass. Weigh down the plastic with bricks or rocks and leave it for at least six weeks. If appearances count, you can cover the plastic with bark mulch in the interim. When the vegetation beneath is dead, the area is ready to be tilled

Raised beds

If the ground is too rocky to till, is compacted, has drainage problems, or the pH cannot be improved enough to grow the plants you want, top it with a layer of good soil. You can build a walled raised bed, or pile up soil for a more natural-looking berm up to 1 foot high without walls. Remove or solarize the existing vegetation, then pile up new soil, level it, and rake the edges so that they gradually slope down to meet the existing soil.

Prevent nitrogen depletion

Uncomposted woody organic mulches, including wood shavings, sawdust, and straw, may deplete soil nitrogen for a short time after spreading. To ensure plants aren't short-changed, apply high-nitrogen fertilizer before applying wood mulches. Signs of nitrogen depletion include pale green or yellowing leaves and stunted plant growth.

Compost

Compost is organic matter that has been broken down into fluffy, nutrient-rich humus by bacteria and other soil microorganisms. A compost pile is, in effect, a factory in which millions of microbes are at work making a product that supplies nearly everything that plants require.

It is inexpensive because it makes use of waste materials that are normally thrown away. Because it is made from a variety of materials, compost contains a wide range of nutrients.

How to use compost Finished compost has a nearly neutral pH and releases nutrients slowly, so you can apply it around plants without harming them. Use it as mulch, as a soil conditioner and fertilizer, or for foliar feeding. You can even use it to fight fungal diseases, because the beneficial bacteria in compost produce antibodies that inhibit the growth of fungi that cause diseases and also of some bacterial organisms. Using compost as mulch also prevents soilborne diseases and insect eggs from splashing onto plants during rain or irrigation.

Make or buy compost? If you don't have room or time to make compost, or if you need more than you can make, you can buy it. Bagged compost and mushroom compost are sold at nurseries and home and garden centers. Many municipalities make compost and offer it free, or at minimal cost, to residents. If you live in an area where mushrooms are grown commercially, you can buy spent mushroom compost from growers.

· HOW TO ·

Ways to dig

Single digging turns the soil over to the depth of one shovel blade. To prepare a new bed, spread a 3-inch-deep layer of organic matter on the soil. Dig a trench one shovel wide, and pile the soil into a cart. Dig a second trench and put the soil from it into the first trench. Proceed like this to the end of the bed, putting the soil from the cart into the last trench. Rake the bed smooth and plant.

Double digging turns the soil two shovel-blades deep. Use this on poor soil. Dig across a bed as directed above, but cover the bottom of each ditch with 3 inches of organic matter and turn it under before filling. When the bed is full, top it with another layer of organic matter, then rake and plant.

Making compost

The ideal mix of materials, moisture, and air enables aerobic soil organisms to process compost rapidly, with no offensive odor. Active, or aerobic, composting happens between 28° and 100° F, when organisms called *thermophiles* take over and raise the compost temperature to a maximum of 160° F, killing weed seeds, insect eggs, and many diseases. The pile then cools, and the previous sets of aerobes work to finish it.

Compost for all seasons

What we consider finished compost is actually only partly decomposed. The first season compost is in contact with soil, it releases about half its nutrients. The process continues in future seasons until all nutrients are released. Most nutrients are released in the heat of summer, just when fast-growing plants need them most.

(Compost continued)

To avoid introducing potential disease-causing organisms into compost, do not compost cat litter or manure other than that of herbivores. Do not compost meat scraps and fat. Leave chemically treated lawn clippings on the lawn to return nitrogen to the soil.

Carbon-rich materials These should make up about two-thirds of the compost pile. Carbon-rich materials, also called brown ingredients, include dried leaves, hay, straw, paper, and sawdust.

Nitrogen-rich ingredients Also called green materials, these enable microbes to break down carbon materials. These include fresh grass clippings, kitchen vegetable and fruit scraps, and manure. Layer these thinly between thick carbon layers—too little nitrogen will slow down decomposition, but too much will create bad-smelling gas. A 1-inch-thick layer of green material alternated with a 3- to 6-inch-thick, or thicker, layer of carbon material works. It is better to layer on too much carbon than too much green material. Too much carbon will slow down, but not sour, the compost.

Moisture Lift the compost with a garden fork to check for moisture at different levels. Water as often as needed to keep the compost barely damp. In dry climates make a depression in the top of the pile to collect water; in wet conditions, mound the pile to shed water, or cover with a tarp.

Aeration Turn the pile with a garden fork a couple of times a week, or make compost in a commercial tumbling composter, which mixes and aerates the compost as you turn the barrel. You can also work a garden fork around in the pile to allow air into the compost, or build a pile up around 4-inch perforated pipes, the kind used for soil drainage. Building a pile on a base of brush and twigs will introduce air into the pile from beneath.

Heat The pile needs to be a minimum of 3 feet across and 3 feet tall to heat up properly.

What to compost

Choose any from the following list of appropriate compost ingredients:

Green ingredients
- **Coffee grounds**
- **Yard trimmings (spoiled vegetables, flower stalks)**
- **Grass clippings**

Common compost ingredients

Kitchen scraps, such as vegetable trimmings, fruit scraps, and coffee grounds, contribute moisture and nitrogen, which speed up composting. Dry leaves and straw contribute all-important carbon. Ideally, these should make up two-thirds of the pile.

Fruit scraps

Fresh grass clippings

Yard waste

Shredded newspaper

Coffee grounds

Vegetable scraps

Freshly pulled weeds

Dried leaves

Weed-free straw

(Compost continued)

- **Vegetable kitchen scraps**
- **Weeds (remove seeds)**

Brown ingredients
- **Dried leaves**
- **Dried seaweed**
- **Newspaper**
- **Pine needles**
- **Spoiled hay**
- **Sawdust (except black walnut, eucalyptus, or cedar, which can inhibit plant growth)**
- **Straw**

Minerals You can either add mineral supplements to your soil, according to soil-test recommendations, or sprinkle them on the compost pile. Wood ashes and eggshells are better sources of calcium than lime. Lime can raise the pH and inhibit the microbial decomposition of compost, and can also cause nitrogen to be released as ammonia gas.

Composting methods

Passive compost Randomly pile up any organic materials, keep them moist, and otherwise ignore the pile. Within four months to a year, the ingredients will be composted. Passive compost will not heat up to the intense temperatures of turned or aerated compost, so weed seeds and plant disease organisms added to the pile will survive.

Layered compost Alternate layers of green and brown material with an activator such as manure. The brown layer should be twice as deep as the green layer, topped off with a thin layer of aged manure—less than a third of a layer. Keep the pile moist and allow it to compost, undisturbed. It will reach temperatures hotter than a random pile but not as hot as a pile that's aerated.

Aerated compost Aerating, the fastest and hottest method of making compost, is also the most labor-intensive. Layer the compost, and moisten as above. Monitor the temperature within the pile with a long, probelike compost thermometer. When it reaches 140° F, turn the pile with a garden fork to introduce more oxygen. Once the pile cools to about 100° F, turn the pile again. With regular turning, compost can break down in two to three weeks.

Three-pile compost This method sets the standard for making, finishing, and renewing compost. It is very efficient and provides an ongoing supply of finished compost. But because it requires at least a 9-foot by 3-foot footprint, it may not be practical for small yards. To make compost this way, put three standard-size compost bins end-to-

healthy garden • healthy garden • healthy garden • healthy

Fungus among us

Don't be alarmed if areas of your nearly finished compost have a cobweblike grayish material growing over them. These are actinomycetes—fungilike bacterial microbes—that work on nearly finished compost. These beneficial organisms are responsible for the earthy fragrance and dusty look of finished compost.

Commercially available compost bins

The key feature to watch for is a lockable lid, an essential if you'll be composting kitchen scraps. Other composting tools include an activator, a thermometer, and an agitator (shown at right).

Stackable plastic compost bins come in pieces, allowing you to add sections to adjust the height as needed and take it apart to access compost.

Tumbling composters aerate and mix ingredients each time they are turned, producing compost in as little as two weeks.

Plastic bins with lockable lids are the type to choose for kitchen wastes. Along with the lid, a hardware cloth screen beneath the bin will exclude scavenging animals.

A wire fencing enclosure prevents dried leaves from blowing away before they can decompose.

Make a compost screen

Finished compost usually still has some clods, making it unsuitable for potting mixes. Sieve compost by covering a wheelbarrow with hardware cloth, bending it over the rim to secure it. Wearing a pair of sturdy gloves, shovel compost onto the hardware cloth and work it through into the wheelbarrow.

(Compost continued)

end. Fill the first with layered compost ingredients. Keep the contents moist. When the pile heats up, turn it into the second bin, and fill the first bin with fresh materials. When the first bin heats to around 100° F (or feels hot at a depth of about 1 foot), turn the second bin into the third bin, and turn the first into the second. Then begin filling the first bin with fresh materials again. When the first bin is hot and ready to be moved, rotate bins as before. The compost in the third bin will be finished by this time, so remove it and use it in the yard. Repeat the process for continual supply of compost.

Sheet compost This method includes mulching and composting rolled into one easy step. Spread uncomposted organic materials over bare soil and work them into the soil, where they will decompose over time. This method is best suited to a new ornamental bed or to food gardens. Sheet composting after the beds are cleared in fall allows the amended bed to compost over the winter and be ready to plant in spring.

Small-scale compost This method is the best solution for small yards and where appearances count, such as in a housing community. You can compost in something as unobtrusive as a trash can by drilling air holes into it, filling it with compost ingredients, and rolling it on its side to aerate the compost. You can also cut the bottom out of a trash can and partially bury it to put your compost in contact with the earth to introduce beneficial microbes and earthworms. Stir the contents regularly to introduce air. You can also choose among dozens of attractive manufactured compost barrels or bins. When composting in a small container, it's most efficient to make a complete batch at one time. Fill the barrel all at once with layers of brown, green, and activator ingredients. Turn it daily, or every other day, to finish the compost in about two weeks. Without turning, the compost will finish in about three months.

The University of California compost method Feed ingredients through a shredder one layer at a time. Aim the shredder output into a three-sided enclosure, filling it as you shred. Moisten the pile. Four days later, turn it, and continue turning every three days. In about two weeks, the compost will be finished.

Mulching

Mulching is an ecologically sound technique for increasing plant health and decreasing yard work. It gives a yard a finished appearance for little money. Mulches are either organic or inorganic materials placed on the soil's surface around plants. Use them to smother or shade out weeds, shade and cool plant roots, conserve water by slowing evaporation, and control pests and diseases. When shopping for mulch, look for porous texture, which will allow water and air to percolate through to the soil.

There are as many kinds of mulch as you can think of—and more. In addition to manufactured, packaged mulches, there are utilitarian mulches such as hay and straw. You can even make your own, using everything from biodegradable newspapers to durable old carpeting (lay the pile side down, exposing the more natural-looking jute backing), aluminum foil, or other materials.

Dark-colored mulch can warm soil in spring to help plants sprout sooner; light-colored mulch will keep soil cool in summer to reduce heat stress. Fluffy-textured mulches such as straw and pine needles used in winter insulate soil against freezing and thawing, which damage plant roots. Use heavy stone mulch to control erosion, and use all mulches to surface paths or support your weight in beds. Lastly, mulch can be a decorative soil covering, offering interesting textures and colors that coordinate with plants, path materials, or the colors of a house.

· HOW TO ·

Using compost

On flower and vegetable beds: Turn a 3-inch-deep layer of compost into the soil before planting. Mulch with compost during the growing season.

On lawns: Incorporate a 3- to 6-inch layer when renovating or seeding. Top dress established lawns annually with a ½-inch layer of compost in fall.

On trees and shrubs: Mulch with a 3-inch-thick layer during the growing season. Keep compost several inches away from the trunk to avoid introducing rot or insects. Azaleas benefit from composted, mildly acidic oak leaves or pine needles.

In potting mix: Mix ⅓ sifted compost, ⅓ sand or perlite, and ⅓ soil. For a soilless mix, substitute peat moss for soil. Use soilless mix for starting seeds.

Organic mulches These types of mulches are made of partially decomposed plants. These mulches break down slowly, releasing nutrients into the soil and improving soil structure. They can last several years before needing to be replaced or topped with a new layer. Fertilize the soil before you apply organic mulch, because fresh mulch depletes nitrogen from the soil.

Inorganic mulches Nonliving materials ranging from gravel and fired-clay pellets to clear or colored plastic sheeting, synthetic landscape fabrics, and even reflective sheeting and metallic foil make up inorganic mulches. These mulches are long-lived. Use them to

(Mulching continued)

absorb the sun's heat and warm up the soil, smother weeds, get plants off to an early start and make them grow faster, and repel insects and plant diseases. On the downside, except for some stone mulches and ground oyster shells, they do not contribute nutrients and are unattractive enough to require a covering of decorative organic mulch such as bark chunks.

Living mulches These may be either a permanent planting of ground cover such as ivy or pachysandra, or what is called *green manure*—an annual crop such as ryegrass or buckwheat sown in a food garden at the end of the season and tilled under the following spring before planting. Living mulches require little maintenance and have all the benefits of other mulches, including preventing soil erosion. Green manures, which are legumes, contribute nitrogen to the soil.

A practical approach to deciding which mulch to put where is to divide the materials into seasonal categories.

Spring and summer mulches These are applied during the growing season. Lay down spring mulches to warm the soil enough for early growth and to smother weeds. Summer mulches are usually attractive organic mulches such as compost or bark chips. Apply them to suppress weeds, cool the soil, reduce evaporation and the need to water, and give a decorative, finished look to beds. Cover utilitarian plastic or fabric mulches with a light-colored organic mulch to cool the soil, or leave them exposed in cool-summer areas to speed the growth of heat-loving plants.

Winter mulches These are used in cold climates to insulate plant roots. Winter mulches are usually fluffy-textured organic mulches such as straw or evergreen boughs, which are heaped around the base of a plant from 6 to 12 inches or more deep. Inorganic winter mulches include plastic foam rose cones, to fill with loose mulch and tip over a pruned rose or other marginally hardy plant. Apply winter mulch after the ground freezes hard in late fall to keep it frozen and avoid cycles of freezing and thawing that can damage plants. Remove this type of mulch in early spring before plants leaf out.

Permanent mulches These include heavy gravel, marble chips, and fired-clay pellets, are best used around permanent plantings such as shrubs and trees, and on beds that won't need to be disturbed for a long time. Remove the mulches temporarily when planting or renewing beds. Avoid putting limestone and crushed oyster shells around acid-loving plants, because they leach lime into the soil, raising the pH.

healthy garden • healthy garden • healthy garden •

Stir things up

Mulch reduces yard maintenance by suppressing weeds and helping keep soil moist, but it will last longer and perform better if it gets a little maintenance itself. Loosen mulch periodically to keep it from crusting and excluding rain. If weed seeds sprout or it becomes moldy, turn the mulch over.

Gallery of mulches

Because mulch is basically a protective layer, the number of possible mulches is nearly limitless. Choose one that serves the purpose you need, is attractive, and is easy to obtain.

Pine needles

Stone

Compost

Wood chips

Leaves

Clean straw

Grass clippings

Shredded bark

Bark chunks

(Mulching continued)

Mulch materials

When choosing mulch, remember that its purpose is to heat or cool the soil, suppress weeds, retain soil moisture, and keep soilborne insects and fungal spores from splashing onto plants. Many materials are potential mulches; favorites are listed here:

- **Bark mulch: an attractive organic mulch that lasts several seasons. Use it in beds, around shrubs and trees, or on slopes.**

- **Cocoa hulls: chocolate fragrance. Use this long-lasting brown mulch decoratively or to warm the soil. Stir to discourage mold.**

- **Compost: dark, fine-textured, all-purpose organic mulch. It repels fungal diseases.**

- **Evergreen boughs: excellent insulating winter mulch for perennials and shrubs.**

- **Grass clippings: nitrogen-rich. Mix with dry leaves or straw to control odor. Leave chemically treated clippings on the lawn.**

- **Landscape fabrics and plastic: permeable or impermeable, and come in black, clear, and colors. Use permeable types to suppress weeds; top them with attractive bark mulch. Use impermeable types to warm soil and control soilborne insects and diseases. Clear plastic heats the soil and kills most pests and diseases in the top few inches.**

- **Leaves: dry and shred so they won't blow away or pack down. Use shredded leaves in landscape beds. Dried leaves can last for two or more seasons.**

- **Pine needles: organic and attractive; decompose slowly. Use them as decorative mulch and as insulating winter mulch.**

- **Stone: protects soil, but also traps and then reflects heat. Especially useful where lighter mulches might wash or blow away.**

- **Straw: used seasonally in food gardens or as an insulating winter mulch elsewhere in the yard. Straw has fewer weed seeds than hay and it outlasts hay.**

Prevent nitrogen depletion

Carbon-rich, dry organic mulches such as wood chips, sawdust, and straw, deplete soil nitrogen for a short time after being put down. Soil microbes that break down the mulch compete with plants for the nitrogen. To keep them from stealing nitrogen from nearby plants, apply a high-nitrogen fertilizer before applying these mulches. Signs of nitrogen depletion include pale green or yellowing leaves or stunted plant growth.

healthy garden • healthy garden • healthy garden •

Mulch color code

Dark-colored mulches, such as black plastic, buckwheat hulls, and dark gravel, absorb the sun's heat. Use them to warm soil in spring for early flowers, or around heat-loving plants such as tomatoes. Pale mulches, including straw and white marble chips, reflect heat. Use them in hot-summer climates and beds in strong sunlight. Some colored mulches pump up vegetable yields. See page 143.

Soil drainage

Soil drainage is essential to maintaining plant health and reducing yard maintenance. When soil is waterlogged, plant roots are deprived of oxygen and suffocate. The plants can also contract fatal root- or crown rot (the plant rots at the ground), or other fungal diseases. Low-lying areas, or valleys, and at the bottom of hills are notorious for poor drainage, because water can pool there.

Hillsides and fast-draining, sandy soil have the opposite problem. Sandy soil may dry out so fast that plants wilt. Hillsides are often dry because rain runs off before it can be absorbed into the soil. In addition, without plantings, they erode.

Ideally, soil should be about one-quarter water and one-quarter air by volume. The rest of the materials in soil are solids: a blend of humus, minerals, and living soil organisms; and these are the key to both moisture retention and good drainage.

Correcting poor drainage

There are several ways you can improve or cope with poor soil drainage, whether soil is too wet or too dry. You can improve drainage in almost any situation by incorporating humus, such as compost or leaf mold, into the top foot of soil to loosen and aerate the soil to a depth that encompasses the root zones of many plants.

You can take drastic and expensive actions by changing the grade of the soil, by either filling in the low spot, or, in the case of a hill, leveling it off or terracing the slope. The heavy equipment and engineering needed to move earth usually require hiring professionals for such jobs. When changing the grade is not feasible, install an underground drainage system called a French drain. This is a sod-covered, gravel-filled ditch that collects and diverts runoff to a storm drain or to better-drained ground.

Coping with wet and dry soils

In some cases, altering soil structure or terrain, or installing a French drain, may prove too expensive or fail to handle the drainage problem. Sandy soil may still drain too fast even with the addition of humus. In these instances, adapt planting and maintenance

· HOW TO ·

Mulching smarts

Use these guidelines to maximize the benefits of mulch:

Mulch thickly (3 to 4 inches deep) on sandy or rocky, dry soil to cool the soil and help conserve water.

Apply thin mulch (1 to 3 inches thick) on heavy clay and poorly draining soil to allow the soil to breathe and dry out between rains.

Don't mulch poorly draining or soggy soil, to allow maximum air circulation to dry the soil and discourage diseases.

Keep a few inches of space between perennial plant stems and mulch to discourage insects, rodents, and diseases.

Apply mulch 1 to 3 inches thick around trees and shrubs, allowing 3 inches between trunks and mulch.

(Soil drainage continued)

techniques to the soil you have, and choose plant species that thrive in those conditions. Well-sited plants are less stressed and less susceptible to disease and insect attack.

Choose plants At the base of a slope and in other wet sites, grow water-loving plants such as blue-flag iris. In very wet sites, consider growing water-loving trees such as maple, willow, or river birch that draw water from the soil. Where erosion is a concern, plant tough, thickly growing ground covers or perennials and shrubs that can also tolerate dry conditions, such as ivy, euonymus, pachysandra, ornamental grasses, daylilies, cotoneaster, yew, and juniper. These plants all have spreading, fibrous roots that hold the soil in place, and their thick top growth will slow the rush of rainwater.

Raised beds Raised beds solve drainage problems in small areas, allowing you to grow plants that can't tolerate wet soils. You can build a traditional raised bed, in which low walls of wood, brick, rock, or other material support the soil. If you prefer a natural-looking island bed, build a mound, or berm, with gradually sloping sides. A berm can be up to 2 feet high in the center without support on the sides. It can be any length and width, and be kidney shaped, circular, or any shape. For additional drainage and aeration, place a layer of brush on the ground before piling on soil.

Move your plants to a spot with well-drained soil. Dig up the plants and relocate them to a site with better drainage. If you later improve the drainage in the boggy area, you can always move the plants back.

Grow thirsty plants River birch, willow, and many other tree species thrive in boggy areas, absorbing vast amounts of moisture through their roots. Or consider attractive, moisture-loving perennials such as astilbe, ferns, ligularia, and lobelia to transform a boggy area into a lush, flowering garden that will attract butterflies and hummingbirds.

Choose drought-tolerant plants When coping with dry soil, look for prairie natives with deep roots, such as purple coneflower and ornamental grasses. Also look for herbs and perennials adapted to dry soil, such as sedums, lavender, and yucca and drought-tolerant woody plants such as bluebeard, Russian sage, and junipers. If dry soil is your problem and you want beautiful but thirsty plants, group them near your house. Cluster extra-thirsty ones, such as ferns and lobelia, near spigots, where they are easy to water and can absorb spilled water. Mulch plants growing in dry soil to reduce moisture evaporation from the soil.

Drainage test

To discover whether your soil drains well, dig a hole 1 foot deep. Fill it with water and let it drain. Fill again. If it empties in less than an hour, drainage is excellent; in less than four hours, good. If the water drains in 12 hours, drainage is adequate; more than 12 hours, you should improve the drainage.

Building a French drain

A piped French drain is an inconspicuous way to drain large amounts of water from a saturated area or to minimize runoff. Expect the system to remain effective for five to 10 years before the spaces between the gravel become filled with soil that has worked its way through the fabric barrier.

1 Dig a ditch that is pitched away from the area you want to drain. The ditch should end at a storm sewer collection grid or empty onto well-drained ground. Make the trench at least 18 inches deep, or below the frost line in your area, and 6 to 12 inches wide.

2 Line the sides of the trench with porous landscape fabric, leaving several inches of excess fabric at the top on both sides. Add a 1-inch-thick layer of gravel to the bottom of the trench.

3 Lay a 4-inch- to 6-inch-diameter perforated plastic drainpipe in the trench. Align holes face down, with the pipe's pitch at least ¼ inch every 10 feet. Cover the pipe with gravel to within 6 inches of the soil's surface, taking care to keep the landscape fabric in place.

4 Fold the landscape fabric from both sides over the top of the gravel and cover with soil. If the trench is in a lawn, you can plant grass or place sod on top.

Planting

To get plants off to a good start, plant on an overcast day or in the evening to prevent newly set-out plants from wilting. When planting small or delicate plants, avoid lifting them by the stem. Lift seedlings into their holes by the leaves; lift larger plants by the root ball.

Perennials and small landscape plants Perennials, annuals, and other small plants need soil prepared to 12 inches deep. Dig a hole that is the same depth as the root ball and two to three times as wide. Work compost into the hole before planting. If the soil is dry, fill the hole with water and let it drain before planting.

Remove the plant from the pot. Instead of pulling it out by the stem, knock the rim of the pot against the edge of a table. This loosens the root ball so it slips out of the pot and into your hand. If roots are tightly wound around the root ball, gently loosen them, then set the plant into the hole. Fill in and firm the soil around the roots.

Mulch the plant with a 3-inch-thick layer of organic mulch (see pages 185–188), which will help it root by reducing evaporation and cooling the roots. Keep soil moist for a week after planting, then water as needed to prevent wilting. If newly planted annuals wilt, shade them with a cardboard box until they recover.

Shrubs and trees Trees and shrubs must adjust to the existing soil. To plant them, dig a hole the same depth as the nursery container and twice as wide. Fill the hole with water and allow it to drain before planting. Loosen the soil around the edges of the hole, set the plant in, fill around it, and firm the soil. Do not fertilize. Water as needed to keep the soil moist the first year. In succeeding years, water during prolonged droughts.

Lawns Begin by cultivating the soil 4 to 6 inches deep until the soil is crumbly. After sowing, mulch lightly with straw to shade seedlings, and water as needed to keep the soil moist until the seeds germinate and the grass grows long enough to mow.

Weeding near plants

Cultivating established beds loosens the soil, which allows water to reach the roots. Depending on the tool used, it also removes weeds and prevents new ones from sprouting. When using a weeding tool, get the cutting edge under the roots and slice off or pry weeds up. Shallow-rooted annual weeds are easier to eradicate than perennial weeds. When digging perennial weeds, avoid breaking the roots; they may sprout at every break.

healthy garden • healthy garden • healthy garden

Well-drained containers

Soil drainage is essential to healthy potted plants. Soggy soil can rot roots. Use packaged potting mix, or incorporate perlite (heat-expanded volcanic rock) or sand to make up one-third of the potting medium. Make sure that pots have drain holes and that they do not sit in water-filled saucers.

Gardening tools have the potential to perform the job well without causing discomfort, and to outlast your need for them. Whether they live up to that potential depends on the quality of the tools and how well they are maintained. It's worth spending the extra money to buy well-made tools, and it's worth spending the extra time needed to keep them clean, sharp, and in good shape.

Start with these tools:
- gloves
- flower shears
- hand pruners
- loppers
- cultivator and hoe
- weeders
- lawn rake
- garden rake
- shovel
- spade
- garden fork
- trowel
- wheelbarrow or cart
- sprayers

Borrow, rent, or buy these tools as the need arises:
- hedge shears or power trimmers
- pruning saw
- dibble
- chain saw
- blower-vac
- rototiller

Hand tools

Hand tools are meant to be an extension of your hand or arm, so they must fit your stature and strength. You'll suffer less fatigue and injury if you choose the appropriate tool. You might be lucky enough to have inherited good-quality hand tools from a parent or grandparent. These are certainly worth cherishing, but if the tool is too large for you to use without strain, it's best to display it in the gardening shed or garage, or pass it on.

Hand tools are best categorized by the job for which they are suited, so this section is divided into tasks and their tools.

• GARDEN GEAR •

Maintaining gear

Here's what you need for keeping tools clean and sharp:
- A stiff brush for removing debris
- Oily rags or antirust lubricant for wiping metal parts
- A bucket of sand mixed with oil for cleaning and oiling digging tool blades
- Boiled linseed oil for wooden handles
- Spray paint in your favorite color to freshen up tools
- Liquid plastic dip to renew plastic coatings on handles
- Vise for holding blades while sharpening
- Fine and coarse flat files, fine and coarse whetstones, and a round file for sharpening
- Wrenches for tightening nuts and bolts

Sizing up pruners

Buy the pruners best suited to your hand size and any physical limitations. They should not open wider than your hand can comfortably extend. Handles should be well-cushioned, and the safety latch that keeps them closed should be easy to flip with your thumb. Ratchets and rotating handles ease hand strain. If you're left-handed, choose a left-hand model.

(Hand tools continued)

Cutting and pruning tools

Every time you cut a stem or branch of a plant, you are pruning that plant. A clean cut can stimulate the growth of more foliage and flowers. A jagged cut or a dull blade can damage the stem, slowing growth and inviting insects and disease to enter the wound. The most basic cutting/pruning tools are flower shears, pruners, and loppers. If you have a hedge, you'll need hedge shears. Pole pruners and pruning saws are needed for tree pruning.

Flower shears Resembling sewing scissors, these shears may look delicate but their steel blades mean business. They are ideal for cutting flowers and thinning stems. They have wide blades for cutting through thin, woody stems. Choose a pair with padded handles and blades that operate smoothly without wobbling.

Hand pruners Sometimes also called *secateurs,* these cut herbaceous and woody stems up to about ¾ inch in diameter, depending on the size of the cutting head. They come in two styles: bypass and anvil. Bypass pruners have one sharpened blade that moves past the other blade—the *hook.* They make clean, close cuts. For the closest cut, put the sharpened blade next to the stem that is staying rather than the hook.

Anvil pruners have one sharpened blade that meets a flat piece of metal—the *anvil*—when the pruners close. The anvil prevents the pruners from making a close cut, so they leave a stub that's more inviting for insects and disease. They also crush the stem as they cut, so they are best suited for use on dead wood. Place these pruners so the anvil is underneath the branch you are cutting off.

Loppers These function much like pruners, but their longer handles give more leverage. Use them for cutting branches that are too large for hand pruners but not large enough to require a saw. Depending on the size of the lopper head and whether it is geared, loppers can cleanly cut branches from 1 to 3 inches in diameter. The longer the handle, the more leverage, but the heavier the loppers will be. These too come in anvil and bypass style.

If you have to frequently reach overhead, consider loppers with lightweight aluminum handles instead of wood. Using loppers can cause sore upper arms and shoulders from the action of squeezing the widely spaced handles together. To ease the strain, choose a model with one long handle and a trigger grip at the end, which you grasp like hand pruners to operate the blade. Ratchet loppers require less strength to operate, and compound-action loppers use gears to increase their power. If pruners are too small for the job but regular loppers are too big, choose shorter-handled mini-loppers. If the

Types of cutting tools

Having the right tool that's sharp and up to the task is the first step in pruning safety. The right tool also makes the job faster and easier to do.

bow saw

folding pruning saw

lightweight pole pruner

compound-action loppers

trimming shears

hedge shears

bypass hand pruner

grass clippers

bypass hand pruner

anvil-style hand pruner

ergonomic hand pruner

(Hand tools continued)

branch is too large for loppers to cut without twisting, switch to a pruning saw.

Pruning saws These are the next step up from loppers, handling large diameter branches. Most saws consist of a long blade with a handle at the end. The blade cuts on the pull stroke. The thicker the branches, the longer the blade should be and the fewer, deeper teeth per inch it should have. A bow saw (which resembles an archery bow) requires more room to work, but the thin blade cuts easily. A good-quality saw has a tempered steel blade with beveled teeth and a comfortable handle. A D-handle is the most comfortable and protects the hand when making cuts. Folding models are handy; just make sure they have a locking mechanism to hold the blade open.

Hedge shears You need these only for maintaining a hedge. Their long blades help ensure even cutting, and the long handles aid reaching into the center of the hedge. Blades of stainless steel or forged carbon steel are the strongest and most long-lasting. Choose the longest pair you can comfortably hold, preferably with a serrated or wavy-edged blade, which helps to grab the stems so they don't slide out from between the blades. Rubber bumpers on the inside of the handles are important for preventing your knuckles from hitting one another as you cut. Although they may be slower than electric models, manual trimmers are more forgiving when you're trying to create a pleasing shape.

Pole pruners These consist of a long pole with a saw or a bypass pruner head at the end. The cutting action is controlled by a rope or lever on the handle. Pole pruners can cut branches up to about 1½ inches thick. They allow you to reach higher than you can with loppers—up to 12 feet or higher with telescoping fiberglass models—so you can avoid using a ladder.

Cutting tool maintenance If you are cutting diseased plant material, clean the blades with a diluted (10 percent) bleach or Lysol solution after every cut to prevent spreading the disease. At the end of the day, clean off the dirt, plant debris, and sap or pitch residue with an emery cloth or a wire brush. If the sap is hard to remove, use rubbing alcohol or paint thinner. Wipe the blade with an oiled cloth to prevent corrosion, especially if using bleach, and tighten any loose screws or nuts. Store tools in a dry place.

Once a month and at the beginning and end of the season, clean off any rust with steel wool, wipe the blades with an oily cloth or spray with an antirust lubricant, and oil the pivot areas (and the spring on pruners).

budget stretcher • budget stretcher • budget stretcher • budget stretcher

Buy quality pruners

If you have lots of woody plants to prune, invest in high-quality pruners. Look for replaceable, tempered carbon steel or stainless-steel blades. They should operate smoothly, the blades passing closely without rubbing or wobbling. Another sign of quality is a groove that directs sap away from the moving parts of the tool.

Cultivating and weeding tools

Cultivators and hoes perform multiple jobs: loosening the soil, weeding, incorporating organic matter, making furrows and mounding soil. Weeders have a single, obvious function, but there are different types for different situations. The basic types of cultivators, hoes, and weeders that you need to maintain your yard and garden include:

Cultivators These are best for soil that has already been tilled or turned over. They are typically curved like a claw to slice through the soil, loosening it and lifting up weeds. If you are cultivating an area prior to planting, or are working around widely spaced plants, you can cover more ground with a tool that has a wider head and more tines. If most of your cultivating will be around plants spaced closely together, you need a tool with a narrow head and only two or three tines.

It's easiest to cultivate standing up using a long-handled tool, but sometimes you may find that you can separate weeds from plants more easily if you kneel and use a short-handled cultivator. Choose a model with short tines if you will be working around perennials, trees, and shrubs, so you don't disturb the roots. Because you have to continually lift up the tool and bring it down into the soil with a hacking motion, the task can become tiring and hard on the back. A spiked-wheel cultivator can make the job easier, as long as your soil is fairly loose to begin with. It has spikes instead of blades, and you simply push or pull it along the ground.

Hoes Hoes come with different blades for different purposes, so you'll want to choose the ones that meet your needs. For cultivating heavy soil, the typical narrow field hoe is best. By turning the pointed corner of the blade into the soil, you can also dig furrows. For making deep furrows and trenches, a hoe such as the triangular, pointed warren hoe can make the job easier. For light weeding and cultivating near the soil's surface, you can use a oscillating-type hoe. Draw hoes, such as the gooseneck hoe, have a blade angled back toward the handle so they slice close to the surface as you draw them toward you. Push or scuffle hoes, such as the Dutch hoe, cut as you push the hoe. The oscillating hoe has a swinging blade that looks somewhat like a stirrup and cuts on both forward and backward strokes. It's best used in a larger area because it can be a bit hard to control. Hand cultivators and hand forks have short handles so you can hoe while sitting or kneeling.

healthy garden • healthy garden • healthy garden

Keeping the edge on pruners

Ease pruning jobs by keeping tools sharp. Start by cleaning the tool, then open it wide or remove the blade. Clamp it in a vise. Soak a medium-grain whetstone or a medium flat file in water or light oil. Lightly move the stone along the edge of the blade from its base to the tip. Repeat until the edge is sharp, taking care to not file it too thin. If you do, the edge will nick easily. Finish with a fine-grain whetstone or file. Remove burrs on the back of the blade. Wipe the blade with an oily rag, or spray with an antirust lubricant.

Tool care tip

A light coating of oil protects tools from rusting. Any lubricant will work, including used motor oil. Also consider synthetic oils. Corona CLP is an example. It repels dirt, protects against rust, and contains a solvent that dissolves sap.

(Hand tools continued)

Hand weeders Because they are designed to be an extension of the hand, most hand weeders consist of a short handle with a blade at the end that pries, slices, or pulls the weed. Use them while kneeling, squatting, or sitting. Here's what you'll need for different situations:

A fishtail weeder (or asparagus weeder) is a must-have tool. Use it for removing dandelions and other plants with taproots. It looks like a screwdriver with a V cut into the business end. Insert the V below the base of the weed and pry it up, removing as much of the taproot as possible.

A dandelion weeder is another handy tool for getting rid of dandelions and other stubborn weeds if you prefer to weed while standing or sitting. The upright handle comes in varying lengths (at least 3 feet long) and contains a lever that controls the two gripper blades at the bottom, which you position on either side of the weed and then clamp together.

A taproot weeder digs under the soil's surface to lift up weeds with its pointed tip. The handle, shaped like a stirrup, is easier to hold than a straight handle for people with any wrist discomfort.

A slicing weeder efficiently removes annual and perennial weeds as you slide the tool along the ground just beneath the soil's surface. The popular Cape Cod weeder has a blade set at about a 45-degree angle to the short handle so the inside of the blade clips the weed as you pull it toward you while kneeling or squatting. A weeder with a wide blade, such as the collinear weeder, can remove more weeds at a time, but it is surprisingly easy to unintentionally cut off good plants along with the weeds. If you space plants close together, choose a tool with a narrow blade.

Tool maintenance Clean off soil and plant debris after every use, and wipe the blades with an oily rag or spray with a lubricant. Once a year, rub wooden handles with boiled linseed oil.

Cultivators and weeders don't need to be sharpened, but hoes do—once a month if they get frequent use. Place the blade in a vise and use a coarse flat file to sharpen the beveled edge at the same angle as the original bevel. Hold the front end of the file at one end of the blade and push the file forward as you move it along the width of the blade from one end to the other. Then use fine-grit sandpaper to remove any burrs on the back of the blade.

Cultivators and weeders

Field hoes and four-prong cultivators are the basic tools in this category. You'll find myriad variations on each one, allowing you to match the tool to the job.

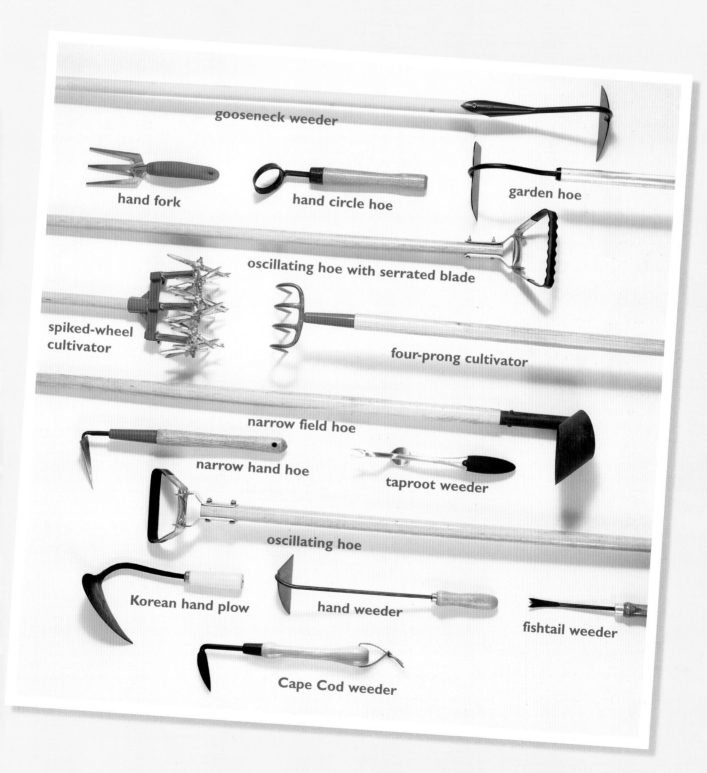

gooseneck weeder

hand fork

hand circle hoe

garden hoe

oscillating hoe with serrated blade

spiked-wheel cultivator

four-prong cultivator

narrow field hoe

narrow hand hoe

taproot weeder

oscillating hoe

Korean hand plow

hand weeder

fishtail weeder

Cape Cod weeder

(Hand tools continued)

Raking tools

If you have both lawn and gardens, you will need at least one lawn rake and one garden rake. They are not interchangeable. There are also specialized rakes that can help out in specific situations.

Lawn rakes With long, flexible tines made of metal, bamboo, or plastic, these are meant for raking leaves, grass clippings, and other lightweight materials. You need a narrow rake for removing leaves from around perennials, shrubs, or other objects; and a wide one for raking lawns. Bamboo rakes aren't durable, but they're inexpensive and easier on the grass blades than metal rakes. Keep them flexible longer by soaking the heads overnight in soapy water every couple of months. If you like the springy action of a metal rake, buy one of good quality so the tines can be straightened if they get bent. Plastic rakes are strong and long-lasting, and don't rust like metal.

Garden rakes For raking up stones, preparing planting beds, and creating raised beds, you need a garden rake. For frequent use, choose a bowhead type; the head is attached to the handle by rods that extend to either side of the head. This is stronger than the type with the head attached directly to the end of the handle. If the need warrants, you can purchase or rent a specialized rake, such as a thatching rake for removing lawn thatch; or a grading, or leveling, rake, which has an extra-wide head for leveling large areas.

Tool maintenance After use, remove debris from rake tines and from the area where the head attaches to the handle. The tines don't need sharpening. Once a year, rub wooden handles with boiled linseed oil.

Digging tools

Digging tools take a lot of abuse as they are plunged into the ground. The force of digging and prying them out of the soil puts pressure on the tool head and handle, and the blade can be damaged from encounters with rocks and other obstacles. This section covers what to look for in selecting the right shovels, spades, forks, and trowels for your situation. You need at least one of each.

Shovels Shovels are made for digging, lifting, and throwing soil, gravel, mulch, or other materials. The shovel you're likely to use the most for digging is a round-point shovel with an 8- or 9-inch-wide, 12-inch-long cupped blade and a handle long enough to allow you to work with minimal bending. A square-point shovel is best for lifting and moving a pile of material or for mixing concrete.

safety alert • safety alert • safety alert • safety alert •

Hand-tool etiquette

To prevent accidents, lay tools blade side down on the ground when you take a break, and bring them inside at day's end. Paint handles of small tools a bright color, or attach orange surveyor's tape so you can spot them easily amid grass or plants. Use a tool organizer bucket, a plastic storage container, or a basket to keep small tools handy and in one place.

Spades A spade differs from a shovel primarily in the shape of the blade and the angle the blade attaches to the handle. Most spades have blades that are flat, rectangular, and with a straight digging edge. However, round-point spades, also called balling shovels, are available. As to attachment, the blade is almost an extension of the handle with very little angle to it. This design of a spade eases the task of digging, especially when slicing into sod and heavy or compacted soil. Most spades have a shorter handle, ending in a D-grip, a YD-grip, or a T-grip. However, round-point spades have long, straight handles. You can also find junior spades sized smaller for a child or small adult to use; it has a T-grip, which is the easiest type for smaller hands to grasp.

Forks A garden fork resembles a spade except for the head, and it's inserted into the soil like a spade—straight up and down. But the four tines allow it to move through the soil more easily than a spade. Nothing beats a garden fork for loosening compacted soil and mixing in compost. Forks with more than four tines are made for moving light, loose material, such as compost, shredded bark, leaves, or grass clippings. There are several versions of the garden fork, including the smaller spading fork with less-durable, flatter tines. It's best suited to digging in soil that has already been improved, and for harvesting potatoes.

Trowels Trowels are essential tools for mixing small quantities of soil, digging planting holes, and mixing in granular fertilizer while you're planting. Narrower transplanting trowels dig holes for transplants and bulbs. Weeding trowels have a pointed tip to pop weeds out of the soil or from between rocks. Extra-long handles reduce the need to bend while working.

Dibbles Resembling long cigars with pointed metal ends, dibbles are useful if you have lots of holes to dig—for seeds, transplants, and small bulbs. You can make a hole quickly with one push, but it's easy to get the holes too deep. These tools are handy but not essential. You can use a trowel or your fingers instead.

Tool maintenance Shovels and spades need to be sharpened only when you see nicks or a rounded edge to the blade. Use a coarse

GARDEN GEAR

Repairing broken wooden handles

A new handle for a typical shovel costs $10 to $20, depending on its style. Take the broken handle with you while shopping to match the shape of the head end. To remove the broken handle, file or grind off the head of the shovel pin (rivet) that connects it to the wood. Then drive the handle out of the socket with a punch or short length of rebar. Tap the handle top on a board on the ground and force the head tightly onto the new handle, then drill holes for a new rivet. Insert the rivet, leaving about ⅜ inch exposed. Heat it with a small torch and then pound the hot metal with a hammer until it mushrooms, forming a tight clamp.

(Hand tools continued)

flat file to sharpen the beveled edge at the same angle as the original bevel. Hold the front end of the file at one end of the blade and push the file forward as you move it along the width of the blade from one end to the other. Then use fine-grit sandpaper to remove any burrs from the back of the blade.

Evaluate quality and comfort

To a small adult, the weight of a tool is crucial. The lighter the tool, the less it will tire and strain you. However, sometimes lightweight tools are of lower quality, because the features that add strength and durability add weight to a tool.

Heads and blades The best-quality tool heads are made from forged steel. The heating and working of the metal during forging greatly strengthens the steel. Stainless steel heads are similar but do not rust. Stamped heads and blades are cut from a single sheet of metal. These are adequate for light- to medium-duty jobs.

Attachment Where the handle joins the blade is a weak spot where a tool has the potential to break. The strongest method of attachment is solid strap. Here, the strap and the blade are forged from one piece of steel. The strap extends up from the blade and is riveted to the handle. Solid-socket attachment is the next strongest. These too are made from one piece of metal. The blade extends up into a socket into which the handle is driven. The least strongest is tang-and-ferrule. A narrow tang (or shank) is driven into the handle; a ring (or ferrule) then is wedged over the end to prevent splitting.

Handles and grips A steel handle is the strongest but also the heaviest. Fiberglass is strong and lighter than steel. Neither steel or fiberglass absorb impact as well as wood, so your arms will feel more shock from contact with rocks and hardpan. Handles made of straight-grain ash are strong and especially comfortable because they're tapered. Hickory is the next best choice for wood handles. Any flaw in the wood of a handle is a weak spot; a handle that's been painted may be hiding defects.

Handles may be a simple straight rod or they may end in a grip. YD, D, and T grips are the three most common style of grips. There is not a lot of difference in grips. Base your choice on comfort. The YD grip dissipates the twisting forces involved in digging through the handle. A solid-wood YD grip is made by splitting the handle at the end. It's important that the handle have a plug to prevent further splitting. Both YD and D grips are held in place by a rivet, which is a weak spot on the tool. A T grip has the potential to work loose.

safety alert • safety alert • safety alert • safety alert •

Hand comfort

To avoid hand or wrist injury, keep your wrist as straight as possible while you work. Wrap your thumb around the handle instead of pointing it along the handle. For added protection, wear a wrist support (available at medical supply stores) that keeps the wrist in the correct position.

Trowels and other digging tools

Digging tools vary in the size and shape
of their blades, the curvature of the blade, the
angle of its attachment, and the length of handle.

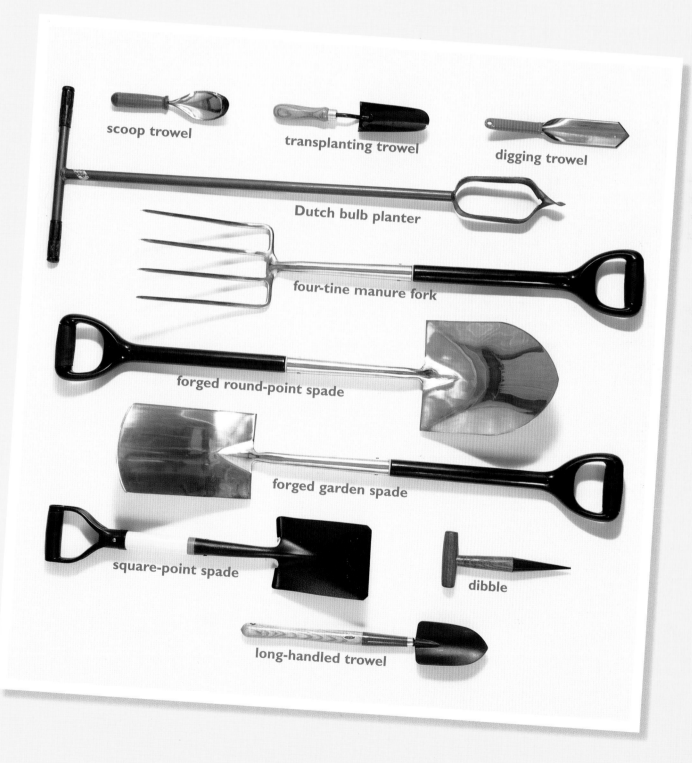

scoop trowel

transplanting trowel

digging trowel

Dutch bulb planter

four-tine manure fork

forged round-point spade

forged garden spade

square-point spade

dibble

long-handled trowel

Choosing quality tools

Superior metals and solid-piece construction
are two indicators of quality. Well-made
tools will last home gardeners a lifetime,
as well as stand up to the rigors of
professional use.

tang, no ferrule

tang-and-ferrule

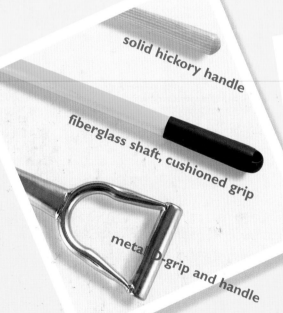

solid hickory handle

fiberglass shaft, cushioned grip

metal D-grip and handle

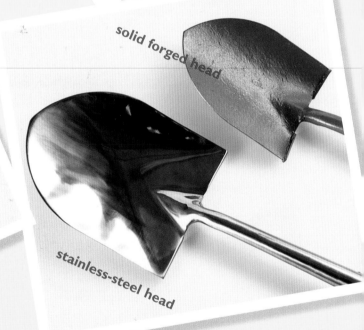

solid forged head

stainless-steel head

solid wood Y-grip handle

plastic and wood
D-grip handle

wooden T-grip handle

wrist-saver trowel

standard trowel

Tool sharpening

Digging and cultivating tools are more effective and easier on you to use when they are sharp. A light coat of oil prevents blades from rusting and handles from drying and splitting.

1 **Clean metal** Use a wire brush or wire steel attached to a bench grinder or power drill.

2 **Sharpen beveled edge** Lock the tool into a vise and use both hands to move a mill file along the edge of the blade toward the shovel's point.

3 **Remove burrs** Flip over the shovel and remove burrs on the back side of the blade with sandpaper. If any rust remains on the blade, remove it with the sandpaper. Also sand old varnish off a wooden handle.

4 **Oil blade and handle** Lightly coat the blade with machine oil. Apply several light coats of linseed oil to the handle, letting the oil soak in after each application.

5 **Grab your gear** You'll need boiled linseed oil, light machine oil, medium-grit sandpaper, steel wool, a mill bastard file (a flat file with medium to coarse serrations), a wire brush, and a vise.

Avoid overtilling

Tilling your garden more than twice a year can damage the soil and compact it just below the reach of the tines. Use a hand cultivator or weeder instead of a tiller whenever possible. Mix in organic matter whenever you till to keep the soil healthy.

Power tools

Blower-vacs, chain saws, hedge trimmers, and tillers can take the place of hand tools to make the job go faster with less effort. Maintenance and safety tips are especially crucial, because the potential for injury is greater than with hand tools. The financial investment also is greater, so you may want to add these as your needs and budget increase.

Chain saws

If you cut your own firewood or frequently need to cut tree limbs too large for other pruning tools, a chain saw might be worth the trouble and expense. Chain saws are dangerous machines that require proper care and use. If you have only occasional need for a chain saw, consider hiring an expert to do the job. If your needs warrant owning one, here are some considerations.

Electric or gas? An electric chain saw can handle light cutting jobs, and it's quiet, easy to start, and emits no fumes. A good-quality electric chain saw costs about as much as a good-quality gasoline chain saw. If you plan to cut a lot of wood, or if you need to use a saw beyond the reach of an electric cord, you need a gas-engine chain saw. Safety bears on your choice of electric versus gas, too. When you stop cutting with gasoline saw, the chain stops right away; it's slowed by friction almost the instant the clutch disengages. In contrast, chains of electric saws coast to a stop.

Sizing The longer the guide bar that holds the chain, the bigger the job it can handle. For cutting small logs and trees, choose a saw with an 8- to 12-inch guide bar. For larger logs and trees, use a saw with a 14- to 20-inch guide bar. Larger saws are for professional use.

Maintenance A chain saw requires extensive and specialized maintenance. Before every use, check the chain's tension and sharpness, and make sure nuts and screws are tight and the saw is well-lubricated. After every use, carefully wipe the bar guide with an oily rag.

Blower-vacs

This electric- or gas-engine tool cleans leaves out of areas that are difficult to reach with a rake, such as perennial and shrub beds, gutters, and roadside ditches. Models vary in size from small, cordless units to backpack versions. Electric ones are adequate for small yards. Wear good-quality ear protectors and eye goggles.

Selection of power tools

When you have a heavy task that needs doing repeatedly, it makes sense to look to a power tool. The following make up a basic outdoor power tool kit. All are available as gas- or electric-powered models.

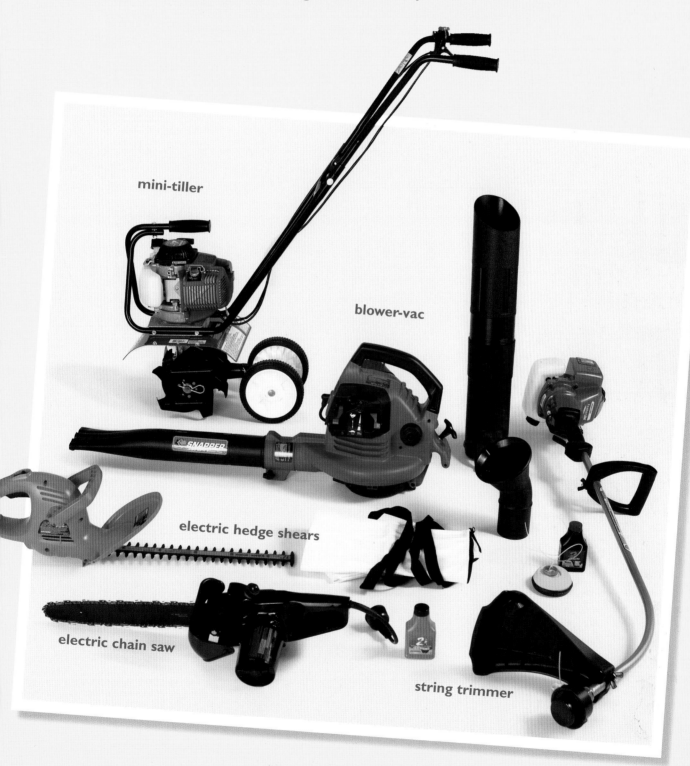

mini-tiller

blower-vac

electric hedge shears

electric chain saw

string trimmer

(Power tools continued)

Hedge trimmers

If you have more than 50 feet of hedge, use this power tool instead of hedge shears. Homeowner models can cut up to about ⅝-inch-thick stems and a 16-inch blade is adequate for most situations. Electric trimmers are lighter and less powerful than the gasoline models but they do the job adequately and are the best choice if your hedge is close enough to a power outlet. Battery-powered trimmers have a detachable, rechargeable battery instead of a cord, making them most maneuverable. These are the least powerful choice. The thicker and denser the hedge, the more power it takes to cut, so the type of hedge will determine how long the battery lasts between charges. Yew and beech are tough to cut; privet will not drain the battery as fast. Gas-engine trimmers are the heaviest and most powerful, but they can be too heavy for some people to use comfortably while reaching over a hedge.

Maintenance After every use, clean debris off cutting blades, tighten any loose nuts or screws, and wipe metal parts with an oily rag. When blades become dull, replace them.

Rototillers

A rototiller can be a worthwhile investment if you have a large garden. These machines have gasoline engines powering rotating tines that break up hardpan, mix in soil amendments, and prepare new beds. In general, the larger the tiller, the wider and deeper the swath it can till. Always cut grass or weeds before tilling them under or they are likely to wrap around the tines, stall the machine, and remain as unsightly clumps.

Mini-tillers Weighing between 20 and 30 pounds, these small tillers are ideal for working the soil in raised beds and in areas that have been previously cultivated. They reach about 6 inches deep and cut a swath 14 to 16 inches wide. The tines propel the tiller forward. Because there are no wheels, the tiller tends to bounce and till unevenly. For best results, till the area twice.

Front- and mid-tine tillers Medium-size tillers have tines in front of or below the engine, so you can till close to plants or other objects. The tines propel the machine forward like the mini-tillers, but this machine requires more strength to handle because the engine is larger, the machine is heavier, and the tines penetrate more deeply—about 8 inches. A tiller this size can be very useful if you have a large vegetable or annual flower garden.

Electric tool safety

Be mindful of the cord, especially when using sharp tools that could sever it. Put away an electric tool when the foliage or ground is wet. Use only three-prong extension cords and outlets with a ground fault circuit interrupter (GFCI) which will immediately shut off power if there's a short in the system.

Safety equipment

Gardening is relatively tame. But power equipment is noisy, and chain saws are clearly dangerous. Take a few moments to protect yourself. Know how to use the tool, then take obvious precautions.

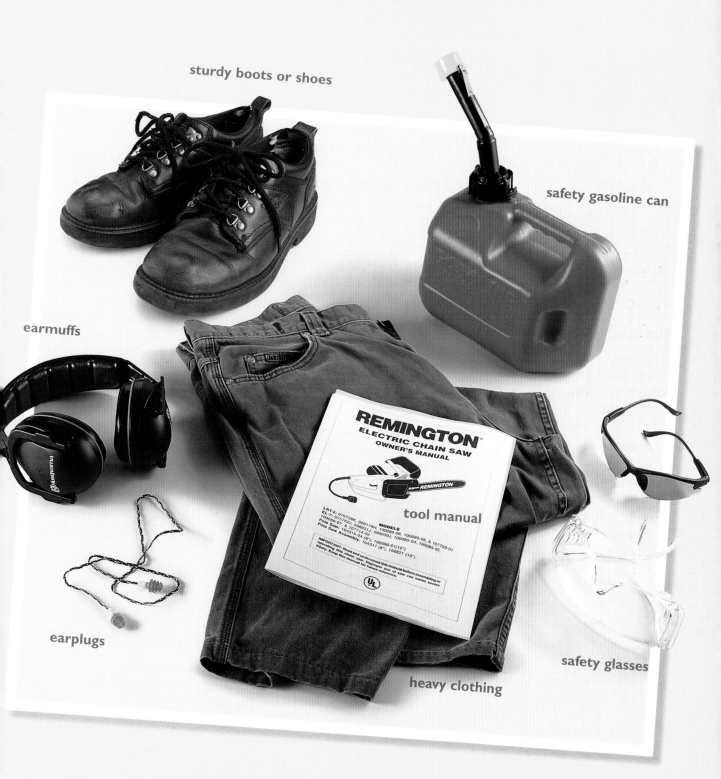

sturdy boots or shoes

safety gasoline can

earmuffs

earplugs

heavy clothing

safety glasses

(Power tools continued)

Rear-tine tillers These heavy-duty tillers, although the biggest of all, can be the easiest to operate. Unlike the other types, the motor of this tiller powers the wheels, so the tiller moves more slowly and smoothly over the ground. These are best suited for turning over unbroken ground, not for tilling in organic matter every year. Consider renting one or hiring someone to do the job for you.

Maintenance After every use, carefully clean any plant debris or wet soil off the tines. When the tines become rounded, remove them and place them in a vise. Use a coarse flat file on each tine to create a bevel of 70 to 80 degrees (not a sharp edge like pruners).

General power equipment maintenance

Spring Change the spark plug if necessary. Clean or replace the air filter (if applicable). Check safety features. With the spark plug disconnected, sharpen dull blades of tillers and mowers; replace the line in string trimmer. Change the oil on 4-cycle engines. Fill the gas tank. Clean all chain-saw fins with a brush.

Summer Before using, clean the engine cooling fins with a brush, and tighten loose nuts and bolts. Disconnect the spark plug before cleaning. Keep the oil tank full.

Fall Clean off the machine. Fill the fuel tank and add stabilizer. Disconnect the spark-plug wire and remove the spark plug. Pour a small amount of oil into the cylinder and turn the engine over several times. Reinstall the spark plug. Store in a dry, ventilated area away from any heat source.

Gloves

Working with soil can quickly dry out hands and cause cracking, not to mention leaving ground-in dirt that's hard to remove, especially under fingernails. Gloves protect hands from dirt and drying, and they provide a barrier to any questionable organisms contained in manure and compost. Gloves also help prevent blisters from using shovels, rakes, and other gardening tools.

The best garden gloves are the ones that best fit your hands and the task. If the gloves are too big, they will limit your dexterity and possibly chafe and cause blisters. Small gloves limit hand movement. No one pair of gloves will be ideally suited to all types of gardening activities. Here are the basic types of gardening gloves and the jobs for which best suited:

budget stretcher • budget stretcher • budget stretcher •

Fitting gloves

For the best fit, try on leather and cloth gloves before you buy. Make a fist and check for any pinching or bulky seams. If trying on isn't possible, hold your hand flat and measure around your hand knuckles (minus thumb) to determine the right size.

$6^1/_2$"– $7^1/_4$" = S
$7^1/_2$"– $7^3/_4$" = M
8"– $8^3/_4$" = L
9"– $9^3/_4$" = XL
10"– $10^3/_4$" = XXL
11"– $11^3/_4$" = XXXL

Everyday gloves

Cloth gloves These are suitable for light planting chores, mixing soil, digging, and raking. They can soak up water and become cold and clammy, but they can also be tossed into the washing machine. They're neither durable nor expensive, so figure on replacing them regularly. Some styles have palms and fingers reinforced with leather or latex, making them longer-lasting, better for gripping, and more impervious to prickles and thorns.

Sheepskin and goatskin gloves Stronger than cloth and very comfortable, these gloves are suited to planting and digging. Sheepskin tears more easily than other leathers, so it's less desirable for pruning trees, shrubs, and brambles. Goatskin gloves are the top of the line in comfort and dexterity. They are ideal for cutting, planting, digging, raking, and shoveling. Both sheepskin and goatskin gloves keep your hands relatively dry and remain supple even after they get wet. Some styles can be machine-washed. They do not stand up well to constant abrasion, so wear heavier-duty cowhide gloves when building a stone wall or patio.

Rubber and PVC-coated gloves Nothing beats these gloves for working with mud and prickly plants. If you are allergic to rubber, choose the PVC option. What these gloves lack in dexterity they make up for in protection. Some styles reach to your elbow.

Heavy-duty gloves

Cowhide and pigskin gloves Traditional work gloves, these are generally more durable than other leather gloves. Use them for handling wood and rocks, planting trees and shrubs, and operating power equipment. Some types are lined with fleece or wool for winter.

Neoprene and nitrile gloves These offer the best protection when working with greases, oils, herbicides, pesticides, and other caustic materials. Make sure your gloves are labeled for use with the chemicals you're using.

Taking care of gloves Knock the dirt off your gloves when you're finished for the day, and bring them inside to keep them dry. To

SMART IDEA

Chain saw safety

By far the most common cause of chain saw accidents is kickback. Kickback occurs when the chain binds up. The chain itself or its teeth may strike a hard substance or get caught in the cut.

Because the chain is moving at a high rate of speed, the whole saw will move with great force. It becomes nearly impossible to control, and may cause an injury.

Most saws in service today have safety features such as chain brakes, safety chains, and deadman switches. However, these improvements on their own are not enough to ensure the safety of the operator. You must take precautions. To avoid kickback:

■ Avoid cutting with the tip or upper quarter of the bar.

■ Use a tip guard that covers the end of the bar.

■ Operate the saw in the correct cutting position, standing at an angle to the saw so that if kickback occurs the saw will miss your head and neck.

(Gloves continued)

remove caked-on mud, dunk cloth and rubber gloves in a bucket of water. Wipe mud off leather gloves with a rag to help keep them from stiffening. Lay leather gloves flat or hang from clothespins so they keep their shape.

Sprayers

Sprayers may be made of plastic, stainless steel, or galvanized metal. Plastic is light and doesn't corrode but can absorb chemicals. Stainless steel is indestructible but heavy. In a typical gardening season, a hand sprayer and either a hose-end sprayer or a small pressure sprayer will be the most useful. Consider having two sprayers, one for spraying herbicides and one for insecticides.

Hand pump These plastic sprayers vary in capacity from a pint to a quart and have a trigger spray head that typically adjusts from a mist to a stream of liquid. Because of their limited capacity, they are useful only for small jobs. The main inconvenience of hand sprayers is that your hand can tire from squeezing the trigger.

Pressurized tank If you have more than the occasional need to spray or have large areas to cover, upgrade to a pressure sprayer. Mix the solution in the container, pump the top to create air pressure inside, then dispense the solution by squeezing the handle. Pressure sprayers for homeowner use range in capacity from 2½ pints to 4 gallons. The 3- and 4-gallon sprayers are necessary only if you are treating many trees and large shrubs or large areas of lawn. They can handle more pressure than a smaller sprayer, creating a more forceful spray that will reach farther. The length of the hose and the wand at the end of it also determine how far the spray will reach. Some models have a telescoping wand, making them more versatile. Because water weighs 8.3 pounds per gallon, 3- and 4-gallon sprayers usually come with a shoulder strap to help distribute weight.

Hose-end This type is convenient and easy to use, but it's limited to areas the hose can reach. Choose one that has an adjustment for different dilution rates. An even easier option is to buy the chemical in its own disposable hose-end sprayer, if available.

Maintenance Residue remaining in a sprayer could damage sensitive plants the next time you use it. Clean the sprayer with every use. Rinse it with soapy water several times. Run the water through the nozzle and hose as well. Hang the sprayer upside down to dry. If the nozzle is obstructed, backflush it with water. Don't try to poke out the clog; that could enlarge the hole. Nor should you blow into the nozzle.

healthy garden • healthy garden • healthy garden

Foliar fertilizing

Plants absorb nutrients through their leaves more quickly than through their roots, so use a sprayer to apply fertilizer when plants are showing signs of a nutrient deficiency or when you just want to provide a boost. Use liquid fertilizer only, and spray early or late in the day, drenching the leaves.

Wheelbarrows, carts, and more

This section is about tools that are absolutely essential—occasionally. You may not need to own these devices that enable you to manage heavy and bulky loads, dispose of quantities of leaves, or reach fruit hanging high in trees. But no section about tools would be complete without mention of some of these favorites.

Wheelbarrows

For maneuvering loads into and out of tight spaces, only a wheelbarrow will do. The tray of the wheelbarrow—either wood, galvanized steel, or plastic—can be used as a container for mixing soil, cement, or other materials, and you can pour out the contents from the front or sides. If you have lots of leaves to rake or grass clippings to collect, choose a model with a front that can rest on the ground so you can rake directly into the tray.

The wheelbarrow frame takes most of the abuse, so for heavy-duty use, choose one made of tubular steel with welded crossbars on the legs. It should have a 4-inch-thick pneumatic tire to carry the load without excessive bumping and jerking.

Carts

With four wheels instead of one, a cart is more stable than a wheelbarrow and can carry heavier loads, but it requires wider clearance. Move planters and large pots in the flat bed of a cart. Push it right up to the back of the car or truck for unloading plants or soil, bricks or lumber. Carts with a removable front panel are especially handy for dumping out the load. For balance and safety, keep the heaviest part of the load centered between the front and back wheels.

Wheelbarrow and cart maintenance Store wheelbarrows and carts upside down, or cover them with tarps so they don't collect water or debris, which can rot the wood and rust the metal parts. Wash out and dry metal carts; clean them of any adhering soil, and coat with a rust preventive. Periodically check the pneumatic tires to see if they need air. Lubricate the wheels once a year if applicable.

· **SMART IDEA** ·

Cleaner machines

In recent years the engines powering garden tools, from lawn mowers to chain saws, have been redesigned with the goal of making them less polluting. And it's worked. The typical small engine today produces 70 percent less air pollution than those of a decade ago. Here's how to do your part:

- Avoid gasoline spills by using non-spill containers and taking the extra care necessary.
- Use lead-free gasoline, 30W oil in summer, and regularly clean or replace air filters.
- For two-cycle engines, use the high-quality engine oil specifically recommended by the manufacturer.
- Keep mower blades sharp.

Children's tools

Provide children with their own tools and a place to dig. Plastic versions are safest for those younger than 5, but older children appreciate a tool that really works. Look for forged-steel heads and wooden handles, which can take some abuse. Kids older than 11 may be able to handle small versions of adult tools, such as a border spade.

(Wheelbarrows, carts, and more continued)

Speciality tools

Kneeler/seat A rectangular foam pad provides the cushioning on this lightweight seat that converts into a kneeler by flipping it upside down. You grasp the side handles to lower yourself up and down. Many variations are available, with either a plastic or tubular steel frame.

Ergonomic supports There are a variety of products on the market that make tools more comfortable to use and reduce injury. Hand trowels and cultivators are available with grips positioned above the handle so you can maneuver the tool without bending your wrist. You can buy add-on handles that attach perpendicular to the handles of long-handled tools and make them easier to hold. Cushioned grips can be slipped onto tool handles to both widen and soften the grip.

Leaf shredder Leaves can present a disposal problem for homeowners who don't have an out-of-the-way place to pile them. Many municipal landfills no longer accept yard waste. Shredders reduce the volume of leaves quickly by cutting them into smaller pieces that decompose faster. Use them as mulch, incorporate them into your garden soil, or add them to the compost pile.

A shredder with a gasoline engine is more than you need for a small yard; an electric model will do the job unless access to an outlet is limited. Shredders use either spinning nylon strings or metal blades. If twigs typically get mixed in with your leaves, choose a model with stronger metal blades. Shredder-vacs also are available; they vacuum up leaves like a blower-vac, then shred them. Chipper-shredders can handle both leaves and small branches, but they are a big step up from simple leaf shredders in size and cost. Consider renting or sharing the cost of one with a neighbor.

To maintain a shredder, clean the hopper and discharge screen (if applicable) after every use. Check the cutting parts at the beginning of each season and replace any broken ones. Follow the manufacturer's instructions for additional maintenance. Use the same safety precautions as with other power tools.

Fruit picker Popular in pick-your-own orchards, this tool reaches into trees so you can retrieve ripe fruit from the ground or from a ladder. The picking end is a wire basket or cloth bag with "fingers" that slip over the fruit and tug it from the tree. Wooden handles reach about 8 feet; telescoping aluminum handles extend up to about 17 feet.

hoses,
sprinklers&
irrigation
systems

Watering is an essential part of gardening. Here's how, and how much.

Keeping your lawn and plants healthy and green adds to your home's value and increases your outdoor enjoyment. All plants must have water to grow and thrive, and rain often provides enough. But where rainfall isn't reliable, you must supplement it with irrigation. Each type of watering system has advantages and disadvantages; some deliver water more slowly or conserve more water than others. A simple hose and sprinkler may suffice for your modest needs. Then again, your climate and lifestyle may lead you to select an underground irrigation system.

Hoses

Every homeowner needs a hose, even if only to rinse out the trash can and fill the birdbath. Hoses come in a range of sizes, compositions, prices, and quality. You have many hose accessories from which to choose, too. Some add convenience and others prolong hose life.

Selecting a hose

Choose a hose to meet your needs by considering what you will use it for, how long you expect it to last, and how much you want to spend. Start by measuring the distance from your outside faucets to the farthest part of the yard where you might use the hose.

Remember to allow for some slack at the faucet and for any objects or areas that the hose will have to circumvent, such as the garage or a flower bed. Manufacturers make 25- to 250-foot-long hoses in increments of 25 to 50 feet, although most stores sell only hoses up to 100 feet long. After measuring your yard, round up to the nearest commonly available hose length, or plan to connect shorter hoses to reach the most distant places. Keep in mind that as hoses increase in length, weight increases and water pressure decreases.

Materials Most hoses are made of polyvinyl chloride (PVC), rubber, or a combination of the two materials. PVC hoses are

▪ SMART IDEA ▪

Faucet access

Outdoor faucets are a great convenience, but can be a nuisance, even a danger, if they are poorly positioned or leaky. Make sure that the area around your faucet is safe by providing good drainage. For secure footing, use gravel or another rough surface under the faucet. A 3-foot-square duckboard pad made of preservative-treated 2×4s makes a suitable dry landing. Keep surfaces free of slippery algae. Plant shrubs and other plants away from the faucet area to give yourself room to work and store hoses. If access to the faucet is difficult, run a short length of hose to a remote faucet mounted on a hose stand or hose cart located in a more convenient place. If necessary, hire a plumber to install a new faucet where it better meets your needs.

(Hoses continued)

lightweight and inexpensive, and work best for light duty or occasional use. They should not be used for hot water and are more prone to rupturing and cracking than rubber hoses. Rubber hoses cost and weigh more but can last many years. Rubber withstands greater water pressure and temperature extremes, and remains more flexible and easy to coil at low temperatures. The most commonly available garden hoses contain layers, or plies, of both PVC and rubber. Neither rubber nor PVC hoses should be used for drinking water unless they are specifically labeled as drinking water safe. Such hoses come with a nontoxic plastic liner.

Construction For strength and durability, hoses contain multiple plies of rubber or vinyl. The number of plies varies from two in the less expensive hoses to six in the highest-quality hoses. The higher the number of plies, the stronger and heavier the hose. To prevent bursting, manufacturers add a layer of reinforcing mesh and spirally wound yarn between the layers of better-quality hoses. Some hoses also have an abrasion-resistant surface.

Flexibility The best hoses form a U-shape easily but do not kink when bent into a tight circle. Hoses that kink are difficult to coil for storage, often split under pressure, and tangle easily when used.

Diameter and length The most commonly sold hoses have an inside diameter of ⅝ inch or ¾ inch. A ¾-inch-diameter hose delivers 65 percent more water than a ⅝-inch hose. Inexpensive PVC hoses may be only ½ inch in diameter, whereas some commercial hoses can be as wide as an inch. Larger-diameter hoses deliver more water pressure and volume but weigh more than narrower hoses. For maximum water pressure, use the shortest hose length possible, because pressure decreases as you get farther from the faucet.

Fittings Hoses often fail at the end fittings when they begin to leak or become misshapen or crushed. The most durable fittings are made of heavy-duty, crush-resistant brass. Round brass fittings can be difficult to tighten and loosen, however. Look for octagonal brass fittings that you can loosen and tighten with a wrench if necessary. Plastic fittings are less durable but can be easier to manipulate. Most high-quality hoses also have a short protective collar at the female end fitting where it attaches to the faucet. The collar relieves stress on the hose and prevents kinking.

Price Generally, a higher-priced hose will last years longer than an inexpensive hose. You pay more for flexibility, strength, durability, and capacity. If you need only a short hose for occasional watering and chores, an inexpensive ½-inch PVC hose may work for you.

safety alert • safety alert • safety alert • safety alert • safety alert

Storing hoses

Coil the hose near the faucet, and pick up sprinklers when not in use to prevent tripping or damage from lawn mowers, cars, or animals. To maximize their useful life, store coiled hoses off the ground and out of direct sunlight.

For rugged, long-term use, choose a ⅝- or ¾-inch rubber and PVC hose with heavy brass fittings.

Many home and garden supply stores also sell specialty hoses, such as permanently coiled spring hoses for light-duty patio use, flat or reel-type hoses for easy storage, and porous or sprinkler hoses for special watering situations.

Repairing hoses

Repairing a good-quality hose is usually much less expensive than buying a new one. The most common and easiest to fix leak occurs at the faucet when the plastic or rubber washer inside the hose-end fitting deteriorates or is lost. Remove the old one and pop in a new one. If the hose still leaks at the faucet, you may need to replace the fitting.

Cracks and holes that appear along the hose can be repaired with tape. The advantage of tape is that the flexibility of the hose and its flow remain intact. Electrical tape will work in a pinch, but much stronger tapes are available. Check with auto repair shops for radiator hose repair tape, or plumbing supply dealers for tape that can be used in water.

For larger leaks and damaged fittings, home and garden supply stores sell hose repair kits to fit any hose or budget. Hoses come in different diameters, wall thicknesses, and materials, making the choice of fittings tricky. When replacing a hose-end fitting or mending a leak, take a short section of the hose or the damaged fitting with you to the store to be sure that you get the pieces that fit your particular hose.

▪ SMART IDEA ▪

Repairing pinhole leaks

If your hose has a pinhole leak, make a temporary repair with a wooden toothpick and some plastic electrical tape. Push the tip of the toothpick into the hole, just through the thickness of the hose wall, then break off the toothpick flush with the outer skin. When the wood becomes wet through normal use, it will swell, firmly plugging the hole.

Next, wrap the hose with hose repair tape over the hole and about 2 inches beyond each side. Stretch the tape tightly over the hole but loosely on either side; this allows the tape to expand if the hose is bent near the puncture point. For larger holes or cuts, as well as for more permanent repairs, use a hose repair kit.

You can find hose repair fittings made of plastic and brass. Some require a screwdriver for assembly; others simply hand-tighten in place. Choose the system that matches the quality of your hose and your budget. If you have an expensive, high-quality rubber hose with heavy brass fittings, buy the best quality brass repair parts. For budget-quality PVC hoses, a less expensive plastic repair kit will do. Look for basic hose repair parts at any home and garden supply store. Choices include:

(Hoses continued)

■ **Male and female hose ends. Hoses need one female fitting and one male fitting.** The female end has threads inside the fitting and is the part that attaches to the faucet. The male end has threads on the outside of the fitting and attaches to the female fittings on sprinklers and other attachments.

■ **In-line repair kits.** These kits join two pieces of hose together by clamping or screwing onto the cut ends of each piece. Use them to repair a leak in a hose or to join two shorter hose pieces together.

Hose connectors and accessories

You can make your hose easier and more convenient to use, and prolong its life and that of other attachments, by adding hose connectors and other accessories. The accessories you might consider include the following:

Quick connectors These connectors screw onto hose-end fittings, faucets, and other hose accessories and allow you to connect and disconnect the parts easily without unscrewing them. Some quick-connect hose-end fittings prevent water from flowing through them until they are connected to another fitting, making them convenient to attach to sprinklers and other accessories without turning off the water. To use, attach a male adapter to the faucet and a female adapter to the hose end and snap together. These systems are especially useful for people with limited manual dexterity or strength, and for yards with multiple hoses and accessories.

Quick connectors come in brass or plastic. Each manufacturer makes its own system, which maybe incompatible with other systems, so choose one manufacturer's system and stick with it.

Gang valves Gang valves allow you to run multiple hoses from one faucet. The simplest ones are Y-shaped and accommodate two hoses, each with its own on/off valve.

Larger gang valves have room for three or more hoses. Use these accessories in conjunction with a water timer when you have different watering zones in your yard, or when you wish to operate more than one hose at a time.

Anti-siphon and back-flow preventers These accessories stop water in a hose, which potentially could be contaminated with fertilizers or pesticides, from siphoning back into household and municipal water systems. Backflow preventers are required for installed irrigation systems, but simpler anti-siphon check valves are good investments for hoses too.

budget stretcher • budget stretcher • budget stretcher •

Winter hose care

Get a long and useful life from your garden hose by storing it in winter. First disconnect and drain it. This prevents bursting and cracking caused by swelling ice. Coil hoses once they're drained, and connect the two ends to keep the coil neat. Store hoses flat, not hanging, ideally in a garage or basement where they won't freeze.

Hose repair

Don't give up on a leaky hose, or worse, put up with one. Replacing couplings takes a few minutes at most.

1 **Cut off bad coupling** Use a sharp knife or heavy-duty cutters to slice through the hose an inch or two past the damaged coupling.

2 **Slide clamp over hose, insert new fitting** Loosen the screws on the clamp if necessary so it slides easily over the hose. Push the new coupling into the hose. It's supposed to fit tightly. Lubricating it with dish soap will help it slide in.

3 **Tighten clamp** Slide the clamp up over the internal portion of the fitting and tighten.

223

(Hoses continued)

In-line valves These allow you to turn the water on or off without returning to the faucet. Screw on one of these inexpensive devices at the end of your hose for convenience when attaching sprinklers and other accessories. Be sure to turn the water off at the faucet when finished for the day. A weak hose may rupture while unattended and waste several hundred gallons of water before you return.

Filters Filters prevent debris in your water supply from flowing through your hose and clogging sprinklers and irrigation equipment. Use them when drawing water from a spring or other nonpublic source. Simple ones made of brass mesh fit into the hose end at the faucet. Filters are a requirement for drip systems using well water.

Hose guides These go into the ground to help prevent hoses from kinking when going around corners and to protect plants from hoses dragging across them. They come in decorative and utilitarian styles.

Hose storage

You have several storage options for your hose. While coiling your hose on the ground in a shady and convenient place is okay, you can prolong its life by keeping it dry and off the ground.

Storing your hose properly prolongs its life, prevents accidents, and keeps your yard tidy. Leaving it stretched out on the ground exposes it to damaging ultraviolet rays from the sun and may promote the growth of unsightly black fungus on its surface. A hose left on your lawn can also damage or even kill the grass beneath it.

Protect hoses from cold temperatures. Water expands when it freezes, splitting hoses and cracking faucets and hose accessories. Disconnect hoses and drain them if you expect freezing weather. Store drained hoses in a basement or garage for the winter to prolong their life. Coil them loosely and remove any kinks.

Wall-mounted L-bracket The simplest and least expensive storage device is a curved piece of metal or plastic that mounts on the side of a building, or a sturdy post with a hanger bracket. Either takes up little space and can hold up to 150 feet of hose, depending on construction.

Mounted hose reel A rotating drum with a crank handle winds up to 225 feet of hose onto a wall-mounted reel. The device has a short length of hose that connects the reel to the outside faucet. The end of the garden hose attaches to an outlet on the reel. Choose from plastic or steel reels that mount parallel or perpendicular to the wall.

healthy garden • healthy garden • healthy garden

Hose guides

Make your own hose guide with an 18-inch length of ½-inch-diameter rebar and a 3-inch-diameter wooden ball. Drive the rebar into the soil at corners or where you need to protect plants, leaving about 8 inches above the soil. Slip a piece of old hose or, to dress it up, copper tubing over the rebar. Drill a hole in the ball to fit the rebar, and glue it in place.

Hose pots, hangers, and reels

Various ways to manage and store hoses have evolved to meet the basic requirements of good looks, convenience, and easy maintenance. Let your situation and preferences be your guide.

Hose pot Attractive ceramic or plastic pots blend in with plant containers and ease coiling. Most hose pots readily accommodate a 50-foot, ⅝-inch hose.

Hose hanger An elaboration on an L-bracket, the curved hanging hose holder helps maintain a hose's shape. Capacity varies with a maximum of 150 feet of ⅝-inch hose.

Hose reel cart Consider one of these if you need to move a length of hose from place to place. The largest versions handle up to 400 feet of ⅝-inch hose.

Hidden storage Benches with storage shelves, built-in benches with hinged seats, and decks with trap doors offer opportunities for storing and hiding hoses.

(Hoses continued)

Hose reel cart When you need to move your hose from one faucet to another, consider a hose cart. The plastic or steel carts have a rotating drum and handle for coiling up to 225 feet of hose, depending on the construction and type of hose. Most carts have two wheels and a stable base that rests on the ground. Some include accessory storage trays. If you have rough terrain, consider a steel cart or one with four wheels.

Hose pots To keep your hose out of sight, coil it in a hose pot or conceal it on a reel mounted inside a decorative box.

Sprinklers and nozzles

In climates where you need to water only occasionally, a sprinkler and hose may be enough to meet your needs. For watering patio containers, hanging baskets, and window boxes, or filling the birdbath, choose a nozzle attachment. Sprinklers and nozzles come in a wide range of styles.

Selecting nozzles

Nozzles work best for small watering jobs, cleaning out trash cans, washing the car, and other odd jobs of short duration. When you shop for a nozzle, consider how you plan to use it. Look for the following features:

Grip types These include straight nozzles, pistol grips, or flashlight grips. Insulated grip handles are more comfortable, especially when using cold water or working in cold weather. Choose a grip style nozzle that fits your hand size and feels comfortable to use at the end of a heavy hose. A lock allows you to run the water continuously without squeezing the trigger.

Pattern controls You'll find pattern controls in three basic styles: a single set pattern, a continuously adjustable jet- to cone-shaped pattern, or a number of set patterns on a dial.

Flow control dials Such dials allow you to adjust the volume of water at the nozzle instead of at the faucet. Usually you can shut off the water completely without changing the spray pattern or releasing the grip lock.

Selecting sprinklers

Sprinklers allow you to water an area thoroughly without holding the end of a hose. They do the best job in landscape situations where you have a large area to cover or anytime water must penetrate the soil deeply to reach plant roots. Manufacturers offer products to meet

Customize your sprinkler

Oscillating sprinklers are preferred by many for the large area they cover with a gentle, rain-like spray. Some oscillators have nozzles that you can open or close individually. This allows you to adjust the spray pattern, making it more narrow by closing the outer nozzles, for instance.

every possible landscape need. Before you head to the store, consider how and where you will use the sprinkler.

The size of the area you plan to water determines the length of the sprinkler's throw radius, or coverage area. The shape of your yard and the proximity to obstacles, pavement, and other nontarget areas should give you an idea of the sprinkler pattern you need.

Your climate may determine the most efficient sprinkler for your yard. Sprinklers that throw water high into the air lose much of it to evaporation in arid climates and do not sprinkle uniformly in windy sites.

Although you will find many different sprinklers at the garden center, they all fall into only four categories. Within each category, sprinklers vary by features and, most notably, by uniformity of coverage. These are the categories:

Oscillating Oscillating sprinklers throw water in a rectangular pattern from a perforated pipe that sweeps back and forth. You can adjust the pattern on the better models. These sprinklers are excellent for seed beds and deep soaking because of their gentle spray. They are most efficient if used in the early morning on windless days.

Stationary Stationary sprinklers offer a fixed spray pattern—usually a circle, square, or rectangle—although some models offer multiple patterns on a turret-style dial. They're inexpensive, cover areas only up to 30 feet in diameter, and lack uniform coverage.

HOW-TO

Watering smarts

Save time, keep your plants healthier, conserve water, and do it all at the same time. It's not magic, and is no more complicated than grouping sun plants with sun plants, and shade plants with shade plants. But especially in arid regions, the savings mount quickly. Group vegetables and other thirsty, exotic plants away from drying winds and shaded from the most intense sun. Still, they are going to need frequent watering, so make it easy and convenient. Set up an automated drip system, or at the least keep a hose with a watering wand nearby. Keep plants that need less water together as well. This way you're less likely to overwater some plants, or waste water and time dragging a hose around the yard.

Revolving Revolving sprinklers throw water in a circular pattern from spinning arms. Some allow you to adjust the spray nozzles to achieve a fine mist to a jet spray. The throwing action of the arms makes revolving sprinklers less uniform than most other types. An exception to this is the traveling sprinkler, which moves along the hose as it sprays to cover a larger and more uniform area.

Impulse Impulse sprinklers, (also called impact sprinklers), give the most uniform coverage of all the sprinkler types. They spray

227

(Sprinklers and nozzles continued)

pulsed drops of water in a circular pattern. You can adjust the water flow from mist to jet, and alter the spray pattern to suit your needs.

Using sprinklers

Healthy plants and efficient water use is the landscape watering ideal. To be efficient, it's important to use only as much water as you need losing the minimum to runoff or evaporation. To do your plants the most good, the water must thoroughly penetrate the soil into their root zone, usually a depth of about 8 inches, depending on the plant.

To use water efficiently, you must know how much water is reaching your plants' roots. Portable sprinklers vary in the uniformity of their spray patterns and in the amount of water they release over a given period of time. The best way to gauge the spray uniformity and measure the output of your sprinkler is to use the catch-can method. (For a picture of the set-up, see page 45.)

1. Gather six or more containers of the same size and capacity, such as straight-sided mugs or tuna cans. Place the containers at regular intervals throughout the spray pattern of your sprinkler, starting within a couple of feet of the sprinkler and extending out to the far reach of the spray. Put containers at the sides of the spray pattern as well as in the center.

2. Turn on the sprinkler and note the amount of time it takes to fill a container with an inch of water. Check the water level in all the containers to determine the uniformity of the spray pattern. If the pattern is very uneven, you will need to move the sprinkler to overlap the deficient areas.

3. To see how deep the water is soaking in, wait a few hours and then use a shovel or trowel to remove a wedge of soil near the catch can with an inch of water in it. Measure the depth of the moisture in the soil. Depending on whether your soil is sandy, clay, or something in between, the moisture will extend from a few inches to nearly a foot deep. Use this measurement and the time it took to apply the water to determine the length of time you need to let your sprinkler run to thoroughly water the plant roots.

The best time of day to water your plants is late evening (after dewfall) to early morning when the air is still and cool. Watering in the middle of the day when wind and evaporation are greatest consumes up to 15 percent more water. Watering on windy days deforms the spray pattern, making the application less uniform.

Runoff occurs when water falls on the ground faster than the soil can absorb it. When water runs off your yard into storm drains and streams, it can spread pollution from lawn and garden chemicals

time saver • time saver • time saver • time saver • time saver • time saver •

Multihose hookup

Attach several hoses to your outside faucet with a gang valve or Y-connectors to configure separate watering zones. Each outlet on the gang valve has a separate control to turn its attached hose on and off. By adding timers to each hose, you can schedule each zone to run at different times.

Hose-end nozzles and sprinklers

Automated in-ground systems notwithstanding, every garden needs the versatility of good hose-end nozzles and portable sprinklers.

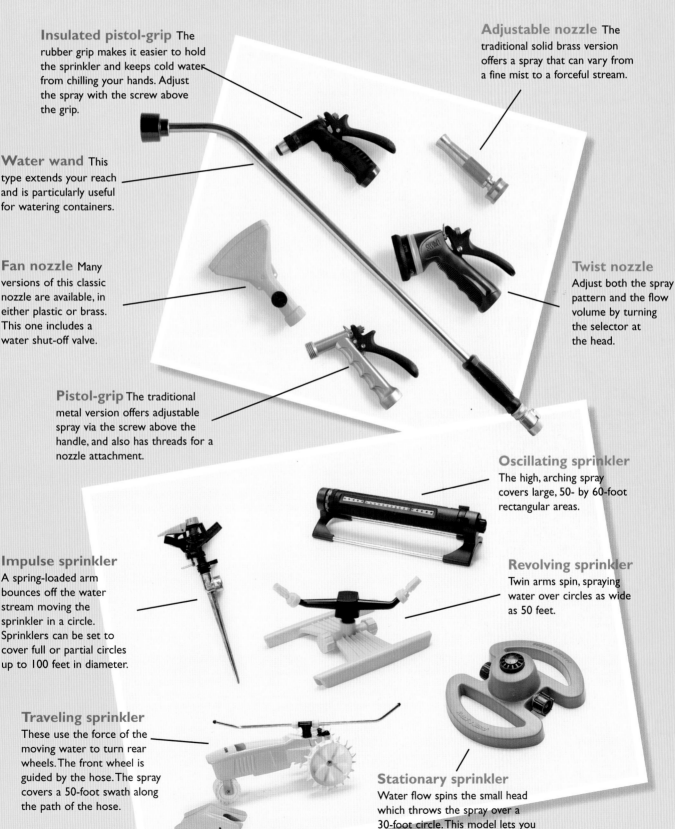

Insulated pistol-grip The rubber grip makes it easier to hold the sprinkler and keeps cold water from chilling your hands. Adjust the spray with the screw above the grip.

Adjustable nozzle The traditional solid brass version offers a spray that can vary from a fine mist to a forceful stream.

Water wand This type extends your reach and is particularly useful for watering containers.

Fan nozzle Many versions of this classic nozzle are available, in either plastic or brass. This one includes a water shut-off valve.

Twist nozzle Adjust both the spray pattern and the flow volume by turning the selector at the head.

Pistol-grip The traditional metal version offers adjustable spray via the screw above the handle, and also has threads for a nozzle attachment.

Oscillating sprinkler The high, arching spray covers large, 50- by 60-foot rectangular areas.

Impulse sprinkler A spring-loaded arm bounces off the water stream moving the sprinkler in a circle. Sprinklers can be set to cover full or partial circles up to 100 feet in diameter.

Revolving sprinkler Twin arms spin, spraying water over circles as wide as 50 feet.

Traveling sprinkler These use the force of the moving water to turn rear wheels. The front wheel is guided by the hose. The spray covers a 50-foot swath along the path of the hose.

Stationary sprinkler Water flow spins the small head which throws the spray over a 30-foot circle. This model lets you connect a series of sprinklers.

229

(Sprinklers and nozzles continued)

and fertilizers, and harm the environment. Clay soil takes longer to absorb water than sandy soil, and may need multiple shorter applications instead of one long watering session. Apply water only until it begins to puddle, then turn off the water and wait until the soil absorbs the water before continuing. Check the depth of the soil moisture and apply only as much water as necessary to the root zone of the target plants.

To conserve water, adjust the spray pattern of your sprinklers so that water falls only on the plants you intend to water. If you cannot adjust the spray pattern, consider purchasing a model that does allow adjustment, such as an oscillating or impact sprinkler. Water that falls on streets, driveways, sidewalks, buildings, and other nontarget areas is wasted and can also lead to pollution from car fluids and other chemicals that wash into downstream waterways.

Fixing clogs and leaks

Water must pass through fine holes in sprinklers and hose-end nozzles, and debris in the water clogs the small openings. To keep dirt and debris out of your hose, keep the open ends of the hose off the ground, and run water through the hose before attaching a sprinkler or nozzle if you suspect that dirt has entered the hose.

If you use irrigation water from a well, you may need particle filters to screen out debris. Purchase faucet screens at any plumbing supply store and install them at the end of the hose that attaches to the faucet. Choose a fine mesh size, such as 150 to 200 openings per inch, for mist sprinklers, soaker hoses, and drip irrigation systems. Check and clean the screens regularly to prevent clogging. If a sprinkler or nozzle becomes plugged, disassemble the spray parts or open them to their widest diameter and back-flush them with water. If lime deposits from hard water accumulate in your hose-end nozzle, you can dissolve the deposits by soaking the nozzle in commercial lime remover or full-strength vinegar. Do not use these products on aluminum, which corrodes when exposed to acid.

If your sprinkler or nozzle leaks at the hose attachment, change or add a rubber washer, or wrap the threads with Teflon tape, which is available at plumbing supply stores.

safety alert • safety alert • safety alert • safety alert •

Drinking water safety

Water in most garden hoses can pick up traces of the chemicals in the PVC or rubber lining, making it unsafe to drink. (Hoses sold as drinking water safe have an inert plastic lining.) Hoses can also pick up unhealthy substances from the ground, such as lawn and garden chemicals and animal waste.

Underground sprinklers

Underground sprinkler systems add convenience and the assurance that your valuable lawn and landscape plants will receive the water they need, when they need it. Once the system is in place and programmed for a sprinkling schedule, it may need little further input for weeks or even months. But to operate efficiently, your system must be monitored for leaks and over- or under-watering, and reset periodically to account for changes in your landscape, seasons of the year, and other factors. It's important to know all the parts of your irrigation system and how they work so that you can make adjustments and minor repairs as needed.

Understanding underground sprinklers

Sprinkler systems use high water pressure to force irrigation water through buried pipes and out of sprinkler heads. The water passes through a number of components from the time it enters the irrigation system to its exit onto the landscape. Here's an overview of the system parts, starting at the water source:

Hookup to water main The beginning of the irrigation pipe should be connected to the main water service line that comes into your property, either near your water meter or the main shutoff valve for the house. It will be located after the main shutoff valve and should have a shutoff valve of its own. In some warm-climate installations, the hookup may be outside the house near a faucet. The pipe may be plastic or metal.

Pipes or lines If you have more than one zone in your system, the main line or pipe from the house will divide into header lines—one for each zone. Lateral lines that feed the sprinkler heads branch off the header lines. Sprinkler heads connect to the lateral lines by riser pipes. Riser pipes may be rigid or flexible, and some have a built-in height adjustment. Each lateral line can have a number of sprinkler heads on it.

Drain valve At the lowest part of the system, usually near the shutoff valve, you may find a drain valve that allows you to empty

• HOW-TO •

Watering math

Lawns and many other landscape plants need an inch of water a week during the growing season. How much is that? If you have a rain gauge—and if it rains—just read the gauge. An inch of water per square foot is just shy of two-thirds of a gallon (.624 to be exact). Therefore, 1,000 square feet of lawn or garden needs 624 gallons of water per week, on average.

If you can't count on rain and need to irrigate, it helps to know how much water is needed. To figure approximately how many gallons of water are needed, calculate the area of your garden (length × width) and multiply that number by .624. To calculate the number of cubic feet (as on most water bills), divide the number of gallons by 7.48.

(Underground sprinklers continued)

the water from the system. If you live in a climate where the ground freezes, you need to drain the water from the system in the fall to prevent damage from frozen water.

Pressure regulator This device prevents excess water pressure from damaging your system. If you have one, it's probably located right after the irrigation shutoff valve.

Backflow preventer Several different kinds exist, but all types will be installed somewhere on the main line in front of the separate zone pipes that go out to the sprinkler heads. Nearly all types must be elevated at least 6 inches above the height of the highest sprinkler head. Backflow preventers keep contaminated irrigation water from flowing back into the household or municipal water supply. All irrigation systems must have one, but municipalities may require or prohibit particular types. The two most common types are the pressure vacuum breaker and antisiphon valves. If your system has a pressure vacuum breaker, you will find just one of them near the beginning of the system, somewhere after the pressure regulator or main shutoff. Systems that use antisiphon valves must have one for each zone of the system. They will be located just past the control valve at the junction of each zone and the main irrigation line.

Control valves If your system has more than one zone off the main irrigation line, you will have automatic or manual control valves that turn each zone on and off. The valves for multiple zones may be grouped together in what is called a manifold. If you have a large yard, you may have manifolds in the front yard and backyard. In an automatic system, each control valve is wired to the master controller and can be programmed to operate independently. Some control valves have built-in antisiphon backflow preventers. Control valves are installed between the header pipe for the zone and the lateral lines that feed the sprinkler heads.

Sprinkler heads Water is ejected from the sprinkler heads and onto your lawn and landscape plantings. Although manufacturers offer scores of different heads, they all fall into one of three main categories, based on how they distribute water. A rotary head resembles an impact sprinkler and shoots out a single jet or multiple jets of water, then slowly rotates to cover a large area around it. Rotary heads are most commonly used for large lawns, parks, and golf courses. Spray heads produce a fine, uniform spray of water that covers an area up to 15 feet away. Most residential systems use this type. Bubbler heads resemble spray heads, but the water floods the ground in a relatively small area instead of spraying outward.

Cycle your sprinkler

Allow water to sink deeply into the soil without puddling or running off by cycling your irrigation system on and off. Use an automatic timer to run the water until it just begins to puddle, then shut it off for an hour or two. Repeat until moisture reaches the target depth.

Installing underground sprinklers

Planning and installing a permanent, underground watering system requires effort. But once up and running it will save you time and energy for years to come.

1 Parts All underground systems have essentially the same parts: tubing, heads, backflow preventer (or antisiphon valve), controllers, and a means to drain the system.

2 Control valve Sprinklers are grouped into circuits so only parts of a yard are watered at a time. Control valves govern the opening and closing of each circuit.

3 Tubing, Ts, and lateral lines Irrigation tubing is buried 6 to 10 inches deep. You can send a circuit into multiple directions with lateral lines, which branch off the main line with Ts and Ys.

4 Backflow preventer Sprinkler systems often connect to the main water supply for the house. A backflow preventer (upper left) must be installed between this connection and the rest of the system. It prevents water within the pipes, which may be contaminated with landscape chemicals or deicing salts, from flowing back into the main supply. To the right of the valve is a coupler, which allows the pipes to be drained to avoid freezing in winter.

5 Sprinkler heads Heads are available in a myriad of styles from popup to stationary, with rotating or fixed patterns, and varying rates of flow. This variety allows you to customize the setup exactly to your yard's requirements. And it results in the most efficient use of water.

233

(Underground sprinklers continued)

Sprinkler heads may pop up from beneath the soil or remain fixed just above the soil. They may distribute water in any pattern, depending on the manufacturer or setting in the field. Your system may use any or all of the different types, but only a single type of head will be on one zone.

Irrigation designers and installers customize each system to fit the property where it will be used. Although the main components of an irrigation system remain the same, you will find a wide variation in the products, techniques, and configurations used in individual systems. Whenever possible, obtain and keep all records about the components, installation, and settings of your system, including product brands and models.

Maintaining a sprinkler system

Sprinkler systems need occasional adjustment and maintenance due to changes in plant growth, the season of the year, and unexpected problems. You can do many of these adjustments yourself, but some may require the help of a professional. Some of the most common problems that you may see and their causes include the following:

Dry spots Lawns develop dry spots when the sprinkler heads deliver water unevenly. Possible reasons for this situation include windy weather; inadequate water coverage due to poorly spaced sprinkler heads or water pressure changes; external obstructions in the spray pattern, such as foliage; and internal blockage from debris inside the sprinkler. If the weather has been drier than usual, your system may not be delivering enough water to maintain the regular level of soil moisture.

Wet spots or puddles When water accumulates faster than the soil can absorb it, wet spots and puddles develop. Causes can include leaking of joints, or valves, holes in any part of the system, irregular sprinkler coverage from wind or external obstructions, and improper adjustment of the heads or timer. You may have to adjust your watering frequency and delivery rate to accommodate soil type and changing weather.

Stuck heads Sand or other debris trapped in the sprinkler body or in wiper seals, which prevent dirt from entering the sprinkler body, may cause heads to not pop up or retract. Turn on the sprinkler and press the head down gently into the fitting a couple of times to dislodge the debris. If the sprinkler head is badly scratched or the wiper seal is damaged, you may have to replace those parts. Some sprinkler heads do not have retraction springs and frequently

budget stretcher • budget stretcher • budget stretcher • budget stretcher

Seasonal tweaks

Monitor the soil moisture and the condition of your landscape plants and irrigation system weekly to be sure that plants receive the correct amount of water. With growth and seasonal changes, plants need more or less water. Check for uniform and efficient irrigation, and unplug or correct any trouble spots.

remain in the up position. You can replace them with spring-loaded pop-up sprinkler heads.

Nonworking circuits or zones When a circuit or zone stops working, suspect problems with the control valve for that zone. Problems often include low water pressure, faulty control wires or solenoids, or blockages in the system. If water gets inside the wire connections on the valve, they will eventually corrode, ruining the solenoid.

You can correct many of these problems yourself. Try these solutions before calling in a professional:

Sprinkler heads Remove debris from sprinkler heads and valves by taking the head or valve apart and carefully cleaning filter screens and outlets. Follow the manufacturer's instructions.

Flow control valve Adjust the valve to correct the amount of water that reaches the sprinklers. Most valves have a handle, screw, or special key fitting in the center of the valve that you turn. Make the adjustments with the sprinklers turned on so that you can see the results. Be aware that overtightening the screw can crack the valve.

Spray pattern Follow the manufacturer's directions to adjust the spray pattern of individual sprinkler heads. Many heads have fixed patterns and cannot be adjusted.

Pipes Excavate the soil away from the area with the broken or leaking pipe. Cut out the damaged section with a hacksaw. Clean dirt and grit off the ends of the pipes that remain. Slip repair couplings over the ends of the pipe and connect a short section of new pipe to them. Apply primer and solvent, according to package directions, if repairing a PVC pipe. Use screw clamps to tighten the new fittings on polyethylene pipe. Test the line for leaks before burying it. You may be able to repair small punctures with a hole plug.

Controller problems When your automated electronic controller fails, it may indicate an electrical failure in some part of the system,

SMART IDEA

Pressure changes

You can thank gravity for the fact that water pressure increases as water flows downhill. Gravity is also the reason that water pressure decreases as water is pushed uphill. Friction is the reason water pressure decreases in a pipe on level ground. Pressure-regulating drip irrigation emitters automatically compensate for the pressure changes so that all the plants on a given circuit receive the same amount of water. But regular sprinklers and soaker hoses are unable to compensate for pressure changes, meaning you have to plan for the discrepancy.

If you're planning a sprinkler system, use the manufacturer's tables to look up compensating factors to use, and avoid long soaker hoses.

Automatic container watering

In hot, sunny weather, plants in containers may need watering twice a day to prevent wilting. Use drip irrigation and an automatic timer to water them regularly. Place one drip emitter in each hanging basket (a microspray stake is more appropriate for pots with very porous, well-drained soil media.) Large pots and long window boxes may need two or three emitters. Select a timer that will briefly cycle on and off at least twice a day.

(Underground sprinklers continued)

usually at the control valves. It's best to call a professional to troubleshoot and fix electrical problems or any other malfunction that eludes a simple repair.

Choosing a contractor

When hiring a contractor, whether to repair or maintain an existing system or to design and install a new one, it's important to find qualified professionals. Sprinkler irrigation systems are complex to design and install, and they require knowledge of soils, plants, hydraulics, electricity, plumbing, local regulations and codes, irrigation products, and more. The professional who designs your system may not necessarily be the person you choose to do the installation. You may choose to hire a landscape architect, a landscape designer, or certified irrigation contractor.

After you have an irrigation layout plan, put the installation out for bid. When shopping for a contractor to install or maintain your system, insist on the following qualifications and standards:

■ **Proof of liability insurance and bonding.**

■ **Licenses required by your state or municipality, including business, plumbing, and electrical. Irrigation industry certification is a plus.**

■ **Verifiable references and a portfolio of finished work. Check out the references.**

■ **Written bids with details of services and products spelled out. Be sure that the bid meets all the requirements of your plan.**

■ **Professional appearance and behavior.**

■ **Written contract that specifies materials and scope of the work; payment arrangements; time line, including when the job will start and how long it will take to complete; warranty for the work and materials; and a guarantee that the contractor will obtain the proper permits, follow the local requirements, and clean up debris.**

Drip irrigation

This is the most efficient watering system gardeners can use for trees, shrubs, gardens, and even container plants. Although similar in some respects to buried sprinkler systems, drip systems differ in important ways: The entire irrigation system can remain above ground, and water is applied directly to the soil under low pressure instead of being sprayed into the air.

Using drip irrigation

The easiest system to set up and use is soaker hose. These pipes come in ¼-, ½-, and ⅝-inch diameters and usually are made of porous rubber. Water oozes out through the pipe walls and can irrigate the soil in a strip 2 to 3 feet wide, making soaker hoses efficient and useful for watering flower and vegetable gardens, trees and shrubs, and narrow planting beds.

Soaker hoses operate at 5 to 15 pounds of water pressure per square inch. Most need a pressure regulator to reduce normal household pressure and prevent the hoses from bursting. To ensure even water coverage, each soaker hose should be no longer than 100 feet and should be laid on level ground. To set up a soaker hose, lay the hose where you want it and hold it in place with U-shaped wire earth staples. You may also bury the hose a few inches deep or cover it with mulch.

The second type of drip irrigation uses drip emitters connected to plastic pipes. Soak systems deliver water slowly so are ideal for clay and other less permeable soils.

Here are the main components of a drip system, beginning at the water source:

■ **The main line from the water source will probably be ½-inch polyethylene pipe. You may need a section of larger-diameter pipe or fittings to connect to the faucet.**

■ **Lateral lines branch off the main line and are connected to it with T fittings. Lateral lines may be further divided into narrower-diameter pipes, depending on the system. To irrigate areas wider than 3 feet, run lateral lines parallel to one another.**

▪ SMART IDEA ▪

Easygoing drip

Drip irrigation systems are a good idea for several reasons, but mostly because they help the plant roots get more water and less is wasted to runoff or weeds. Drip irrigation systems are common in arid regions, but they also find favor where soils are heavy, slow-absorbing clay and where small wells provide a limited amount of water flow. The easiest way to get started with drip irrigation is with drip tape or emitter lines. These have factory-installed, clog-free emitters at predetermined intervals. Use them around trees, shrubs, flower and vegetable gardens, and narrow plantings near buildings. For durability, choose drip tape with thick walls. If you don't like the look of the plastic pipe snaking through your garden, cover it with an inch of mulch.

(Drip irrigation continued)

■ Emitters or water outlets fit into the lateral lines, either directly or at the ends of short, narrow tubing called spaghetti tubes. Spaghetti tubes work best for containers and other places where they are unlikely to be damaged by yard and garden tools or animals. You can choose from two types of emitters: pressure compensating or regular. The pressure regulating types maintain the same drip capacity regardless of changing water pressure, making them useful for installations where the elevation changes from one end of the system to the other, including for hanging baskets. Emitters are rated based on the amount of water they allow to pass through, usually 1/2 gallon, 1 gallon, or 2 gallons per hour. Use the lower-capacity emitters near plants requiring less water and higher capacity emitters near plants requiring more water to tailor your drip system to your landscape plantings. Some systems use emitters that are incorporated directly into the pipe at predetermined intervals. For customized systems, however, you can insert emitters wherever you want them, using either in-line or punch-in types. You can also find microsprinkler emitters, which work much like a regular sprinkler but at lower pressure. Microsprinklers are well suited to sandy, well-drained soils. Water drains downward so quickly that it does not move well laterally (sideways), making root zone coverage with an emitter difficult. The spray pattern of the microsprinkler allows it to cover a larger root zone area in these situations.

■ Backflow preventers keep irrigation water from flowing back into the main water source and causing contamination. Install one right after the faucet or water source.

■ Pressure regulators reduce normal household water pressure to a lower, safer level for drip irrigation (usually 20–30 psi). Install one on the main line after the backflow preventer.

■ Screens and filters prevent small bits of soil and debris from clogging the emitters. Insert a filter into the system before branching off to the drip zones. The filter should be at least 150 openings per linear inch (150 mesh). The time interval between filter cleanings will depend on the quality of your water source.

■ Adapters and fittings allow transitions from the water source to the narrower irrigation pipes.

Calculating the capacity and number of emitters to use in each situation can be complicated. For help designing a custom system for your garden or landscape, hire an irrigation professional. Take a map of your yard, showing distances and locations of water sources, obstacles, and areas to be watered. When purchasing a system, it's a good idea to choose one manufacturer for all your system parts because parts may not be compatible between manufacturers.

Maintaining drip irrigation systems

To prevent clogging, flush out the system once a month. Clean or backwash the filter, then remove the end caps and pressure regulator from the lines and run water through the system until it runs clear. If water is flowing out of a soaker hose at a lower volume than it

budget stretcher • budget stretcher • budget stretcher

Kits or custom?

Irrigation system kits are tempting because you're assured of having a complete, functioning system in the box. On the other hand, a kit may not fit your needs exactly. Some kits are designed to work only with the number of emitters included. If you expand the system, it won't function properly. Drip systems are easy to assemble, and buying parts individually is likely to save you money.

Drip system for containers

Container plants need small amounts of water frequently, which is why an automated drip system is so practical for them. You can easily set up a system like this in a day.

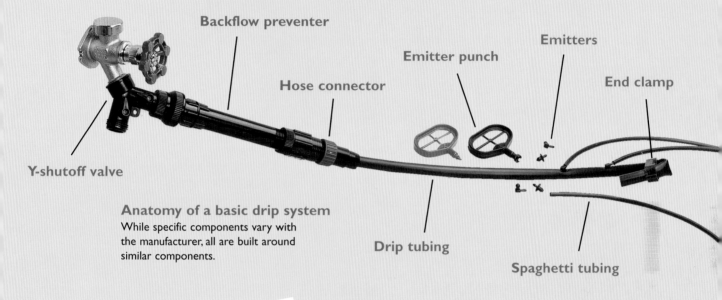

Backflow preventer

Emitters

Emitter punch

Hose connector

End clamp

Y-shutoff valve

Anatomy of a basic drip system
While specific components vary with the manufacturer, all are built around similar components.

Drip tubing

Spaghetti tubing

1 Automatic shutoff Set the timer and turn the water on. Valve will shut off according to time elapsed or water consumed.

2 Run drip tubing Bring a line from the nearest convenient location to where your container plants are grouped. Slip on an end clamp.

3 Add emitters Use a punch to make a hole in the drip tubing in order to connect ¼-inch tubing .

4 Place drip line in pot An easy way to hide the emitter is to thread the tubing up through the pot's drainage hole, but this requires that the pot be slightly elevated (you can buy "pot feet" for this purpose) to keep the tube from flattening.

5 Raised pot Neatly hidden from sight, tubing disappears below a deck. Beyond basic black, drip tubing is available in colors such as brown and white to better match house colors.

(Drip irrigation continued

once did, flush it out as described. Check the flow from drip emitters every few weeks by measuring their output along the system. Catch the emitted water in a small container for a specific period of time and compare the outputs of different emitters. Flush the system or unplug the emitters if some emitters in the system fail to work or have low output. Remove plugged emitters and soak them in water to remove the debris, or blow through them. Replace with new or spare emitters. If your emitters need frequent unplugging, shop for self-cleaning emitters, or upgrade your filter.

If you live where the watering season ends in the fall and freezing weather is ahead, roll up the drip lines and store them for the winter. Otherwise mice and other rodents may chew holes in the pipes.

Automating sprinkler systems

Adding a timer to your irrigation system can save you time and water if set up and used properly. You can choose from a wide range of prices and features, depending on your watering system and individual needs.

When shopping for an automatic water timer, consider what kind of irrigation system you have, how often you will use it, and how much time you have to monitor your system. Prices vary widely with the level of automation, quality of the components, and number of features and accessories you choose.

The simplest water timers for hose-and-sprinkler and drip irrigation systems work like mechanical kitchen timers. They attach to the system between the faucet and the hose and shut off the water when the timer runs out. You can choose from two types: one kind measures the amount of water and the other measures the amount of time. To operate, simply twist the dial to set the number of gallons or hours to operate. These inexpensive timers can only shut off the water, however, and must be set each time you use them. They are useful when you water at night or any other time when you won't be available to shut off the water.

Electronic, battery, or electrically operated water timers can turn the water both on and off. You can program most models to cycle on and off many times a day, and choose which days of the week you want to irrigate. In portable hose-and-sprinkler systems, the unit fits between the hose and the faucet and controls only one zone, like a mechanical timer. Some offer a mist feature that turns the water on briefly several times an hour, making them useful for establishing new lawns. Some offer accessories, such as soil moisture or rain

healthy garden • healthy garden • healthy garden

Sensing soil moisture

Invest in a sensor that measures the soil moisture and overrides your automatic timer to prevent overwatering. Without a sensor, the automatic timer applies water regardless of rainfall and other weather conditions. The excess water may run off, resulting in waste and possible pollution from fertilizers and lawn chemicals.

Water timers

Sprinkler controllers are essential for gardeners who travel frequently or who simply don't want to spend much time managing sprinklers. The options range from the simple to elaborate.

Battery-powered timer No wiring or setup is required beyond inserting batteries. Program it to operate portable or drip sprinklers on a fixed schedule.

Volume regulator Some portable sprinklers include built-in timers. Set them for the length of time or amount of water to apply and they turn themselves off.

Multistation timer Located in the garage or basement, they operate more than one watering circuit. Some go further, allowing two or more watering programs.

Making connections Multistation timers are complicated pieces of equipment. It's smart to hire an irrigation contractor to set up the circuits for you. But once that's done, setting the timer is a breeze.

(Drip irrigation continued)

sensors that override the programmed irrigation schedule to prevent watering when none is needed.

Buried sprinkler systems have even more choices available for controlling water distribution. Some work much like those for hose-and-sprinkler systems; others can control many zones. These low-voltage, multistation controllers electronically turn water valves on and off in each part of the system, and each zone can have a different schedule. You can even control some from your home computer. Get more information about the options for your system from your installer or a professional who is familiar with your setup and needs.

Programming automatic timers

Automatic timers save time and water, but only if they are programmed and managed properly. (Everyone has laughed at the sprinklers coming on during a rain). Ideally, you want the sprinklers to come on only when plants need the additional water. The amount of irrigation water your landscape needs changes with the temperature, the amount of natural rainfall, the type of plants and their stage of growth, and the soil type.

First, consider attaching the timer to sensors that can detect dry soil, rain, or both. Then program the timer to water every day. The sensors will override the timer whenever the soil is moist.

Short of using sensors, monitor and record the amount of time or gallons of water needed to obtain the desired level of soil moisture in different situations, and also the amount of time it takes for the soil to dry out after irrigation. Use your records to set the timer so that your system will deliver the correct amount of water to moisten the soil to a depth of 6 to 8 inches.

Water as seldom as possible to promote a healthy landscape. Newly established plants and new sod may need daily water for a week or so, but daily watering of established landscapes promotes shallow root growth and results in poor plant health. Use these rules of thumb, depending on climate and water need: Irrigate clay or loam soils once or twice a week. Sandy or sandy loam soils should be irrigated two to three times a week. Check the depth of the soil moisture regularly. Change the timer's program as needed.

Favorite programs

In the world of irrigation timers, a program is a watering schedule. If your timer has one program and six stations, you can only set the amount of time each station should run. Each time the timer begins, all six stations will run, irrigating for the time you have set for each one. A multiprogram timer allows more flexibility, allowing you to program zones for different days, times of day, and irrigation length of time. Many new timers have at least three programs for flexible scheduling.

Water conservation

In some regions, water is always a scarce and expensive commodity; other places experience only occasional drought. But even where water appears ample, watering landscape plants often has hidden costs. Water used for watering lawns and shrubs is water lost for drinking, manufacturing, and agriculture. Wasting water depletes the underground supply and contributes to the contamination of rivers and other aboveground water sources.

Reducing water use

Many strategies exist for decreasing water use in your garden and landscape. Some require only a change of habits. Other techniques involve choices in watering equipment, plants, and other landscape features.

Use efficient watering techniques Drip irrigation and soaker hoses lose less water to evaporation than overhead sprinklers, as does applying water early in the morning and in the evening instead of watering in the heat of mid-day. Drip irrigation and soaker hoses also apply water only where it's needed. Irrigate only when the soil is dry, and avoid relying solely on automatic timers. See "Using sprinklers" on page 228 for more information.

Avoid runoff Turn off the sprinklers as soon as puddles begin to form, to allow water to soak into the soil. Apply water slowly to clay soils, and use berms to retain water on hillsides. Also monitor the moisture in the soil, and stop watering when it reaches the desired depth. Adjust sprinklers so that water falls only on target areas, avoiding driveways and other pavement.

Group plants by water needs Organize your landscape into planting zones based on water needs. Group plants with high water requirements in one zone, those with moderate needs in another zone, and the most drought-tolerant in a third zone. This system simplifies watering and conserves water.

Choose locally adapted plants Plants that are native to your area or places with a similar climate will thrive without additional

· SMART IDEA ·

Irrigating with well water

If you plan to use well water with your drip irrigation system first check your water for iron content. Iron will remain dissolved in water and move through filters until it contacts air. It then oxidizes into solid iron oxide. Iron usually does not cause a problem (except for unsightly staining of driveways or plants in some cases), but the small openings in drip systems make them susceptible to plugging from iron. The iron oxidizes as it touches air—right in the emitter outlet—and plugs up the emitter over a short time. If your water contains more than 0.3 parts per million of iron, you will need some type of water treatment to use drip irrigation. Water with less than 0.1 ppm will not cause a problem.

(Water conservation continued)

water. Ask at local nurseries for plants that require little water after they become established.

Reduce your lawn area Retain only enough lawn for your needs, and replace the rest with landscape plants that require less water. You can find many attractive ground covers, perennial plants, shrubs, and trees with low water—and maintenance—needs. Some turfgrasses require much less water than others and may be more suitable for your climate.

Use mulch Bare ground gives up water to evaporation and weed growth. Cover the soil among landscape plants with organic mulch, such as bark or seed hulls, to conserve water and keep down the weed population.

Shelter plants with a windbreak Plants lose more water in windy sites. Reduce the wind velocity in your yard with a windbreak fence or hedge, and put the thirstiest plants in sheltered spots. To reduce water loss in winter, wrap dormant evergreen shrubs with burlap.

Improve your soil Soil that contains plenty of organic matter holds moisture better than depleted soils. Apply compost, aged manure, shredded leaves, and other organic materials around landscape and garden plants, and mix it into the soil at every opportunity.

Free water

The traditional source of free water is rain collected in a cistern or barrels. Set a rain barrel under the downspout and dip the water out with a watering can, or attach a spigot near the bottom of the barrel that will accept a hose. Cover the top of the downspout with a screen to filter out debris. You can connect multiple barrels with PVC pipe for more storage. Cover the barrels securely to deter mosquitoes, small animals, and children.

Graywater is the soapy used water collected from the washing machine, shower, or bathtub. Using it involves plumbing that can divert the desired water through a filter and onto the landscape. Gray water is safe to use on nonedible plants and should be applied below ground via a filtered drip irrigation system or directly to the soil, never through sprinklers. Some communities prohibit or regulate the use of graywater, so check with the health officer in your town before setting up a graywater recycling system. For more information, contact a licensed plumber or county extension agent.

healthy garden • healthy garden • healthy garden

Graywater savvy

Using it to water plants makes good sense wherever water supplies are limited or often interrupted. But you'll need to think twice about what you send down the drain. Soaps and detergents that contain boron, bleach, or sodium will harm plants, but similar ones containing potassium or magnesium do not.

water
features
& ponds

Healthy water gardens need little maintenance. Here's how to get yours in shape, and keep it that way.

A well-maintained pond adds value to your home and provides a tranquil retreat. Small water gardens take only minutes of care a week. Larger ponds and those with fish can require an hour or more to maintain, but they reward your efforts with color, movement, and an even more dramatic element for your landscape. With some care and a few hours of work, even neglected ponds can come alive again and resume their place as jewels in your landscape.

Caring for ponds

Ponds, whether installed in the ground or raised slightly above it, require maintenance throughout the year. The amount of time required by yours depends on its size, location, construction, and contents. The basic parts of a pond that need regular attention include the liner, edging, pump, filter, plants, and fish.

Most ponds have a liner made of flexible synthetic rubber or PVC sheeting, or rigid plastic or fiberglass, to contain the water and prevent it from leaking into the surrounding soil. Both flexible and rigid liners usually rest on a bed of sand covered by an underlayment or pad to protect the liner from stones. Some ponds may be lined with clay or concrete, although this is less common. Stones or concrete pavers are used to disguise the pond's edge where the liner meets the lawn or garden surrounding it. The edging also helps to prevent surface water from draining into the pond and possibly contaminating it with soil, fertilizer, or lawn chemicals.

Routine pond maintenance

Large ponds often need less frequent attention than small ponds, because the greater volume of water leaves them more stable. The ecology and chemistry of a small volume of water are more prone to fluctuate. Weekly chores vary throughout the year, but they fit a predictable pattern. The most time-consuming jobs take place at the beginning and end of the growing season in cold-winter climates.

▪ SMART IDEA ▪

Still waters breed mosquitoes

Mosquitoes are unpleasant, cause allergic reactions, and carry diseases. If you suspect that mosquitoes are breeding in your pond, here's what to do: Mosquitoes won't lay eggs in moving water, so add a fountain, bubbler, or anything that will keep the water circulating and in motion. Even a small amount of water movement discourages mosquitoes from laying eggs. If moving water is impractical, add goldfish, koi, or the mosquito-eating fish, gambusia, to your pond. They're widely available and dine with gusto on mosquito larvae. Another option: use a floating mosquito doughnut to infect immature mosquitoes and prevent them from growing to adulthood.

Pond maintenance calendar

Task	What to do	Why
SPRING		
Locate and patch leaks	use a pond repair kit	prevent ongoing water loss
Top up water level	trickle water at bottom of pond	avoid buildup of salts and minerals
Clean up the water	skim leaves and debris	decaying debris creates toxic gases
Refresh plantings	add oxygenating bunch plants	increase oxygen in water
Divide potted plants	treat like perennials in the garden	keep plants growing vigorously
Begin feeding fish	use a high-carbohydrate food	fish become more active as weather warms
Reinstall pump and filter	check and replace if necessary	maintain proper functioning
Clean pond bottom if needed	drain pond and hose down liner	more than an inch of muck is detrimental
SUMMER		
Top water level as needed	add small amounts often, not large amounts rarely	help maintain proper water balance by preventing salt and mineral buildup
Test water chemistry weekly	use a test kit for ammonia, chloramines, and chlorine	fish will die if these chemicals are excessive
Trim plants	remove dead leaves, flowers, overgrown plants as needed	prevent fast growers and plant debris from overwhelming the pond
Clean filters, pump intakes	check weekly for clogs	clog can damage plumbing
Increase aeration for fish	add a fountain or bubbler	hot water can be oxygen depleted
Routinely check fish	look for sores, unusual behavior	catch problems early
Control plant pests	depends on the pest	ensure good health of plants
AUTUMN		
Skim or net falling leaves	spread net over pond	protect water quality
Reduce fish feeding	stop when water temperature drops to 50° F	digestion slows in winter, and undigested food in their guts can kill fish
Remove nonhardy plants, fish	move them indoors	ensure survival over the winter
Disconnect filter, pumps	drain, store inside	prevent damage
Drain water lines, fountains	use a siphon or let water drain	prevent freezing and cracking
Prepare hardy plants for winter	move hardy plants to deepest portion of pond bottom	protect them from freezing if the pond is deep enough
WINTER		
Protect pond	float wood or ball on surface	absorb pressure from expanding ice
Keep air hole open for fish	use a bubbler or air stone to keep water moving slowly	release toxic gases; prevent water from freezing

Routine pond care

A well-designed pond with fish and plants in balance requires little care. Routine tasks include keeping debris from accumulating in the water, and deterring pests.

Move frost-sensitive tropical plants from winter storage and return them to ponds in spring after the threat of cold weather has passed.

Trim damaged leaves, spent flowers, and overgrown plants throughout summer to keep the water garden tidy and prevent material from getting into the water.

Remove debris frequently. In fall, you can avoid skimming the pond daily by stretching netting over it to catch leaves. Secure the netting in place with bricks or rocks. Enlist a helper to remove and dump the net when it is full.

Control algae. String algae will run amok if nutrients in the water are excessive. Scoop up algae with a long-handled bristle brush, a rake, or a pole.

Gravel in ponds

Avoid placing layers of gravel, stones, or cobbles in your pond. Debris accumulates in the crevices between stones, creating stagnant areas that produce toxic gases. Cleaning is more difficult, too, and must be done more frequently. Sharp stones may pierce the liner, causing leaks.

(Caring for ponds continued)

Treating neglected ponds

Ponds that do not receive regular maintenance and those that haven't been thoroughly cleaned for several years often become polluted from decaying plants, leaves, fish or animals, and other debris. The bottom may be covered in muck and the water or surfaces green with thick algae. The water may appear murky, black, or bluish and have an unpleasant odor. If any of these situations describes your pond, you can rejuvenate it.

1. Remove all potted and floating plants and fish. Place them in buckets or a water-filled wading pool to keep them wet. Trim off dead and yellowing foliage. Scoop out a bucket or two of pond water in which to place the fish. Also reserve several buckets of clear pond water to add back to the pond after cleaning.

2. Drain the pond as shown on the opposite page. Check with your city before draining into a storm sewer or the street.

3. Lift out fish, snails, and other creatures with a net or bucket before the water level gets too low and put them in a bucket of clear pond water.

4. Scoop the muck gently out of the bottom of the pond with a plastic bucket or scoop, taking care not to damage the liner. Add the muck to the compost pile. Rinse the sides of plastic and synthetic ponds with a garden hose, but do not scrub with a brush. The film of residue on the sides contains beneficial bacteria and algae. If the algae is too thick, you can rub some of it off with an old towel. If the pond is concrete or fiberglass, scrub it with a brush if you plan to resurface or reseal the liner.

5. Examine the liner for damage, including the perimeter where it meets the edging. A leak here may undermine the side of the pool or allow surface water to enter. If the liner is made of polyethylene or other short-lived plastic, consider replacing it with a more durable synthetic rubber liner.

6. Clean the filter and pump. If you use a biological filter, retain some of the old, dirty filter material and put it back with the new filter to help restore the beneficial bacteria.

7. Refill the pond with water, adding a few bucketfuls of the old pond water to help restore the ecological balance. If you have a municipal water source, find out if the waste is treated with chloramines and if so, add a neutralizer. Set up the pump and filter.

Rejuvenating a neglected pond

The best time to clean a water garden is in early fall. Cleaning then ensures that the fish fully recover and are healthy before the stressful winter season sets in.

Drain pond Use a pump to drain average size ponds. Scooping water out with a bucket will serve for small ponds.

Hold fish Place fish and snails in a bucket or wading pool filled with pond water. Aerate the water with an air pump, and keep the container cool and out of the sun.

Rinse liner Once the pond is drained, scoop out accumulated silt and rinse algae and plant debris from the walls.

Repair leaks Match the patch to the type of liner used in making the pond. Your supplier can recommend the right one.

(Caring for ponds continued)

Allow the water to circulate for a day or two before adding plants. Wait one to two weeks before adding fish; while waiting, keep the fish in a cool spot out of the sun. Add an air stone to the filter system to ensure they have enough oxygen.

8. Sort the rescued plants, trimming, dividing, and repotting as needed. Wipe or prune off algae-covered leaves. Put plants back into the pond. Add fish and snails only after the temperature has returned to normal and the chemicals have been neutralized. Work inside the pond in bare feet or water shoes to avoid puncturing or tearing the liner. If possible, rejuvenate your pond in fall or early spring.

Finding and repairing leaks

The water level in your pond may drop for several reasons: evaporation; misdirected fountain spray; or leaks in the liner, waterfall, or plumbing. If the weather has been hot, dry, and windy, you may suspect evaporation. To rule out misdirected fountain spray, turn off the fountain and observe the water level for a couple of days. If the water continues to drop, your pond has likely sprung a leak.

To find the source of the leak, eliminate the possibilities one by one. Walk around the pond and look for wet spots where water may be splashing out of bounds. If you have a waterfall, turn it off. If the water level no longer drops after shutting off the waterfall, look for leaks in the pond's lining or plumbing, and also check for misdirected water that could be splashing out of the system.

If the leak is in the pond lining, the water will drop until it reaches the level of the leak. When the water level has stabilized, check around the perimeter for obvious punctures or tears. If you can't find any, turn off all pumps and aerators. Add an inch of water to the pond, then drip droplets of food-grade dye (or milk) into the water at intervals around the perimeter to find the trouble spot.

Repair PVC and synthetic rubber liners with patch kits sold for this purpose. Follow the instructions included with the kit. Plastic preformed pools and brittle PVC liners most often must be replaced when they start to crack. Repair concrete-lined ponds with cement, then paint with a waterproof masonry paint. Painting is important because cement contains lime, which will alter the pH of the water and perhaps damage the fish or plants. Consider installing a synthetic rubber liner inside a concrete pond to prevent future cracks and leaks.

budget stretcher • budget stretcher • budget stretcher • budget stretcher

Choosing a pond liner

All ponds need a liner to retain the water and prevent it from leaking into the surrounding soil. Pond experts prefer 45 mil EPDM-SF, a kind of synthetic rubber. It's available in widths from 5 to 30 feet, and because it comes on rolls, the length is your choice. Don't confuse the similar material roofers use for waterproofing with pond liner—it's toxic to fish.

Water balance

Ponds and water gardens contain more than just water. A complex web of bacteria, microorganisms, algae, plants, and creatures inhabit the water, interacting constantly to affect the water chemistry and quality. Water quality influences the appearance of the pond and the ability of fish and plants to live in it. Understanding water quality and how to control it is the most important key to water gardening maintenance and success.

Water cycles

As animals live and die, they release ammonia and other waste products. Bacteria and microorganisms process these materials as well as those released by decaying plant matter, turning them into harmless nitrogen compounds that plants can use for food. The process in which waste becomes plant food is called the nitrogen cycle. Here's how it works:

- **Fish waste, dead plants, uneaten fish food, and other organic debris accumulate in the water. This waste matter contains nitrogen in the form of ammonia. Ammonia also comes from water-purifying chemicals, called chloramines, that municipalities commonly add to the water supply. Ammonia is toxic to fish and cannot be absorbed by plants.**

- **Bacteria break down the ammonia into another form of nitrogen called nitrite, which is also toxic.**

- **A second kind of bacteria uses oxygen to turn the nitrites into nitrates, chemicals that are harmless to fish. Plants absorb nitrates from the water and use them to grow.**

The amount of oxygen in the water also affects the health of your pond. Here's how the oxygen cycle works:

- **Oxygen enters the water wherever the water's surface is exposed to air. Waterfalls, bubblers, and fountains increase water surface area, which increases the amount of oxygen in the water.**

- **Bacteria that convert nitrites into nitrates use oxygen. Fish and other aquatic animals also use the oxygen and give off carbon dioxide.**

- **Plants absorb carbon dioxide during the day and release oxygen. At night, plants use oxygen.**

▪ POND SAVVY ▪

EPDM: How to make a seam, or fix a leak

The virtue of this synthetic rubber is that it comes in rolls so wide that seams are rarely necessary, and it's resilient enough that punctures or tears are rare. (The manufacturer, Firestone, guarantees the material for 20 years.) But splicing and repairing can be done. Once the damaged area is clean and dry, measure how much repair tape you need. Order the tape by the foot, in either 2-inch or 6-inch widths. Peel the paper backing off the tape and press it over the liner, applying even pressure as you work. (Use double-sided tape if you plan to overlap and join to sections of liner.) Once the tape is applied, run a bead of e6000 adhesive the full length of all seams. It's a clear, polystyrene glue, available from many pond suppliers as well as craft stores.

(Water balance continued)

When the level of oxygen and the number of bacteria in the water are sufficient to process all of the available waste, and the water contains enough plants to absorb the food, the water is considered balanced.

Pond problems develop when any part of the cycle cannot function properly, usually due to lack of oxygen, too much waste, and insufficient bacteria, or too much plant food and not enough plants. Symptoms of unbalanced water include excessive algae growth or green water, dying fish, and smelly or cloudy water.

Testing water quality

It's a good idea to test your pond water for ammonia and nitrites before adding fish and whenever you have problems with dying fish or plants or suspect any other troubles. You can either test the water yourself with a purchased kit or take a sample to a pond or fish supply store and have someone test it for you.

If the test results show high levels of ammonia or nitrite, avoid adding fish until the levels come down. If you have fish already, the population may be higher than the water ecology can sustain. Increase the amount of oxygen in the water and remove excess fish waste and plant debris. Reduce the level of ammonia by removing about 10 percent of the pond water and replacing it with fresh water. Using ammonia-neutralizing chemicals and adding ammonia-absorbing granules to your filter may also help. The pond may need more time to grow beneficial bacteria. Add bacteria starter, purchased from a pond supplier, to speed the process.

Chloramines Municipalities treat water supplies with chlorine chemicals to purify the water and kill disease organisms. Many add plain chlorine; others use chemical combinations of chlorine and ammonia, called chloramines. Both chloramines and chlorine are toxic to fish and plants, and must be removed from pond water. Small amounts of plain chlorine will not cause harm when topping off a pond, so it's a good idea to frequently add small amounts of water. Plain chlorine will dissipate into the air within a day or two and does not need chemical neutralizing unless you add a lot all at once. Chloramines, on the other hand, must be neutralized whenever you add water to your pond. Pond supply stores sell the appropriate products. Consult your water district to find out what chemicals it uses to treat your water.

Dying fish

If you've observed fish gulping for air at the surface, they are most likely suffering from lack of oxygen. The remedy is a pump with an air stone or aerator. But suspect disease if you see any of the following: sluggish behavior, clamped fins, blotches or ragged fins. Take the affected fish to a professional for diagnosis and treatment.

Pumps and filters

Pumps create current, which circulates water through fountains and filters, over waterfalls, and throughout the pond. Ideally, the current mixes water thoroughly so that fresh oxygen reaches all parts of the pond, and toxic gases and waste are not allowed to accumulate. Filters help remove waste from the water either by straining out the debris or by providing a medium for beneficial bacteria to grow and decompose the waste. Pumps and filters need regular maintenance throughout the year to keep them safe and operating efficiently, and to maintain pond health.

Maintaining pumps and filters

Pumps may be submerged in the water or sit outside the pond on the ground, depending on the pump design. Both types use spinning blades, called impellers, to pull water from the pond through a screened intake and expel it from an outlet pipe. Very large ponds most often use external pumps; smaller ponds and water gardens, as well as fountains, use submersible pumps.

Most pumps remain trouble-free, but all require attention to their intake filters and screens to prevent clogging. The most labor-intensive submersible pumps use built-in foam prefilters, which can clog up quickly with debris. In dirty water, these may need rinsing every few days. To cut down on maintenance, replace foam prefilters with filter screens whenever possible, or put submersible pumps inside a filter box. Check these weekly and rinse off any debris. Clogged filters reduce the water intake, which can stress the motor and even cause it to fail. Avoid running a pump without a filter, because debris lodged inside the pump could damage the impeller.

Ice will crack the pump housing and damage the internal parts. Remove your pump from the water and drain it thoroughly as soon as freezing temperatures threaten. Clean algae from the pump's surfaces with plain water and store the pump indoors until spring. Avoid using detergents or soap to clean anything that will come in contact with the pond water. Also take care to avoid lifting or dragging a submersible pump by its power cord, because you could break the watertight seal into the pump body, thereby voiding the warranty and ruining the pump.

▪ GARDEN GEAR ▪

How much does a pump cost to operate?

Ponds that use a pump and other electrical equipment consume electricity, so they will increase your monthly electrical bill. Some pumps, however, cost less to operate than others.

Look for pumps that move the same amount of water while using fewer watts. If your pump does not list the wattage, multiply volts times amps to determine watts.

To calculate the cost of operating a pump, use the following formula: watts ÷ 1,000 × electricity cost ($.08 is average) × 24 hours × number of days of operation = cost. For example, a 300-watt pump operating all day every day for a 31-day month costs about $18 to run.

(Pumps and filters continued)

Filter maintenance varies with the type of filter you have and the size and contents of your pond. Mechanical filters that trap debris need weekly cleaning to remove leaves and other matter. Check the filter more frequently when the autumn foliage falls. Biological filters usually employ a combination of foam and other materials to strain debris out of the water, and to provide surfaces on which beneficial bacteria can grow and decompose the debris. To maintain your biofilter, beginning about eight weeks after setting it up, rinse about one-fourth to one-third of the foam or other media each month. Rinsing more than that at one time will disrupt the filter's efficiency. Rinse with pond water rather than tap water.

If you must replace a pump or filter, take your old one to a pond supply dealer along with information about your pond. You will need to know how many gallons your pond holds, the height of waterfalls or other water features, the dimensions and depth of the pond, the size and length of the tubing that connects the pump to filters or accessories, and the distance to the electrical outlet. If your pond needs cleaning too frequently, or you plan to add fountains or other water-driven accessories, or fish, consider buying a larger pump or filter. Pumps and filters need to match each other's capacity when used together, so take information about your pump, such as capacity in gallons per hour, when shopping for a filter, and vice versa.

Choosing and sizing a pump

Choose your pump based on your needs and budget. Determine what you expect the pump to do in your pond, and how much you are willing to spend on the initial purchase and for its long-term energy consumption. Before you shop for a pump, you need to know the capacity of your pond in gallons and the vertical height of any pump outlets, such as waterfalls, above the pond's surface.

To calculate the capacity of a rectangular pond, use this formula: pond length (in feet) × width (in feet) × average depth (in feet) × 7.48 = gallons. For a circular pond, use radius × radius (in feet) × 3.14 × average depth (in feet) × 7.48 = gallons. For irregularly shaped ponds, divide it into easier-to-calculate geometric shapes and add the gallons from each measured section. If you measured in inches, multiply the total by 231 instead of 7.48.

Manufacturers offer pumps in a wide range of sizes and styles, from those suitable for patio tubs to ones able to handle a large pond. Look for the following attributes when shopping for pumps:

Capacity Manufacturers rate pumps by the gallons of water per hour they can circulate, measured at 1 foot above the pump. The

budget stretcher • budget stretcher • budget stretcher • budget stretcher

Pump types

There are two kinds of electric pumps: submersible and aboveground. The former are less expensive, quieter, and easier to install, but they're not as powerful. Larger ponds usually need larger, aboveground pumps. Magnetic-drive pumps are more efficient than direct-drive, and water-cooled is preferred over oil-cooled. Of course, the more efficient pumps cost more. Your dealer will help you make the final choice.

Pond pumps and filters

Hidden or behind the scenes of your pond are these essential tools that together keep the water clean and healthy.

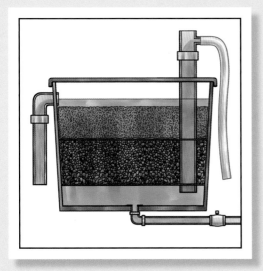

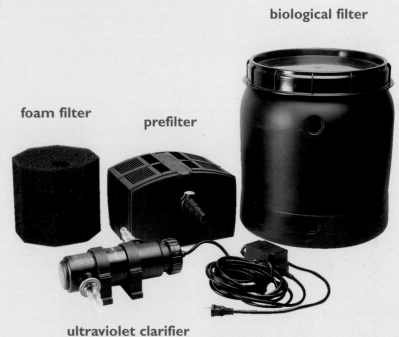

biological filter

foam filter

prefilter

ultraviolet clarifier

Inside a biological filter Water enters from the right, passing first over coarse media, then through finer layer, exiting on the left. Bacteria that grow on the filtering media remove the ammonia and nitrates that would otherwise accumulate in the pond.

submersible pumps

Inside a submersible pump Water enters from the right moving first through a foam strainer. The spinning, finned impeller pushes the water, in this case, up and out of a decorative nozzle.

(Pumps and filters continued)

entire pond capacity should be circulated through the pump every one to two hours, depending on the pond size, contents, water-powered features, and location. Ponds with fish or waterfalls, and those in warmer climates, need greater circulation capacity than water features in cooler climates and those without fish. Ponds under 250 gallons should have the water circulated once an hour.

The height at which water is discharged is called the head height. Pump capacity decreases as the head height increases, so manufacturers also list the gallon outputs at various head heights. To calculate the head height of a waterfall, for example, measure the vertical distance from the surface of the pond to the top of the discharge pipe, perpendicular to the pond's surface. Add 1 foot to the head height for every 10 feet of pipe. Your pump's capacity at the required head height should circulate the gallon capacity of the pond at least every two hours. In other words, if a pump's output at 4 feet of head height is 500 gallons, it can service a pond between 500 and 1,000 gallons in size if the discharge pipe is 4 feet above the pond's surface.

There's an alternate way to determine pump size for a pond with waterfalls. First, measure the width (in inches) of all spillways. For a light, ¼-inch-deep sheet of water going over the falls, figure 50 gallons per hour for each inch of width.

Submersible versus external Pumps either sit outside the pond or are submerged in the water. Very large ponds often require larger and more expensive external pumps. If you need an external pump, consult a pond professional for the plumbing and wiring needed to install it. Submersible pumps generally cost less, are readily available at most garden and pond supply stores, can stay out of sight, and serve most pond owners' needs. Look for one with a sturdy stainless-steel or heavy-duty plastic case and a long power cord. Plug the cord into an outlet with a ground fault circuit interrupter (GFCI).

Warranty Look for pump with the longest warranty. The best manufacturer warranties cover pumps for as long as five years, although one- to three-year warranties are more common.

Installing pumps and filters

Consider ease of maintenance as well as maximum water filtration and circulation when purchasing a pump or filter. The best place for submerged filter is usually in the deepest part of the pond, where debris typically accumulates. Many ponds have a deeper section built just for this purpose. To make retrieving the filter from the pond easier, attach a rope to it and anchor the rope on the side of

healthy garden • healthy garden • healthy garden

Counting gallons

There's an easy way to figure out the water volume of your pond, but it only works when you're filling it. Before filling your pond, jot down the reading on your water meter. With all other water in the house turned off, fill the pond. Check the reading again and subtract to find how many cubic feet of water were used. Convert to gallons by multiplying by 7.48.

the a pond. If your filter sits outside the pond, put the end of the intake pipe into the deep part of the pond. To circulate the water thoroughly, put the pump discharge as far away from the intake as possible. Adjust the positions of the pipes to avoid dead zones and to ensure that all parts of the pond receive freshly circulating water. Raise pumps that are not enclosed in a filter box a few inches off the bottom of the pond to prevent clogging from debris. Set them on stones or bricks.

To connect the pump to the filter and other accessories, such as fountains and waterfalls, use flexible black tubing. Tubing comes in standard internal diameters from ½ to 2 inches. Pumps vary in their output, depending on the diameter of the tubing attached to them, so manufacturers and retailers provide charts that show their pump's flow using different tubing diameters. In general, use tubing that's one size larger than the output fitting on the pump. For example, if the output fitting on your pump is ½ inch, use ⅝-inch-diameter tubing. Use adapters and hose clamps to attach tubing to pumps and accessories with different fitting sizes. To divide the pump's output and operate two different accessories, purchase a T-fitting and two flow-control valves. Some fountain pipes also offer a diverter valve that allows you to operate the fountain and send the excess flow to another part of the pond. Always install flow control valves to the tubing on the output side of the pump to avoid straining the motor.

Avoid using extension cords to power your pump. Whenever possible, plug the pump directly into a ground fault circuit interrupter (GFCI) protected outlet. If the pond is too far from the nearest GFCI outlet, hire an electrician to install one for the pump motor.

· HOW-TO ·

Pond pump longevity

Given proper care, a good-quality water garden pump should last for several years. There are a few steps you can take to ensure its maximum life. Prevent debris or algae from clogging and overworking the motor by cleaning the prefilter and intake filter about once a week in spring, more often in summer and fall. If algae clogging is a problem, fashion a prefilter by wrapping the entire pump in a large section of fiberglass window screen; then place it inside a black plastic bucket. Avoid setting the pump directly on the bottom of the pond, where it will pick up more silt. Set it on a brick or flat stone. Finally, submersible pumps should always be in water when running. Letting it run dry will shorten its life.

Choosing and sizing a pond filter

Filters help maintain clear water and are essential for keeping fish healthy. If you must replace the filter in your pond, or plan to add one for the first time, match the filter to the pump's output and to the capacity of the pond. Manufacturers rate filters for the size of the pond, in gallons, that the filter can effectively handle, but other factors also affect the size of the filter each pond requires. Small

Natural filtration

You can use nature's own water purifiers, plants, even if your pond doesn't include any. Such a natural filter is a small, plant-filled tub that's plumbed to the main pond so that water recirculates through it. The plants' roots consume surplus nitrogen, reducing algae growth in the main pond.

(Pumps and filters continued)

Small ponds need proportionately bigger filters than large ponds because they have less stable water ecology. For example, if your pond holds 200 gallons, look for a filter that can handle 300 to 400 gallons per hour. If your pond contains 1,000 gallons, a filter rated for at least 1,000 gallons should work fine, unless you have fish, which require larger filters due to the amount of waste they produce.

Filters sit inside or outside the pond, depending on their design. These are the three basic types. Some manufacturers combine types within one unit, or you may combine more than one type in your own system.

Mechanical filters These types of filters physically strain debris out of the water as it passes through screens, brushes, pads, nets, or other media. The filters range in expense and complexity from a screen over a pump intake to a plumbed pool skimmer. Mechanical filters require frequent cleaning to remove the captured debris from the water. One common mechanical filter consists of a pump installed inside a perforated or slotted box filled with filter media.

Biological filters These filters also trap material out of the water, but they take the process one step further by providing a home for beneficial bacteria that decompose waste. Biofilters use media that provide maximum surface area for the bacteria, and they are more sensitive to the flow rate of the pump than mechanical filters. Water that flows through the filter too fast keeps the bacteria from reaching their potential and could wash the bacteria out of the media.

Ultraviolet (UV) clarifiers UV clarifiers work by killing algae and microorganisms as they pass over a UV bulb. The dead organic material clumps together and can be strained out of the water by mechanical filtration. UV filters are especially effective at removing suspended algae. The units may sit inside or outside the pond, depending on the model, and have intake and output nozzles so that they can fit into the water circulation system. Be sure to match the UV filter's recommended flow rate with your pump's output, and install it in the system between the pump output and the mechanical or biological filter. These filters need little maintenance. Change the bulb annually to keep the clarifier running efficiently.

Fish and water plants

Plants play an integral role in balancing your pond's natural ecology and its water cycles. They provide oxygen for fish, snails, and other aquatic creatures. Plants use the by-products of fish waste and decomposing plants as food and help to keep algae growth in check. Many aquatic and marsh plants have ornamental foliage and flowers, and provide habitat for birds, dragonflies, frogs, and other animals. Add fish to your pond for their lively movement and color, and to help control insects, such as mosquitoes.

Choosing plants

Aquatic plants have growth habits that allow them to inhabit certain parts of the pond ecosystem. Marsh plants grow at the water's edge, with their roots constantly moist and their leaves rising into the air. Other types root in the soil at the bottom of ponds and let their leaves float on the water's surface. Some float on the surface but do not take root. Others grow below the water's surface, sometimes rooting in soil, sometimes drifting.

The most important plants may be the ones that decrease maintenance chores by competing with algae and keeping it under control. Submerged plants and those with floating leaves fill that role particularly well. Plants that grow along the water's edge also filter nutrients from the water with their submerged roots and may shade the pool from excess sunlight.

Free-floating plants Free-floating plants shade the water's surface and are highly effective at reducing algae in a pond. Some, however, including duckweed *(Lemna minor),* water lettuce *(Pistia stratiotes),* water hyacinth *(Eichhornia crassipes),* and fairy moss *(Azolla caroliniana),* increase rapidly, often becoming invasive, and are banned in some states. These may be suitable for smaller, aboveground water gardens. Frogbit *(Hydrocharis morsus-ranae)* and water poppy *(Hydrocleys nymphoides)* have more subdued growth habits.

Rooted floating plants Plants that root in the soil and have floating leaves also shade the water and compete with algae for

· GOOD PLANTS ·

Beware the invaders

Some water garden plants grow so vigorously or spread so prolifically that they may escape into the wild and become a threat to the local ecology by displacing native plants and disrupting natural plant and animal habitats. These invasive plants usually come from other parts of the world and are introduced through the garden and landscape trade. Federal and state agencies maintain lists of prohibited and invasive plants. A few commonly restricted plants include water hyacinth (Eichhornia crassipes), common reed (Phragmites australis), Eurasian milfoil (Myriophyllum spicatum), purple loosestrife (Lythrum salicaria), and yellow flag iris (Iris pseudacorus). Avoid adding these plants to your water garden.

(Fish and water plants continued)

nutrients. These include water clover *(Marsilea* spp.), sacred lotus *(Nelumbo nucifera),* American lotus *(Nelumbo lutea),* and hardy and tropical water lilies *(Nymphaea* spp.). Many water lily hybrids exist, in a range of colors. Dwarf water lilies remain small enough for patio tubs; other species have leaves more than 3 feet across.

Submerged or oxygenating, plants These compete with algae for nutrients and add more oxygen to the water than other types of aquatic plants. Most suppliers sell these plants in bunches, consisting of several stems bound with a rubber band. One bunch per square foot of water surface area can effectively reduce or even eliminate suspended algae. Submerged plants include hornwort *(Ceratophyllum demersum),* anacharis *(Egeria densa* or *Elodea densa),* and fanwort *(Cabomba caroliniana).* Fish enjoy nibbling on these plants.

Marginal plants These are the plants that grow in the shallow water at the pond's edge and add a vertical dimension to the water feature. Their roots absorb nutrients from the water and may filter surface water from outside the pond. Some help keep nuisance animals out of the pond and provide wildlife habitat. Marginal plants include papyrus *(Cyperus* spp.), flowering rush *(Butomus umbellatus),* blue flag iris *(Iris versicolor),* Japanese iris *(Iris ensata),* variegated sweet flag *(Acorus calamus* 'Variegatus'), arrowhead *(Sagittaria sagittifolia),* and marsh marigold *(Caltha palustris).*

Buy plants through mail-order nurseries or local pond suppliers and garden centers. Water garden clubs and societies exist in nearly every state and can also be a good source of water plants and information. Enthusiasts frequently swap plants and are eager to share their knowledge. Plants collected from the wild may harbor diseases that can infect your other pond plants and fish or introduce unwanted pests and parasites, such as leeches and snails.

Many of the water plants cultivated in ornamental ponds have been imported from other parts of the world. Some grow so vigorously they can displace native plants and disrupt the local ecology if they escape into the wild. For this reason, all states ban certain plants and prohibit nurseries from selling them or importing them into the state. If you have one of these plants, dispose of them, and don't dump plants from your pond into a waterway or storm drain. For more information on prohibited plants in your state, see Resources.

As with other garden plants, some aquatic plants live year after year as perennials, whereas others succumb to freezing temperatures and must be overwintered indoors or replaced in spring.

healthy garden · healthy garden · healthy garden · healthy garden

Potting up

After planting any water plant in its pot, top off the soil with pea gravel or similar material. Topping off keeps the soil from washing in moving water, and prevents fish from poking around roots too. Make the layer about ½ inch deep, just up to or slightly below the pot's rim.

Choose and replace pond plants using the same creative design considerations discussed for flower gardens in Chapter 5. Contrast and blend flower and foliage colors, textures, and growth habits. Use vertical marsh plants to offset horizontal floating plants, for example. Balance the size of the plants with the size of the water feature. Select large, bold plants for bigger ponds and smaller or more refined plants for patio-size pools. Limit your plant palette to avoid a cluttered display. Smaller and more formal water gardens often feature only one or two dramatic plants; informal ponds usually contain many different plants to imitate a natural setting.

Maintaining water garden plants

Aquatic plants need regular maintenance to stay healthy and looking good. Some tasks require weekly attention, others much less frequently. Follow a schedule to care for your plants.

Spring Divide and replant water lilies, lotus, and marsh plants (see directions on page 264–265). When the water has warmed to at least 50° F and the frost danger has passed, add new floating and submerged plants to keep algae in check. Fertilize potted plants.

Daily or weekly Throughout the summer, snip off spent flowers and yellowing leaves to prevent them from spoiling the water. Remove any submerged plants that appear to be dying. If floating plants, such as duckweed, have grown too thick, net some out and add to your compost pile. Replace or add plants as needed or desired. Check for insect pests, especially aphids, Japanese beetles, and plant-eating snails. If possible, look under water lily leaves for clear, jellylike masses of snail eggs and wipe them off. See "Pests and problems" on page 267 for more information on pest controls. Fertilize potted plants monthly with aquatic plant fertilizer tablets.

Autumn Move frost-sensitive marsh plants and tropical water lilies indoors for the winter. Net out floating and submerged plants that will not survive the winter in your climate and either discard or move them indoors. If your pond does not freeze solid, move hardy submerged plants and hardy water lilies and lotus to the deepest part of the pond after trimming off the foliage.

■ SMART IDEA ■

Plants in the deep

To grow water plants at the right depth, set their pots on stacks of weathered exterior bricks, old pots, or on non-floating plastic crates, such as milk crates.

When planting new water lilies, lotuses, and other deep-water aquatics, start plants out at a shallow depth, gradually moving them deeper as they grow. To do this, support the pots on bricks, then remove the bricks one layer at a time until each pot reaches its permanent depth, making sure that the leaves always remain on the water surface.

Before buying water plants, ask the nursery staff how many plants are optimal for your size pond, the size container they need, and how deep they should sit in the water when full-size.

(Fish and water plants continued)

For ease of maintenance and cleaning, grow rooted water plants in round pots or tubs, using containers large enough for each plant. Standard-size lotus, large water lilies, and tall, vigorous marsh plants, for example, need tubs 2 to 3 feet in diameter. Dwarf lotus and water lilies and smaller marsh plants can grow in 1- to 2-foot-wide containers. You may purchase special planting baskets for aquatic plants or use standard plastic nursery pots.

In most cases, shallow pots work best, because water plants tend to grow most of their roots close to the soil's surface. Cover drainage holes and line baskets with a couple of layers of newspaper before adding soil to prevent clouding the pond water with silt.

Use a soil mix made especially for water plants, or mix your own using heavy garden soil, composted manure, and coarse sand. Avoid peat moss, perlite, and other materials that float or could cloud the water. Place fertilizer tablets at the bottom of pots before adding soil and plants. Top off each pot with a thin layer of pebbles to keep the soil in place and prevent fish from uprooting plants. Don't cover the growing shoots of the plants. Set pots directly on the bottom of the pond or support them on plastic crates or bricks.

As potted plants grow, they often become crowded in their pots and need dividing and repotting. Divide water lilies and marsh plants by removing them from their containers and pulling or cutting the clump apart into two or more well-rooted pieces, each with one or more leafy crowns. Wash the soil off the roots with a stream of water from a hose to help untangle the roots. Replant each piece in a clean pot, setting the cut end of tubers or runners against the side of the pot and pointing the growing tip toward the center.

Choosing and keeping fish

A few fish in your pond will improve the water balance and decrease the number of nuisance snails and mosquitoes. Stocking too many fish adds to maintenance and demands larger pumps and filters to keep the water clear. The most common ornamental pond fish are goldfish and koi, and each has its pros and cons.

Goldfish Goldfish come in a range of colors, fin conformations, and body shapes. Those with long bodies and single tails, such as comets and shubunkins, grow up to 12 inches long and tolerate water temperatures between 40° and 80° F. They can even live under ice if provided with an air hole to the surface. Types with short bodies and double tails, such as fantails and orandas, stay smaller but are less hardy, preferring temperatures between 55° and 75° F. Prices for

Water lilies

Hardy water lilies go dormant in winter and can survive below the ice in cold climates. In season, their floating white, yellow, or pink blooms open in the morning and close by late afternoon each day for several days. Tropical water lilies need water above 70° F. They hold their flowers above the water and bloom in a range of colors that includes white, pink, purple, blue, yellow, and red. Some bloom during the day; others at night.

Planting a water lily

Grow lilies like most other water plants, in plastic containers filled with topsoil that's covered with gravel or rocks. Start hardy kinds from dormant tubers, and tropical kinds (shown) from growing plants.

1 Supplies You'll need pots—black nursery, terra-cotta, plastic-mesh, or fabric containers—potting soil formulated for water gardens, and gravel. If you use a plastic-mesh type container, line the inside with landscape fabric before planting.

2 Preparing to plant Once it's removed from its nursery pot, rinse the plant and roots thoroughly to wash off hitchhiking pests. Add a layer of pea gravel to the bottom of the pot, and fill the container about two-thirds full of soil.

3 Planting For tropical water lilies, form a mound of soil in the center of the pot. Place the plant on the mound and spread its roots over the mound. Place hardy lilies at the edge of the pot with their roots spread out so they are not under the rhizome. Lightly cover the roots.

4 Gravel Top off with a ½-inch layer of gravel. Avoid burying the crown of hardy lilies. Look for the point on tropical lily stems where the color changes from light to dark. The gravel should be even with this point.

5 Place in water Position the plant in the pond at the correct level. To raise a plant, stack a few weathered bricks underneath it, or put the pot on a black plastic storage crate

265

(Fish and water plants continued)

goldfish depend on the size and type, but most small ones cost from less than a dollar to under $10. Goldfish nibble at submerged plants and eat some kinds of algae. Two or three goldfish can survive in a patio-size tub if protected from sudden temperature swings.

Koi Koi can grow to 2 feet in length and live for decades in suitable conditions. Prices range considerably—depending on the size and quality of the individual fish—from just a few dollars for small pets to thousands of dollars for mature, show-quality fish. They prefer cool water, about 40° to 70° F, and will live under ice with an air hole to release gases from the water. Koi eat plants and root around in the soil in pots and in the debris at the bottom of ponds. They produce lots of waste and demand plenty of oxygen in the water, requiring a large pond with a high-capacity pump and filter.

Some states and municipalities restrict the introduction of fish into ponds, even goldfish into home water gardens. Check with local authorities before stocking your pond, and never dump fish into a stream or other natural body of water or storm drain.

Eliminating chlorine and chloramines from the water and monitoring nitrites and ammonia is particularly important when keeping fish. All these chemicals are toxic to fish. When introducing fish to your pond, allow them to adjust gradually to your pond's water chemistry and temperature. Half-fill a pail with pond water and place it in a shady spot. Float the bag of fish in the bucket for 15 minutes to allow the water temperatures to equalize. Open the bag and release the fish into the bucket. After an hour or so, add more pond water to the bucket to fill it three-quarters full. Observe the fish for signs of disease and parasites before releasing them into the pond.

Feed fish only as much as they will eat in a few minutes. Use floating food made specifically for goldfish or koi so that you can easily skim out any that remains uneaten. Stop feeding fish when the water temperature drops below 50° F.

Winter care

Most goldfish and koi, hardy water lilies, lotus, and other water plants, can remain in ponds year-round if the pond is deep enough. In cold northern climates, ponds should be 3 to 4 feet deep to overwinter fish and plants. To promote air exchange and prevent the buildup of toxic gases, you must provide a hole in the ice throughout the winter. Use a water heater made for that purpose.

To overwinter fish and plants indoors, keep fish in an aquarium with a filter and an aerator, no more than 1 inch of fish per gallon of

Pond and pool safety

Most municipalities regulate the installation of pools and ponds that could pose a danger to children. They often require fencing around the water feature. Check with local authorities to learn what your town requires, and obtain a permit before building or expanding your pond.

water. Store water plants in buckets, watertight tubs, or even wading pools under artificial lights. Many water plants, such as hardy water lilies, become dormant in winter and do not need light.

Pests and problems

Ponds probably present more challenges to homeowners than any other landscape feature. Although a regularly maintained pond may remain trouble-free for long periods of time, eventually some problem will require solving. The most common dilemmas are animal and insect pests, algae, and leaking water. Consult a pond expert in your area if you have difficulty solving these problems on your own. Pond society and club members, as well as experienced pond supply store clerks, can offer a wealth of advice.

Ponds and water features attract animals and other creatures in search of food, water, and a place to live. You may welcome some of the wildlife, but not every visitor is harmless. To prevent most animals and predatory birds from entering your pond, cover the pond with netting. Provide overhanging rocks and other hiding places for fish away from the perimeter, in the center of the pond. Devices with motion sensors, that spray water or play the radio, can also act as deterrents. Animals and herons avoid ponds with steep sides—a factor to consider when building a new pond.

Fish parasites and diseases are difficult to diagnose and treat. The most common problems occur when fish are stressed, such as when new fish are added to the pond, or when water chemistry becomes toxic or has changed. If fish are sick, check the ammonia and nitrite levels and increase the aeration by adding a fountain spray. To examine a fish more closely, net it out and put it in a bucket of clean pond water for observation, or take it to an expert for diagnosis.

Many of the same pests—such as aphids, leaf-eating beetles, and thrips—that bother terrestrial plants also attack water plants, especially the exposed parts above the water. The only safe way to remove the pests is manually or with nontoxic treatments, such as horticultural oil. Chemical pesticides have no place in or around a

GARDEN GEAR

Outwitting predators

Raccoons, cats, and herons love to eat fish and are programmed to hunt for them. That means they'll find and catch any in your pond that they can reach.

Cats and raccoons depend on shallow water at the edge of the pond to gain access to the fish that gather in the shallow waters around the margins. Similarly, herons prefer to land in shallow water or on land, then wade into the pond. Therefore ponds with sides that drop straight down will save many pond fish from all three predators. If you have an established pond with shallow sides, install an unobtrusive black mesh net over the pond's surface or around the perimeter. You'll save your fish and keep falling leaves out as well.

(Pests and problems continued)

pond, and organic pesticides may kill fish and other aquatic creatures. You can purchase aquatic chemicals that kill pest snails, but they kill harmless snails as well as the nuisance kinds.

Controlling mosquitoes

Mosquitoes lay their eggs in water, and their first life stages live in water before they become winged, airborne pests. Adult mosquitoes not only ruin an evening outdoors, they carry a number of serious parasites and diseases, including canine heartworm, West Nile virus, viral encephalitis, and malaria. The best way to control mosquitoes in ponds is to eliminate their aquatic life stages. Fish will seek out and eat both mosquito eggs and wiggling larvae. If you don't have fish, use floating pellets called bacillus dunks to kill the larvae.

Clearing up algae

Algae grow in every pond. Most kinds of algae are beneficial to water ecology, such as those that grow on underwater surfaces, helping to oxygenate the water. Two types, however, can become a nuisance. Suspended algae cloud the water; string algae or blanket weed grows in long strands or mats that may cover surfaces, clog filters, and create an unsightly mess. Both are more common in spring and whenever the pond contains insufficient plants to compete for the sunlight and nutrients in the water. Algae use oxygen, which may deprive and suffocate fish. Moreover, large amounts of algae dying suddenly add toxic nitrite to the water as they decompose.

To control all types of algae, increase the competition for food by adding bunches of submerged water plants, up to one bunch for each square foot or two of pond surface. As the plants grow and compete, the algae will gradually diminish. Decrease the amount of nutrients in the water by removing decomposing debris. Shade the water with a water-coloring chemical or netting to decrease the amount of sunlight. You can wind string algae filaments on a stick and remove them manually.

Another natural algae control is barley straw. One 8-ounce bale treats up to 1,500 gallons of water. Allow two to eight weeks for it to become effective after placing it in the pond.

Eliminating string algae takes time. When the pond water achieves a balance between the available nutrients and desirable plants, the algae will naturally subside. Be patient and allow at least three to four weeks in spring and for newly renovated or established ponds to adjust and establish a healthy water cycle.

Algae and UV light

Green algae is the kind that turns pond water as green as pea soup. Even small amounts of it makes the pond look sickly. Too much, and it will consume all the pond's oxygen, suffocating the fish. UV clarifiers are the simplest, quickest way to eliminate green algae (see page 260).

Eliminating pond pests

Natural checks and balances between plants, fish, and insects keep most problems from getting out of hand. These are practical remedies for some of the most common pond problems.

Motion detector scarecrow Motion detectors that activate a sprinkler can serve to chase away browsing fish predators.

Bacillus dunks The floating cakes contain a natural insecticide that is specific to mosquitoes. One doughnut treats 100 square feet and is effective for about a month.

Barley straw pellets As the straw begins to rot, a chemical is released that prevents or slows growth of green and string algae without harming other plants. Allow about a month for it to become active.

Oxygenating plants Anacharis breaks dormancy earlier than other submerged plants and so competes for oxygen with algae, limiting the algae's growth.

269

Plants for container gardens

How many water plants and fish can a container support? It depends on the size of the pot. For example, a pot that is about 2½ feet in diameter can easily support a water lily, water iris, a floating water hyacinth, and a clump of parrots feather. Dwarf varieties of cattail, lotus, and water lilies will fit easily in most pots and leave room for companion plants.

Caring for patio tubs and fountains

Water gardens in containers offer a creative solution if your space is limited, and they require less time commitment than larger water features. They are also the easiest sort of starter garden if you're just getting interested and want to try water gardening on a small scale. There's no digging and little expense. You can place it on a deck or balcony. As with ponds, you can add plants, fish, and even a waterfall or fountain. Depending on the container and accessories, a small water feature can be inexpensive to set up and maintain.

Choosing containers

Any watertight container can be suitable for water gardening as long as it does not leach anything toxic into the water. Check for cracks, leaks, and rust. You can waterproof wooden and unglazed ceramic containers with a water sealant that's available at pond supply and paint stores. Plug drainage holes with plumber's epoxy. If you will need to move the filled water garden, choose one with rigid walls that won't twist or crack and that's light enough to carry.

After choosing your container, check it for watertightness before planting. Let it sit filled for a day or more, then check for leaks. If there are minor leaks, drain it and seal the cracks from the inside with fish-safe silicone caulk. Make wooden and porous containers watertight with either flexible liner or a brush-on sealant designed for water gardens. Be wary of recycled whiskey-barrel halves or copper pots. Both need lining before they'll support fish and plants.

Look for a container that's large enough to house what you want to put in it. Miniature water lilies and dwarf lotus need only a 24-inch-wide container, whereas full-size specimens require twice the space. Small marsh plants can grow in pots as narrow as 12 inches.

Larger volumes of water retain more stable temperatures and water chemistry than smaller amounts of water, an important consideration for keeping fish. Fish also need as much surface area as possible for air exchange, and may require a pump to aerate the pond water. If you plan to add moving water, select a container that's wide enough to contain the splashing droplets.

If you're planning to include fish in an aboveground water garden, locate it where it will be shaded in the afternoon, to prevent the water's heating beyond the tolerance of the fish.

Planting a container water garden

The beauty of a water garden in a container is that you can have it almost wherever you want. Watertight containers of any kind can serve. Here's how to do it.

1 Prepare container
Paint the inside of the pot with water-garden paint, then check it for leaks. Fill it with water and let it sit for a day on a dry surface. If water seeps out, repaint. Once seepage stops, move the pot to a level surface capable of holding the weight of the water. The final location should be near a GFCI outlet.

2 Position pump and plants Set the pump in the container, lodging it securely between bricks. Adjust the nozzle height to just below the final water level. Drape the power cord over the back of the container. Set potted plants on bricks.

3 Fill and fine-tune Add floating plants as well as some that will drape slightly over the pot edge to conceal the power cord. Adjust nozzle height and flow as needed.

4 Landscape Dress up the pot and cover its bare sides with smaller container plants.

Tub plants in winter

If sustaining your water garden indoors isn't an option, here's what to do: Lift pots of hardy plants, cut them back, and wrap them in a plastic bag. Set them where they'll stay cool but not freeze, and cover with straw. Similarly, lift and cut back tender tropicals, but also remove them from pots, rinse soil off roots, and replant in pots of damp sand. Store these plants where temperatures remain above 55° F.

(Caring for patios tubs and fountains continued)

Seasonal maintenance

If you live where the average winter minimum temperature is 30° F or higher, your container water garden is fine outdoors all year. If there's just a little more winter chill, down to 20° F, bury the container in garden soil, leaving only the top 2 or 3 inches above the ground. That will be enough insulation to prevent freezing. But if you live where temperatures are routinely 10° F or lower, you should bring your container water garden indoors. (This is especially true if it is made of breakable terra-cotta or ceramic.)

You can take patio tubs inside for the winter and keep them going in a sunny window or under grow lights. As the weather cools in autumn, decide whether you will overwinter your fish and plants indoors or replace them in spring. Some plants will continue to live and grow all winter under artificial lights or in a sunny window. Here's how to keep them going:

1. Empty the water and its contents from the container and move it to a place in your house where it can remain during the cold season. It's a good idea to keep your fish in an aquarium for the winter, where you can provide adequate filtration and aeration. When choosing the aquarium and needed supplies for overwintering your fish, ask for advice at a pet store. Do not release your pond or water garden fish into a stream, pond, or other natural body of water, or pour them into a storm drain. Doing so violates the law.

2. Clean and drain the pump as well as any tubing and other accessories, and put them in nonfreezing storage for the winter. Empty any debris from the bottom of the water garden container, but do not scrub the algae and bacteria off the inside.

3. Set the container back up without the pump and fountain, and place a fluorescent grow-light fixture about 6 to 12 inches above the water's surface or tallest plant. Provide about 12 hours of light per day. Some plants, including hardy water lilies and lotus, may become dormant for the winter and lose most or all of their leaves. They need no supplemental light and will resume growing in spring.

4. Monitor the plants and water for aphids and other pests. Trim dying leaves promptly and cut back overgrown plants. Don't expect growth to be as vigorous as during the summer.

caring
for your yard's
structures

Here are some tricks and techniques to keep your outdoor rooms looking their best.

The hardscape areas around your house—the driveway, walkways, paths, patio, and deck—need as much attention as your landscape. Once serious problems develop with paving materials, repairs can be time-consuming and expensive. Regular maintenance is the way to make sure such scenarios don't happen.

Paving

The single biggest threat to any form of paving—including concrete, asphalt, and brick—is water. When it freezes, water expands with enough power to crack almost anything, including sidewalks and mortared stone walls. In its liquid form, water can cause damage by softening and eroding the ground beneath patios, foundations, and driveways.

By repairing cracks when they appear and directing standing or running water away from potential trouble areas, you can keep your paved areas as good as new for many years.

Concrete

Concrete is a cost-effective and long-lasting product, but certain problems peculiar to concrete can arise. First, no matter how carefully it's poured, concrete will sooner or later crack to some degree. The cracks may be hairline or small, which generally do not indicate any serious problems, or they may be deep and wide. There is no fixed rule on what constitutes a wide crack, but consider any crack ½ inch wide or more a problem. The next step is to determine whether the crack is dormant or active. Dormant cracks may be the result of natural shrinkage during curing or initial settling, and the concrete is no longer moving. Active cracks continue to widen and lengthen, indicating potentially more serious problems, such as settling or heaving ground. Careful observation and measurement over a few weeks will help determine the nature of the crack.

• HOW-TO •

Resurfacing concrete

Resurfacing concrete is an intermediate repair, more substantial than patching but less work than tearing up the damaged concrete and starting over. Use this technique only if the damaged concrete still has a strong structure. Set new forms around the section to be resurfaced but about an inch higher. Use a paint roller to apply a layer of latex concrete-bonding agent. Then mix a batch of stiff, extra strong concrete by adding two shovelfuls of portland cement to each 60-pound bag of sand-mix cement. Add just enough water to wet the mix, then shovel it over the damaged area, occasionally smacking it with the back of the shovel to ensure a good bond. Level the area, and then finish it with a steel trowel.

Splash test

**Weather-protecting
your concrete
is as important as
protecting a deck. It
can help prevent
cracking and block
stains. Pour a glass
of water onto the
concrete to see if it
is waterproofed.
If the water soaks
in and makes the
surface darker, the
surface is not
waterproofed. In
that case, apply a
concrete sealer.**

(Paving continued)

Preventing cracks

The main cause of significant concrete cracking is ground movement, which may have several causes. For example, it occurs in what is known as expansive soil, which expands significantly when wet and shrinks when dry. Wet soil also expands as it freezes. Earth underlying concrete that is washed away or settles, removing the supporting base, can also cause concrete to crack. Tree roots close to a sidewalk or foundation will eventually push the concrete out of line until it cracks. The power of these forces is enormous, enough to move houses as well as crack driveways and sidewalks.

Spalling occurs when the surface layer of concrete breaks away, usually in thin plate-size pieces and sometimes in long runs. When small pieces of concrete spall, it is often a result of poor finishing and curing. Long spalling runs often indicate that iron reinforcing bars within the concrete are rusting, causing surface expansion and cracks.

Maintaining proper drainage around concrete, whether a foundation, driveway, or path, is an essential part of long-term care. Water can be diverted and controlled in a number of ways:

1. If rainwater runs beside or over your sloping driveway, install 4-inch-diameter perforated drainpipe in a gravel-filled trench beside the driveway. Dig the trench about 8 inches deep, put down 2 inches of crushed rock, then place the drainpipe with the holes facing down. Cover the drainpipe with crushed rock. If you wish to sod over the trench, cover the rock with landscape fabric to keep dirt from clogging the drain holes.

2. On sloping property, build swales or shallow trenches above the driveway to divert water toward the street or to a natural drainage area before it can undermine the driveway or patio.

3. If you are building a patio or other hardscape beside the house, install a drainage trench and pipe beneath it in advance. This allows you to later connect any nearby rain gutter downspouts to the drain line so water will not wash across the hardscape.

Repairing and cleaning concrete

In areas where freezing occurs, cracks in concrete need to be repaired before ice makes them worse. For do-it-yourself concrete repairs, there are a number of products available at home supply centers that are effective and easy to use. These include tubes of prepared concrete patching material, epoxy mixes, stain and rust removers, and self-leveling concrete. Cracks in a driveway are not structurally dangerous, but a growing crack in a brick or concrete retaining wall needs immediate attention.

Before you start Because new mortar will not adhere to existing concrete if the surface is oily or dusty, brush or vacuum large cracks clean of dust and debris. An air hose or high-pressure water sprayer will do the job well.

Repairing cracked concrete Hardware and home supply stores sell concrete repair material in caulking tubes. Clean the crack thoroughly and apply the mixture with a caulking gun. For larger cracks, press foam rope into the crack to fill much of the gap before applying the repair caulk. For large and active cracks, call a concrete contractor.

Resurfacing old concrete Worn, chipped, or spalled concrete surfaces can be repaired by most homeowners, but if an entire driveway or concrete slab must be resurfaced, turn the job over to a concrete contractor.

There are a number of resurfacing materials on the market; most contain a combination of portland cement, sand, and acrylic polymers. Others may use a blend of epoxy adhesives. One effective resurfacing product is self-leveling concrete, which is poured over the surface in a liquid form. The concrete is then spread evenly across the surface with a special squeegee that adjusts to the desired thickness.

Repairing steps If a discrete piece of concrete has broken off that is salvageable, gluing it back with epoxy cement is the most straightforward repair. Depending to some degree upon how well the pieces fit, a crack will still be visible, but at least the colors will match. Clean both surfaces and allow them to dry. Once dry, mix the epoxy and apply a thin layer to both pieces. Press the chip into place; wipe away excess epoxy with a rag soaked in mineral spirits.

safety alert · safety alert · safety alert · safety alert

Cracks in walls

Some cracks widen imperceptibly. If you have a concrete crack that you suspect is worsening, check it by measuring and recording the width and the length every week for two to four months. If the crack continues to expand, it may be time to call in a concrete contractor.

Concrete fixes

Sturdy as it is, concrete is hardly invulnerable.
Freeze-thaw cycles, expanding and contracting clay
soil, tree roots, and soil settling are common causes of
splits and cracks.

Repairing a crack

1 Open and widen the crack to ease filling. Use a wire brush, stone chisel, or hand grinder.

2 Remove loose or flaking material. An indoor-outdoor vacuum will do the fastest and easiest job.

3 Fill the crack with a prepackaged patching material. Wipe or squeegee off the excess. Sprinkling on a little dry concrete mix helps disguise color variations.

Cleaning an oil spill

1 Pour clay-based kitty litter over the oil stain until it is covered completely. Pulverize the litter underfoot. As a powder, it can absorb more oil. Leave the powder in place for 24 hours.

2 Sweep up the powder, then pour a can of regular cola over the stain. Let it sit for several hours to bleach what the litter did not absorb.

3 Rinse with water to remove any remaining litter or cola residue. If the stain is still visible, repeat the process.

(*Paving continued*)

Cleaning specific stains

Oil and grease Commercial stain removers, available at hardware or automotive supply stores, effectively clean oil and grease stains on concrete. Typically, the powdered, liquid, or spray-on chemical is spread over the stain, allowed to penetrate for a few hours, then hosed away. Using a high-pressure hose nozzle speeds the removal. A surprisingly effective home remedy for removing oil stains from concrete involves kitty litter and a can of cola.

Paint spatters Paint is difficult to remove from concrete and bricks because masonry is porous. Scrape away as much excess paint as possible with a putty knife, then use a chemical paint stripper. A portable high-pressure water sprayer will help blast paint particles from the concrete pores after the stripper has loosened them.

Mildew Mildew commonly grows in damp areas that receive little or no sunshine. If you are not sure whether a stain is dirt or mildew, put a few drops of bleach on it. Mildew will turn white; dirt will not change. Scrub mildew away with a mix of 1 part bleach to 3 parts warm water. If the area is routinely damp, scrub it once a month with the bleach mixture to keep the area mildew-free. Avoid getting bleach on plants.

Removing accumulated grime If you move a flower pot that has been on a concrete surface for a long time, you will likely see a lighter colored circle where it sat. Concrete often turns dark from accumulated airborne grime. A portable high-pressure water sprayer is an excellent tool for cleaning driveways, walkways, and patios. A stiff brush, soap, water, and elbow grease also work.

Embedded stains and rust Various heavy-duty, acidic cleaners are available that will remove the toughest stains from concrete. Be aware that most can damage concrete as well as clean it, particularly smooth-finish concrete, especially if the cleaner is not diluted or otherwise used improperly. Test the cleaner in an out-of-the-way area first. Then follow directions carefully.

HOW-TO

Removing moss from concrete

Moss will grow on any outdoor concrete surface that is moist and shaded. Pouring boiling water over the moss usually kills it, though this may not be practical for large areas. Full strength laundry bleach is also effective. Swab it over the area with a mop, but be sure to wear rubber boots and old clothes. Rinse the concrete thoroughly afterward, and wash off any plants that may have been splattered.

Moss-killing products containing iron, zinc, copper, or fatty acids of potassium salts are also available. Look for products labeled for moss control on concrete. Follow all product directions.

For best results, seal the concrete after treating it. Moss will grow back but will be easier to remove.

Brick by brick

Unlike concrete—which must be formed, poured, finished, and cured quickly—bricks can be dealt with one at a time, at your own pace. That's why a brick-on-sand patio or walkway is an ideal project for the whole family, including children. Also, because bricks on sand are loose and not mortared permanently, maintenance such as resetting or replacing loose or crooked bricks, is easy to do.

(Paving continued)

Asphalt

Asphalt is made from crushed rock mixed with bitumen, a sticky petroleum byproduct. Ultraviolet rays and heat combine to degrade the bitumen, allowing water to penetrate it, which further accelerates the damage. The first line of defense is to keep the surface clean of moss, dirt, and debris. Equally important in protecting the surface is to coat it with sealer every three or four years. An established maintenance program for an asphalt driveway or walkway will help prevent major problems from developing.

Asphalt problems

Indications that asphalt is in distress include numerous cracks, a wavy surface, wheel ruts, and potholes. Water seeping through cracks in the asphalt's surface can weaken the base, which in turn can lead to erosion, settling, and potholes. An extreme problem is known as alligatoring, when many small cracks begin to connect. This generally indicates the entire driveway needs replacing.

Prevention Seal the asphalt. Asphalt sealer and repair products are either asphalt- or coal tar-based. Coal tar is considered longer-lasting and more resistant to oil and gasoline spills. Whichever product you choose, check the warranty for an idea of the quality. The better products will have warranties of four to six years.

Start the project by cleaning the surface well. Use a degreaser on all oil stains to ensure that the sealer will adhere. If water pools on the surface, treat the oil stain until it is removed. Spread the sealer evenly and smoothly with a special long-handled squeegee, available where you buy the sealer. An old paint roller attached to an extension rod also works well. Apply the sealer in dry weather when the temperature is above 45° F. One thin coat is all that is needed.

Repairing small cracks Liquid crack fillers work well for a few cracks ⅛ inch wide or less. For cracks up to an inch wide, it is best to use a flexible, puttylike material that is pressed into the crack, then melted with a propane torch. Cold-patch materials, as used for repairing potholes, will also work in larger cracks.

Patching potholes To repair a pothole or sunken area, dig out and remove all loose and broken asphalt down to the base. Keep all sides of the hole vertical as you dig. For patching material, select any of the brands available at your home supply center. Ideally, the patch should be no more than 2 inches thick.

Cold-patching asphalt

Because asphalt is fairly soft, cracks and small potholes are likely to appear nearly every year. They're easy to repair, and are one of the simplest household fixes.

1 **Clean out loose debris** with a trowel, digging down to the gravel base, if possible. For small cracks that are wider than ¼ inch, use a hammer and chisel to widen the bottom of the crack so that it is wider at the base than at the top.

2 **Fill with asphalt patch** For larger repairs, use a masons trowel to draw and spread the asphalt patch from the tub. For thin cracks, apply the material directly from a caulking tube.

3 **Tamp cold-mix asphalt** into the patch compound, and finish by leaving the area about ½ inch above grade. Seal the patch and the surrounding area with asphalt sealer.

(Paving continued)

Brick, pavers, and flagstone

Classic and durable patios and garden pathways are made from brick, flagstone, or the increasingly popular interlocking pavers. The materials can be mortared in place, which takes some skill, or laid directly on to sand or crushed rock, a project within the range of many homeowners.

Bricks Traditional bricks are made of clay and come in a variety of colors, including red, red and black, and tan. There are also half-thickness bricks, which are excellent for patios and walkways. Concrete bricks are less expensive, but their coarse finish and dull uniformity make them less appealing. Used bricks still spattered with mortar or paint make excellent pathway materials and have the look of having been in place for years. Used bricks may cost more because of the labor needed to remove old mortar.

There are many brick styles and grades, but for landscaping purposes the most important styles are face and common bricks. Common bricks, also called building bricks, are made of clay and are designed for the inner layer of a brick wall. Face bricks are higher quality and have a smooth face to resist weathering. Bricks are also made in three primary grades: SW, designed to withstand severe weathering and below-freezing temperatures; MW, designed to withstand freezing in dry climates; and NW, for areas with no freezing and low rainfall.

Flagstone and bluestone Durable and attractive flagstone and bluestone are also widely used for pathways and patios. They are best set in mortar but can also be bedded in sand or crushed rock. These paving materials need no care other than sweeping and periodic washing.

Pavers Concrete pavers are manufactured in a number of different patterns, many of which interlock for increased stability. Less expensive than brick or flagstone, concrete pavers can be laid in place quickly on any smooth, firm surface. Interlocking pavers do not need to be set in mortar, and they don't require a border to hold them in place, as do bricks or flagstone laid on sand.

Rock Crushed rock is also an excellent choice for a patio or walkway. As with a sand base for bricks or flagstone, crushed rock must have a rigid border to keep the material in place. Crushed rock is a better choice than gravel for a walking surface because its irregular edges lock firmly together. Rounder and smoother gravel rolls underfoot and does not stay in place.

budget stretcher • budget stretcher • budget stretcher •

Removing paint from brick

Brick is porous, making paint removal a problem. To remove small spots, scrape away as much dried paint as possible, then apply paint stripper to the remainder. Test stripper for staining by applying a small amount in an unobtrusive location. Remove a full coat of paint from brick by sandblasting. Be aware that the process destroys the bricks' protective surface, so they will be more vulnerable to the elements.

Maintenance

Inspect brick, flagstone, and pavers regularly for broken or loose mortar or paving units. These should be repaired before water and ice do more extensive damage. Garden areas that are continually damp and shady promote the growth of mildew, which in addition to being unsightly can be dangerously slippery. Remove moss and algae by scrubbing the surface with a long-handled brush or broom dipped in a 50–50 mix of bleach and water. Avoid spattering the leaves of adjoining garden plants with the mix, which can damage the plants. If this is a risk, cover the plants with an old sheet first.

Fixing problems

Although brick or flagstone paving will last for decades, individual pieces occasionally crack or come loose. If the loose piece has been mortared in place, use a cold chisel to break out the surrounding mortar, then pry the piece out. Vacuum or brush out loose material from the hole, then reset the piece in mortar as follows: To ready-mix mortar, available at home supply centers, add enough water to make the mortar the consistency of toothpaste. Spread an inch-thick layer in the hole, then press the brick or flagstone into it until level. The following day, use a grout bag to squeeze mortar around the brick or stone; smooth it with the back of an old spoon.

If a brick, flagstone, or paver placed on sand has sunk or become otherwise displaced, pry it out with a screwdriver, then add dry sand under it until level. Press the brick or stone back in place, then sweep dry sand over it to fill the spaces between it and adjoining pavers.

Efflorescence is often a problem with new brick patios, walkways, and walls. A crystalline white substance is pushed to the bricks' surface by moisture in the bricks or the soil. Although unsightly, it is not structurally harmful. Remove efflorescence by scrubbing bricks with a stiff brush dipped in a bucket containing 1 part muriatic acid to 3 parts water. Rinse the surface with a hose after scrubbing. You may have to repeat this process several times over a year or two until all the salts are forced from the brick and mortar.

■ SMART IDEA ■

Keeping weeds out of paving

Weeds that grow in the cracks between pavers are a common nuisance. The best solution is preventive: Spread a layer of landscape fabric under the pavers. The fabric allows water to drain through but prevents weeds from rooting. Any that do start are easy to scrap away.

If landscape fabric is not an option, plant ground covers such as creeping thyme in the spaces. Once established, the thyme will prevent weeds from finding growing space.

A third option is to simply kill the weeds. Various herbicides are available, or use a propane weed torch to scorch weeds. In either case, exercise caution.

Do you need an engineered wall?

Any retaining wall more than 4 feet high should be designed or approved by a structural engineer. For safety and to ensure structural reliability, a licensed professional should build the wall. The chief elements always working against any retaining wall, regardless of the height, are water and gravity. The steeper the slope and the heavier the wet soil, the greater the pressure on the wall.

Retaining walls

A retaining wall is designed to hold back an earthen bank that gravity otherwise compels to move downhill. As such, the wall must have a solid base, be tilted back (called battering), and have drains to keep water from damming up behind it. Because so many forces are continually putting pressure on retaining walls, they require regular maintenance and occasional repairs.

General maintenance

A leading cause of failure among retaining walls is improper drainage, which allows water and wet soil to build up behind the wall. The steeper the slope, the greater will be the force against the wall. Ideally, a retaining wall should be built with a 6- to 8-inch-wide band of gravel fill behind it and a perforated drainpipe along the base to carry water away.

Some walls are built with weep holes along the base that allow water to run through the wall. Clean these openings with a length of wire or screwdriver to ensure that they stay open. If a drainpipe exists behind your wall, check during the rainy months that the pipe is not plugged.

Retaining wall problems

Tilted wall If a retaining wall is leaning downhill instead of being tilted back uphill, it is losing the battle with gravity and the weight of earth behind it. The same holds true if a section of the wall has become bowed out of line. Retaining walls cannot be simply pushed back into proper alignment; they must be torn down and rebuilt. In such cases, it is best to have a licensed professional specialist, such as a landscape contractor, do the job.

Loose material If a brick in a mortared wall has come loose, remove it and chip away the old mortar around it. Apply a layer of ready-mix mortar, available at home supply stores, to the bottom and the ends of the brick, then slide the brick back into the opening. Add mortar to the top of the brick by pushing mortar from your trowel into the space with a jointing tool or the back of an old spoon. Scrape the excess mortar from the brick with the trowel, then wipe the brick clean with a wet rag. Loose rocks in a mortared stone wall are repaired in the same manner.

Another common problem of stone walls is a loose cap rock. Repair it by chipping off the old mortar, then setting the cap rock in a new bed of mortar. Fill gaps around the cap rock with mortar.

Repointing a brick wall

Removing and replacing deteriorated mortar restores the visual and physical integrity of the masonry.

1 Chip out damaged mortar For most damaged brick joints, remove the mortar to a depth of ½ to 1 inch, including any damaged mortar beyond that depth. Use a hammer and chisel for small areas, a power saw or a grinder and small pneumatic chisel for repointing entire walls.

2 Spread mortar into the hole and press it into the space. If the gap is deeper than an inch, add the mortar in layers.

3 Smooth mortar with a convex jointer. If the bricks have worn or rounded edges, recess the mortar slightly from the face of the masonry to avoid creating a joint that is visibly wider than the joints surrounding it.

Pressure-treated wood

Pressure-treated wood, which is widely used to build deck substructures, has chemicals forced into it to prevent it from rotting when in contact with soil. Wood that has been treated with chromated copper arsenate is being phased out because arsenic, a known carcinogen, is used in the mix. New types of pressure-treated woods replace the arsenic with copper.

Decks

A deck, like a patio, is essentially an outdoor room. It's the ideal place for entertaining friends, simply lazing about, or holding casual family gatherings. Rather than being just a wide expanse of boards, a deck can be segmented into different use areas. One part may be partially covered to provide refuge from the sun or rain. Multiple deck levels form areas that are distinct yet still connected. A deck can extend over steep and otherwise unusable land, or be tucked away in a little grove of trees as a private retreat. Regardless of the deck's size and style, a good quality deck, if given proper care, will last for decades.

Deck maintenance

The most important part of a deck is the supporting substructure. Any loose connections or broken elements could result in a collapse. Check under the deck annually to inspect for loose nails, screws, or bolts. Tighten loose bolts or screws; if a nail is loose, pull it, then drive in a larger one. Pay particular attention to crossbracing, ensuring that all pieces are tightly nailed or bolted and there are no cracked or rotted boards. Also inspect the joists and beams for cracks.

If the deck is attached to the house or garage, check that the ledger board—the supporting board fixed to the side of the house—is tightly bolted to the house. Because water can run down behind the ledger unless it's properly flashed, it is subject to rot. If you see carpenter ants, other evidence of wood-eating insects, or evidence of rot, remove the deck planking closest to the house, inspect the ledger board and replace it if necessary.

Check the joists and the underside of the decking for mold, usually a white or gray discoloration. If you find mold, scrape it clean, then spray the spot with a 50-50 mix of bleach and water. At the same time, use a small, sharp screwdriver to probe for signs of dry rot, which is often associated with mold. Push the tip into suspect areas. If the tip readily penetrates ½ inch or more, it may be a sign of rot. Call a decking contractor to further inspect the structure and recommend needed repairs.

On the decking itself, tighten any loose screws. If a nail is loose, replace it with a nail one size larger, or a screw. Similarly, check the railings and tighten loose posts or rails.

Decking materials

A variety of low-maintenance decking materials are available, ranging from all-natural wood to vinyl, plastic, and recycled wood-and-plastic combinations. These latter types of planks don't rot. Some are nailed like wood; some require special fasteners; and others have predrilled holes for screws.

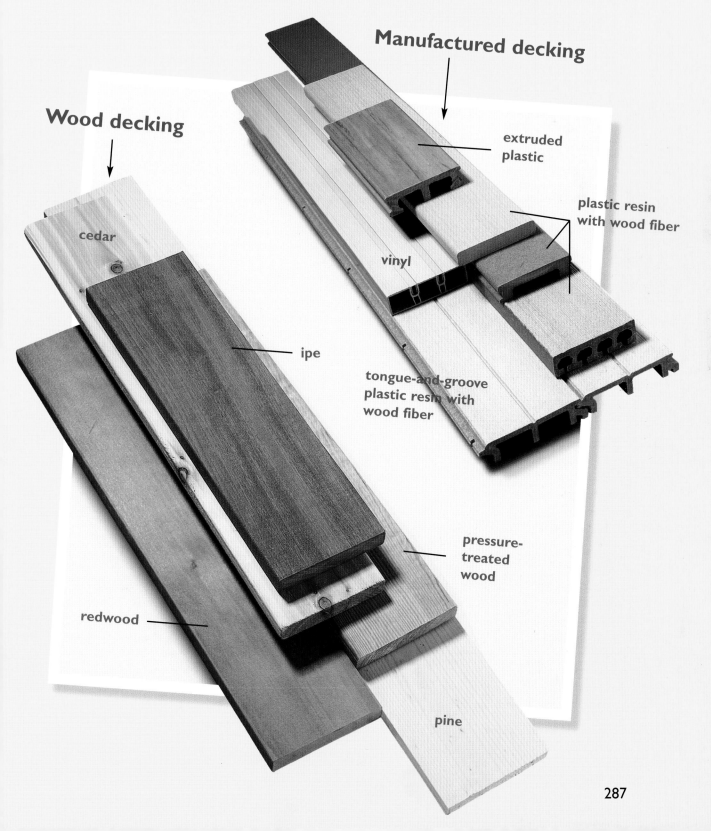

Manufactured decking

extruded plastic

plastic resin with wood fiber

vinyl

tongue-and-groove plastic resin with wood fiber

Wood decking

cedar

ipe

pressure-treated wood

redwood

pine

Put the paintbrush away

Avoid using paint or polyurethane on decks or outdoor wood structures. Polyurethane breaks down when exposed to direct sunlight. It will quickly yellow, then crack and peel away from the wood. Although exterior paint withstands the effects of sunlight and weathering, it is easily marred by regular foot traffic.

(Decks continued)

Sealing and staining your deck

New decks should be sealed promptly after installation, regardless of the type of wood used, including pressure-treated wood. Decks should also be sealed even if the wood is *green,* meaning freshly milled and still containing sap. Although the sap will evaporate and force some of the sealer out when it does, the sealer still benefits the wood. After the decking material has cured, seal it again.

Ideally, apply all protective stains or water repellents to the decking lumber before it is installed. In particular, the substance should be applied to the ends, edges, and underside of the decking first, because once the decking is down, these places are not accessible.

Types of stains and sealers

Clear water repellent Since it does not protect wood from ultraviolet light, the deck will weather to the soft gray of redwood and cedar. This repellent tends to remain on the surface of the wood rather than penetrating, so it should be applied annually to protect the wood. This is a popular choice for pressure-treated yellow pine decks.

Semitransparent stain This product contains small amounts of pigments that alter the color of the wood when it is applied, leaving the wood grain visible. These stains, combined with UV blockers and water repellents, generally last from two to three years and are a top choice for protecting new redwood or cedar decks.

Solid-color stain This product contains enough pigment to obscure the wood grain. It provides a smooth finish similar in appearance to paint but is more durable. It generally lasts two to three years. As with semitransparent stains, select varieties that include water repellents and UV blockers. Although stains hide the grain, the pigments add protection.

Bleaching To turn redwood, cedar, or tropical hardwoods a soft gray in a few months, use commercial bleaching and weathering stains, according to product directions.

Teak oils Hard-finish teak oils penetrate dense tropical hardwoods, such as ipe and meranti, better than sealers designed for redwood or cedar. The oil must be reapplied annually.

Care of your deck

You have a wealth of choices when it comes to deck cleaners and wood protectors. In addition, you will need either a sprayer or paint brushes and rollers, gloves to protect your hands, and typical cleaning supplies.

preservative sprayer

deck cleaners

wood protectors

deck cleaners

gloves

applicators

Best
deck
cleaner

The best way to
clean most wood
decks is with
products that
contain oxygen
bleach, also known
as sodium
percarbonate.
Mix with water
and apply with a
soft, sponge-like
applicator or a
pump sprayer.
Leave in place
exactly as long
as the directions
specify, usually
about 10 minutes,
then rinse
thoroughly.

(Decks continued)

Restoring an old deck

The first line of defense in maintaining a deck is to keep it clean. Dirt and sand tracked onto a deck will soon mar the finish, allowing UV rays and water to begin damaging the wood. Regular staining and sealing will slow this process, but it will still occur. Redwood, cedar, and tropical hardwoods will turn a soft gray when exposed to regular sunshine but will turn dark when used in a damp and shady area. Pressure-treated southern yellow pine will change from light green to light gray to dark gray over the years. Neglected decks will suffer even more quickly. Regardless, most wood decks can be restored almost to their original appearance in one of several different ways.

Bleaching Because wood fibers can be damaged during these processes, the best way to clean an old deck is the gentlest way, using a sprayer, scrub brushes, and common cleaning products. There are faster ways, but this technique puts color back into the wood with the least harm.

After sweeping the deck clean, spray the deck and railings with straight household bleach. Use a 2-gallon garden pump sprayer and adjust the nozzle to a mist. Be sure to cover surrounding plants with old sheets to protect them from the bleach. Plastic will also work, but on hot days there is a danger that the plants will overheat.

Use the sprayer to coat the deck and all parts of the railing, particularly the undersides of the top and bottom rails. The bleach should show almost immediate results by lightening the color of the wood. The bleach kills mold and mildew, which help turn the wood dark.

Immediately after spraying with bleach, hose the deck with water. Experts agree that bleach can be harmful to wood fibers, but little damage is done if it's rinsed away promptly. After rinsing, mix 12 ounces of oxalic acid, also called wood bleach, per gallon of water, and use a long-handled nylon brush dipped in the mixture to scrub the deck. Avoid using a metal brush, which could add black stains to the deck. In addition to further lightening the wood, the oxalic acid will remove the dark stains that develop around nongalvanized or poorly galvanized nailheads.

Inspect the deck to see that it is evenly bleached, and rescrub sections of wood that did not sufficiently lighten on the first round. Rinse the deck again thoroughly, and remove coverings from the plants.

When the deck is well dried, usually in a day or two, stain can be applied. Bleach damages wood fibers to some degree, which in turn makes penetrating stains less effective. For best results, use a semitransparent stain that contains UV blockers, water repellent, and mildewcides. Apply the stain with a long-handled paint pad or a roller, or brush it on. Be generous with the stain, allowing it to soak in until it begins to puddle on the surface.

Other methods

Pressure washing Portable high-pressure water sprayers will blast away ingrained dirt and sun-damaged surface fibers to turn a darkened wood deck back to its original color. High-pressure sprayers, both electric and gasoline-powered, can be rented in most areas. Use the sprayer also to clean the railings, posts, and steps.

Although this process is fast, many deck experts caution against it. Pressure washing to some degree cuts wood fibers and causes them to mat, which in turn reduces the penetrating abilities of deck stains. If you use the sprayer, protect the deck with a coat of sealer or stain as soon as the wood has dried.

Commercial cleaners There are a number of chemical deck cleaners and brighteners on the market that are designed to remove mildew, stains, and dirt ground into the deck's surface. Deck brightening products often contain bleach that may be disguised under its chemical name, sodium hypochlorite. These cleaners use only a percentage of bleach in the mix, not undiluted bleach. If you use a chemical cleaner, rinse it off after allowing it to set for the time specified in the instructions. Results will vary according to the product and the condition of the deck.

TSP You can clean and brighten a deck with materials commonly found in your house. In many cases, they are the same products found in commercial deck cleaners. One such material is trisodium phosphate (TSP). First wet the deck, then sprinkle it with the TSP. Scrub the deck with a brush or an old broom dipped in a bucket containing a 50-50 mix of water and bleach. Hose the deck clean, then let it dry before applying new coats of protective sealer or stain.

HOW-TO

Repairing deck knots

A loose knot in a deck—or an actual knothole—is unsightly more than it is a problem, but it can be readily fixed using these techniques.

To keep a loose knot in place, tack an aluminum can lid over the knot from the underside of the deck. Attach it with a few daubs of all-weather adhesive and use small nails to tack it in place.

If the knot has fallen out and you can recover it, put it back and hold it in place with the can lid, small nails, and all-weather adhesive.

If the knot is lost, tack the can lid in place and then fill the hole with wood putty. To make sure the putty matches your deck, mix sawdust from your deck planking into its surface before it dries.

(*Decks continued*)

Common deck repairs

Even with the best maintenance, decks will need some repairs and upgrades. Deck boards become loose or cracked, railings need replacing, support posts rot—the list can be depressingly long. If you can handle a hammer, screwdriver, and wrench, you can do many of the tasks yourself.

Loose deck board Deck boards are commonly attached to the joists with nails or screws, which can break or work their way out. If you do not see fasteners on the surface of the loose plank, the fastener may be hidden. Look at the deck boards from underneath to see what type of fastener is used.

If a nail comes loose, pull it out rather than hammering it down again. When pulling the nail, place a piece of scrap wood under the hammerhead to avoid marring the deck board. To securely fasten the board down again, use a nail one size larger than the original. Many builders recommend hot-dipped galvanized nails, but even these will leave black stains around the nailhead in redwood and cedar. A better choice for holding power and appearance is deck screws covered with a vinyl coating that matches the wood color.

Warped boards Some boards will warp with sufficient strength to pull the nails loose. To straighten an out-of-line deck board, remove the nails or screws from other boards for several feet on each side of the warped section. To push the warped board back into line, drive a chisel into the joist below the board where it is most out of line, then pry the board straight again by pushing on the chisel handle.

Broken or cracked boards These are hazardous and need to be removed and replaced as soon as you notice them. Remove all nails or screws holding the board in place and lift the board away from the joists. Replace the plank with the same kind of wood.

Damaged joists If a support joist is rotten or cracked, it lacks strength and needs to be bolstered. If rot is the problem, scrape away rotted material and treat the area with a wood preservative. Attach a new joist of the same size and length to the original joist with nails and all-weather adhesive. With the new joist installed, nail or screw the deck planking to the new joist.

Loose posts or rails Any problems should be repaired as soon as they are discovered. Posts are attached to the deck in different ways: Some are bolted at the base to a deck joist; others are sandwiched between two joists. In most cases they are *through-bolted,* meaning

Deck stains

According to the Forest Products Laboratory, penetrating oil-base, semitransparent stains that are formulated for decks last longest. These soak into the wood without forming a continuous layer that will later peel or crack. Plus the pigment protects the wood from sunlight.

that holes have been drilled through the post and the joist, and the two are joined with nuts and bolts. Others may be fastened with large lag screws. Tightening a loose post may be as simple as tightening a loose bolt. If the post has been nailed to the joist, remove the nails and through-bolt the post for greater stability.

Loose rails should be reaffixed with screws rather than nails. Replace cracked rails or balusters immediately with matching material. Stain and seal the replacement pieces before they are put in place, being careful to stain and seal the ends of the boards as well.

Stair repairs Regularly check that both the treads and the risers are securely in place. If nails have worked loose, replace them with deck screws, which are much more permanent.

Rotten or cracked stair stringers often go unnoticed because the treads and risers cover them. You may have to lie down beside the steps or crawl under the stringers to actually see what is going on. Inspect stringers for significant cracks. Some stringers are bolted to the deck substructure, and some are placed in metal joist hangers. Either way, inspect for loose connections, rot, or cracked stringers and repair as needed. Suspected weak areas can often be repaired by *sistering* (attaching) a length of wood, such as a 2×4, to the inside length of the stringer. Use pressure-treated wood and affix it with wood screws.

Also check the bottom of the stair stringer for rot. Wood that is in direct contact with the ground is subject to both rot and boring insects, such as termites. If this is the case, cut off damaged wood and set the bottom of the stringers on masonry, such as bricks or old pieces of concrete.

If an entire stringer must be replaced, remove the stair treads and risers first, then remove the stringer. Do this without breaking the stringer, then use it as a pattern for marking a new stringer. Stair stringers are almost always cut from pressure-treated 2×12 wood.

· HOW-TO ·

Updating deck railings

For safety, most building codes require a railing around any deck that is 36 inches or more above the ground. Additionally, codes require that the space between balusters or railings be 4 inches or less. This is primarily to prevent small children from wriggling through.

If several railings are loose or broken, take the opportunity to install all new railings and balusters in a different design. The new wood and new pattern will give the deck an updated appearance. You might wish to place screening over the balusters or install latticework between the cap rail and the deck—excellent means of protecting small children.

Fences and gates

There are ordinary fences, and there are fences that are works of art. Elegant or rustic, a fine fence enhances the entire yard. Similarly, a unique gate can bring life to an otherwise mundane fence. There are fences for privacy, for security, to hide unsightly areas, to define a boundary, or to contain livestock or pets. A fence need not be strictly utilitarian when it can also be eye-catching.

Fence boards

Clean and maintain Over the years, wind, rain, and ultraviolet (UV) rays combine to degrade both painted and natural-finish fence boards. Slowing this process can be as simple as washing away accumulated summer dust from a painted fence. Painted fences, like house siding, benefit from an annual washing with a brush and hot soapy water, followed by a rinse from a hose. Vinyl fences should be cleaned in the same manner, using a soft-bristle brush to avoid scratching the vinyl.

Unpainted fences are generally constructed with rot-resistant wood such as redwood or cedar, both of which mellow over time to a soft gray. In some cases, the wood turns nearly black. To lighten wood that has turned dark, use a garden sprayer to coat it with straight bleach. You will likely see the wood lighten right away as the bleach kills accumulated mildew. Rinse with the hose immediately after the treatment. If you have plants or lawn beside the fence, use plastic or old sheets to protect them from the bleach. Avoid using plastic on a hot day when it could cook the plants.

Like wood decks, wood fences should be protected with sealers and stains if they are not painted. For best results in applying a stain or sealer, use both a brush and a paint roller. Roll the stain over about a 4-foot-wide section and follow immediately with a brush for deeper stain penetration. The roller is fast, but it leaves the stain resting on top of the wood. The brush works the stain in. For proper maintenance, recoat the fence every two to three years.

Repaint When repainting your fence, first scrape or sand away any loose paint or drip marks. For best results, use a random-orbit sander to remove most of the old paint. Brush the fence clean, then apply a primer. When that is dry, lightly sand the surface to provide better adhesion, then apply a gloss or semigloss finish coat, which will give better protection than a flat finish. Be sure to paint the bottom ends of the fence boards, where moisture damage often begins.

family friendly · family friendly · family friendly · family friendly

Building fences

Regardless of the type of fence you want, there are two key factors to consider: local codes and your neighbors. In the first instance, city regulations commonly restrict the style and height of fences, especially in the front yard. Second, it's courteous to discuss fence plans with your adjoining neighbors, because the fence will affect them too.

Fence posts

Fence posts are usually made of either pressure-treated wood or a naturally rot-resistant wood such as redwood or cedar. Either way, moisture and earth are continually working against them.

If your fence posts are set in concrete, look where the concrete is formed around the wood at or slightly above ground level. Usually there is a space of ⅛ inch to ¼ inch between wood and concrete, which is a result of the concrete shrinking as it dries. Water will run down into that gap and be trapped against the post, inducing rot. To prevent this, fill the gap with a bead of silicone caulk and repeat annually or as needed.

If your posts are set directly in earth, build the dirt up on all four sides in a pyramid fashion to keep water from pooling at the base. Tamp the earth firmly in place against the post with your foot.

Replacing a support post A broken or rotted fence post must be replaced. Use a posthole digger to dig next to the weakened post to a depth of 30 to 36 inches. The support post should extend above the ground one-third to one-half the height of the damaged post. The support post must be positioned tightly against the weakened post and be of equivalent dimensions.

If the weakened post is set in concrete, either break away the concrete or half-lap the lower portion of the support post so it fits over the concrete. Bolt the two posts together, then fill the hole with packed dirt or a bag of ready-mix post-setting concrete.

If the post is instead set into the ground, use a metal support, which fits around three sides of a 4×4 post at the base. Drive the long, pointed tail section into the ground, and then bolt it to the post.

Straightening a fence post Even a perfectly sound fence post may lean out of line, dragging the fence with it. To straighten a post, dig down to the base on the side opposite the lean. Push the post upright and brace it with one or two temporary 2×4 supports. Reset the post with earth (pack it down) or ready-mix concrete. Leave the supports in place until the concrete has thoroughly hardened.

HOW-TO

Set a strong fence post

The key to setting a post that won't wobble after it is set in dirt or gravel is a lot of hard tamping. Once the post is held vertical with a few inches of dirt or gravel around its base, use the shovel handle to pack the dirt down hard.

Add another few inches of filler and pack it down hard again before adding more. Continue in this manner until the post is set. Mound some dirt up around the base of the post so water will drain away.

Concrete does not have to be pounded down like dirt, but you still need to work it to ensure that it's firm. When setting a post in concrete, use a stick instead of the shovel handle to work out any bubbles in the concrete after you add each layer.

295

(Fences and gates continued)

Gates

Wood fence gates habitually get out of line and don't close properly. Here are some methods to correct the problem:

Loose post A post can be pulled over by the weight of the gate. To correct this, remove the gate and the fence rails and boards where they are attached to the post. Reset the post as described on page 295, preferably in concrete. Reconnect the fence rails and boards to the post, using screws longer than the original ones. Reinstall the gate.

Loose hinges If a gate will not close properly because the hinges have worked loose from the post or the gate, use new screws slightly longer than the original ones for better holding power. If that doesn't work, attach the hinge somewhere else, especially if the hinge was in the wrong place to begin with. But if the hinge is where it needs to be, drill through the wood with a bit that just slides through the screw hole in the hinge plate. Then, install the hardware with machine bolts, nuts, and washers.

A loose hinge problem may not originate with the fastener. It may be loose because it's carrying more weight than it is designed for. (Gates higher than 5 feet or wider than 3 feet need three hinges.) Add a new hinge of the same strength or perhaps three new, heavier ones.

Gate sticks If the gate sticks on the latch side even though the posts and gate are properly installed, use a hand plane or wood rasp to shave away wood on the gate until it fits properly. Be sure to paint or stain the bare wood promptly. For minor sticking, just rub the area with paraffin.

Gate sags Gates are commonly made from four pieces of wood formed in a square or rectangle that is then covered with fence boards. Unless the gate frame is properly crossbraced, it will eventually sag. The crossbrace should extend from the lower hinged side of the rectangle to the upper latch side. In many instances, the brace is placed just the opposite of this, which fails to provide proper support. To repair a sagging gate, take it down and remove the boards from the frame. Straighten the frame until it is square, then affix metal L-braces (or triangular wooden gussets) to all four corners. To determine whether the frame is square, measure both diagonals; when they are the same, the frame is square. If the frame did not have a crossbrace, add one now to help keep the gate square.

Gate repairs

To make the repair as easy as possible, look in hardware and home stores for repair kits for sagging gates. These kits include corner brackets, gate truss cable, a turnbuckle, and screws. Install the kit so that the cable extends from the latch to the opposite bottom corner so it pulls up the latch side of the gate.

Repairing a sagging gate

Gates take a lot of abuse, so it's no surprise that most eventually sag or bind. Fortunately, most gate repairs are not very complicated.

File or plane Some gates bind only in wet weather, as wood swells. Mark the spot and file it down later once wood dries. File any spots where clearance is less than ¼ inch.

Install brace Fix a sagging gate by squaring it and bracing it in place; remove it if necessary. Attach a diagonal support as shown, from the upper latch-side corner to the lower hinge-side.

Reset hinges and latch If tightening no longer is sufficient, an easy fix is to install new hardware in a slightly different location.

Realign the support post If the gate opening is not square, the likely cause is a leaning post. With the post re-plumbed and braced, dig out the footing and reset it in concrete. Keep braces in place until the concrete cures.

297

Bathing beauty

Got a sun worshipper in your house, or rather on your patio? If you have vinyl patio furniture, take precautions. Tanning oil and sunscreens penetrate vinyl, causing it to crack and break. Cover vinyl furniture with a towel before stretching out on it. Clean it with a mild dish soap and warm water to remove lotion residue.

Maintaining outdoor furniture

Outdoor living and loafing on the deck or patio involve furniture that may be plastic, wood, cast iron, aluminum, fabric wicker, or a combination of materials. Each variety needs some regular care to look its best.

Plastic Those ubiquitous white or green plastic lawn chairs serve their purpose well: They're inexpensive and stack easily for storage. If they are left outdoors for a few winters, however, the finish will deteriorate. White furniture is particularly susceptible to staining from mildew and grime. Although the chair cannot be scrubbed back to its original color, it can be revived with a coat of paint.

The fastest and easiest way is to spray the furniture with a glossy acrylic paint. Krylon has developed a paint specifically for plastic furniture and children's play equipment. The company says it is not necessary to sand and prime the surfaces first; just spray and play.

Exterior glossy latex paint also holds up well on plastic furniture. Clean the furniture first with a rag and a 50-50 solution of vinegar and water. Let dry, then either paint with a brush or use an aerosol spray. The paint goes on smoothly and adheres well.

Cast iron This outdoor furniture is valued for its durability and solid appearance, but it must be kept painted to prevent rust. If existing paint is flaking, scrub it with a wire brush to remove all loose pieces. Wash the surface with a 50-50 mix of water and white vinegar to help prime the metal; let dry, then apply a thin coat of acrylic latex metal primer. When the primer is dry, brush or spray on a coat of glossy acrylic latex paint. Remove any adjoining wood that is attached to the cast iron or protect it with newspaper and masking tape. If rust shows up in spots under the paint, scrape and sand down to bare metal, then prime and touch up with matching paint.

Aluminum Aluminum furniture can be painted in the same manner as cast iron. Glossy exterior acrylic latex paint is the best choice for aluminum. Wipe the aluminum first with a 50-50 mix of water and white vinegar. Apply a primer coat, then the finish coat. Aerosol paint comes in a variety of colors, so be as daring as you wish.

Wood Whether painted or stained, wood needs regular attention to prevent it from cracking and splitting. Touch up painted wood as necessary, but if the paint is cracked and peeling, it's best to strip and refinish the wood. Wearing rubber gloves and working in

Furniture care basics

With regular cleaning and periodic maintenance, outdoor furniture looks better and lasts longer.

Fabric Brush loose particles from fabric-covered cushions. Spot clean with a stiff brush and a mild solution of dish soap in warm water.

Wood Renew wooden furniture by stripping off old, peeling paint. Then either prime and repaint or stain and seal.

Metal Renew metal furniture with a steel brush to remove rust, followed by spray primer and paint.

Aluminum Clean aluminum with soapy water and a mildly abrasive scrub pad. Prime and paint for a new look.

Plastic Renew stained plastic by spraying with paints specifically intended for that purpose.

299

Powder coat

If you have old metal patio furniture to restore, consider powder coating. Special equipment is required, meaning it's only done by professionals, but it looks good and lasts. Dry, finely ground particles of pigment and resin are electrostatically charged and sprayed onto the furniture. Then the furniture is baked, and the particles melt and fuse together.

(Maintaining outdoor furniture continued)

a well-ventilated area, coat the wood with paint stripper and let it soak in to soften the paint. Some strippers will penetrate 10 or more coats of paint, so give the paint stripper time to work. Use a paint scraper to remove the softened paint, then sand away any remaining residue. If repainting, be sure to first apply a primer coat, then the finish coat. If you are staining the wood, apply a sealer first, or use a combination sealer/stain for best results.

Redwood and cedar commonly weather to a soft gray. If the wood has turned nearly black, it can be cleaned and restored to its original beauty. For details on this process, see deck restoring techniques on page 290. Teak is a popular choice for outdoor furniture because it readily withstands severe weathering with little or no maintenance. New teak is light yellow in color but weathers to a soft gray. Special teak cleaners, brighteners, and sealers are available.

Fabric To clean pillows, hammocks, and patio umbrellas, use a stiff brush to spot-wash the problem area with detergent and water. Be sure to let the material dry thoroughly to prevent mildew. For stubborn spots, use a commercial spot remover, or wash the fabric with a mix of 3 parts water to 1 part bleach. Always test the cleaner on a small inconspicuous area of the fabric first.

Teak The polished appearance of teak furniture comes from oil occurring naturally in the wood. The surface oil will evaporate after a few days outdoors but it is the sub-surface oil gives that gives the wood its durability. After a short time outdoors, six to nine months, depending on the amount of exposure, the untreated furniture acquires an attractive silver-gray patina. Water spots or other discoloration may also occur during weathering. Once the teak has this patina, it is advisable not to apply any oil at all because it may invite mildew or cause irregular coloring.

Periodically cleaning teak furniture is beneficial. Use a solution of 4 parts dishwashing soap and 1 part bleach applied with a soft-bristle brush; rinse thoroughly. For deeper cleaning, use a cleaner specifically designed for teak; check with your dealer. It's possible to keep the furniture its original golden color—or restore it—with a teak sealer, but this will require annual applications. These cleaners restore the furniture to its natural golden color regardless of how long the piece has been outside.

outdoor
lighting

Lighting enhances the beauty of your yard and adds to safety and security.

Not long ago, outdoor lighting meant floodlights over the back door. Today, landscape lighting greatly expands your living space, allowing you to enjoy outdoor rooms in your yard. Whether you have a system that you want to upgrade, or you want to start from scratch, here's how lighting works and how to care for it.

Outdoor lighting

Outdoor lighting systems include 120-volt power; 12-volt or low-voltage power, which is the simplest and most widely used system; solar-powered lights; and light-emitting diodes (LED). You can use any of the above or a combination of systems. Each type has its own requirements and benefits.

How much voltage?

120-volt These systems run on the same electrical supply as your house. They are versatile because the fixtures available for them range from dim to brilliant in brightness. 120-volt systems are especially useful for security lighting. Have a licensed electrician install them.

Low-voltage In low-voltage systems, household current is reduced to 12-volts so these systems are much safer and more economical for homeowners to work with. Lighting tends to be dimmer than 120-volt systems, but the effects can be dramatic.

Solar-powered Photovoltaic panels on a solar light charge a small battery during daylight, and the battery operates the light at night. Because no wiring is involved, the lights can be readily moved to a new location as needed. Most need at least six hours of sun daily for a full charge.

LEDs Light-emitting diodes for outdoor use are relatively new to the field but are gaining in popularity. They will far outlast a standard incandescent bulb. LEDS produce only about one-tenth of a watt of power, comparable to the light put out by lightning bugs. Group several together to cast more light.

· HOW-TO ·

Extending connections

The standard way to extend 120-volt electricity to a yard is to run the wiring underground to posts set at strategic locations in the yard. and then mount an outdoor receptacle on the post.

For safety's sake, 120-volt wire must either be encased in electrical conduit or rated for direct burial. In most communities, local codes specify how deep the wire is to be buried.

Additionally, all receptacles must be in weatherproof boxes and must be GFCI (ground fault circuit interrupter) receptacles or wired to a GFCI breaker. GFCI receptacles cut off power in about one one-hundredth of a second, before any harm can be done, if it senses a short circuit.

Low-voltage equipment

Low-voltage lighting can be purchased in a kit form or by individual elements. For a fast and simple setup—the job can be completed in an hour or so—the kit systems are a good choice. For $50 to $100 you get a transformer, about 100 feet of wire, and six to 12 lights of varying styles, usually some basic tiered lights and spotlights. The relatively low price is offset by the fact that kit systems cannot be expanded, and the quality is below what you could obtain by buying the elements individually.

Kit systems cannot normally be expanded because of the limitations of the transformer and the lights. Kit transformers usually are designed with a limited amount of wattage, which is matched to the watts on the kit lamps. Adding more lights or ones with higher wattage would overload the transformer. Also, kit transformers usually have only one circuit available for the low-voltage lights, and the wire is incapable of handling more lights. If you want to add more lights later, you will have to buy another kit or, better, purchase a lighting system designed for your specific needs.

For more professional quality and a wider choice, spend time at a lighting store to see what lamps are available and determine which will best fit your lighting plans. Selecting the transformer, the wiring, and all the lights individually, gives you the freedom to choose exactly what you need. When you want to add more lights, you will be able to do so if you bought a powerful enough transformer (see "Stretching watts" at left).

Low-voltage bulbs are brighter, watt for watt, than incandescent bulbs and last much longer—routinely 2,000 to 4,000 hours and up to 20,000 hours. Wattage ranges from 10 to 100 watts, with the most widely used bulbs in the 20- to 50-watt range. Keep in mind that the total wattage of your lamps cannot exceed the transformer's wattage limitation. If it does, your system will either function below par or not at all.

Whether you have a system you want to upgrade or you want to start from scratch, you will find all the details on getting under way, from planning to installation, in the following pages. With these and a design plan, you can have a superior landscape lighting system.

Transformers

A transformer is the heart of a low-voltage system. It's the device that reduces the 120-volt alternating current for the house to a harmless 12 volts of direct current. Different transformers are designed to

budget stretcher • **budget stretcher** • **budget stretcher** • **budget stretcher**

Stretching watts

When planning a low-voltage system, count the total number of watts the bulbs will use, then select a transformer that will handle at least 50 percent more. This allows you to expand the system significantly without having to purchase another transformer. Kit systems already have the wattage-to-transformer size worked out.

Deck and patio fixtures

When lighting decks and patios, aim for an effect similar to interior lighting. Choose a variety of fixtures to support the way you will use the space. For example, use brighter lights where you will be cooking or playing games, dimmer lights where you want to create a mood, and the brightest lights where security is a concern.

Security light fixtures provide bright, far-reaching light. Use them to eliminate shadows where intruders could hide or where you want to ensure safe passage. Built-in motion detectors turn on the lamp whenever someone or something comes near.

Rope lights These small, low-wattage lights are set in flexible plastic tubing that can be readily bent or curved to follow any form. They are particularly effective under benches or along deck railings.

Deck lights are usually mounted on walls or posts. They can also be recessed into the wall. Typically, they are hooded or have frosted glass to prevent glare. Mount them below seated eye level.

Floodlights and spotlights are versatile fixtures, useful for security lighting or for creating dramatic effects with shadows. This one is a 120-volt, stake-mounted fixture. Better-quality floodlights have an adjustable beam that ranges from a moderate to a wide spread. They are among the most widely used yard lights, for everything from grazing lights on walls to lighting trees.

Post lights direct their illumination downward. They can be mounted on deck posts to illuminate work areas on the deck or on separate posts to mark pathways or the bottom of the deck stairs.

(*Low-voltage equipment continued*)

handle different amounts of wattage, usually ranging from 50 watts to 1,000 watts.

The least expensive transformers are entirely manual: You have to turn them on and off each time you use them. Better transformers have timers to control the hours in use. Others have a photoelectric cell that turns the lights on at dusk, plus timers to switch them off at the appointed hour. Good transformers have a memory chip that restores the lighting schedule in the event of a power outage. These top transformers also have breaker switches to prevent power overloads.

To install a transformer, you hang it on a wall near an outlet and plug it in. Depending on its quality, the transformer will handle from one to four low-voltage circuits, each controlled by an individual switch. This allows you to operate all yard lighting at once or to select just one or two lights.

Wiring

Low-voltage-system wiring normally ranges in size from 16-gauge to 10-gauge wire. The lower the gauge number, the thicker the wire, which means it can carry more electricity with less resistance. The most common size is 12-gauge wire, the same size widely used for residential wiring. This thicker wire prevents a voltage drop, or insufficient power, at the end of the wiring over long runs. A voltage drop causes lights at the end of the wiring run to be noticeably dimmer than others on that line. In such instances, you may have to remove the last one or two lamps, or install larger-gauge wiring.

For small yards with 50 feet or less of wiring, 14-gauge wire is sufficient. For wiring runs up to 150 feet, 12-gauge wire will suffice, but beyond that, use 10-gauge wire. Even for runs to 150 feet, 10-gauge wire will be more efficient.

Low-voltage wiring can be laid directly on the ground or buried without the special protection that is required for 120-volt wiring. The wire can be lightly covered by soil or decorative bark, or completely buried. Where the wire must cross a lawn, use a square-point shovel to cut a slot in the sod and fold it back. Use a stick to push the wire down about 6 inches into the earth, then push the sod back in place with your foot.

Fixtures

Tiered lights Among the most common, tiered or pagoda lights have louvers on them that cast a pool of light downward to prevent glare. They are often used to outline walkways and driveways.

Lamp rehab

Low-voltage lamps are exposed to the elements year-round, which can take a toll on the finish. Plastic is particularly susceptible to damage from ultraviolet rays. To brighten a worn-looking lamp, clean it well, then give it a light coating of spray paint.

Yard and garden fixtures

With a few adjustments, the fixtures used in the yard and garden are the same as those used on decks and patios. Away from the house, though, you can take advantage of their full range of effects.

Spotlights focus intense beams on an object. They can be used in the yard to dramatic effect, illuminating focal points, creating shadows, and lighting large areas from above. When you need a strong, direct light, choose spotlights. Use them sparingly, however, because they tend to overwhelm the rest of your yard lights. They can be angled up into trees and plants or positioned overhead to provide area lighting.

Path lights direct their beams downward. They come in many styles, such as this tulip light, the bollard light below, and the post light on page 305. Use them wherever you'd like a muted pool of light.

Well lights are low-profile lights that are set in a shallow well below ground level and pointed up to light trees, shrubs, or walls. The well shields the bulb and prevents glare. Some take on the shape of other objects, such as this stone.

Halogen spotlight bulbs shine whiter and brighter than ordinary incandescent bulbs. Because they are so efficient, they can be small enough to use in a low-voltage system yet produce as much light as a regular bulb.

Specialty lights Specialty lights inspire special uses. This one, mounted on the side of a turtle, fits alongside a pond or waterfall.

Bollard lights are akin to post lights, and in fact the terms are often used interchangeably for any fixture on a short stem. This example casts light in a 360-degree pattern. The light is usually diffused and not intrusive.

Adjustable spotlights can be placed on the ground or in trees.

(Low-voltage equipment continued)

Twig lights These tall, slim lights closely resemble a twig stuck in the ground. Group them together or mix them among tall plants.

Underwater lights These are designed to be placed in a garden pond, behind a waterfall, or in a fountain. Most have an extra-long cord in order to reach a low-voltage connection beyond the water.

Riser lights Small, low-wattage lights are inset into stair risers, marking where the stairs are at night and improving safety.

Post cap lights Ranging in style from large globes to low-profile caps, these lights are effective on top of any post, such as gate posts, deck posts, or posts that are artistically positioned in the yard.

Lamp types

Lamps are constructed from a wide variety of materials ranging from plastic to cast aluminum to copper to actual rock. There are scores of styles. Top-of-the-line low-voltage fixtures will last for years without suffering weather damage. Freestanding yard lamps are commonly mounted on a plastic stake, and the whole unit is positioned by pushing the stake into the ground. Other lamps may rest on the ground, nestle beside rocks or plants, or attach to a vertical surface.

Here is a rundown of the materials used in low-voltage lamps and what to look for in terms of quality.

Plastic Plastic is the least durable of lamp materials. The lamps are more flimsily constructed than their metal counterparts. The sun's ultraviolet light and the mix of rain and sun will discolor the plastic in a few years. Plastic can be painted with glossy exterior acrylic latex, however, to help restore its appearance.

Steel This is the next step up from plastic. Steel is more durable than plastic, but it will rust if the exterior coating is scratched or worn. It needs periodic rust removal and painting to keep it in good shape. Steel is being phased out in favor of other metals.

Aluminum More costly than plastic or steel, aluminum is a better choice in terms of durability. The additional expense is offset by the need to buy fewer replacement lamps. There are two types of aluminum: spinning and cast. Spinning produces a lighter and tinnier product; cast aluminum is heavier and thicker. Cast aluminum is more expensive, but it has a more imposing appearance. Aluminum can oxidize in harsh climates, particularly near the seacoast.

Copper, bronze, and brass These materials are the high end of lamp materials in terms of both quality and cost. All withstand severe

Long-lasting bulbs

Because it is made of quartz rather than glass, a halogen bulb can withstand higher internal heat and pressure than standard incandescent bulbs. The bulb contains inert halogen gas, which makes the bulb burn brighter and last longer than standard bulbs.

climates and are a top choice for areas near the sea, where the salt air damages steel and aluminum. Copper will naturally take on an attractively weathered green patina; it requires little or no care.

Bulb types

Bulbs for low-voltage systems range in wattage from 10 to 100 or more watts. The most common range is 20 to 50 watts. Low-voltage bulbs are less expensive to operate than bulbs for 120-volt systems, and they far outlast them. Most are rated for at least 2,000 hours, and some up to 20,000 hours. The combination of low-voltage power and long-lasting bulbs means that the operating costs for outdoor lighting are low.

Standard incandescent bulbs have now been largely replaced by brighter and longer-lasting low-voltage halogen bulbs. Incandescent bulbs are less expensive than halogen bulbs and don't burn as hot. Their life span is 600 to 1,000 hours.

Halogen bulbs are technically incandescent, but they burn hotter and more efficiently than standard incandescent bulbs. Don't touch the glass bulb with your bare hands during installation, because the slight amount of oil transferred to the bulb from your fingers will cause it to overheat at that point and burst. If you do touch the bulb, clean it with rubbing alcohol. Halogen bulbs usually last in the 1,000- to 4,000-hour range. They come in several styles. The industry standard is the mirror-reflector MR-16, which is available in a variety of wattages and beam spreads. Being the industry standard, it is less expensive.

▪ SMART IDEA ▪

Lighting kit or custom?

Outdoor lighting kits are relatively inexpensive and can be set up quickly. If you find one that suits exactly your needs, good. But kits have limitations. Typically the wiring in a kit is 16-gauge, which is so small it may cause the voltage to drop at the lamps farthest from the transformer, causing them to dim.

If you select components—transformer, wiring, and lamps—separately, you will get just what you need for your project, assuming you planned in advance. The cost is likely to be slightly greater than a kit, but the benefit is being able to choose lamp styles that meet your specific needs. Plus, the equipment will be better quality and last longer.

Metal halide This casts a bright bluish-white light more like sunlight than a regular halogen bulb. A metal halide bulb can be expected to last about 10,000 hours.

High-pressure sodium This light is a favorite for the moonlight effect it creates when beaming down from tall trees. The light is yellow-orange, and the bulb has a standard life of about 24,000 hours.

Both metal halide and high-pressure sodium bulbs have tubes containing a light-emitting gas that takes three to four minutes to reach full brilliance.

Making connections

Sometimes pierce-point connectors bend or miss the wire inside. Fix them the old-fashioned way: Cut the low-voltage wire and strip ¼ inch from the end of the wires. Do the same with the lamp wires. Then connect the wires with wire nuts. Protect the connections with heat-shrink rubber tubing.

Low-voltage system maintenance

Although outdoor low-voltage lighting is constantly exposed to the elements, it is surprisingly resistant to failure. Periodically cleaning lens elements and checking the wiring and connections will give you better and longer-lasting lights.

Transformer Although it has no moving parts, keep it clean inside and out to minimize the chance of dirt and moisture interfering with the electrical connections. If the transformer is mounted on a post, keep it at least a foot above ground so water runoff will not affect it. Once or twice a year, unplug the transformer and check that all the wire connections are clean and tight.

Outdoor receptacle If the transformer is connected to an outdoor receptacle, that receptacle must be GFCI protected or must be connected to a GFCI breaker at the residence. Both receptacles and breakers have test buttons on them. Check that the system is working properly by pushing the test button, which will shut down the connection. To resume operations, push the reset button. Ensure that the receptacle's weatherproof box has not been damaged.

Wiring Follow the wires from the transformer to all the lamps, looking for signs of wear or nicks. If the wire's insulation has been just slightly nicked, perhaps by a shovel, wrap the damaged area tightly with black electrical tape. If the wire is exposed, strip the ends of the wires back ½ inch and reconnect them with weatherproof twist connectors.

Wire connections If using the standard-issue, pushpin-style wire connections for the lamps, squeeze them between your fingers to ensure that the needles are firmly connecting with the wires. If you switched to weatherproof twist connectors, give each one a slight clockwise twist to tighten the wire connections.

Lamps Because dust and grime on lens covers will impair the light output, wipe the covers with a damp, clean cloth as often as necessary. Using a little water rather than just a dry cloth will help prevent scratches on plastic covers.

Bulbs Bulbs sometimes work loose, causing the light to flicker. Periodic tightening will help prevent this. If rust develops on or around a bulb socket, shut off that circuit, remove the bulb, and sand away the rust. A light spray of oil will improve the electrical connection and help prevent further rust. If you touch a halogen bulb with bare fingers, you must wipe it with rubbing alcohol.

Troubleshooting guide

Problem	What to do
The last few lights at the end of the wiring run are less bright than the other lights.	Dim lights at the end of a run indicate that electrical resistance is high, meaning insufficient electricity is reaching the lamp. This is caused by the wire being too thin for that distance. Run 10-gauge wire from the transformer to the first lamp, then continue with the existing wiring. Alternatively, you can replace all the wiring on that run with a heavier gauge. In other words, if you were using 14-gauge wire, change to 12-gauge.
One light on the circuit flickers.	The lightbulb is probably loose. Remove the lamp's cover and tighten the bulb. If that doesn't work, the connection between the lamp and the wiring is loose. Press pushpin connectors tightly so the pins make contact with the wires. If you have weatherproof twist connectors, tighten them. If that does not work, replace the twist connectors with new ones.
One light in the middle of a circuit is dim.	This may be just a dirty lens cover. Check and clean the cover. It may also be a poor connection between bulb and socket or between lamp and wiring. Unplug the transformer, remove the bulb, and clean its base and the socket with sandpaper or a small wire brush. Confirm that the lamp wires are tightly connected to the wiring.
The transformer is plugged in, the GFCI is functioning, but the system does not work.	The timing mechanism on the transformer is switched to OFF. Turn the timer to ON.
The transformer is plugged in, the GFCI is functioning, the breaker is okay, but the system still does not work.	If the transformer is equipped with a photoelectric cell and it is still daylight, the photocell can override the on-off functions. Hold your finger over the photoelectric cell for a minute or two to see if the system switches on.
The photocell is okay, the terminal connections are tight, but the system will not work.	A loose wire or a faulty transformer is often the cause. Unplug the transformer, open it up, and check that all wire connections and fittings are tight. If you have a continuity tester, check all the connections. If you still have no success, return the transformer for repairs or replacement.
The transformer is plugged in but the lights don't work.	The GFCI device may have been tripped. At the GFCI receptacle, press the reset button. Do the same if the GFCI is in a breaker panel.
The GFCI receptacle or breaker clicks off as soon as the transformer is plugged in.	The GFCI device will shut off in a fraction of a second if it detects a short circuit. Unplug the transformer and check all the wiring, starting with the low-voltage wires attached to the transformer. Confirm that all connections along the wiring runs are tight. Check the wiring for a cut or nick that has exposed wire.
The GFCI or breaker in the panel trips a minute or two after the system is turned on.	The circuit is overloaded, meaning that the total wattage of bulbs on the circuit is more than the transformer can carry. Reduce the electrical load by removing one or more lamps until the total wattage is within the transformer's rating. Another solution is to add another transformer to establish new circuits, or install a larger transformer.

family friendly · family friendly · family friendly · family friendly

The shadows know

It is the shadow that lends substance and form to an object, not the light that illuminates it. Consider a photograph of a person's face at midday compared to one taken early in the morning or late in the afternoon. The interesting shadows in the latter situations create the same depth of lighting effect you want in your yard and garden.

Lighting effects

One of the best things about outdoor lighting is the chance to experiment, because in most cases it is easy to reposition lights. If your present landscape lighting system no longer fits your needs, or you are planning an entirely new one, keep in mind that you will be creating an atmosphere. Remember that, in outdoor lighting, less is better. Subtle lighting is the key to success, as is accenting only special parts of the house or yard with light.

How the light is angled will also influence the overall lighting design. In this regard, there are two primary types of yard lighting: up or down. Within these parameters, of course, there are many variations.

Uplighting

Angling the light up is the most dramatic approach, because it is the opposite of what happens during the day, with the sun shining down from above. Uplighting, such as a flashlight held beneath someone's chin, literally casts everything in a different light, which immediately captures attention. Lights that are angled sharply up are particularly effective on trees, large plants, fountains, and waterfalls.

Graze lighting When an object is lit from a close angle rather than full on, the surface is cast into strong relief, which brings out details that would otherwise go unnoticed. A grazing light angled up against a brick or stone wall will cast distinct shadows. It is the shadow, not the light that provides the impact.

Silhouetting Place a light in front or behind an object, such as a large plant or small tree, to present that object in stark outline. The lamp can be aimed up at the plant from behind, which emphasizes the plant itself (backlighting), or the light can be aimed at a wall close to and behind the plant, which silhouettes the plant against the wall (shadow lighting).

Ambient lighting Provide a soft background and set the stage for more directed types of lighting. A light washing across rock or a brick wall will cause the ambient light to bounce attractively onto a nearby plant or tree. Similarly, ambient light reflecting from a tree can cast a warm glow over a seating area beneath the tree canopy.

Accent lighting Emphasize and enhance particular objects by setting them apart from their surroundings. Accent lights are often small fixtures that can be hidden behind a plant, placed flush with the ground or below ground level, or tucked into a row of flowerpots. The light itself is not seen, just the object it is focused on.

Outdoor lighting

Night lighting will alter your landscape quickly and dramatically, not to mention allowing use of the garden after dark. These are the basic techniques.

Shadow lighting Place lights low, in front of plants or sculptures so that shadows appear behind the objects.

Uplighting Place a well light, floodlight or spotlight at the base of the object you want to illuminate. Aim the light skyward to create dramatic shadows.

Path lighting Gentle pools of light direct visitors along a sidewalk to ensure safe travel. The effect can be achieved with path lights, bollards, and overhead lights.

Graze lighting Place a light close to an interesting surface so that the light washes over it, casting the surface into bold relief.

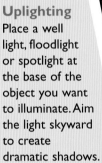

Moonlighting This type of downlighting is intended to emulate moonlight. It is particularly effective when mounted high in a tree so that light cascades through the canopy.

Backlighting Place a light behind the item you wish to highlight to create a silhouette.

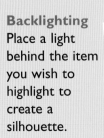

Accent lighting Aim floodlights upward to focus attention on an object or area.

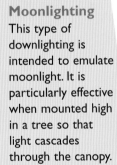
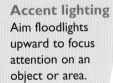

Central power

Putting the transformer in a central location means shorter and more efficient runs of low-voltage wire. Run 120-volt power from the house underground to areas nearer the center of your planned lighting. The shorter the low-voltage wiring, or the larger the gauge of wire, the more efficient the lighting.

(Lighting effects continued)

Downlighting

Although generally less dramatic than uplighting, lights pointed down are ideal for such things as illuminating pathways or a wide expanse of deck or patio where people gather to socialize.

Moonlighting One of the most effective uses of downlighting. One or two flood lamps placed high in a tree spill light through the branches in a manner similar to the light cast by a full moon. Position the lights so that branches and leaves are in front of the light, to diffuse it and cause a dappled effect below.

Task lighting A form of downlighting sometimes necessary to light an area being used for specific purposes. Typically, a barbecue area will need a light positioned overhead so the cook can see properly. The danger with task lights is that they may overwhelm other garden lights. Remembering to turn off task lights when not in use can mitigate their potential for intrusion.

Task lights are also effective for yard structures, such as a trellis, an arbor, or a gazebo—places where people may wish to sit and read or may otherwise need overhead lights. Additionally, a task light casting a glow from within a structure such as a gazebo is a preferred alternative to lighting the building from the outside. Shadows provide the definition.

Path lighting These downlights provide light for safely maneuvering in the yard, but their soft light and low profile are not objectionable. They come in such a wide range of styles that it is worth your time to visit several stores or search online for the pathway lights that best fit your design.

Floodlighting Lighting the entire backyard is the least effective form of yard lighting, but it is commonly seen in the form of motion sensor lights aimed at front yards and backyards. Some of these lights are installed for security. Apart from resembling prison-yard lighting, the glare can annoy neighbors. If motion sensor lights need to be installed, a more effective use is to have the motion switch turn on the porch light or a lamp in the house, suggesting that someone inside is aware of the movement.

1 Assemble system components
They include a transformer, low-voltage cable, fixtures, and accessories. You'll also need tools including screwdriver, pliers, wire cutters, and a spade.

Installing low-voltage lighting

Whether a kit or individual components, low-voltage systems are easy to install. Most installations can be completed in an afternoon.

2 Mount the transformer
Follow manufacturers' directions and guidelines for setting up the transformer. If the transformer is weatherproof, it can be mounted on an outside wall near an outdoor GFCI receptacle.

3 Bury the cable
In lawns, ground cover beds, or other areas where you are likely to dig or mow, bury cable at least 4 inches deep.

4 Attach fixtures
Assemble fixtures, taking care to not touch halogen bulbs directly. Leads from the lamps attach to the main cable. Connectors vary; some are press-on and others require wire stripping. In the latter case, use gel-filled wire nuts to make weather-proof connections. Adjust the fixture in place to achieve the desired lighting effect.

315

Planning sense

To make an accurate landscape plan, use a 100-foot tape to measure the yard, the house, and all key elements in the yard. Transfer these figures to graph paper, letting each ¼-inch square represent 1 foot. Now you can draw the yard and all it contains to scale.

Planning outdoor lighting

The first step in planning outdoor lighting, whether you are updating an existing system or starting anew, is to view your property as if for the first time. Look for features that appeal to you, such as particular plants, trees, or open spaces.

Next, carry a light chair around the yard and sit down to inspect certain viewpoints more carefully. Position yourself in several places to see how even a slight relocation changes the perspective. Take your time, perhaps making notes or simple sketches of the main focus this viewpoint provides, and the secondary areas. Come back to these spots a day or two later for a second opinion.

As you begin thinking about the lighting itself, concentrate on just one or two primary focal areas from a particular viewpoint, and one or two secondary areas. Don't assume you need to light all or even most of your yard. The primary focal areas will be the most dramatically lighted; the secondary areas should appear subtler, as if in a supporting role.

Remember that the garden is enjoyed at night from inside the house as well as outside. Even in cold or inclement weather, a well-lighted garden seen at night from within the house adds a new dimension to your residence. A nightscape of freshly fallen snow or backlit rain will only reinforce how nice it is to be warm and dry inside. The view from inside your house, whether from the living room, kitchen, or bedroom, should be part of your planning.

To work on a concept of the lighting effect, place some flashlights or lanterns in the yard where you think lights should go. Position some lights to shine up, others to shine down, and a few to accent plants or objects. Also, consider that you can light multiple areas simultaneously or switch off certain areas for a more intimate feel. This can be accomplished by having different and independently switched outdoor lighting circuits. Your final results will be much more sophisticated than what the temporary flashlights or lanterns can show, but these rough tools will give you a sense of the possibilities.

When planning your light placement, also evaluate how formal or informal your yard is. The more formal the garden, the more formal the lighting should be. This means specifically spacing and aligning the lights in accordance with your yard's layout. In a casual setting, the lights can be more randomly placed while still providing the needed attention to focal areas.

Pleasing effects

To ensure pleasant results from outdoor lighting, there are two main considerations. One, shield light sources so they are not visible, and two, don't overpower objects with light.

Subtle is best A low-voltage system amply serves this yard. A path light at the edge of the deck marks steps. Small lights graze the wall. Others highlight shrubs and show off the sculptural quality of tree limbs. The overall result is a backyard with a warm and relaxing nighttime atmosphere.

Front landscape Lighting is part of the welcoming appearance of your house. Locate wall lights where they look best on the house. Use several low-wattage fixtures rather than one glaring light. Space path lights so they create gentle pools of light leading people to your door.

Avoid glare High-mounted post lights and opaque coverings keep the light out of people's eyes. Even though bright, this deck is comfortable to use.

317

(Planning outdoor lighting continued)

Lighting specific areas

Your yard is not just a single expanse, but actually several units combined. There are paths, trees, a driveway, and perhaps garden areas and a pool. Each has its own lighting needs and those needs ideally should be combined so they balance one another.

Paths and driveways A row of lights marking a driveway or pathway outline is much more attractive than bright overhead lights that look as if a runway were being lit. Commonly used for path lights are the low-voltage tiered or pagoda lights that cast small pools of light, making them naturals for paths and walkways, or outlining a driveway. Small bollard lights low to the ground beside a pathway or driveway are equally effective. If a garden or house wall is near the path, a spotlight on the wall can bounce enough light back for the path.

Trees Spotlights aimed up into a tree from the ground are one of the most dramatic uses of outdoor lighting. The ambient light reflecting back down from beneath the tree canopy provides a pleasant atmosphere for relaxing on a summer evening. Lights angled up into trees need to be bright, such as metal halide. Such lights should also have ample housing around the bulb to prevent glare, or they should be placed below ground level. For tall trees, a second light mounted about halfway up the tree and angled skyward may be necessary to provide the full effect of tree lighting.

For the moonlight effect, the lamp, usually about 50 watts, needs to be positioned in the tree so that branches and leaves are in front of the light, diffusing the light so that it is more than a floodlight mounted on a tree trunk.

Sculptures, rocks, and walls A light placed close to a sculpture or a rock or brick wall and angled either up or down will cast the object in sharp relief, allowing shadows to enhance the details. Spotlights are ideal for this purpose. Walls are also excellent for applying a long wash of light, which in turn will provide a soft bounce of ambient light.

Large plants Placing a light either behind or in front of a large plant will show it off, but in markedly different ways. A light behind the plant will silhouette it. A light aimed at a wall close behind the plant will also silhouette the plant while at the same time lighting the wall. And a spotlight aimed at the front of the plant will show off the plant itself, which is ideal for flowering or beautifully shaped plants.

budget stretcher • budget stretcher • budget stretcher

How much light is bright?

How bright a light is depends on more than just the watts being used. A 20-watt bulb in a narrow spotlight is brighter than a 50-watt bulb in a wide floodlight. To keep your lighting cost-effective, plan it with the proper wattage for the object being lighted.

Lighting situations

It's important to determine your lighting goals. Are the lights to be utilitarian, decorative, or mood enhancing? All are important functions.

Paths The type of path and the amount of traffic it receives influence the type and number of path lights you use. The rougher and more frequent use it gets, the more light is required for safety. Here only one light is needed for an occasionally used stone path.

Stairs Any place that has a change in level is an accident waiting to happen. Riser lights clearly but unobtrusively mark steps. Here rope lights fill that role.

Fence On their own, fences need no extra lighting. But where a fence lines a heavily traveled sidewalk, path, or driveway, lights on each post ensure safe travel.

Water lights lend a mystical mood to outdoor lighting. The sealed lights can be placed in ponds to light underwater features such as rocks, or aimed up into a waterfall.

(Planning outdoor lighting continued)

Lighting water

The glow that emanates from underwater lighting, whether in a swimming pool or a fountain, is a hypnotic centerpiece for landscape lighting. Underwater lighting of waterfalls, streams, or small fishponds adds drama to the night landscape. The full effect of underwater lighting depends on the water clarity, so regular maintenance of the water feature is necessary.

Ponds Low-voltage underwater lights come in a range of wattages; the larger the pool or waterfall, the more wattage you will need. Some models sit on the bottom of the pool and put out a wide, unfocused light. Others are spotlights mounted in weighted bases that can be swiveled into numerous positions. Among the more unusual pond lights available are floating "lilies."

Waterfalls and fountains When lighting a waterfall, you can best enhance the falling water by angling an underwater halogen light upward and into a waterfall from behind. If that is not possible, place the light to one side rather than directly facing the waterfall.

For fountains, upwardly angled light, whether in the pool beneath the fountain or on the fountain itself, will best capture the rising and falling water.

Running water Streams running from a waterfall down to a garden pond are often overlooked when it comes to lighting. To catch the full effect of a stream at night, place small lights nearly even with the water. This will cast the ripples into relief and add to the sense of movement.

You can enhance still water, such as in garden pools, with underwater lights and a single overhead light that creates a soft moonlight effect. For a small pond, a few lights angled to highlight underwater rocks or plants are particularly effective, as is silhouetting an underwater plant or object.

Another dramatic lighting approach for still water is to use an accent light to illuminate an object on the far side of the pond, such as a statue or plant. Lighting a single object in this manner will cause it to be attractively mirrored on the water's black surface.

Portable lighting ideas

Lights that are easily moved about provide numerous opportunities for adding light to parties and special occasions.

Track lights—the kind in which low-watt halogen fixtures are snapped onto cables—highlight an arbor.

Hurricane lights come in a variety of styles, from the traditional shown here to modern cones. All can be strung overhead to lend a festive air to any gathering.

Candles are most effective outdoors when shielded from wind. These colorful candleholders are like tall cocktail glasses.

Fairy or holiday lights twinkle all year. Here they're wrapped around twig stars and greenery for a winter welcome.

321

budget stretcher • budget stretcher • budget stretcher •

Best beam spread

Common beam spreads are 8 to 12 degrees, 14 to 20 degrees, 24 to 30 degrees, 32 to 40 degrees, and 60 degrees. To light a tall, slender tree, use a 10- to 12- degree beam spread so all the light is focused on the tree. Use a 60-degree beam spread for a low, broad tree.

Enjoying your outdoor areas

Once the outdoor lights are in place and you have had time to enjoy them, you might decide the effect wasn't what you expected. You don't have to be locked into maintaining the status quo. One of the many values of low voltage lighting is that both the lamps and the wiring are easy to move. Periodic changes in the arrangement for both practical and aesthetic reasons will give the area a refreshing new look. Experiment with different arrangements or different fixtures as often as you desire.

Temporary lighting

Special occasions and changes in routine may affect your outdoor lighting needs. For instance, say you need to move the barbecue from its normal location to another spot that is not sufficiently lit. The answer is to simply add a temporary overhead lamp clamped to a handy tree branch or patio cover. Consider getting a special tree-mount fixture called a shielded directional light that comes with a strap and a hook. You position the light, wrap the strap around the limb and snap the two strap ends together. Or perhaps you could use several strings of ribbon lights to light the area.

For entertaining, add Japanese lanterns or candle lanterns to tree limbs to give the scene a new and festive look. In these cases, the lights don't have to be low voltage; you can set them up with an extension cord and standard incandescent lights. The idea is to be flexible and innovative.

Candles add a warm glow to any situation. You can find all sorts of holders suitable for using outdoors, or you can create your own with items from around the house, such as buckets, jars, punched-tin cans, or frosted ceiling-fan bulb covers.

Dining alfresco as weather permits is one of the prime benefits of outdoor lighting. The area needs to be comfortably lighted, balanced between having enough light to see the meal yet not disrupting the mood. A few freestanding low-voltage coach lights, resembling gas street lamps from days of yore, can provide just the balance of light and atmosphere. Or consider an umbrella lamp. This double-bulb fixture is an uplight that attaches to the pole of your patio umbrella.

Outdoor lighting will turn your yard into a great "new" space for evening and nighttime enjoyment, whether relaxing with just the family or entertaining friends.

critters

Most insects and animals are harmless passersby, even a pleasure. But some aren't. Here's what you need to know.

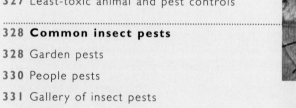

Pests are inevitable visitors to any yard or garden. But rarely is a bug—or a woodchuck, for that matter—a disaster. Instead, its presence is an opportunity to match wits, to see if you can outmaneuver your challenger without turning your garden into a war zone.

An ounce of prevention

In nature, a balance of natural predators and a healthy environment keeps pests under control, whether they bug our pets, our plants, or us. And many pests are avoided simply by using good gardening practices: keeping plants healthy and gardens clean.

But like a seesaw, a perfect balance is easily tipped. Weather, especially unusually mild winters or rainy summers, is a chief culprit. These are opportunities for pest populations to explode. When preventive measures are not enough, use the least intrusive measures first, turning to heavy-duty ones only as required. For instance, try washing the aphids off with a hose before pulling out the insecticide. Today there is a wide range of remedies available for specific pests—barriers, traps, predators, and parasites, not to mention pesticides. This chapter is about the most common yard and garden pests, and the smartest ways to deal with them.

Controlling pests safely

Integrated pest management (IPM for short) is the basic approach recommended by experts. It's basically what's described above: Working through pest problems by starting with the simplest remedies first. IPM is an environmentally savvy way to use pest controls that combines information and a stair-step approach from least toxic to most toxic. Although powerful pesticides are good at quickly stopping an infestation, they kill the beneficials at the same time. That's the reason some pesticides turn out to provide only short-term control at best. In fact, their use can cause more difficult-to-manage pest problems down the road. When a pest is out of control, work first with the least toxic controls. Nudge the system, rather than hammering it. That's the way you're most likely to reestablish a healthy balance in your yard.

■ SMART IDEA ■

Call for help

If you have questions about using, storing, or disposing of a pesticide, provide the Environmental Protection Agency's EPA Code Number listed on the product label to authorities when you talk to them.

Call the manufacturer's telephone number, which is listed on the product label, or the National Pesticide Information Center (NPIC), at Oregon State University, Corvallis, OR, at 800-858-7378, or visit the website: http://npic.orst.edu/map.htm. The NPIC is a telephone hotline, partly funded by the EPA, for answering consumer questions concerning pesticides, pesticide ingredients, uses, storage, and disposal. In case of emergency, call your local poison control center (call 4-1-1 information for that number), or call: 9-1-1.

(An ounce of prevention, continued)

Read labels Study pesticide package labels for important information about how to use the products, their toxicity, and what to do in case of emergency. Note the brand name and the active ingredient (chemical name). The active ingredient is the name you will need to give to a poison control center or doctor in case of skin exposure, inhalation, or ingestion. One of three "signal words" on the label designates the toxicity level. Ratings for over-the-counter pesticides range from danger (most toxic) to warning (less toxic than danger) to caution (least toxic). All pesticide labels carry the warning "keep out of reach of children." Other information listed on the label includes first-aid instructions and directions for use, storage, and disposal. Make sure the pesticide package mentions the pest you are targeting and the plants you plan to treat.

Safe pesticide practices

Handling Mix and apply pesticides only as directed on the product label. Applying an extra strength solution is illegal and can be harmful. Mix pesticides outdoors. Use dedicated sprayers and keep them locked up with the pesticide after use. Apply pesticides on a windless, dry day to avoid having the product drift onto nontarget areas of your yard or a neighbor's. Wear old, preferably disposable clothing. Cover your hair. Wear long sleeves, long pants, socks, impermeable rubber boots and gloves, a dust mask or ventilator (as recommended by the product), and goggles.

Cleanup After application, dispose of your clothing or launder it separately and lock it up with the pesticide. Wash gloves and boots outdoors. Wash your face and hands carefully, then shower and shampoo. Keep children, pets, and others away from the treated area for as long as the product label indicates.

Storage Dispose of pesticides or store unused pesticides in their original container. Write the date of purchase on the container and put it in a locked cabinet in a dark, cool but not freezing area. Post a large sign on the storage area: "keep out, pesticides." Store herbicides separately from pesticides to avoid vapor contamination. Contact your local sanitation company or government regulators for disposal requirements.

Spills If a pesticide spills, do not hose the area with water, which could spread it. Instead, absorb the pesticide with kitty litter. Sweep up the litter and dispose of it as directed by your local authorities. If a pesticide spills onto soil, remove and dispose of the contaminated soil according to municipal sanitation guidelines.

healthy garden • healthy garden • healthy garden •

Pesticide outfits

- **Long pants**
- **Long-sleeved shirts**
- **Rubber shoes and gloves**
- **Head covering**
- **Respirator**
- **Goggles and no contact lenses**
- **Avoid eating, drinking, smoking, or touching your face when using pesticides**

Least-toxic animal and pest controls

Gardeners can choose among a wide variety of products and techniques to discourage pests of various kinds, and do it safely. These are some of the basic tools for dealing with pests.

Bt (Bacillus thuringiensis) is a bacteria. One type is a stomach poison targeting leaf-eating caterpillars and larvae. Another controls mosquito larvae in ponds.

Sulfur This element is a naturally occurring fungicide and miticide. Dust it on and around plants.

Traps Sticky traps, such as fly paper, let you know when certain pests are active and it's time to start using controls. Catch small animals in baited traps but check local regulations before relocating them.

Diatomaceous earth is made up of sharp-edged, fossilized shells of tiny sea creatures. Sprinkle it around plants to kill or block slugs and other soft-bodied insects that try to crawl over it.

Iron phosphate Slug and snail baits containing iron phosphate are safe for use around wildlife and pets.

Oil Spray it to smother mites and other insect pests and their eggs.

Barriers Physically prevent pests from reaching plants. Row cover stops insect pests. Chicken wire, and tree wrap netting shields plants from animals.

Insecticidal soap Spray insecticidal soap on mites and soft-bodied insect pests to kill them on contact.

Neem is a natural poison derived from an East Indian tree.

Copper strip Snails and slugs can't cross it, so it makes a highly effective deterrent.

327

healthy garden • healthy garden • healthy garden •

Dear diary...

Insects do pretty much the same things year after year, or try to. Keep track of infestations as they appear around your home and garden. Note the type of pest, the date, and where the pest was seen. Then next year—because you'll know when and where they are likely to appear— you'll be a step ahead.

Common insect pests
Garden pests

Aphids Aphids are pear-shaped, soft-bodied winged or wingless insects about ⅛ inch long. There is also a white cottony form that attacks fruit trees. Often clustering on the growing tips of stems, these sap-sucking insects yellow and distort leaves and flowers, and can spread plant viruses as they feed. They secrete clear, sticky "honeydew," which attracts ants and irritates car owners who have parked under infested trees. Beneficial insects, such as ladybugs, often bring aphids under control by midsummer (for more on beneficial insects, see page 332). Aphids are fragile and easily controlled. Knock them off plants with a strong spray of water from a hose, or spray insecticidal soap.

Caterpillars and worms These are the larval stage of moths and butterflies. You may wish to take the time to identify those feeding on your plants. Many turn into beautiful butterflies. Parsleyworms, for example, are 1-inch-long green caterpillars that mature into black swallowtail butterflies. Because butterflies are nice to have around and generally don't damage plants, most gardeners leave their larvae alone. But if they become a nuisance, simply pick them off plants.

If caterpillars are persistent problems, there are various controls you can use, starting with calling on natural predators such as birds. A birdbath attracts birds and the result is fewer caterpillars. Parasites, such as some tiny wasps, also keep caterpillar numbers in check. You will see evidence of their work if the caterpillars have small white eggs attached to their backs. Leave affected caterpillars alone so the wasps can continue their work.

To prevent moths from laying eggs on plants, cover plants with floating row covers (available at garden centers). (But remove the row cover when food plants that need to be pollinated to produce fruit, such as tomatoes, start to bloom.) Control young caterpillars with the biological material Bt *(Bacillus thuringiensis),* which is harmless to people, animals, and beneficial insects. As an alternative, spray pyrethrum, a botanical contact insecticide, or pyrethrin (its synthetic form). Apply all pesticides following package instructions.

Earwigs Earwigs are ¾-inch-long brown insects with pincers at the rear of their bodies. During the day earwigs hide in crevices and under garden debris. At night, they chew holes in leaves, stems, flowers, and fruit. Earwig adults sometimes consume other pests, which is good, but they can get out of hand. Trap them by laying pieces of cardboard on the soil overnight; in the morning, collect and dispose of the insects. As an alternative, spray infestations with an over-the-counter pesticide, or scatter insect bait pellets labeled for earwigs on the ground. Follow all label directions.

Japanese beetles At ½-inch-long, these metallic blue or green beetles with coppery wings are voracious pests. The adults consume leaves and flowers, leaving only leaf veins. The grubs overwinter in the soil and eat grass roots in spring. Handpick and dispose of beetles by dropping them into a container of soapy water. (They drop to the ground when alarmed so just hold the container under them.) To reduce their numbers, spread beneficial nematodes (*Heterorhabditis bacteriophora*) over lawns in early spring. Spray the botanical insecticide neem on adults, or a synthetic pesticide containing malathion or carbaryl. Place beetle traps far from susceptible plants to avoid attracting the pests in their direction.

Mealybugs These are small, sap-sucking, cottony insects. They can transmit plant diseases as they feed, and their sticky secretions invite sooty mold and ants. Dab mealybugs on indoor plants with rubbing alcohol. Outdoors, encourage natural predators—including ladybugs, mealybug destroyers, and green lacewing larvae—by growing small-flowered nectar plants, such as sweet alyssum and scabiosa. Spray insecticidal soap, summer oil, the botanical insecticide neem, or an insecticide containing the active ingredient carbaryl.

Scale insects Scales are ¹⁄₁₆-inch-long, immobile insects encased in hard, oval shells. Their small shells are hard to distinguish from bark. Spray woody plants with dormant oil in late winter to suffocate the pests. During the growing season, spray plants outdoors with the botanical insecticide neem, a synthetic insecticide containing the active ingredient carbaryl, or lightweight horticultural oil. Apply all materials according to package directions, and only on plants listed on the label.

Slugs and snails Both are moisture-loving creatures that rasp holes into leaves and flowers. Discourage them by removing garden debris and mulch, where they hide during the day. Handpick and dispose of them at dusk. Scatter wood ashes or diatomaceous earth around plants to dehydrate and lacerate them. Set shallow saucers of beer

SMART IDEA

Finish off fungal diseases

- Site plants far enough apart to allow air to circulate.
- Water plants before noon so leaves can dry before sundown.
- Mulch to keeps spores from splashing onto plants.
- Spray healthy leaves with a homemade fungicide solution (I teaspoon of baking soda and I teaspoon of insecticidal soap dissolved in a quart of warm water).

To treat infected plants:
- Pick off and dispose of infected leaves.
- Stay out of the garden on wet days to avoid spreading spores.
- Cut off infected parts of plants to spur new growth.
- Apply a commercial fungicide containing sulfur or lime or one formulated for roses or the disease you are targeting.

(Common insect pests, continued)

under plants in the evening to lure and drown them. Use snail baits; ones containing iron phosphate are not toxic to birds and pets, while those with metaldehyde are. Or surround beds with copper strips, which shock these moist mollusks on contact.

Tent caterpillars These are larvae of several types of moths. The eastern tent caterpillar moth is dark with a white-striped back and blue-spotted sides. The western species is blue-and-white spotted. A similar pest, the fall webworm, builds webs in autumn. These small, fuzzy caterpillars build webs that span several tree branches. At night and in stormy weather they stay in their nests, and on clear days they emerge to eat leaves. Severe infestations can defoliate trees. Natural predators, including birds and wasps, pick them out of treetops. To control caterpillars that are within reach, remove and burn nests. If nests are in treetops, rely on natural predators, or use a high-pressure sprayer to apply the biological insecticide Btk *(Bacillus thuringiensis* var. *kurstaki)* when the caterpillars are small. As an alternative, open and spray the insides of nests with the botanical insecticide pyrethrum, or the synthetic version, pyrethrin. Ornamental trees listed on the product label can be sprayed with a synthetic insecticide containing the active ingredients acephate, carbaryl, or malathion. In winter, spray infested trees with dormant oil to smother the eggs. Follow all pesticide label directions carefully when applying, and use only on plants listed on the product label.

People pests

Bees and wasps These insects are primarily beneficial. Bees are important pollinators of garden plants and fruit trees; wasps prey on insect pests, especially caterpillars. Beneficial wasps are so small that they cannot sting people, but to avoid close encounters, avoid wearing perfume and pink, red, purple, or yellow clothing while working in the yard.

If you find a wasp's nest on or near your house, take action. Spray a powerful insecticide formulated for wasps or yellow jackets that contains the botanical insecticide pyrethrum or pyrethrin, or one containing the synthetic active ingredient resmethrin. Apply in the evening or early morning, when the insects are lethargic. Use pesticides only as directed on the product label. If in doubt about spraying a wasp's nest, call a licensed exterminator. Call a beekeeper to relocate beehives.

Fire ants Fire ants are ⅛-inch-long red or black ants that live underground, creating large anthills; they live where winters are warm. Their painful bites develop into blisters that take several weeks to heal. Use commercial chemical growth regulators

If stung, take action

If you are stung by a bee, don't grasp the stinger with tweezers or fingers. That's likely to inject more venom. Instead, scrape the stinger away with the edge of a knife or credit card. Apply an antibiotic cream to help prevent infection.

Gallery of insect pests

Most of the insects in a garden are harmless. They aren't noticed because they don't attract our attention. In contrast, a few routinely live at the expense of garden plants. These six are among the most common.

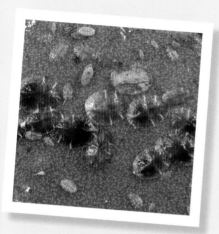

Scale insects There are several kinds of scale insects. All begin as *crawlers*, which are mobile until they find a good location to feed on plants. Adults are immobile and protected by a shell, which may be hard or soft. Control with soap or oil sprays.

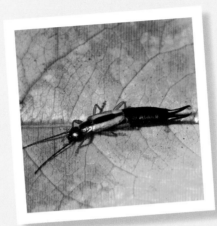

Earwigs These ¾-inch-long brown pincer-equipped insects are less fearsome than they look. Adults prey on other pests. Immature ones feed on plants at night, making holes in leaves, stems, flowers, and fruits. Set and empty traps daily.

Slugs and snails Famously moisture-loving, these pests feed at night and on cloudy days, eating holes in the leaves and flowers of plants and leaving shiny slime trails as they crawl across plants and damp soil. Reduce numbers with bait; exclude with copper barrier strips or diatomaceous earth.

Japanese beetles These ½-inch-long metallic blue or green beetles with coppery wings are the nemesis of many gardeners. Their grubs overwinter in soil and eat lawn roots in spring. The adults consume leaves and flowers, especially those of roses and hibiscus. Reduce numbers by controlling grubs in early spring. Handpick adults or knock off plants with water streams. Or spray with neem, malathion, or carbaryl.

Tent caterpillars They're more nuisance than threat. These small, fuzzy caterpillars build webs in spring that span several branches. When it is dark, they stay in the nest; when sunny, they emerge to eat the leaves. Foil them by wrapping barriers around trunks to stop migration from ground to leaves.

Aphids Populations explode in spring but usually fall back quickly by summer. They are pear-shaped, soft-bodied tiny insects that feed on most plants, causing pale, distorted leaves and flowers. They can spread plant viruses as they feed. Aphids also secrete clear, sticky *honeydew*, which attracts ants.

(Common insect pests, continued)

formulated for fire ants, or a synthetic pesticide (formulated for fire ants) containing the active ingredients acephate. Apply only as directed on the package label. If in doubt about controlling these aggressive ants, call a licensed pesticide applicator.

Mosquitoes Mosquitoes are a nuisance, both in the home and around the yard, and they can transmit many diseases. Female mosquitoes lay eggs in shallow water. Eggs hatch in about five days, so frequently empty plant saucers and containers. Add mosquito-eating goldfish, or mosquito fish, to ornamental pools, or use small, floating, doughnut-shaped products designed to keep eggs from hatching. Encourage (or at least tolerate) bats, which eat mosquitoes.

Minimize your exposure to mosquitoes by staying inside during the early morning or evening when mosquitoes are most active. Wear long sleeves and long pants, and a hat with a brim. Consider using personal repellents, such as those containing deet. Running an electric fan on a patio or balcony helps to keep mosquitoes away. Propane-powered traps are highly effective on most, but not all, species of mosquitoes. These traps work by releasing heat, carbon dioxide, and a scent that lures mosquitoes.

Some municipalities spray for mosquitoes. You can also buy pesticides for yards that contain the botanical insecticide pyrethrum or its synthetic form, pyrethrin, or pesticides with the active ingredient malathion. Apply outdoors only as directed on the label, or call a licensed pesticide professional to treat your lawn or house.

Beneficial insects

Many insects are beneficial. Some are pollinators, such as bees, that are essential to setting fruits on food plants. Others are predators or parasites that prey on plant-eating insect pests, keeping pest populations small enough that the damage they cause is minimal. Learn to recognize beneficial insects and encourage them, through good gardening practices or reintroduction (to buy beneficials, see Resources page 355), to take up residence in your yard.

Assassin bugs Assassin are ½-inch-long, brown- or black-winged insects with flat bodies and sharp beaks. Both adults and nymphs eat flies, leafhoppers, Japanese beetles, tomato hornworms, and other caterpillars. Plant flowering perennials to attract them.

Centipedes Centipedes are 1-inch-long insect relatives that eat various insects and spiders. Encourage them by providing hiding places under rotten pieces of wood placed on moist soil.

safety alert · safety alert · safety alert · safety alert

Take care in tick country

In the United States, ticks inhabit the northeast, mid-Atlantic and upper north-central states, and northwestern California. If you spend time in wooded areas in spring, take precautions. Wear deet repellent, a hat, and long sleeves, and tuck pants into socks. Remove attached ticks with fine-tipped tweezers, pulling slowly. See the Centers for Disease Control and Prevention web site at www.cdc.gov.

Flies Beneficial flies are tiny; they prey on, or parasitize, insects. Some species of beneficial flies have evolved to mimic the appearance of other insects in order to fool their prey. *Aphid midges* are 1/10-inch-long mosquitolike insects that need a moist, windless site. Adults eat pollen and nectar from small-flowered plants such as dill, mustard, and thyme. Their aphid-eating orange maggots pupate in the soil; protect them by mulching. *Hover flies* are ½ inch long with a yellow-and-black-striped body. The adults look similar to wasps and are excellent pollinators. Their aphid-eating maggots resemble slugs. *Robber flies* resemble bumblebees and damselflies. The adults eat beetles and grasshoppers. The maggots live in the soil, where they eat beetle larvae. *Tachinid flies* look like small houseflies with bigger eyes and fuzzy abdomens. The adults feed on nectar. They lay white eggs on caterpillars and the larvae of beetles, borers, and fall webworms. Grow small-flowered nectar plants to attract these beneficials.

Ground beetles The larvae of these 1-inch-long, shiny black beetles live underground and eat cutworms, gypsy moth larvae, root maggots, and their eggs. Adults eat slugs and snails, caterpillars, and potato beetles. Attract ground beetles by growing white clover or by placing a compost pile near the garden.

Lacewings These fragile, long-bodied insects with transparent wings may be brown or green and are about ½ inch long, with a smooth body and narrow wings. The larvae, called aphid wolves, eat as many as 60 aphids per hour. Adults also eat aphids and mealybugs. You can purchase lacewings from mail-order insectaries.

Ladybugs Also called *lady beetles* and *ladybird beetles,* these ⅜-inch-long beetles have a rounded shape with shiny, black-spotted red wing covers, or they may be yellow, orange, gray, or black, depending on the species. Adults and larvae eat aphids, mealybugs, scales, thrips, mites, and other small insects. To keep purchased ladybugs from flying away, spritz infested plants with water or a carbohydrate-rich lemon-lime soft drink (regular, not diet) before releasing the insects. To attract native ladybugs, grow the small-flowered nectar plants tansy, angelica, or scented geraniums.

▪ GOOD PLANTS ▪

Companion planting

Companion planting is a practice that pairs species of plants to create an environment that insect pests find unfavorable. Many pungent herbs have a fragrance that people find attractive but insect pests do not. Planting these herbs around susceptible plants is thought to confuse and repel pests. Likewise, some plants are favorite foods, or hosts, of certain insect pests. By segregating these from the garden, you can protect the majority of your garden, or even use the host plants as "trap plants."

Repelling plants:
Mint, basil, marigold, garlic and other members of the onion family

Trap plants:
Nasturtium (aphids); fennel, dill, and parsley (caterpillars); eggplant (flea beetles)

(Beneficial insects, continued)

Praying mantis Praying mantises are green or brownish insects that look like leafy sticks with large, upraised forelegs. They sit, camouflaged, until insects are within reach, then grab and eat them. Praying mantises range in size from ¾ inch to 5 inches long. They inhabit most gardens.

Beneficial nematodes These microscopic, soilborne worms kill pests that live underground or lay their eggs underground. Beneficial nematodes attack a number of pests, including fleas, cabbage root maggots, iris borers, and strawberry root weevils. The species *Steinernema carpocapsae* targets billbugs, caterpillars, cutworms, and webworms. A different species of nematode, *Heterorhabditis bacteriophora,* targets Japanese beetle grubs. Native populations will be attracted to soil-dwelling pests, but if pest infestations are heavy, consider buying beneficial nematodes from a mail-order insectary.

Minute pirate bugs These ⅛-inch-long black bugs have white chevron markings on their backs. Adults and nymphs eat aphids, thrips, spider mites, small caterpillars, whiteflies, and insect eggs. Adults also eat pollen; attract them with flat-flowered plants such as daisies and yarrow. When purchasing these voracious insect predators, plan on one bug per plant.

Wasps All wasps are beneficial insects that prey on pest insects. The large species can pose a problem to people. Smaller species are harmless to people and can be encouraged to live in your yard, or you can purchase them from a mail-order insectary. If you decide to buy live beneficial wasps, read the catalog descriptions carefully to match wasp species to the pest species that are causing problems in your yard. Attract local populations of wasps by growing small-flowered pollen and nectar plants, such as black-eyed Susan, lovage, Queen Anne's lace, scabiosa, sweet alyssum, and tansy. Allow herb and vegetable plants such as dill, fennel, and carrot to set flowers.

Beneficial wasps include a number of species that can live in the yard or garden. *Aphid wasps,* which are ⅛ inch long with long antennae, lay their eggs exclusively in aphids, where the hatching larvae eat and kill the aphids. *Braconid wasps* are ⅒- to ⅛-inch-long brown- or black-winged insects. They similarly parasitize armyworms, cabbageworms, coddling moths, gypsy moths, tomato hornworms, and other insects. *Encarsia formosa* are ⅟₂₅-inch-long black wasps with yellow abdomens. The adults parasitize whiteflies and sweet potato flies and eat whiteflies. These wasps are not native but can be ordered from mail-order sources (see Resources, page 355). *Ichneumon wasps* are ⅛- to 1-inch-long red or brownish wasps that

family friendly • family friendly • family friendly • family friendly

Attracting butterflies

To entice butterflies, choose a site protected from wind, and set up a "puddle feeder." Cover the bottom of a saucer with a mix of sand and garden soil. Add water to create mud that offers firm footing. Top it with a few slices of ripe fruit, such as banana, orange, mango or peach.

Gallery of beneficial insects

Ladybug adult The familiar adult eats aphids and other small pests.

Ladybug eggs If you see these clustered on the undersides of a leaf, leave them alone.

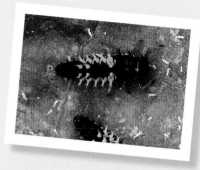

Ladybug larvae In this alligator-like stage, they feed voraciously on aphids and other pests.

Ladybug pupa Pupas attach to a stem and are immobile. The adult emerges after about a week.

Lacewing adult Green and brown forms are common; both are delicate creatures that feed mostly on pollen.

Lacewing larva The larva consumes aphids, insect eggs, mites, leafhoppers, whiteflies, and caterpillars.

Soldier beetle The ¾-inch-long beetles regularly dine on aphids and other small and soft insects.

Syrphid fly adult Syrphids look like bees but are flies that hover in one spot. Adults feed mostly on pollen and nectar.

Syrphid fly larva Called *maggots*, the legless, slug-like larvae eat aphids and other small insects.

Tachinid fly It looks like a hairy housefly. Adults feed on nectar but lay eggs in armyworms and cutworms.

Braconid wasp cocoon Wasps may sting multiple times, each resulting in a cocoon with a developing larva.

Braconid wasp The wasp injects an egg into an aphid. The larvae feeds on the aphid, leaving an empty *mummy* done.

Glowing beneficials

Fireflies—or lightning bugs—are fun to watch flashing their familiar lights on summer evenings. Their larvae are also voracious predators of some of the worst garden pests: slugs, snails, cutworms, and mites. Fireflies are very sensitive to pesticides, so read pesticide labels carefully, and apply pesticides frugally to protect these harbingers of summer.

(Beneficial insects continued)

parasitize caterpillars, insects, and spider eggs. Adult ichneumon wasps feed on pollen and thrive in sites that have high humidity. *Trichogramma wasps* are minute yellow, orange, or brown wasps with red eyes. They parasitize the eggs of cabbageworms, fruitworms, hornworms, loopers, and other caterpillars. Adults eat insect eggs, nectar, and pollen.

Mites Beneficial mites encompass a group of tiny, spider relatives that prey on small pests, including harmful sap-sucking spider mites and thrips. The adults eat pollen and nectar; attract them to your yard by growing plants with small, pollen-rich, flowers, such as sweet alyssum and scabiosa. Several species are commercially available; combining several produces the best results. Commercially available mites require humidity and are not recommended for dry climates.

Decollate snails These types of snails voraciously consume common brown garden snails. They are not native to North America, but are imported from Europe. Order them from mail-order insectaries. Check with the supplier and local entomologists when ordering, because their sale is restricted in some areas of the country. When releasing decollate snails, set clay flowerpots, rocks, or other small shelters on moist ground to provide them with shady hiding places during the day.

Spiders Most spiders pose little threat to humans. They eat many kinds of insects, including both beneficials and pests. Two types build webs: orb weavers, which build large, circular webs often seen sparkling with dew, and dome weavers, which build delicate, dome-shaped webs. A few don't build webs. Wolf spiders are distinguished by eraser-size egg sacs, which females carry on their back. Jumping spiders pounce or grab insects when they come within range. Crab spiders move sideways like crabs. They hide in flowers where they catch insects, changing color to match the flowers. Crab spiders prefer pastel flowers; attract them by planting cosmos, daisies, or goldenrod. Green lynx spiders, which mostly inhabit the warmer southern states, are translucent green with red spots. They do not build webs but sit with their front legs raised, poised to catch insects.

To attract spiders, cover planting beds with loose, dry mulch, such as straw or shredded bark, and leave some perennials and grasses standing over the winter as places for them to hibernate.

Although indoor spiders also eat insect pests, their webs can be unsightly. When possible, catch them by sweeping them into a jar with a sheet of paper, and set the open jar on the ground outdoors to release them.

Plants that attract beneficial insects

The adults of many beneficial insects require a diet of carbohydrate-rich nectar and pollen. To attract these insects to your yard, grow plants that produce clusters of small flowers. Also, combine plants to have blooms from spring through fall.

Sweet alyssum The tiny flowers are important because they appear early in the season.

Cilantro The midseason blooms are small and in flat-topped clusters, which make it easy for beneficial insects to retrieve the nectar.

Fennel Blooming midseason through fall, fennel provides a steady source of food for beneficial insects.

Yarrow Flat-topped flowers of common yarrow support a variety of beneficial insects.

Common animal pests

Watching wildlife visitors from the kitchen window or deck is an entertaining and educational activity for family members. For the most part, backyard wildlife can coexist with people and pets. But there are conditions under which wild animals can cause destruction to landscapes, gardens, and homes, or pose a health threat to pets or family members. It is important to be able to identify the cause of damage that you find in order to know what animal is responsible and how to control it. It is often possible to find a humane way to repel an animal pest or to trap it for relocation. Keep in mind that all wild animals can bite, and be sure to keep children away from them. If you have any doubts about controlling an animal pest, call your local animal control office or a local wildlife sanctuary, or look up a professional wildlife management specialist in the Yellow Pages of the telephone book.

Chipmunks Chipmunks are small brown rodents distinguished by tan stripes that run from head to tail. They live in underground colonies and can become prolific pests, raiding gardens, eating bird eggs, and chewing on young trees. They damage lawns and homes by digging holes, building nests, and chewing woodwork and wiring.

Repel chipmunks with commercially packaged fox urine (purchase it at a sporting-goods store) dabbed on a rag and placed near their trails, bird feeders, or burrows. Or use a commercial repellent formulated for chipmunks, applied according to label instructions.

Erect fencing around planting beds or individual plants to protect them from gnawing. Chipmunks can climb over and dig under a fence, so make it at least 4 feet tall, and extend it 1 foot underground. A smooth wooden fence is hard for chipmunks to climb, but a strand of electric fence placed close to the ground also works. Avoid electric fencing if small children or pets play in the yard. Wrap young tree trunks with smooth tree wrap to deter gnawing.

Capture chipmunks in a box trap, such as Havahart brand, baited with nuts, and release them more than a mile away. Check first with authorities to determine whether relocating wild animals is legal in your area.

Deer Deer are graceful and endearing animals to observe, but increasing populations and decreasing habitats are driving them into suburbs and urban areas, where their feeding causes substantial damage to landscaping. Toward the end of summer and the beginning of the breeding season, bucks can kill young trees by

safety alert · safety alert · safety alert · safety alert

Ticks and disease

Deer ticks feed on pets and people and can transmit the diseases ehrlichiosis, Lyme disease, and Rocky Mountain spotted fever. Symptoms include fever, aches, and, in some cases of Lyme disease, a rash around the bite. All but Rocky Mountain spotted fever can be treated with antibiotics in the early stages. If bitten, save the tick for examination.

Gallery of animal pests

While having a certain amount of backyard wildlife is enjoyable, some animals quickly wear out their welcome, especially when they turn a garden into an all-you-can-eat buffet.

Deer As their predators have waned in numbers, deer populations have exploded. Their feeding damages plants, and they host deer ticks, which can transmit Lyme disease to pets and people.

Mice Small but prolific, they contaminate food, pet supplies, and birdseed. They damage houses, chewing on wood and wiring. Their nests are a source of fleas indoors. In winter, they can gnaw the bark off young trees with fatal results. Mice reproduce year-round.

Rabbits They live in burrows and forage during the day. They are notorious for eating garden vegetables and gnawing the bark of young trees in winter. A female can give birth to as many as 20 young per year.

Woodchucks True vegetarians, woodchucks (or groundhogs) will quickly consume a row of green beans, peas, or any other plant material. Live-trap them with lures of banana or apple. Check with animal control agents before relocating.

healthy garden · healthy garden · healthy garden · healthy garden

Deer-repellent plants

It is easy to discover which plants deer prefer when you see the roughly torn branches they leave. Substitute ornamentals that deer do not relish. Usually, deer don't like plants with fuzzy leaves or a pungent fragrance, such as butterfly bush, calla lily, columbine, daffodils, ferns, herbs, Japanese maple, iris, black-eyed Susan, and plants native to the Mediterranean region.

(Common animal pests continued)

aggressively rubbing their antlers against the trunks, and they can threaten people who confront them. Deer also host deer ticks, which can transmit Lyme disease to pets and people.

Repel or deter deer in your yard with commercial or homemade repellents. Renew repellents after rain, because they lose their scent. Alternate repellents throughout the year for maximum effect, as deer lose their fear of the familiar. The key to a deterrent's success against deer (and other browsers) is random motion, because deer learn to ignore predictable sounds and sights. White flags tied to string and allowed to flutter in the wind scare deer because they mimic the lifted-tail warning signal of deer. Hanging pie tins or shiny can lids on a string, so that they twirl in the breeze, can also deter deer, because they mimic the flashing eyes of a predator. A number of commercial deterrents also use noise or motion to repel deer. One effective commercial device combines a battery operated motion detector with a high-pressure water nozzle to harmlessly spray cold water on any moving animal within a range of 30 feet.

To make your property less likely to be raided by deer, use landscaping techniques to create an environment they consider inhospitable. In the wild, deer are edge dwellers, grazing in open areas and dashing to nearby woods for safety. If your yard borders a wooded area, avoid planting fruit trees, vegetable plants, or susceptible ornamental plants such as roses along the property lines. Site plants deer find tasty in the interior of the yard, surrounded by lawn. Select unpalatable species (see "Deer-repellent plants" at left) to plant along property lines.

Walk your dog, or encourage neighbors to walk theirs, along the boundaries of your property daily to lay down the fresh scent of this resident predator.

Fence your property to effectively keep deer out. Deer routinely clear 6-foot fences, so to exclude deer, a fence should be at least 8 feet tall. Topping a privacy fence with several rows of wire can deer-proof an existing fence. If installing a new deer fence, consider any standard fencing or special black plastic deer fencing, which can be fastened inconspicuously to trees. Heavy-duty nylon fishing line strung from tree to tree is an effective, invisible fence; tie a few white flags to it to keep from tripping family members. An electric fence 3 feet above the ground and daubed with peanut butter is an effective deterrent but should not be used if children live nearby. Deer can jump a width of 4 feet, making a wide fence as effective as a tall one. To build this type of fence, erect 4-foot posts that have additional posts attached to each upright post at a 45-degree angle. String fencing along the slanted posts.

Ways to deter animal pests

Often, a barrier is the best way to outmaneuver a pesky animal. But half-way measures won't work. Learn the dimensions and features of barriers that really work—before building.

Deer fencing Deer are excellent jumpers, meaning any fence meant to deter them must be at least 8 feet tall; 10 feet tall is better.

Deep fence To thwart rabbits and other animals from digging under a fence to get into the garden, bend fencing into an L-shape at the base. Bury the L under soil or mulch.

Tree wrap Start wrapping just below the soil's surface, and continue until the wrap is above the snow line. Treat it with a thiram repellent to deter mice, rabbits, and deer.

Root basket Protect tulip bulbs, or the roots of roses and young fruit trees, from pocket gophers by planting them in wire baskets and burying the basket in the soil.

(Common animal pests continued)

To control deer, contact your local fish and wildlife department (see government listings in the telephone book) for information and regulations on legally hunting deer, or for how to obtain a permit to allow a professional to hunt deer on your property (see "Using lethal controls" on page 343 for more details).

Gophers Gophers are prolific inhabitants of western states. These rodents can grow to 1 foot long: they have a ratlike tail and cheek pouches in which they stash food. Gophers are destructive, digging holes and burrowing in lawns, as well as gnawing on trees and underground wires.

Wrap fine-mesh hardware cloth loosely around tree trunks to discourage gnawing. Fence garden areas with hardware cloth, and bury it 1 foot underground to discourage burrowing. Protect individual plants and bulbs by encasing root balls in boxes made of hardware cloth, planting hardware cloth and all. Encase underground wiring in metal conduit to prevent gnawing. Tolerate natural predators such as snakes, skunks, and foxes.

To kill gophers, use Macabee traps, which fit into tunnels, or poisons formulated for gophers. Apply poisons according to package directions, and keep any excess in a locked cabinet. If in doubt about lethal controls, call a wildlife control specialist.

Moles Moles damage lawns by tunneling extensively, but because there are usually only one or two moles per yard, it is possible to eradicate them. Moles eat insects and lawn grubs exclusively and show little interest in poisoned bait and deterrents.

To force moles to move elsewhere, eradicate lawn grubs. Apply the biological controls milky spore disease or beneficial nematodes, or a synthetic commercial grub killer to lawns in early spring. Use a product that lists lawn grubs on the label, and follow package instructions carefully.

To capture a mole for relocation, use a shovel to scoop it quickly from a tunnel into a bucket for relocation. If you study tunnels carefully, you can see where the mole is because the grass above it vibrates. Release moles a mile or more away, but check with local authorities first to see whether relocating wild animals is legal in your area.

To kill moles, set lethal spear traps above active tunnels. These animals have sharp claws and teeth; if in doubt about trapping them, consult the business pages of the telephone book for a wildlife control specialist.

budget stretcher • budget stretcher • budget stretcher •

Deer repellents

Repellents mimic the scent of predators, or taint plants with an unappetizing scent or flavor.

USE
- **Blood meal:** scatter it around plants
- **Deodorant soap:** hang bars in plants

AVOID
- **Mothballs:** they are toxic if eaten
- **Hot pepper:** these are painful and potentially blinding to animals

Opossums Possums are large, ratlike gray animals with white faces. These omnivorous animals are mostly nocturnal and are famous for raiding trash cans, pet food bowls, chicken coops, and gardens. Although they rarely carry rabies, opossums can spread mange, a skin disease that causes hair loss, appetite loss, and severe itching. To deter opossums, patrol the yard daily with a dog to renew its predator scent. To keep opossums away from plants, install a fence. The best fence is a wooden one that is at least 4 feet tall and that extends a foot underground, to deter climbing over or digging under. Electric fencing near the ground can also work, but if small children or pets play in the yard, avoid electric fences.

If relocating animals is legal in your area, consider trapping opossums in a box trap, such as Havahart brand, baiting it with canned cat food. Release the opossum at least 10 miles away. Shooting is the only effective lethal control for opossums. Check with local authorities to determine whether using firearms in your area is legal, or contact a wildlife control specialist. (See "Using lethal controls" at right.)

Rabbits Rabbits can become pests around food gardens, fruit trees, and flowers. They'll strip the bark of young trees in winter, and in summer will feast on succulent tulips and carrots.

Repel rabbits by scattering blood meal or commercial repellents labeled for rabbits, but you'll have to reapply them after rain. Walk a dog around the garden daily to renew its scent. Hang pie tins or shiny aluminum can lids on a string, so that they twirl in the breeze, mimicking the flashing eyes of predators. One effective commercial deterrent combines a battery-operated motion detector with a high-pressure water nozzle to spray any moving animal within a range of 30 feet. To ensure protection, fence beds, extending small-mesh fencing 1 foot underground. Encircle young tree trunks with commercial tree wrap or hardware cloth. Electric fences, with one strand hung 4 inches above the ground and another about 1 foot above the ground, are effective in deterring rabbits.

▪ SMART IDEA ▪

Using lethal controls

Especially when an animal poses a health or safety threat, lethal control may be necessary. Lethal controls include fumigants, poisons, traps, and shooting. If you have any doubts about controlling an animal pest, call the animal control office of your municipality or the local wildlife sanctuary, or look up a professional wildlife management specialist in the Yellow Pages. Buy poisons labeled for the species to be controlled, and apply according to directions. Keep poisons away from children and pets, and keep any excess in a locked cabinet. Keep children away from dead animals, and wear disposable gloves if you must handle them.

family friendly · family friendly · family friendly · family friendly

Skunk stink cure

Tomato juice or vinegar are the old home remedies for a dog that's had an encounter with a skunk. Here's a more practical recipe developed by the Nebraska cooperative extension service:

- **1 quart hydrogen peroxide**
- **¼ cup baking soda**
- **1 teaspoon liquid soap**

Combine ingredients. Hose off the dog, then put it into a washtub; lather with the mixture, and rinse.

(Common animal pests continued)

Trap and relocate rabbits using box traps such as Havahart brand baited with vegetables. Relocate the rabbits several miles away, but first check with authorities to determine whether relocating is legal in your area.

Tolerate natural enemies, such as cats, dogs, owls, and hawks. To kill rabbits, insert gas bombs formulated for rabbits into their tunnels, or use lethal traps. If it is legal to use firearms in your area, you may shoot rabbits.

Raccoons Raccoons are easily recognized by the black bandit mask around their eyes. They can grow to 35 pounds and are very strong. Raccoons forage at night, raiding garbage cans, and eating pet food, bird eggs, fruits, and vegetable plants. They can tear their way into buildings, and they can carry diseases, including mange and rabies. If you see a raccoon in the open during daylight, report it to local authorities, because it may have rabies. Deter raccoons by walking a dog around the yard daily. To keep the raccoons out of a garden, encircle it with an electric fence that has two strands less than a foot above ground; avoid using an electric fence if young children or pets play in the yard. Install metal caps on chimneys to keep raccoons out.

To trap raccoons for relocation, use box traps such as Havahart brand, baited with fresh corn or bread, and relocate them several miles away. Check with authorities first to see whether relocating is legal in your area. To eliminate raccoons, use lethal traps, shoot them, or hire a wildlife control specialist (see "Using lethal controls" on page 343 for more details).

Mice, rats, and voles These animals are prolific breeders that can cause tremendous damage if not controlled. They chew on and nest in houses, and they foul food and gnaw trees. Repel them indoors with an ultrasonic-noise machine. Outdoors, use commercial repellents labeled for rats and mice, which contain the chemical ingredient thiram. Deter mice and rats with hardware-cloth fencing and tree wraps, and seal holes with hardware cloth or expandable foam. Keep grass and weeds mowed and under control.

Trap and relocate these animals using small live traps, such as Havahart brand, baited with peanut butter. Relocate them more than a mile away, but first check with local authorities to determine whether relocating is legal in your area.

Lethal solutions include tolerating natural enemies such as hawks, owls, and house cats, and using snap traps, glue boards, or commercial rat and mouse poisons.

Skunks Skunks are pests when they dig holes in lawns in search of insects to eat, raid trash bags and pet bowls, or nest in or under buildings. If threatened, skunks release a foul-smelling spray, and they can carry diseases, including mange and rabies. To repel skunks, keep trash and pet food contained. Control grubs in the lawn. Contact a wildlife control specialist to trap or eradicate skunks.

Squirrels Squirrels are more a nuisance than a pest. They raid bird feeders and trash bags, and nest in attics and garages. There are many homemade and commercial deterrents, but few are effective for long. To keep squirrels out of an attic, trim tree branches a distance of 10 feet or more from the roof, and cover the chimney with a metal cap. Seal entry holes with hardware cloth or expandable foam. Trap and release squirrels, using live traps such as Havahart brand, baited with birdseed. Release squirrels 10 miles away, but first check with local authorities to be certain that relocating wild animals is legal.

Woodchucks Also called *groundhogs,* these are bushy-tailed brown rodents weighing up to 14 pounds. They damage landscapes by digging holes and eating plants. They can carry diseases, including distemper, mange, and rabies.

These seemingly fearless animals respond poorly to deterrents, but one of the more successful is a commercial device that combines a battery-operated motion detector with a high-pressure water nozzle that sprays any moving animal within a range of 30 feet. To keep woodchucks out of a garden bed, surround it with a tall fence that is also buried at least 1 foot deep. To repel woodchucks and other small animals, install electric fencing with two rows of wire spaced less than a foot from the ground. Warn your family, especially young children, to stay away from the fence. It won't harm them, but the shock is not pleasant.

Trap and relocate woodchucks using a live trap baited with fresh fruit or vegetables. If you plan to relocate the animal, check first with authorities to determine whether that is legal in your area. To kill woodchucks, use lethal traps or shoot them.

SMART IDEA

Squirrel-proof bird feeder

Many squirrel-proof feeders are available, as are baffles designed to keep squirrels from raiding existing feeders. Few deterrents work perfectly in every case. Squirrels give the word persistence new meaning. There is one style of bird feeder, however, that excludes squirrels and large bird pests while allowing songbirds access to the seed. The design incorporates a standard tube-type feeder, surrounded by a cage of wire. Birds can enter through the cage to access the feeder, but the squirrels are kept out. Available in garden centers, bird supply stores, mail-order catalogs, and on the Web from several manufacturers. Consider this heavy-duty feeder a lifetime investment.

Certify your backyard

To learn about attracting wildlife, or for children's activities, contact the National Wildlife Federation, a charitable, educational organization. For an application to certify your yard with the Backyard Wildlife Habitat Program, write to National Wildlife Federation, Backyard Wildlife Habitat Questions, 11100 Wildlife Center Dr., Reston, VA 20190-5362, call 800-822-9919, or see www.nwf.org

Attracting animals

Small wildlife are appealing backyard visitors. A surprising number of species will visit a suburban setting, or even the balcony of a housing complex or high rise. Some are benign and beautiful; others are beneficial and keep unwanted insect pests and rodents under control. By meeting their basic needs, you can entice birds; butterflies; toads; turtles, lizards, and other reptiles; and small mammals into your yard. At the same time, you will be helping to preserve local creatures and improving the diversity of your own neighborhood.

Seasonal abundance

It is fairly easy to attract animals to your yard in summer. To attract them year-round and encourage them to take up residence and raise their young, you must enhance your landscape so that it meets their needs in every season. Plant clumps of grasses, shrubs, and trees to provide nesting places in spring. Supply a rich variety of nesting materials, such as clothes-dryer lint, stuffing from old pillows, and bits of fluffy string. In summer, plant shrubs and ornamental grasses as shady resting places, grow nectar flowers, and set out hummingbird feeders and fresh water. Leave some grasses and perennials standing in fall to provide seeds for birds and winter homes for beneficial spiders and small mammals. In winter, supplement whatever berry-producing shrubs you have in your yard with birdseed, suet feeders, and cracked corn for turkeys and browsing animals.

Shared habitats

All forms of wildlife have the same basic needs for food, water, and shelter. Many species share similar habitats. To attract specific animals or birds, provide their favored foods and shelter, and place water close enough to shrubs and trees so that they can approach it safely.

Many small mammals, amphibians, reptiles, birds, and even deer are edge dwellers, living along the edge of wooded areas, where they can enter open meadows to feed, then dash to the woods if threatened. To duplicate this habitat in a natural-looking landscape, choose plants by mature height, and arrange them in vertical layers. To extend the edge throughout a neighborhood, plant the layers along property lines and encourage neighbors to do the same. Layered plantings along property lines create a wildlife corridor. These edges are also called flyways, and will become home to year-round wildlife residents.

Landscaping in layers

Landscaping in vertical layers is nature's version of high-density housing. Birds and other animal species live at different heights; some are ground dwellers, others spend most of their time in bushes, still others live in trees. Planting in vertical layers allows many species to occupy the same small area of land, even a small backyard. When planting in layers, set plants close enough together so that birds and small animals can scurry or fly easily from the ground covers to the tallest trees without being exposed to predators. Include native plants in your groupings, because wild animals are adapted to eating the fruits of native plants.

Create the lowest layer by planting some open lawn and some ground covers; incorporate flowering bulbs and short perennials, such as hostas, for color and interest. Devoting an area of your yard to lawn and ground covers will attract purple martins, swallows, chimney swifts, and even bluebirds, all of which fly over open areas to catch insects on the wing. Include berry-producing, evergreen ground covers such as cotoneaster, which provides a layer shelter and edible berries for ground-feeding birds, such as mourning doves, and also shelters small animals, such as toads and chipmunks.

Plant the second layer with a knee-to-waist-high combination of annuals and perennials. Include some native seed-bearing species such as ornamental grasses, coreopsis, purple coneflower, and black-eyed Susan, and some nectar plants such as salvia and butterfly weed, to attract butterflies and hummingbirds.

Devote the third layer to shrubs and small trees that naturally grow in the shade of taller trees along woodland edges. This important layer must provide food and shelter in winter as well as summer. Grow understory natives such as azalea, dogwood, hydrangea, lilac, redbud, rhododendron, and viburnum. The blossoms of hydrangea, azalea, and rhododendron provide nectar for hummingbirds, and the plants shelter a variety of animals in winter. Dogwood and viburnum produce berries that birds relish in winter; shrubby conifers, such as berry-producing junipers, provide both shelter and food in winter.

■ SMART IDEA ■

Critter watching at night

Watching nocturnal animals takes a bit of detective work. They are naturally shy, and some will wait to visit your yard until after lights-out, leaving only their footprints as evidence. Armed with a footprint identification guidebook and the two techniques below, you can enjoy the full range of wildlife in your neighborhood:

■ Turn off the house lights and turn on an outdoor light in the evening. Sit in a darkened room and patiently watch the lighted area for an animal parade.

■ Collect footprints. Set a shallow tray of damp sand in the yard and put a treat, such as peanut butter, in the center of the tray. Animals tempted by the treat will leave their footprints in the sand.

(Attracting animals continued)

Small animals

Small animals, such as chipmunks, rabbits, turtles, and toads, evade predators by remaining under cover much of the time. Some are nocturnal, which makes them harder to spot. But if you sit quietly and watch, you can see them. To attract small wildlife, set up the kind of habitat in which they feel secure. Grow ground covers such as ivy, pachysandra, and cotoneaster for birds and chipmunks; provide dry, sunny spots for reptiles, and moist, shady ones for amphibians. Meeting their small needs is easy, and it makes a good family activity. Most small animals eat insects so you do not need to put out additional food to attract them.

There's a fine line between the animals being a fun diversion and becoming a garden pest. You might want to consider limiting the amount of yard space you devote to attracting small animals. Avoid setting food out on the ground at night, because it could attract raccoons and vermin. And be prepared to accept the bad with the good.

Amphibians This group includes toads, salamanders, newts, frogs, and the little tree frogs called spring peepers. These animals need to keep their skin moist, so they gravitate toward shady, moist places with damp leaf litter to hide in. To attract them, supply water at ground level and loose organic mulch, such as shredded bark or leaf mold. Hollow out small, cavelike areas in the soil under rocks or overturned clay flowerpots. Turn on an outdoor light at night to attract a feast of swirling insects for toads to eat. Plant iris or cattails near a small pond to attract spring peepers, which like to cling to these plants with their sticky toes.

Bats Bats are a night-flying insect-control squad, with mosquitoes being high on their list of favorite menu items. To attract them, all you need are mosquitoes and roosting places outdoors. If bats do not already live nearby, you may attract them by installing bat houses, which are available at garden centers and from mail-order and online catalogs. Bats can carry rabies, so avoid handling them.

Chipmunks These charming little brown-and-tan-striped animals are active during the day. They help keep insect pests at bay, but they can also get into mischief by nibbling garden plants and nesting where they are not wanted (for more on deterring chipmunks, see page 338). To attract them, build rock piles or a small rock garden, leaving gaps for them to hide in between the rocks, or set out decorative tree stumps, driftwood, or hollow logs to provide them with places to sun and hide from predators. Neighborhood cats are the most serious predators of chipmunks. To protect chipmunks, put

---

safety alert

Dealing with domestic predators

The most dangerous predators that small animals encounter are cats, raccoons, and dogs. To deter predators:

- **Place feeders 6 feet from trees**
- **Bell cats**
- **Keep pets indoors in the early morning and early evening, when small wildlife feed**
- **Erect a fence at least 6 feet high that touches the ground, to keep domestic animals from running wild**

bells on cats' collars, and monitor neighborhood dogs, which can also kill them.

Reptiles These include garter snakes and other insect-eating nonpoisonous snakes, lizards, terrapins, and turtles. To attract these cold-blooded beneficials, provide a source of water at ground level and exposed rocks and logs for them to sit on and bask in the sun. Lizards especially enjoy hiding in rock crevices. If you do not have a rock wall, you can build a pile of rocks or a small rock garden, leaving big enough gaps among the rocks for lizards to dart in and out of.

Squirrels Squirrels spend most of their lives in trees. Red and gray squirrels are easy to spot because they are active during the day; flying squirrels are nocturnal. To attract squirrels, plant nut-producing trees—hardwood and evergreen. In spring, tie bundles of nesting materials, such as clothes-dryer lint, scraps of soft fabric, or bird-nesting material (sold in pet stores), to trees. To offer a flying squirrel a nesting site, fasten a bluebird house to the trunk of a tree (squirrels will likely claim it by gnawing around the entry hole). If you want to feed squirrels in winter, set out dried corn on the cob, peanuts, and sunflower seeds. Squirrels can become pests when they raid bird feeders or nest in unwanted areas.

Opossums These nocturnal, omnivorous animals are noteworthy for a couple of reasons. They are America's only true marsupial; after their young are born, they carry them in a pouch on their stomach for a couple of months. They also have long prehensile tails, which they wrap around tree and shrub branches then hang from the branch They also have nimble, handlike paws. These extremely intelligent animals are excellent climbers, and you can frequently see them on a tree branch or fence post at night. Although they are interesting to watch and will eat nearly anything, you should not set out food for them, because they can easily become pests, raiding trash cans, pet food bowls, and gardens. If they appear in your yard, they will likely return even without a handout. For how to repel opossums, see page 343.

• HOW-TO •

Build a platform feeder

"Ground-feeding" birds such as robins and mourning doves browse at ground level in natural areas, but aren't served well by being fed on the ground, unless the area is changed frequently. Scattering seed on the ground may help spread some bird diseases. That's where ground-type platform bird feeders fit in. To make one, build a shallow wooden frame (or use a sturdy wooden picture frame) at least 2 feet square, and staple aluminum window screening to the bottom of it. Attach legs at each corner to raise it 1 foot above the ground. Fill the tray with cracked corn, sunflower seeds, and scraps of bread. The screening will allow air and rainwater to pass through, keeping food from spoiling.

(Attracting animals continued)

Rabbits Rabbits can be a delight to watch. They cause little damage as long as there's no vegetable garden for them to invade. They live and raise their young in the "borrowed" burrows of other animals, and are most active in the morning, when you can see them browsing on dewy grass, and again in the cool shadows of evening. If they live in your neighborhood, and you have a lawn, there is little need to put out food to attract them, but they will appreciate a small salt block and fresh fruit or vegetable scraps. To provide a home for rabbits, bury a 2-foot-long section of clay or plastic pipe that is about 6 inches in diameter, at a shallow angle, leaving an open end exposed as an entry.

Raccoons Children will enjoy watching raccoons washing their food before eating it. To attract a raccoon, in the evening set unbreakable bowls containing fresh water and a raw egg on a fence post or other perch. Although it is interesting to watch these intelligent, nimble-fingered animals, they can easily become nuisances, damaging property or transmitting diseases (see page 344). Do not attract them or provide a home for them unless you have a very large property and can do so at a distance from your house. To provide a home, place a hollow log in a wooded area. If you see a raccoon wandering aimlessly during the day, report it to your municipal authorities, because it may have rabies.

Attracting larger animals

Deer, elk, and moose These graceful animals are a joy to observe in the wild. To attract them to your yard without putting too much of the landscape plantings at risk takes thoughtful planning. Place attractions at the farthest reaches of your property so these animals won't be tempted to enter the yard's interior. Once they lose their fear of humans, they can eat your favorite plants or venture far enough to eat foundation plantings. Site ornamental plants that these animals are particularly fond of eating, such as daylilies, roses, and tulips, close to the house, where the animals will be less likely to venture. Set out a livestock salt block, shelled corn, and a trough of fresh water to attract them. Plant groups of deciduous and evergreen shrubs and trees of varying heights along the outer edges of your property to offer them protective cover. Look for deer and other browsers when they are most active, in the early morning and early evening hours.

Attracting birds

Birds will delight you with their songs and colorful antics, if you supply them with a combination of their five essential needs: food, water, shelter, cover, and nesting sites. Birds will visit a balcony or

budget stretcher • budget stretcher • budget stretcher

Nectar for hummers

Hummingbird food is simple to make but it needs to be fresh and clean:

- **2 cups water**
- **½ cup granulated sugar**

Boil water in a pan. Stir in sugar until it dissolves. Let the syrup cool, then pour it into a jar and keep refrigerated. Use it to fill a clean hummingbird feeder. Clean the feeder by pouring boiling water through it, and refill it every three days.

Ways to attract friendly animals

Water, food, and shelter: Help neighborhood creatures meet their basic needs and you're sure to see them often.

Birdbaths These attract many birds and small animals, especially in dry climates. The best kinds are elevated, such as the pedestal style shown, and include a trickle of moving water.

Berries Fruiting shrubs and trees, such as winterberry, pyracantha, and crabapple, will encourage robins and other birds to stay through winter rather than migrate south.

Brush piles Birds and other wildlife will often find temporary cover, and sometimes food and nesting sites, within a haphazard pile of brush.

Tree snags Leave dead trees in place, assuming they pose no threat of falling. They are preferred nesting sites for woodpeckers.

Plants for bird food and shelter

To learn which native plants are best suited to your area, contact the following societies: North Carolina Wildflower Preservation Society, www.ncwildlfower. org; New England Wildflower Society, www.newfs.org; National Wildflower Research Center, www.wildflower.org; or the California Native Plant Society, www.cnps.org. Examples of suitable plants are bee balm and butterfly bush for hummingbird nectar, and dogwoods and junipers for shelter and berries.

(Attracting animals continued)

deck supplied with feeders and water, taking advantage of cover provided by potted plants. Even in a small garden, if there's room for a tree, some shrubs, and ground covers, birds may build nests and raise young.

Water is the basic requirement for birds, and a reliable source of fresh water is essential to attracting them. Set out a 1- to 3-inch-deep saucer or birdbath, because small birds are afraid of deep water. Select a container with gradually sloping sides and sure footing.

Water should be available in all seasons. Natural sources shift, dry up, or freeze with changing weather. In winter, renew frozen water, or use a heating element to prevent freezing.

Birds are especially attracted to splashing water, so add a fountain or suspend a jug of dripping water above a birdbath for extra allure. Change the water and scrub off any scum several times a week to prevent spreading avian diseases and mosquito outbreaks. A small decorative pond with a sandy beach area will attract birds as well as other small wildlife, such as toads, frogs, and turtles.

Food is a strong attraction to birds, and a bird feeder may be the only reason they have to visit a balcony or other area without a natural food source such as seed- or berry-producing plants. There are many types of feeders and birdseed available. The feeder style is less important than the quality of seed; many birds will gather around a clay flowerpot saucer if it is filled with sunflower seed, thistle seed (niger), and peanut hearts. Avoid inexpensive seed mixes that are primarily composed of millet, which few native birds favor.

To round out their menu, offer suet cakes in winter (use wire suet holders to exclude greedy squirrels). If you have hummingbirds in your area, hang out a hummingbird feeder in early spring, because the birds often migrate northward before the earliest nectar flowers, such as azaleas and rhododendrons, are open, and will appreciate the energy boost. Buy commercial nectar mix, or make your own (see recipe on page 350). Be sure to change the nectar every three days, and rinse the feeder with boiling water before refilling to avoid fermentation and pathogens. Birds will stop long enough to eat and drink but will not stay long if there is no protective cover, shelter from the elements, or nesting sites, so if there is room, grow a habitat.

Grow plants that produce food in all seasons to round out a backyard bird habitat. In spring and early summer, hummingbirds will be attracted to the nectar in pink- and red-flowered plants. Other birds will enjoy early fruit, and the insects that the plants attract. In

Bird feeding stations

No longer a winter-only activity, feeding birds has less to do with helping them survive, and more with the desire to watch birds close up. Set up one or more feeders, sit back, and enjoy.

Specialty feeders
Red and yellow feeders for hummingbirds are well known. Suet feeders come in a variety of configurations, most with some intent to exclude marauders. Also available are corn feeders for squirrels, fruit feeders for orioles, and nesting material offerings.

Seed feeders The key distinction among them is between those that deliver only large seeds, such as sunflower, or only small seeds, such as niger. Baffles to deter squirrels are essential in most areas, and various methods of hanging or supporting the feeders are available.

Ground and platform feeders
For the many birds that feed at or near the ground, feeding stations like these are much cleaner and healthier than scattering seeds on the ground. See instructions, page 349.

353

Windows and birds

Territorial birds, such as robins and cardinals, often charge windows, mistaking their reflections for rivals. To protect the birds and your windows, buy or make silhouettes in the shape of large black birds with outstretched wings, and tape them to windows. Birds will mistake the decals for predators and avoid the windows.

(Attracting animals continued)

fall and winter, birds enjoy the seeds of ornamental grasses, native flowering plants such as sunflowers and black-eyed Susan, and the berries of dogwood, juniper, viburnum, and other plants.

Cover and nesting sites combine various landscape plants, or even container plants, in vertical layers. Grow a variety of plants. Include native plants that produce edible seeds or berries, because native birds are not adapted to eating the fruits of plants imported from other continents. To provide shelter from wind, rain, and cold, include broadleaf and needled evergreens. If you want to attract birds to a deck, patio, or balcony, group a collection of potted plants together, and include some tall plants such as roses or vines climbing on trellises so that birds will have a secluded place to perch. Plant along property lines and encourage neighbors to do the same to create flyways, which can extend for miles. Migrating birds will fly above these shelter belts as they travel from north to south and back each year, visiting yards all along the way.

Birds to attract

Some birds are so widely distributed that they populate nearly all parts of the continent. Look for chickadees, goldfinches, mourning doves, robins, song sparrows, and woodpeckers in your neighborhood. Attract them with feeders filled with sunflower seeds, thistle seeds, and peanut hearts. In early spring, hang out feeders for hummingbirds, because these long-distance travelers will be arriving hungry from their Mexican and South American wintering grounds. Some birds have special needs, so read about them before attempting to attract them. Purple martins, for example, require a sizable source of water nearby. It would be futile to erect a martin house if your property is not near a pond or lake.

Squirrels and cats are the most common pests of bird feeding stations. The former are looking for their share of the bird food; the latter for the birds themselves. To discourage squirrels, elevate the feeder at least 5 feet off the ground and place it 8 to 10 feet away from the nearest building or tree. Baffles of sheet metal discs will discourage squirrels from running down wires and hanging chains.

If you own a cat, keep it inside during the morning and evening when feeding birds are most active, and hang a bell from its collar. To discourage neighborhood cats, place feeders high and at least 15 feet from places where a cat might hide before pouncing.

resources

Seeking an expert or looking for a supplier? This is the place for more information.

USDA Plant Hardiness Zone Map

This map of climate zones helps you select plants for your garden that will survive a typical winter in your region. The United States Department of Agriculture (USDA) developed the map, basing the zones on the lowest recorded temperatures across North America. Zone 1 is the coldest area and Zone 11 is the warmest.

Plants are classified by the coldest temperature and zone they can endure. For example, plants hardy to Zone 6 survive where winter temperatures drop to −10° F. Those hardy to Zone 8 die long before it's that cold. These plants may grow in colder regions but must be replaced each year. Plants rated for a range of hardiness zones can usually survive winter in the coldest region as well as tolerate the summer heat of the warmest one.

To find your hardiness zone, note the approximate location of your community on the map, then match the color band marking that area to the key.

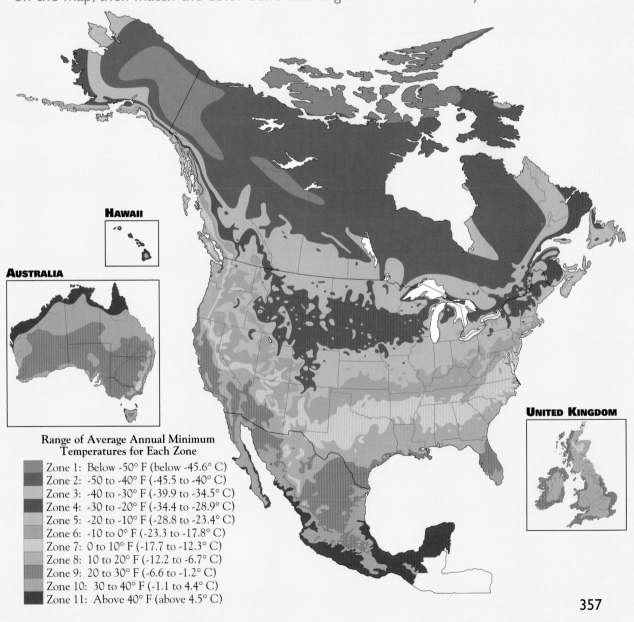

HAWAII

AUSTRALIA

UNITED KINGDOM

Range of Average Annual Minimum Temperatures for Each Zone

Zone 1: Below -50° F (below -45.6° C)
Zone 2: -50 to -40° F (-45.5 to -40° C)
Zone 3: -40 to -30° F (-39.9 to -34.5° C)
Zone 4: -30 to -20° F (-34.4 to -28.9° C)
Zone 5: -20 to -10° F (-28.8 to -23.4° C)
Zone 6: -10 to 0° F (-23.3 to -17.8° C)
Zone 7: 0 to 10° F (-17.7 to -12.3° C)
Zone 8: 10 to 20° F (-12.2 to -6.7° C)
Zone 9: 20 to 30° F (-6.6 to -1.2° C)
Zone 10: 30 to 40° F (-1.1 to 4.4° C)
Zone 11: Above 40° F (above 4.5° C)

357

American Horticultural Society
Plant Heat-Zone Map

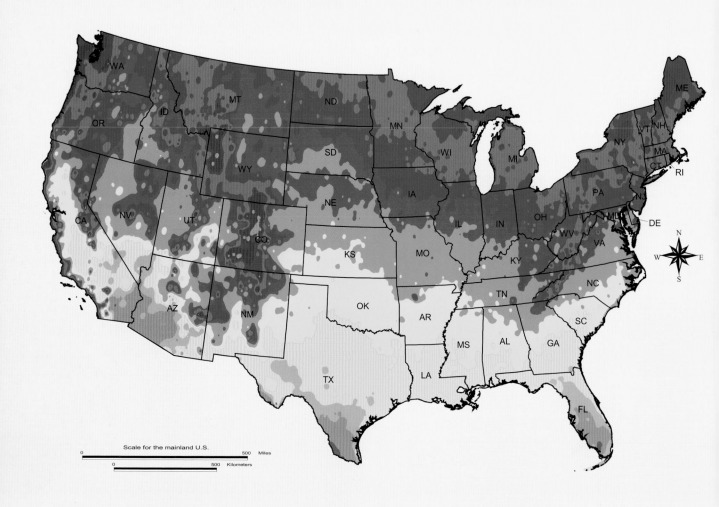

Scale for the mainland U.S.

0 _____ 500 Miles

0 _____ 500 Kilometers

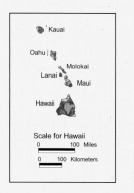

Kauai

Oahu

Molokai

Lanai · Maui

Hawaii

Scale for Hawaii

0 ___ 100 Miles

0 ___ 100 Kilometers

Scale for Alaska

0 ___ 500 Miles

0 ___ 500 Kilometers

AMERICAN HORTICULTURAL SOCIETY

7931 East Boulevard Drive
Alexandria, VA 22308 U.S.A.
(703) 768-5700 Fax (703) 768-8700

Coordinated by:
Dr. H. Marc Cathey, President Emeritus

Compiled by:
Meteorological Evaluation Services Co., Inc.

Underwriting by:
American Horticultural Society
Goldsmith Seed Company
Horticultural Research Institute of the
American Nursery and Landscape Association
Monrovia
Time Life Inc.

Copyright © 1997 by the American Horticultural Society

Average Number
of Days per Year
Above 86° F (30°C) | Zone

< 1	1
1 to 7	2
> 7 to 14	3
> 14 to 30	4
> 30 to 45	5
> 45 to 60	6
> 60 to 90	7
> 90 to 120	8
> 120 to 150	9
> 150 to 180	10
> 180 to 210	11
> 210	12

General resources

Extension services

The Cooperative State Research, Education and Extension is an agency of the U.S. Department of Agriculture, located at each state's land-grant university. Your county's extension office is listed in your local telephone directory, usually in the government listings or under the university's name. These offices offer a variety of horticultural programs, publications, garden problem-solving, and soil-testing services.

In addition to the extension service indexes and specific websites listed for each chapter, the following website includes annotated lists of extension websites around the country:

www.ext.colostate.edu/links/linkexte.html

Gardening search engine

Ohio State University Plant Facts is a search engine for online publications from universities, extension services and other government organizations around the country. It is perhaps the best single online connection (searchable by subject) to noncommercial information on yard care:

plantfacts.osu.edu/web/

Garden discussion forum

GardenWeb discussion forums, forums.gardenweb.com/forums/

Mail-order gardening resources

Cyndi's Catalog of Garden Catalogs

More than 2,000 mail-order catalogs listed and evaluated
www.qnet.com/~johnsonj

Mail-order and online catalogs (seeds and plants)

Vegetables and herbs seeds and plants

Burpee
300 Park Ave.
Warminster, PA 18974
800-888-1447
www.burpee.com

Companion Plants
7247 N. Coolville Ridge Rd.,
Athens, OH 45701
740/592-4643
www.companionplants.com

Gurney's Seed & Nursery
P.O. Box 4178
Greendale, IN 47025-4178
513/354-1491
www.gurneys.com

Johnny's Selected Seeds
955 Benton Ave.
Winslow, ME 04910
207/861-3900
www.johnnyseeds.com/catalog

Nichols Garden Nursery
Old Salem Road NE
Albany, OR 97321-4580
800/422-3985
www.nicholsgardennursery.com

Park Seed Company
1 Parkton Ave.
Greenwood, SC 29647
800/213-0076
www.parkseed.com

Richters Herbs
375 Hwy. 47
Goodwood, Ontario
LOC 1AO, Canada
905/640-6677
www.richters.com

Seeds of Change
P.O. Box 15700
Santa Fe, NM 87592-1500
888/762-7333
www.seedsofchange.com

Seed Savers Exchange
3076 North Winn Rd.
Decorah, IA 52101
563/382-5990
www.seedsavers.org

Southern Exposure Seed Exchange
P.O. Box 460
Mineral, VA 23117
540/894-9480
www.southernexposure.com

Territorial Seed Company
P.O. Box 158
Cottage Grove, OR 97424-0061
541/942-9547
www.territorialseed.com

Willhite Seed, Inc.
P.O. Box 23
Poolville, TX 76487-0023
800/828-1840
www.willhiteseed.com

Fruit trees and berries

Four Winds Nursery
Fremont, CA
www.fourwindsgrowers.com

Indiana Berry & Plant Company
5218 W. 500 South
Huntingburg, IN 47542
800/295-2226
www.inberry.com/index2.html

Johnson Nursery
1352 Big Creek Rd.
Ellijay, GA 30540
888/276-3187
www.johnsonnursery.com

Miller Nurseries
5060 West Lake Rd.
Canandaigua, NY 14424-8904
800/836-9630
www.millernurseries.com

Nourse Farms
41 River Rd.
South Deerfield, MA 01373
413/665-2658
www.noursefarms.com

One Green World Nursery
28696 South Cramer Rd.
Molalla, OR 97038
877/353-4028
www.onegreenworld.com

Pacific Tree Farms
4301 Lynwood Dr.
Chula Vista, CA 91910-3226
619/422-2400
www.kyburg.com/ptf/index.html

Raintree Nursery
391 Butts Rd.
Morton, WA 98356
360/496-6400
www.raintreenursery.com

St. Lawrence Nursery
325 State Hwy. 345
Potsdam, NY 13676
315/265-6739
www.sln.potsdam.ny.us

Stark Bro's Nursery
P.O. Box 1800
Louisiana, MO 63353
800/325-4180
www.starkbros.com

Whitman Farms
3995 Gibson Rd. NW
Salem, OR 97304
503/585-8728
whitmanfarms.com

Tools and Garden Supplies

A.M. Leonard, Inc.
241 Fox Drive
Piqua, OH 45356-0816
800/543-8955
www.amleo.com
Composters and composting supplies, garden hand tools, fertilizers, landscape fabrics, soil amendments, outdoor power equipment

Bountiful Gardens
18001 Shafer Ranch Rd.
Willits, CA 95490-9626
707/459-6410
www.bountifulgardens.org
Gardening supplies, natural pest controls

The Eclectic Gardener
store.yahoo.com/eclectic-gardener/index.html
Online garden tool shopping.

Gardener's Supply Company
128 Intervale Rd.
Burlington, VT 05401
888/833-1412
www.gardeners.com
Gardening supplies, tools, natural pest controls

Gardens Alive!
5100 Schenley Pl.
Lawrenceburg, IN 47025
513/354-1482
www.gardensalive.com
Organic, nontoxic, and biological pest controls including live insect predators and beneficial nematodes, animal repellents, and other garden supplies

Gempler's
1210 Fourier Dr.
Suite 150
Madison, WI 53717
800/382-8473
www.gemplers.com
Garden and landscape tools, work clothes, safety equipment, pest controls

Harmony Farm Supply & Nursery
3244 Hwy. 116 North
Sebastopol, CA 95472
707/823-9125
www.harmonyfarm.com
Natural pest controls, garden tools and supplies

Lee Valley Tools
P.O. Box 1780
Ogdensburg, NY 13669-6780
800/871-8158
www.leevalley.com
High quality garden hand tools

Mellinger's
2310 W. South Range Rd.
(P.O. Box 157)
North Lima, OH 44452
800/321-7444
www.mellingers.com
Lawn and garden supplies, composters, seeds, plants

Peaceful Valley Farm Supply
P.O. Box 2209
Grass Valley, CA 95945
888/784-1722
www.groworganic.com
Organic pest control and live insect predators, animal repellents, soil testing, tools, and gardening equipment

Seeds of Change
See page 359
Composters, soil-testing kits, soil amendments

Smith & Hawken
25 Corte Madera
Mill Valley, CA 94941
800/776-3336
www.smithandhawken.com
Garden tools, composting products

Snow Pond Farm Supply
699 Adams St.
P.O. Box 115
North Abington, MA 02351
781/878-5581
www.snow-pond.com
Garden supplies, tools, soil amendments, pest controls, weed controls, composting supplies

Resources by chapter

Chapter 2: Caring For Your Lawn

Get more ideas at BHG.com
For more advice on lawn care, see
■ www.bhg.com/landscape

Budd Seed, Inc.
199 Budd Blvd.
Winston-Salem, NC 27103
www.turf.com
Lawn seed supplier, lawn care information

The Scotts Company
Scotts Consumer Service
14111 Scottslawn Rd.
Marysville, OH 43041
888/270-3714 (answers to lawn care questions, 800/543-8873)
www.scotts.com
Lawn products, information

Seedland
9895 Adams Rd.
Wellborn, FL 32094
888/820-2080
www.lawngrass.com
Online lawn seed and supply source

The National Turfgrass Evaluation Program
10300 Baltimore Ave.
Bldg. 003, Room. 218
Beltsville Agricultural Research Center-West
Beltsville, MD 20705
301/504-5125
www.ntep.org
Evaluates turfgrass varieties and publishes results

Outsidepride.com Inc.
2430 McGilchrist St. SE
Salem, OR 97302
877/255-8470
www.outsidepride.com
Online lawn seed source

Pennington Seed Inc.
P.O. Box 290
Madison, GA 30650
800/285-7333
www.penningtonseed.com
Lawn seed, lawn care information

SeedSuperStore.com
P.O. Box 812
Buffalo, NY 14225
866/634-0001
www.seedsuperstore.com
Online lawn seed source

Southland Sod Farms
P.O. Box 579
Port Hueneme, CA 93044-0579
805/488-3585
www.sod.com/html/seed_store.html
Sod supplier

Turfgrass Information Center
Michigan State University
www.lib.msu.edu/tgif

Turfgrass Producers International
1855-A Hicks Rd.
Rolling Meadows, IL 60008
800/405-8873,
www.turfgrasssod.org/links.html

Turfseed
P.O. Box 250
Hubbard, OR 79032
800/247-6910
www.turfseed.com/home/
Online lawn seed source

Online publications

Colorado State University Turf Program
http://csuturf.colostate.edu

The Lawn Institute
www.turfgrasssod.org/lawninstitute/digest.html

Ohio State University
http://ohioline.osu.edu/lines/lawns.html

Penn State Agricultural Sciences
www.agronomy.psu.edu/extension/turf/diagnose.html#mowing

Purdue Turfgrass Program
www.agry.purdue.edu/turf

Texas A&M University Turfgrass Programs
http://aggieturf.tamu.edu

Chapter 3: Trees & Shrub Care

Get more ideas at BHG.com
For more advice on trees and shrubs, see
■ www.bhg.com/treeshrub

American Association of Botanical Gardens and Arboreta
100 West 10th St., Ste. 614
Wilmington, DE 19801
302/655-7100
www.aabga.org
Links to research, organizations, and publications

American Conifer Society
P.O. Box 3422
Crofton, MD 21114-0422
410/721-6611
www.conifersociety.org

American Rose Society
P.O. Box 30,000
Shreveport, LA 71130-0030
318/938-5402
www.ars.org

Corona Clipper
1540 East Sixth St.
Corona, CA 92879
909/737-6515
www.coronaclipper.com
Pruning tools

Fiskars Garden Tools
780 Carolina St.
Sauk City, WI 53583
800/500-4849
http://gardening.fiskars.com/index.html
Pruning tools

Online publications

Clemson University Extension
http://hgic.clemson.edu
Searchable database

Colorado State University Cooperative Extension
www.ext.colostate.edu/menugard.html
Links to publications by topic

International Society of Arboriculture
www.isa-arbor.com/consumer/
consumer.html
Tree-care links

North Carolina State Department of Horticultural Science
www.ces.ncsu.edu/depts/hort/
consumer/hortinternet
Search database by plant name or topic

Ohio State University Extension
http://ohioline.osu.edu/hyg-fact/1000/
index.html
Links to bulletins by title

University of Florida Cooperative Extension
http://edis.ifas.ufl.edu/topic_lawns_and_
landscapes
Links to fact sheets

Chapter 4: Caring For Vines & Ground Covers

Get more ideas at BHG.com
For tips on vine and ground covers, see
■ www.bhg.com/vines

American Association of Botanical Gardens and Arboreta
See under Chapter 3: Trees & Shrub Care

Corona Clipper
See under Chapter 3: Trees & Shrub Care
Pruning tools

Fiskars Garden Tools
See under Chapter 3: Trees & Shrub Care
Pruning tools

Online publications

Clemson University Extension
See under Chapter 3: Trees & Shrub Care

Colorado State University Cooperative Extension
See under Chapter 3: Trees & Shrub Care

North Carolina State Department of Horticultural Science
See under Chapter 3: Trees & Shrub Care

Ohio State University Extension
See under Chapter 3: Trees & Shrub Care

University of Florida Cooperative Extension
See under Chapter 3: Trees & Shrub Care

Chapter 5: Flower Gardens

Get more ideas at BHG.com
For more advice on flower gardening, see
■ www.bhg.com/flowers

American Association of Botanical Gardens and Arboreta
See under Chapter 3: Trees & Shrub Care

Better Homes and Gardens magazine
www.bhg.com/bhg/gardening/
index.jhtml
Searchable database

Netherlands Flower Bulb Information Center
www.bulb.com

National Garden Clubs
4401 Magnolia Ave.
St. Louis, MO 63110
314/776-7574
www.gardenclub.org

National Garden Bureau
www.ngb.org
Links to wholesale and retail seed companies

National Gardening Association
1100 Dorset St.
South Burlington, VT 05403
802/863-5251
www.garden.org

Proven Winners
1117 N. 14th St.
Dekalb, IL 60115
877/865-5818
www.provenwinners.com
Wholesale plant supplier; information

Online publications

Clemson University Extension
See under Chapter 3: Trees & Shrub Care

Colorado State University Cooperative Extension
See under Chapter 3: Trees & Shrub Care

North Carolina State University Extension
See under Chapter 3: Trees & Shrub Care

Ohio State University Extension
See under Chapter 3: Trees & Shrub Care

Perry's Perennial Pages
University of Vermont Extension
www.uvm.edu/~pass/perry

University of Florida Cooperative Extension
See under Chapter 3: Trees & Shrub Care

Chapter 6: Harvest Gardening

Get more ideas at BHG.com
For more advice on harvest gardening, see
■ www.bhg.com/gardening

California Rare Fruit Growers
E-mail: admin@crfg.org
www.crfg.org
Information about tropical and subtropical fruits

National Garden Bureau
See under Chapter 5: Flower Gardens

National Gardening Association
See under Chapter 5: Flower Gardens

The Herb Society of America
9019 Kirtland Chardon Rd.
Kirtland, OH 44094
440/256-0514
www.herbsociety.org

Tree Fruit & Extension Center

Washington State University
1100 N. Western Ave.
Wenatchee, WA, 98801
509/663-8181
www.tfrec.wsu.edu

Online publications

National Gardening Association

www.nationalgardening.com/special/
veggieguide.asp
Vegetable gardening guide

North Carolina State University Cooperative Extension

www.ces.ncsu.edu/depts/hort/hil/
hvegnew.html

Ohio State University Extension

See under Chapter 3: Trees & Shrub Care

University of Georgia

www.ces.uga.edu

University of Missouri

muextension.missouri.edu/explore/
http://agguides/hort/index.htm

Colorado State University

www.colostate.edu/Depts/CoopExt/
4DMG/VegFruit/vegs.htm
Frequently asked vegetable questions

Texas Agricultural Extension Service

http://horticulture.tamu.edu:7998/
vegetable/search.html
IPM for vegetables

University of Arizona

http://ag.arizona.edu/pubs/garden/mg/
vegetable
The vegetable garden

University of Florida

http://edis.ifas.ufl.edu/TOPIC_
Vegetable_Gardening

University of California at Davis

http://vric.ucdavis.edu/veginfo/
homegarden.htm

Michigan State University

www.msue.msu.edu/iac/agnic/lgrntlst/
consvege.html

Oregon State University

www.ippc.orst.edu/cicp/Vegetable/
vegindex.htm
Vegetable Integrated Pest Management

Texas A&M University Extension Service

http://aggie-horticulture.tamu.edu/
extension/ container/container.html
Vegetable gardening containers

Virginia Cooperative Extension

www.ext.vt.edu/resources

Online publications (herbs)

National Gardening Association

www.nationalgardening.com/special/
herbguide.asp
Herb gardening guide

Pennsylvania State University

http://hortweb.cas.psu.edu/extension/
vegcrops/herb_directory.html
Directory of herbs

Massachusetts Department of Food & Agriculture

www.state.ma.us/dfa/gardening/herbs
Home gardening—herbs

West Virginia University

www.wvu.edu/~agexten/hortcult/herbs
/ne208hrb.htm
Growing herbs in the home garden

University of Wisconsin

www.wcfls.lib.wi.us/newberlin/
gardening.htm
Vegetable and herb gardening

Online publications (tree fruits)

National Gardening Association

www.nationalgardening.com/special/
fruitguide.asp
Fruit gardening guide

Auburn University

www.seedman.com/Tips/fruitspy.htm
Home fruit spray guide

Virginia Tech University

www.ento.vt.edu/Fruitfiles/
SprayGuide/HomeFruitSprays.html
2003 Spray guide for home

University of California-Davis

http://homeorchard.ucdavis.edu/
links.shtml

University of Minnesota

www.extension.umn.edu/distribution/
horticulture/DG0675.html
Home fruit spray guide

California Rare Fruit Growers

www.crfg.org/pubs/frtfacts.html
"Fruit Facts" publications

Massachusetts Department of Agricultural Resources

www.state.ma.us/dfa/gardening/fruits/
index.htm
Home gardening: fruits

Chapter 7: Managing Soils and Compost

Get more ideas at BHG.com
For more tips on soils and compost, see
■ www.bhg.com/bksoil

A & L Analytical Labs

2790 Whitten Rd.
Memphis, TN 38133
800/264-4522
Soil-testing laboratory

U.S. Composting Council

4250 Veterans Memorial Hwy.
Suite 275
Holbrook, NY 11741
631/737-4931
Information about composting

National Cooperative Soil Survey

National Soil Survey Center
USDA-Natural Resources Conservation Service
Federal building, room 152
100 Centennial Mall North
Lincoln, NE 685085-3866
402/437-4149
http://soils.usda.gov/soil_survey/main.htm
County-by-county scientific inventory of U.S. soils on nearly all public and private land. A soil survey includes soil maps and descriptions of each type of soil in the county, as well as interpretations of the soil's characteristics and potential for community planning, agricultural land management, engineering, and wildlife management

Cornell University Composting

www.cfe.cornell.edu/compost/Composting_Homepage.html
Information, resources, and contacts

Seattle Tilth Association

4649 Sunnyside Ave. North, Room 1
Seattle, WA 98103
206/633-0451
www.seattletilth.org
Organization offering supplies and information about composting and organic gardening

The Rodale Institute

611 Siegfriedale Rd.
Kutztown, PA 19530
610/683-1400
www.rodaleinstitute.org
Information on organic gardening, soil improvement, and composting

University of Massachusetts Cooperative Extension Service

Umass Soil Test Laboratory
West Experiment Station
University of Massachusetts
Amherst, MA 01003-8020
413/545-2311
www.umass.edu/plsoils/soiltest (click on list of services)
Compost testing service

Wood's End Research Laboratory

P.O. Box 297
Mt. Vernon, ME 04352
207/293-2457
www.woodsend.org
Compost testing and compost analysis equipment

Suppliers of Soil Amendments, Soil Testing, and Composting Supplies

A.M. Leonard, Inc.
See under Tools and Garden Supplies

Bountiful Gardens
See under Tools and Garden Supplies

Burpee
See under Vegetables and herbs seeds

Gardens Alive!
See under Tools and Garden Supplies

Gardener's Supply Company
See under Tools and Garden Supplies

Harmony Farm Supply
See under Tools and Garden Supplies

Lee Valley Tools, Ltd.
See under Tools and Garden Supplies

Mellinger's
See under Tools and Garden Supplies

Nitron Industries, Inc.
P.O. Box 1447
5703 S. Hewitt
Fayetteville, AR 72701-1447
800/835-0123
www.nitron.com
Organic soil amendments, fertilizers, composting supplies, and equipment

Peaceful Valley Farm Supply
See under Tools and Garden Supplies

Seeds of Change
See under Tools and Garden Supplies

Smith & Hawken
See under Tools and Garden Supplies

Solarcone, Inc.

P.O. Box 67
Seward, IL 61077-0067
815/247-8454
http://solarcone.house8.net
Commercial compost bin

Online publications

Colorado State University
www.ext.colostate.edu/ptlk/ptlk1600.html
Index and links to guides on soils, amendments, and composting.

Ohio State University
http://ohioline.osu.edu/lines/hygs.html#LANDS
Links to bulletins on soil management

Chapter 8: Garden Tools

Get more ideas at BHG.com
For more tips on garden tools, see
■ www.bhg.com/gardentools

A.M. Leonard, Inc.
See under Tools and Garden Supplies
Hand tools, outdoor power equipment

Corona Clipper
See under Chapter 3: Trees & Shrub Care
Hand tools

Echo
400 Oakwood Rd.
Lake Zurich, IL 60047-1584
800/673-1558
www.echo-usa.com/start.asp
Outdoor power equipment

The Eclectic Gardener
See under Tools and Garden Supplies
Hand tools

Gardener's Supply Company
See under Tools and Garden Supplies
Hand tools

Gempler's
See under Tools and Garden Supplies
Hand tools

Husqvarna
www.usa.husqvarna.com
Outdoor power equipment

Lee Valley Tools
See under Tools and Garden Supplies
Hand tools

Mantis
1028 Street Rd.
Southampton, PA 18966
800/366-6268
www.mantisgardentools.com/home.asp
Rototillers

MTD
www.mtdproducts.com/home.jsp
Outdoor power equipment

Outdoor Power Equipment Institute, Inc.
341 S. Patrick St.
Old Town Alexandria, VA 22314
703/549-7600
opei.mow.org
Outdoor power equipment trade group

Mellingers
See under Tools and Garden Supplies
Hand tools

Smith & Hawken
See under Tools and Garden Supplies
Hand tools

U.S. Consumer Product Safety Commission
www.cpsc.gov/search.html
Safety tips for operating outdoor
power equipment

The Toro Company
8111 Lyndale Ave. South
Bloomington, MN 55420
800/348-2424
www.toro.com
Outdoor power equipment

Chapter 9: Hoses, Sprinklers, and Irrigation Systems

Get more ideas at BHG.com
For more tips on irrigation systems, see
■ www.bhg.com/regionaltips

Clemson University Extension
See under Chapter 3: Trees & Shrub Care
Searchable online bulletins

Colorado State University Cooperative Extension
www.ext.colostate.edu/pubs/garden/
04702.html
Drip irrigation fact sheet

DripWorks
190 Sanhedrin Circle
Willits, CA 95490
800/522-3747
www.dripworksusa.com
Mail-order irrigation supplies

Fiskars Garden Tools
See under Chapter 3: Trees & Shrub Care

Home Depot
800/553-3199
www.homedepot.com

Hunter Industries
www.hunterindustries.com/hunter/
Resources/resource.htm
Sprinkler manufacturer; information

The Irrigation Association
6540 Arlington Blvd.
Falls Church, VA 22042-6638
703/536-7080
www.irrigation.org

Irritrol Systems
www.irritrolsystems.com
Manufacturer of watering system timers

Lowe's
800/445-6937
www.lowes.com

L.R. Nelson Corporation
One Sprinkler Lane
Peoria, IL 61615-9544
309/690-2200
www.lrnelson.com

Melnor, Inc.
P.O. Box 2840
Winchester, VA 22604
540/722-5600
www.melnor.com

Rain Bird Corporation
800/724-6247
www.rainbird.com

Swan Hose Co.
800/848-8707
www.swanhose.com

The Toro Company
See under Chapter 8: Garden Tools
Sprinkler and watering equipment

The Urban Farmer Store
2833 Vicente St.
San Francisco, CA 94114
415/661-2204
www.urbanfarmerstore.com
Irrigation supplies and information

Victor Valley Water District
17185 Yuma St.
Victorville, CA 92392-5887
760/245-6424
www.vvwater.org/guide/index.htm
Guide to high desert landscaping

Online publications (irrigation)

University of Georgia
www.ces.uga.edu/pubcd/b894-w.html
Irrigation for lawns and gardens

Chapter 10: Water Features & Ponds

Get more ideas at BHG.com
For more advice on water gardens, see
■ www.bhg.com/watergarden

Associated Koi Clubs of America
www.akca.org

Beckett Pond Supplies
www.888beckett.com

Goldfish Society of America
P.O. Box 551373
Fort Lauderdale, FL 33355
www.goldfishsociety.org

Hagen pond supplies
www.hagen.com/usa/ponds

International Waterlily and Water Gardening Society
6828 26th St. W.
Bradenton, FL 34207
941/756-0880
www.iwgs.org

Lilypons Water Gardens

P.O. Box 10
6800 Lilypons Rd.
Buckeystown, MD 21717-0010
800/999-5459
www.lilypons.com
Aquatic plants, water-garden supplies

Little Giant Pump Co.

P.O. Box 12010,
Oklahoma City, OK 73157-2010
888/956-0000
www.littlegiant.com
Water garden pumps

OASE

1607 Carmen Dr., Suite 207
Camarillo, CA 93010
805/383-1888
www.oase-pumpen.com/us
Pond supplies

Paradise Water Gardens

14 May St.
Whitman, MA 02382-1841
800/955-0161
www.paradisewatergardens.com
Aquatic plants, water-garden supplies

Perry's Water Gardens

136 Leatherman Gap Rd.
Franklin , NC 28734
828/524-3264
www.tcfb.com/perwatg
Aquatic plants, water-garden supplies

William Tricker, Inc.

7125 Tanglewood Dr.
Independence, OH 44131
800/524-3492
www.tricker.com/
Aquatic plants, water-garden supplies

Online publications
(ponds and water features)

Clemson University Extension
See under Chapter 3: Trees & Shrub Care

North Carolina State University Extension
See under Chapter 3: Trees & Shrub Care

University of Florida, Center for Aquatic and Invasive Plants

http://aquat1.ifas.ufl.edu/welcome.html

U.S. Geological Survey

Nonindigenous Aquatic species
nas.er.usgs.gov
Invasive species information

Chapter 11: Caring For Your Yard's Structures

Get more ideas at BHG.com
For more advice on yard structures, see
■ www.bhg.com/gardenprojects

National Ready Mix Concrete Association

900 Spring St.
Silver Spring, MD 20910
301/587-1400
www.nrmca.org/concrete_basics/index.htm

The Concrete Network

www.concretenetwork.com
Products, service providers

Moxie International

800/356-3476
www.moxie-intl.com/tutorial.htm
Concrete cleaning supplies

Online publications

University of Wisconsin Madison
http://aec.engr.wisc.edu/resources/rsrc07.html
Q and A on concrete repairs

Online publications

Asphalt
National Pavement Contractors Association
www.pavementpro.org/surveyguide.htm
and /eosso_article.htm
Guide to repairing asphalt

Bricks
Radon Seal
www.radonseal.com/concrete-cleaner.htm
Brick-cleaning supplies, online shopping

Decks

DeckTechs
www.decktechs.com/products.htm
Deck cleaners, online shopping

California Redwood Association
405 Enfrente Dr., Ste. 200
Novato, CA 94949
888/225-7339
www.calredwood.org
Deck construction and maintenance

Western Red Cedar Lumber Association
1501-700 W. Pender St.
Pender Place 1, Business Bldg.,
Vancouver, B.C.
Canada V6C 1G8
604/684-0266
www.wrcla.org/index.asp
Cedar projects and care

Trex
www.trex.com
Alternative deck product

TimberTech Limited
894 Prairie Rd.
Wilmington, OH 45177
800/307-7780
www.timbertech.com
Alternative deck product

CertainTeed Corp.
P.O. Box 860
750 E. Swedesford Rd.
Valley Forge, PA 19482
800/782-8777
www.certainteed.com/cfence
Alternative deck product

E-Z Deck
800/990-3099
www.ezdeck.com
Alternative deck product

Nexwood Industries Ltd.
1327 Clark Blvd.
Brampton, ON, Canada, L6T 5R5
888/763-9966
www.nexwood.com/home.html
Alternative deck product

Deck and Fence Sealers

Wolman-Zinsser Co., Inc.
173 Belmont Dr.
Somerset, NJ 08875
800/556-7737
www.wolman.com
Wood-care product

BEHR Process Corporation
3400 W. Segerstrom Ave.
Santa Ana, CA 92704
800/854-0133
www.behr.com/behrx/act/view/products_main
Paints, stains, wood and concrete finishes

Chapter 12: Outdoor Lighting

Get more ideas at BHG.com
For more advice on yard structures, see
■ www.bhg.com/outdoorliving

B&K Lighting
www.bklighting.com
Outdoor lighting products

USA Light & Electric
800/854 8794
www.usalight.com
Outdoor lighting supplies

Low Voltage Lighting Forum
www.lowvolt.org/manufacturers.html
Links to manufacturers, industry
standards, low-voltage-lighting
designers and installers

Cooper Lighting
1121 Hwy. 74 South
Peachtree City, GA 30269
770/486-4800,
www.cooperlighting.com/home.asp
Outdoor lighting product

Residential Landscape Lighting & Design
4912 Blossom St.
Houston, TX 77007
800/239-2939
www.residential-landscape-lighting-design.com
Online shopping

The Urban Farmer Store
2833 Vicente St.
San Francisco, CA 94114
415/661-2204
www.urbanfarmerstore.com/lighting/lighting.html
Outdoor lighting equipment/supplies

Chapter 13: Critter Control

Get more ideas at BHG.com
For more advice on controlling wildlife, see
■ www.bhg.com/bkwildlife

Agrobiologicals
www.agrobiologicals.com
Pest problems, solutions, and suppliers
of alternatives to agrochemicals

Bio-Integral Resource Center
P.O. Box 7414
Berkeley, CA 94707
510/-524-2567
www.keyed.com/birc
Information on integrated pest
management

California Environmental Protection Agency
Department of Pesticide Regulation
Environmental Monitoring and Pest
Management Branch,
1020 North St., Room 161,
Sacramento, CA, 95814-5624
916/324-4100
List of beneficial organisms in North
America

Entomological Society of America
301/731-4535
www.entsoc.org/catalog/2002/general.asp

IPM Laboratories, Inc.
Main Street
Locke, NY 13092-0300
315/497-2063
www.ipmlabs.com
Information on pest control, including
a newsletter

National Pesticide Information Center
Oregon State University
333 Weniger
Corvallis, OR 97331-6502
800/858-7378
http://npic.orst.edu
Telephone hotline for questions
concerning pesticides, pesticide
ingredients, uses, storage, and disposal

Ortho Consumer Service
P.O. Box 1749
Columbus, OH 43216
888/295-0671
www.ortho.com
Information on Ortho brand pesticide
products, online Ortho Problem Solver,
gardening advice

U.S. Environmental Protection Agency
Ariel Rios Building
1200 Pennsylvania Ave. NW
Washington, DC 20460
202/272-0167
www.epa.gov
Information on commercially
manufactured and distributed chemical
and organic pesticides

The Rodale Institute
See under Chapter 7: Managing Soils
Information on organic pest control

Pest-Control Supplies

Biologic Company
P.O. Box 177
Willow Hill, PA 17271-0177
717/349-2789
www.biologicco.com
Biological pest control

Bonide Products, Inc.
6301 Sutliff Rd.
Oriskany, NY 13424
315/736-8231
www.bonideproducts.com
Pesticides, fungicides, and herbicides

Bountiful Gardens
See under Tools and Garden Supplies
Natural pest controls

Charley's Greenhouse Supply
1569 Memorial Hwy.
Mt. Vernon, WA 98273
800/322-4707
www.charleysgreenhouse.com
Gardening and greenhouse supplies;
pest control products.

DeerBusters
888/422-3337
www.deerbusters.com
Deer- and animal-control products

Gardens Alive!
See under Tools and Garden Supplies
Biological pest controls

Gardener's Supply Company
See under Tools and Garden Supplies
Natural pest controls

Harmony Farm Supply
See under Tools and Garden Supplies
Natural pest controls

Mellinger's
See under Tools and Garden Supplies
Manufactured, organic, and biological
pest controls

Nitron Industries, Inc.
See under Suppliers of Soil Amendments

Peaceful Valley Farm Supply
See under Tools and Garden Supplies
Organic pest control and live insect
predators; animal repellents

Plow & Hearth
P.O. Box 5000
Madison, VA 22727
800/627-1712
www.plowandhearth.com
Pest controls and lures for
beneficial insects

Reed-Joseph International Co.
P.O. Box 894
Greenville, MS 38702
800/647-5554
www.reedjoseph.com
Bird scare devices

Rincon-Vitova Insectaries, Inc.
P.O. Box 1555
Ventura, CA 93022
800/248-2847
www.agrobiologicals.com/company/
C319.htm
Biological pest management

Snow Pond Farm Supply
See under Tools and Garden Supplies
Animal repellents, biological controls

The Tanglefoot Co.
314 Straight Ave. SW
Grand Rapids, MI 49504
616/459-4130
www.tanglefoot.com
Sticky trapping systems

Victorpest.com
800/800-1819
www.victorpest.com
Low- and non-toxic pest controls

Woodstream Corp.
800/800-1819
Animal traps including Havahart Traps

Online publications

California Environmental Protection Agency
Department of Pesticide Regulation
www.cdpr.ca.gov/docs/label/
prodnam.htm
Search pesticide products by partial
product name

Oregon State University Integrated Plants Protection Center
www.ippc.orst.edu/cicp/pests/
rodents.htm
Database of IPM Resources; pest
management for the Pacific Northwest

Maryland Department of Agriculture
www.mda.state.md.us/plant/bmps.htm
Pesticide best-management practices

North Dakota State University Extension Service
http://ndsuext.nodak.edu/extnews/
askext/wildpest.htm
Information on insect and animal pests
including rabbits, rodents, and snakes.

North Carolina Cooperative Extension Service
http://ipm.ncsu.edu/urban/cropsci/
toc.html
Urban integrated pest management

The Scotts Company
See under Chapter 2: Caring for Your Lawn
Pest and animal control information

Alabama Cooperative Extension System
www.acenet.auburn.edu/department/
ipm/mammal.htm
Control of mammals and birds in the
vegetable garden

U.S. Fish and Wildlife Service
www.fws.gov/index.html
Animal control

15

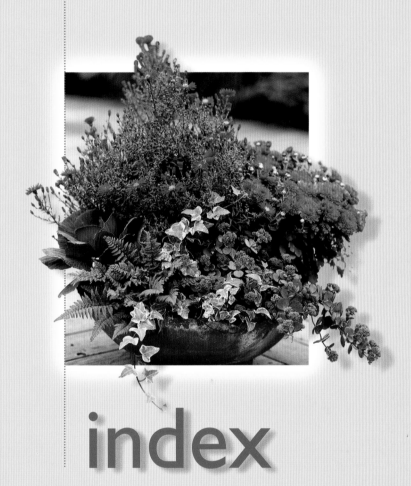

index

References to photographs are printed in boldface type.
References to tip boxes are in italicized type

credits

Yard & Garden Owners Manual
Editor: Marilyn Rogers
Project Manager: Michael MacCaskey
Writers: Kathy Bond Borie, Charlie Nardozzi, Delilah Smittle,
   Ann Whitman, T. Jeff Williams
Contributing Editor: Lynn Ocone
Contributing Assistant Editor: Diane A. Witosky
Design Director: Ernie Shelton
Copy Chief: Terri Fredrickson
Copy and Production Editor: Victoria Forlini
Editorial Operations Manager: Karen Schirm
Managers, Book Production: Pam Kvitne, Marjorie J. Schenkelberg,
   Rick von Holdt
Contributing Copy Editor: Barbara Feller-Roth
Contributing Proofreaders: Kathy Roth Eastman, Fran Gardner,
   Alison M. Glascock, Mindy Kralicek, Barbara Stokes
Photographers: Marty Baldwin, Scott Little, Blaine Moats, Jay Wilde
Contributing Photographer: Rob Cardillo
Technical Consultants: Tom Bressan, Marcia Eames-Sheavly, Margaret McKinnon,
   Bob Polomski, Bryan Smith, Thomas L. Watschke
Indexer: Mary Pelletier-Hunyadi
Researcher: Rosemary Kautzky
Editorial and Design Assistants: Kathleen Stevens,
   Mary Lee Gavin, Karen McFadden

Meredith® Books
Editor in Chief: Linda Raglan Cunningham
Design Director: Matt Strelecki
Executive Editor, Home Improvement and Gardening: Benjamin W. Allen
Executive Editor, Gardening: Michael McKinley

Publisher: James D. Blume
Executive Director, Marketing: Jeffrey Myers
Executive Director, New Business Development: Todd M. Davis
Executive Director, Sales: Ken Zagor
Director, Operations: George A. Susral
Director, Production: Douglas M. Johnston
Business Director: Jim Leonard

Vice President and General Manager: Douglas J. Guendel

Better Homes and Gardens® Magazine
Editor in Chief: Karol DeWulf Nickell
Deputy Editor, Gardens and Outdoor Living: Elvin McDonald

Meredith Publishing Group
President, Publishing Group: Stephen M. Lacy
Vice President-Publishing Director: Bob Mate

Meredith Corporation
Chairman and Chief Executive Officer: William T. Kerr

In Memoriam: E. T. Meredith III (1933-2003)

Thanks to: Janet Anderson; Patrick Cobbs; Doug
Fender, Turfgrass Producers International; Sandra
Gerdes, Better Homes and Gardens Test Garden
Manager; A.M. Leonard; Michele Newkirk; Mary Irene
Swartz; Greg Phillips at Earl May Garden Center.

Photographers: (Photographers credited may retain
copyright © to the listed photographs.)
L = Left, R = Right, C = Center, B = Bottom,
T = Top, i = Inset

William D. Adams: 26BL, 51TRC, 56TL, 162BLi, 162BL,
162BR, 163Row2#4; **Cathy Barash:** 173TL, 173TC,
173TR; **Gay Bumgarner/Positive Images:** 324BL,
351TR; **Rex Butcher/Positive Images:** cover BL, 2BL,
4TCL, 53; **Rob Cardillo:** cover BR, 4TR, 7#1R, 8TL,
8BLT, 9R#2, 9R#3, 10L#2, 10L#3, 26BLC, 45TR, 45L,
54BR, 61BL, 61BR, 69L, 69BR, 81, 84BL, 84R, 93, 97,
102, 104, 117TL, 117TR, 117BR, 119, 125BR, 131TL,
135TR, 142TL, 145TL, 145TR, 145BR, 166BR, 169BL,
191, 217, 218TL, 223, 225, 239TCL, 241, 246CL, 246BL,
246BR, 251TL, 251TR, 251BR, 269TR, 269BR, 271,
274TR, 297, 341TR, 341BR; **David Cavagnaro:** 6BL,
8BL, 12BL, 19TR, 127BL; **Crandall & Crandall:** 162TL;
E.R. Degginger: 51BLC, 335Row4#1; **James F. Dill:**
149Row4#1, 163Row1#1, 163 Row1#3, 163Row3#1,2,3,
163Row4#1, 163Row5#1; **Derek Fell:** 17BR,
149Row1#3, 149Row2#4, 149Row3#2, 163Row2#3,
163Row3#4, 163R5#2, 341TL; **Nigel Francis/Garden
Picture Library:** 331TR; **John Glover:** 87BR, 331BR;
Jerry Harpur: 19TL (Christopher Masson), 56TR (Mrs.
Arelt), 100BR (Patrick Miller), 319BR (James Aldridge),
321BL (Lisette Pleasance); **Meredith Hebden/Positive
Images:** 335Row2#1; **Neil Holmes/Garden Picture
Library:** 131TRC; **Saxon Holt:** 100TL, 142BL,
149Row2#1, 159, 162TR; **Rowan Isaac/Garden
Picture Library:** 112BL, 131BR; **Bill Johnson:** 67TC;
Gene Joyner: 51BRC, 51BR; **Wolfgang Kaehler:**
331BC; **Dency Kane:** 127TR, 163R5#3; **Rosemary
Kautzky:** 5TL, 61TR, 301, 302BL, 313TL; **Dwight
Kuhn:** 149Row1#1, 149Row2#2, 149Row3#1,
149Row4#2, 324BR, 331TL, 335Row1#1, 335Row1#2,
335Row2#2, 335Row3#2, 335Row3#3, 335Row4#3,
339TR, 339BL; **Andrew Lawson:** 12CL, 19BR
(Designers: Oehme & Van); 100TR, 112TL, 115TR,
121TL, 121BR, 337BL; **Scott Leonhart/Positive
Images:** 10L#4, 149Row3#3, 339TL, 339TL; **David
Liebman:** 7#5R, 51TL, 51TLC, 100TLi, 100TCL, 127BR,
149Row2#3, 149Row3#4, 173BL, 173BC, 173BR, 324CL,
331BL, 335Row3#1; **Janet Loughrey:** 6TL, 9BL, 19BL,
87TR, 115TL; **Charles Mann:** 87TL; **Elvin McDonald:**
5BL, 355; **Clive Nichols:** 8B, 73R, 115BR. 319BR, 321TL
(Joe Swift); **Philip L. Nixon:** 67TL, 67CL, 163Row1#2,
163Row1#4; **NouN/Garden Picture Library:**
149Row4#3; **Jerry Pavia:** 337TL, 337TR, 351BL, 351BR;
Phyllis Picard/Photo Network: 100BL; **Diane A.
Pratt/Positive Images:** 335Row4#2; **James Robinson:**
149Row4#4, 324TR, 331TC; **Richard Shiell:** 67BC,
131TLC, 131BL; **Neil Soderstrom:** 9R#4, 166TL, 169CL;
Pam Spaulding/Positive Images: 339BR; **Michael
Thompson:** 100CR, 149Row1#4, 163Row2#2, 337BR;
Connie Toops: 51TR; **Mark Turner:** 56BR, 313BL;
Ron West: 51BL, 149Row1,#2; **Rick Wetherbee:** 8TR,
12TR, 17TR, 54TL, 56BL, 84TL, 87CR, 112TR, 127TL,
142BR, 163Row2#1; **Justyn Willsmore:** 67CR, 115BL,
131BRC, 169TL. 313CL, 313TR, back cover top

Cover Photography: (clockwise from top left) Jay
Wilde, Rex Butcher/Positive Images, Rob Cardillo,
Povy Kendal Atchison

metric conversions

To Convert From	Multiply By	To Get	To Convert From	Multiply By	To Get
Inches	25.4	Millimeters	Millimeters	0.0394	Inches
Inches	2.54	Centimeters	Centimeters	0.3937	Inches
Feet	30.48	Centimeters	Centimeters	0.0328	Feet
Feet	0.3048	Meters	Meters	3.2808	Feet
Yards	0.9144	Meters	Meters	1.0936	Yards
Square inches	6.4516	Square centimeters	Square centimeters	0.1550	Square inches
Square feet	0.0929	Square meters	Square meters	10.764	Square feet
Square yards	0.8361	Square meters	Square meters	1.1960	Square yards
Acres	0.4047	Hectares	Hectares	2.4711	Acres
Cubic inches	16.387	Cubic centimeters	Cubic centimeters	0.0610	Cubic inches
Cubic feet	0.0283	Cubic meters	Cubic meters	35.315	Cubic feet
Cubic feet	28.316	Liters	Liters	0.0353	Cubic feet
Cubic yards	0.7646	Cubic meters	Cubic meters	1.308	Cubic yards
Cubic yards	764.55	Liters	Liters	0.0013	Cubic yards

To convert from degrees Fahrenheit (F) to degrees Celsius (C), first subtract 32, then multiply by $\frac{5}{9}$.

To convert from degrees Celsius to degrees Fahrenheit, multiply by $\frac{9}{5}$, then add 32.